Recreational Use
of Wild Lands

McGraw-Hill Series in Forest Resources

Avery   Natural Resource Measurements
Boyce   Forest Pathology
Brockman and Merriam   Recreational Use of Wild Lands
Brown and Davis   Forest Fire: Control and Use
Chapman and Meyer   Forest Mensuration
Dana   Forest and Range Policy
Daniel, Helms, and Baker   Principles of Silviculture
Davis   Forest Management
Davis   Land Use
Duerr   Fundamentals of Forestry Economics
Graham and Knight   Forest Entomology
Guise   The Management of Farm Woodlands
Harlow, Harrar, and White   Textbook of Dendrology
Heady   Rangeland Management
Panshin and De Zeeuw   Textbook of Wood Technology
  Volume I—Structure, Identification, Uses, and Properties of the Commercial
  Woods of the United States
Panshin, Harrar, Bethel, and Baker   Forest Products
Rich   Marketing of Forest Products: Text and Cases
Sharpe, Hendee, and Allen   An Introduction to Forestry
Shirley   Forestry and Its Career Opportunities
Stoddart, Smith, and Box   Range Management
Trippensee   Wildlife Management
  Volume I—Upland Game and General Principles
  Volume II—Fur Bearers, Waterfowl, and Fish
Wackerman, Hagenstein, and Mitchell   Harvesting Timber Crops
Worrell   Principles of Forest Policy

Walter Mulford was Consulting Editor of this series from its inception in 1931
  until January 1, 1952.
Henry J. Vaux was Consulting Editor of this series from January 1, 1952, until
  July 1, 1976.

Recreational Use of Wild Lands

Third Edition

C. Frank Brockman
Professor of Forestry, Emeritus
College of Forest Resources
University of Washington

Lawrence C. Merriam, Jr.
Professor of Forestry
College of Forestry
University of Minnesota

With two specially prepared chapters by

William R. Catton, Jr.
Professor of Sociology
Washington State University

Barney Dowdle
Professor of Forest Resources and
Adjunct Professor of Economics
University of Washington

McGraw-Hill Book Company

New York   St. Louis   San Francisco   Auckland   Bogotá   Düsseldorf   Johannesburg
London   Madrid   Mexico   Montreal   New Delhi   Panama   Paris   São Paulo
Singapore   Sydney   Tokyo   Toronto

Library of Congress Cataloging in Publication Data

Brockman, Christian Frank, date
  Recreational use of wild lands.

  (McGraw-Hill series in forest resources)
  Includes bibliographies and index.
  1. Wilderness areas—Recreational use.
2. Recreation areas—Management. 3. Recreational
leadership. 4. National parks and reserves.
I. Merriam, Lawrence C., joint author. II. Title.
GV191.67.W5B76   1979   333.7'8   78-15712
ISBN 0-07-007982-X

RECREATIONAL USE OF WILD LANDS

1 2 3 4 5 6 7 8 9 0 DODO 7 8 3 2 1 0 9

This book was set in Times Roman by The Total Book (ECU/BTI).
The editors were Jean Smith and Marian D. Provenzano;
the production supervisor was Dominick Petrellese.
R. R. Donnelley & Sons Company was printer and binder.

Contents

3

PEOPLE RELATIONSHIPS

4

RECREATIONAL RESOURCES

Administration of National Forests / Distinction between
National Forests and National Parks / Recreational
Resources of the National Forests / Coordination of Use
of National Forest Lands / Public Recreational Use of
National Forests

5

ECONOMICS

6

PROVIDING RECREATIONAL OPPORTUNITIES

7

INTERNATIONAL RELATIONSHIPS

Preface

Recreational management of wild lands, as a professional activity, has been developing for many years. Since its inception it has been accelerated by a number of progressive steps which, undoubtedly, will continue in the future. However, this profession came of age in the 1960s. The publication of the report of the Outdoor Recreation Resources Review Commission in 1962 sparked a notable advance. The effect of this report was significantly different from that of earlier efforts, since it crystallized many years of increasing public concern over varied ills related to deterioration of the countryside, expanding urbanization, air and water pollution and similar factors.

For the first time there was a broad general groundswell of public and official awareness of the values inherent in the perpetuation of environmental quality and of recreation as a valid wild-land resource. Such subjects rapidly became "fashionable" and "politically expedient." The ORRRC report served as a catalyst that resulted in well-defined concerted action toward amelioration of past mistakes in the allocation of varied land uses and toward the formulation of adequate safeguards for avoiding other mistakes in the future. One particular result was that the Bureau of Outdoor Recreation was established.[1] The National Park Service, the U.S. Forest Service, many state park organizations, and industrial timberland owners, long associated with wild-land recreation, expanded their activities; and other public and private agencies, previously little concerned with recreation, became deeply involved. Such increased emphasis on wild-land recreation was favored by new legislation, including the Land and Water Conservation Fund Act, the bill establishing the National Wilderness Preservation System, bills establishing several new national parks, the Wild and Scenic Rivers Act, and the National Scenic Trails Act. These events, together with a phenomenal increase in public use of wild-lands for recreation, stimulated great interest in the career possibilities of outdoor recreation. This interest prompted improvement of early relevant curricula and the formation of new programs at numerous colleges and universities, designed to prepare a large number of qualified workers for many necessary and complicated tasks related to the recreational management of wild lands.

The first edition of *Recreational Use of Wild Lands* was published in 1959. Somewhat ahead of its time, it sought to bring together, in concise, organized form, basic concepts and ideas on recreational management of wild-lands developed by pioneers in that field. The intent was to provide early instructors in wild-land recreation with a foundation for their varied individualized instructional programs. The pattern of that first edition placed strong emphasis on the historical background and philosophical aspects of recreational use of wild lands; on the distinctive differences in types of recreational lands, ranging from wilderness areas and national parks to areas provided for intensive mass use. Such an approach is basic to the nature of activities and facilities that can be accommodated on specific types of recreational lands if the particular attractions of such areas are to provide maximum enjoyment and be protected and preserved for use by future generations in the most economical manner.

The second edition, published in 1973, although retaining the basic purposes, objectives and philosophy of the first edition, was an overhaul of its predecessor. Its content profited from the leadership of the ORRRC and the phenomenal upsurge of public interest in environmental protection, as well as in recreational use of wild lands resulting from such leadership. It was also favored by the assistance of Dr. Lawrence C. Merriam, Jr., as coauthor; by the interest of a number of instructors of wild-land recreational management at certain western universities; and by the contribution of chapters on specialized recreational relationships by Dr. William R. Catton, Jr. and Dr. Barney Dowdle. The authors of the second edition were also aided by the cooperation of various land-management agencies and numerous individuals who provided information concerning their particular interests and activities.

The third edition of *Recreational Use of Wild Lands* builds upon its

[1]In 1978 it became the Heritage Conservation and Recreation Service (see pp. 75; 125-129).

predecessors. Much material included in the first and second edition is still valid; this has been retained, although reorganized in certain instances. Significant information has been updated. Recent ideas, concepts, and policies, resulting from experience in recent years, have been added or have replaced outmoded viewpoints or programs.

SCOPE AND ORGANIZATION OF THE THIRD EDITION

The third edition of *Recreational Use of Wild Lands*, like its two predecessors, is intended as a basic introduction to this subject—as an overview of salient highlights of recreational use of wild lands for students entering that growing profession or contemplating such action. Discussion of all aspects, in depth, is not and cannot be accomodated within the necessary limitations of this general introductory text. However, material contained herein should aid students in an assessment of this field of endeavor and, should their initial interest persist, help them in deciding upon some particular aspect for later specialization.

Despite growing specialization in recreational management of wild lands a generalized introductory text on that subject is valid. Students planning a career in wild-land recreation should profit from an understanding of the historical background and basic philosophical concepts of their chosen profession, as well as its ramifications, before concentrating upon some particular area. In large measure, success in all aspects of recreational land management, from planning to detailed operation, its predicted upon such understanding. The reasons underlying past mistakes as well as those basic to current procedures may be clarified. As a result, policies and procedures can be developed which promote the most advantageous public recreational benefits, minimize the impact of increasing public recreational use on the environment, and foster economy of operation.

Further, students majoring in the related fields of land management should benefit from an understanding of recreation as one form of wild-land use so that they may better relate recreational requirements to those of their major activities. Such understanding is particularly important for students majoring in forestry, wildlife management, and water-resource management, since areas with which they will deal have high outdoor recreational values. A generalized treatment of the recreational use of wild lands should also assist interested laymen in recognizing the complicated ecological, social, economic, and political problems involved. This is important in developing necessary public understanding and support which, in turn, favors formulation of logical balances in land-use allocations, policies, and procedures.

Each of the various chapters in the third edition of *Recreational Use of Wild Lands* represents a skeletonized treatment of a particular aspect of this subject; each is worthy of elaboration in depth. However, elaboration of specific details is the province of specialized publications and the responsibility of individual instructors. Instructors should expand upon basic generalized material in this volume, adapting it to specific teaching procedures and course outlines, amplifying it in the light of their own experience and research and the requirements of their particular situation. Reference lists at the end of each chapter should aid those who wish to go more deeply into individual topics. Further, the accompanying suggested

Suggested Course Organization

Chapters	General Subject	Topical Outline
1 and 2	Recreation—relation to wild lands	Benefits, influences; leadership; education
3, 4 and 5	Historical background	Evolution of modern policies, procedures
6	People—relationships	Visitor motivation, behavior, impact
7 through 12	Recreation resources	Knowledge and land; land classes; policies of relevant agencies

Federal, state, local and private lands } Resource manager — Environment — Communication — Policy; programs — Resource user { Recreation visitors and others indirectly concerned

Chapters	General Subject	Topical Outline
13	Economics	Basic relation to recreational land allocation and use
14	Planning—basic principles	National, regional, site; recreational objective
15	Management—basic "tools"	Zoning; nature and degree of development; environmental manipulation; regulations; public relations and involvement; interpretation; research
16	Management—basic operation	Protection of area and visitor health, safety; facilities; maintenance; interpretive program; commercial services; budgets; personnel
17	Foreign parks and equivalent reserves	Importance, background; policies in relation to areas in the United States

course outline will guide the reader logically through material contained in various chapters. The authors hope and expect that instructors and students will supplement this text with detailed discussions and reading on specific topics, and on updated information in rapidly changing situations related to public recreational use and management of wild lands.

ACKNOWLEDGMENTS

To give adequate credit to all who have assisted in the preparation of the three editions of *Recreational Use of Wild Lands* would be impossible. Many people, directly and indirectly, have made vital contributions which are gratefully acknowledged by the authors.

Considerable information required in updating the third edition was derived from various public and private agencies concerned with recreational land use. Tentative revised outlines relating to those agencies most concerned with recreational use of wild lands were checked by responsible employees before being readied for publication. In such instances the authors are particularly grateful for the help of Robert M. Artz (National Park and Recreation Association), Roy H. Boyd (Bureau of Reclamation), Robert D. Buechner (National Society for Park Resources), Dale Brammer (National Park Service), Frederick B. Fields (Tennessee Valley Authority), Kenneth I. Fredericks (Bureau of Indian Affairs), Fred Isbell and Dr. D. W. Lime (Forest Service), Robert E. Jones (American Forest Institute), Frances X. Kelly (Army Corps of Engineers), Darrell E. Lewis (Bureau of Land Management), David McCraney (Heritage Conservation and Recreation Service), Marcus C. Nelson (Fish and Wildlife Service), and Diane Yokel (Nature Conservancy). Others who provided assistance included Eugene Hinds (Bureau of Reclamation), Richard S. Meyer and Rose P. Kranak (Army Corps of Engineers), and Dr. John Hendee and Mack Hogans (Forest Service).

Suggestions by a number of professors who have examined or used this text are also appreciated. Those made by Dean R. A. Skok and Dr. T. N. Knopp (College of Forestry, University of Minnesota), Dr. Grant W. Sharpe (College of Forest Resources, University of Washington), Dr. C. R. Crowther (Michigan Technological University), Dr. Richard W. Jones (School of Forest Resources, University of Georgia), and Dr. J. Lamar Teate (School of Forestry, Louisiana Tech University) were particularly helpful. Also acknowledged is the continued interest and cooperation of Dr. William Catton, Jr. and Dr. Barney Dowdle, who provided the two special chapters.

Finally, the authors express their sincere appreciation for the patience, cooperative support, and help in manuscript preparation provided by their wives, Evelyn G. Brockman and Katherine W. Merriam.

C. Frank Brockman
Lawrence C. Merriam, Jr.

Section One

Underlying Recreational Relationships

Recreation on wild lands is focused on environment; it is resource-oriented, as illustrated in this view of the John Muir Wilderness, Sierra National Forest, California (Class V, Primitive Area). *(U.S. Forest Service.)*

Chapter 1

The Importance of Recreation

Recreation may be defined as the pleasurable and constructive use of spare time. Formulation of an all-inclusive, concise definition of this apparently simple term is not as easy as it might appear, for a multitude of personal, as well as social and philosophical, concepts and interpretations must be considered.

CONCEPTS AND INTERPRETATIONS OF RECREATION

Many people feel that recreation is merely fun or some activity which varies from the routine of their daily lives. Dictionaries define the term in some such manner as "the act of recreating, or state of being recreated; refreshment of the strength and spirits after toil; diversion, play."[1] Similarly, recreation is defined as "activity that rests men from work, often giving them a change (distraction, diversion), and restores (re-creates) them for work"[4].

Recreation is many things. It involves any activity which is participated in, anytime and anywhere, merely for the enjoyment it affords. Re-

---

[1] "Webster's Third New International Dictionary," unabridged, G. & C. Merriam Company, Springfield, Mass., 1968.

creation may be purely physical; it may provide intellectual, esthetic, or emotional outlets; or it may include combinations of these. In its broadest sense, it encompasses much more than simple amusement or play. Moreover, the way free time is used is very definitely individual and personal. An activity which serves as recreation for one person may be work, or a bore, for another. Further, recreational needs of specific individuals vary at different times. They not only change during periods of life, in accordance with physical ability and intellectual capacity, but often at different periods in one day, depending upon personal needs, preferences, and options.

In our definition of recreation the word "pleasurable" signifies that recreation is fun. Benefit will accrue to the individual only if one voluntarily selects some spare-time recreational activity because of the pleasure it affords. But recreation can do more than merely enable an individual to occupy idle time, to loaf. For this reason the word "constructive" is included in our definition. In this sense recreation has a purpose beneficial to the individual and society, whether consciously recognized or not, and is necessarily related to leisure.

Relation of Leisure and Spare Time

Leisure and spare time, periods not directly involved with work or personal care, are synonymous to many people. But there is a difference [4,12]. Leisure is positive and, in a broad sense, productive. It does not denote aimless indolence; sterile or mismanaged free time may have negative implications. While some uses of spare time may be beneficial, other spare-time activities may be detrimental; in either case the effects may be temporary or lifelong. Leisure implies freedom from the necessity of labor; it is time during which one is free to choose what one wishes to do. Thus, it involves responsibility in proper choice from the entire range of both passive and energetic interests and activities made possible by modern technological advances. Leisure interests and activities may often require expenditure of more time and energy than are demanded by earning a living.

RECREATIONAL BENEFITS

The rewards of recreational activities, whatever their nature, depend upon the degree to which they provide outlets for personal needs and interests not attainable in daily routine. In addition to involving rest and relaxation they provide a change of pace from normal workday activities, important to individual physical and mental well-being and productive capacity. Recreation may also operate as a potent teaching force—it may be creative as well as re-creative. It may improve individual personality and social relationships. By supplementing routine often imposed by modern, highly specialized tasks, it can give balance to life by enhancing personal accomplishment and importance. Recreation can also challenge and stimulate by enriching and broadening individual outlook and horizons, developing individual capabilities, and gratifying a person's natural desire for new and more satisfying objectives and ambitions. Indeed, more than a few individuals can credit their interest in a particular vocation to the germ of an idea planted during their early years by inspired direction in some sort of recreational program.

EXPANDING OPPORTUNITIES FOR RECREATION AND LEISURE

Early social systems provided leisure for only a small percentage of the population [4,12]. Many people lived close to a subsistence level, in certain cases as slaves. Modern technological society with its varied mechanical devices for saving time and accomplishing difficult or disagreeable tasks provides increasing opportunities for recreation and leisure for far greater numbers of people.

That each individual needs some form of recreation requires little elaboration; it is axiomatic. If maximum efficiency in the business of living is to be achieved, the stresses and strains of modern life must be relieved by periods of physical and mental relaxation properly coordinated with routine tasks. However, it should be recognized that certain aspects of some jobs may be basically classed as leisure or recreation, particularly if a high degree of personal selection were involved in such employment.

The greatly increased amount of free time now available as a result of technological progress will be used in some way, beneficially or otherwise. The way it will be used and the kind of recreational outlets chosen by various people will depend upon numerous factors: (1) cultural background, (2) physical and intellectual capability, (3) education, training, and experience, (4) age and sex, (5) marital status and family relationships, (6) occupation, (7) economic status, (8) free time, (9) residence, whether urban or rural, (10) varying moods and emotional needs, (11) available opportunities, and (12) the manner in which recreational interests and opportunities are presented.

RESPONSIBILITY OF SOCIETY FOR PUBLIC RECREATIONAL NEEDS

The public sector of society has properly assumed an increasing share of responsibility for providing opportunities for constructive spare-time activities. The acreage of various types of both public and private lands available for recreation has greatly increased during the past several decades. Museums, art galleries, zoological gardens, arboretums, and similarly specialized institutions are important adjuncts of recreation. Schools, churches, and a variety of other organizations sponsor a wide assortment of recreational programs for different age groups and promote spare-time activities of almost every conceivable type. The cost of these publicly and privately sponsored recreation opportunities has been great; however, the cost of *not* providing meaningful outlets for the energies, interests, and abilities of all segments of the population could be much greater.

As outlined more fully later, many factors contribute to the expanding need for adequate recreational opportunities, facilities, and services. More people have more spare time and greater opportunity for leisure as a result of modern technological advances. Our population has increased greatly; it is now primarily urban rather than rural, and consequently the general nature of occupations has changed from largely active to primarily sedentary. There are also more old and more young people, and both of these groups require outlets for their energies and interests. Further, our standard of living is higher so that more people can afford necessary costs. We also have faster, more dependable, and more diversified means of transportation, making it possible for us to reach places far beyond the dreams of our parents, and to do so easily, in comparative comfort, and within a shorter span of time. In addition, public attitude toward work and recreation has changed significantly over the years.

These changes, which began to develop slowly almost from the time the first colonists established themselves on the Atlantic seaboard, have continued at an accelerated pace in recent years and will undoubtedly be even more rapid in the future [15]. By way of prediction, consider this statement by David Sarnoff, former chairman of Radio Corporation of America, in the January 1955, issue of *Fortune* [10]:

> Leisure, of course, will be greatly extended. A much shorter work week will no doubt prevail in 1980, and another ten or fifteen years will have been added to the average life span . . . .
>
> Not labor but leisure will be the great problem in the decades ahead. That prospect should be accepted as a God-given opportunity to add dimensions of enjoyment and grace to life.

This concern for the future of our society has been increasingly noted by other responsible, informed writers [1-8,12,16,17]. The growing importance of recreation in connection with leisure, together with the requisite maintenance of environmental quality, is not lost on growing numbers of citizens. Public interest is reflected in attitudes and activities of legislators. This is indicated by the growth in number of recreational areas and increasing restrictions relative to improper utilization of natural resources, dangers of air and water pollution, needless environmental destruction in expansion of highways and industrial and urban developments, and related matters affecting the natural interest and beauty of the countryside.

MAJOR INFLUENCES ON PUBLIC RECREATIONAL REQUIREMENTS

Factors which have contributed to our growing recreational needs in the past, and which will exert great influence in the future, include the nature, density, and distribution of our population, as well as the relation between different groups and age classes. Equally significant are the amount of leisure time available to the individual, the amount of a person's income, the nature of education, occupation, and means of transportation. Change in public attitude toward work and recreation has been another important influence.

Population Changes and Their Effects upon Recreational Patterns

Our expanding population has brought about a phenomenal increase in the number of potential users of recreational lands. Within a few years after the American Revolution the population of the United States was nearly 4 million, largely confined to the Atlantic seaboard. Since that time, with the western boundary of our country extended to the Pacific, our population has increased manyfold. In 1960 it was about 180 million; by 1976 it had increased to over 214 million. It is predicted that by the year 2000 the population of the United States will be between 246 and 283 million and by 2050 it could range upward to 488 million [13].

Although the population of the United States has increased tremendously over the years, it is not uniformly distributed. In 1976 about 42 percent of our people lived in the New England, Middle Atlantic, and East North Central sections of our country, a region embracing less than 12 percent of our area. By way of contrast, the Mountain section has about 24 percent of the area of the United States but less than 5 percent of our population.

By 1976 population density within the various states ranged from a low of 0.7 people per square mile in Alaska to a high of 975.4 people per square mile in New Jersey. Other examples of extreme variations in population were high densities per square mile in Rhode Island, 883.7; Massachusetts, 742.3; and Connecticut, 641.1. Such high densities were in sharp contrast to extremely low densities per square mile in Wyoming, 4.0; Montana, 5.2; and Nevada, 5.6. Of the Eastern states, Maine had the lowest population density per square mile, 34.6; greatest concentration of people per square mile in the West was in California, 137.6. The state of Hawaii had a density of 138.1 people per square mile [13].

The change in the population pattern in the United States from primarily rural to primarily urban, at about the time of World War I, has profoundly affected the living habits and occupational pursuits of our people. Today most Americans are crowded onto relatively limited areas of land where natural conditions are largely nonexistent; employment is primarily in industrial, commercial, clerical, or professional activities which are essentially sedentary. Thus, many Americans are removed from regular contact with open spaces and to a considerable degree have lost the ability of their forefathers to conduct themselves properly and safely in a truly natural environment. Modern, largely urbanized civilization divorces many people from intimate contact with nature, from recognition of the inherent difficulties and hazards as well as interests involved. Uncomfortable, unpleasant and, on occasion, disastrous experiences result from lack of understanding.

The rapid growth and irregular distribution of our population, together with their effects upon the habits and occupations of the people, have greatly influenced our need for diverse recreational opportunities. It is obvious that we require a greater number of properly distributed recreational areas of widely varying types suited to different spare-time interests and activities. Recreational lands readily accessible to people in more densely populated areas are most important. Overcrowded conditions typical of most recreational lands, particularly those in and near major centers of population, emphasize this need. The growth of metropolitan, county, and state park systems in many sections of the country is a direct result of this demand. Changes in population patterns and living habits also indicate why there is a constantly increasing pressure for the reservation of large unspoiled tracts, such as wilderness areas, where people can completely escape the confines of the city and obtain the benefits of recreation in truly natural surroundings. We cannot afford to overlook the damage done to recreational lands of unique quality, such as national parks, through pressure of increased use together with unenlightened public demand for facilities and services which are inappropriate to such areas.

Effects of Variations in Age Classes

Since people of different ages have varying interests and physical abilities, the relation between various age classes comprised in our population is another factor which bears upon their recreational preferences and, consequently, the nature of recreational facilities required. Of particular importance is the recent increase in number of young people and old people. These two groups at opposite extremes of physical ability, experience, and maturity, obviously have widely divergent recreational interests.

Young people prefer, and need, facilities for active recreation; the emphasis here is on sports, team play, and active group programs. Declining vigor of more mature years prompts increasingly greater emphasis upon physical moderation and more passive interests and activities; further, areas of our country typified by less rigorous climates have greater appeal to older people.

Improvement of Living Standards and Increase in Leisure Time

Activities of modern people are highly specialized. In our work today most of us contribute to the welfare of society largely through detailed tasks which are but parts of a broad, overall project. Creative elements are largely lacking in our daily routine; many individual workers have little or no idea

Table 1-1   Gross National Product and Personal Consumption Expenditures[a]

	GNP	PCE		GNP	PCE
1929	103.4	77.3	1955	399.3	253.6
1930	90.7	69.9	1960	506.0	324.9
1935	72.5	55.8	1965	688.1	430.2
1940	100.0	71.0	1970	982.4	618.8
1945	212.3	119.5	1975	1,516.3	973.2
1950	286.2	192.0	1976	1,691.6	—

[a]In billions of dollars; Alaska and Hawaii excluded prior to 1960.
Source: "Statistical Abstracts of the United States, 1977," U.S. Bureau of the Census, Washington, 1977.

of how their efforts are related to the finished product. In short, a modern individual's existence is considerably regimented by an industrialized civilization in which personal satisfaction is often sacrificed for greater productive capacity.

Such a system, however, has many compensations. Together with various technical innovations, modern techniques have materially improved our living standards so that we are better able to afford the costs of spare-time activities of our own choosing. Over the years there has been a noticeable change in the affluence of the American people. Except for the Depression years of the 1930s, the Gross National Product (GNP) and personal consumption expenditures have risen sharply since 1929 (Table 1-1).

Modern technology also makes it possible for us to produce more goods with far less effort and in much less time than formerly. As a result, the amount of spare time available to the individual has been greatly increased.

During the early days of America, when the population was essentially rural in character, people had to labor long hours each day in order to provide the necessities of life for themselves and their families. About 125 years ago the average workweek was seventy-four hours [14]; of the remaining ninety-four hours in each week, eighty-four were required for personal care (eating, sleeping, etc.). Opportunities for those activities now termed "recreation" were severely limited in a schedule which permitted only about ten hours of free time weekly.

It should be stated, however, that the long hours of work characteristic of early America were not without their compensations. A new home, a new community, a new nation were literally being carved from the wilderness. To a degree, such work represented personal achievement, and the long hours may not have had the debilitating effect upon the worker that many routine tasks have today.

Nevertheless, although time for personal care has remained fairly constant over the years, developing technological progress has brought a gradual reduction in the effort required to supply a person's basic needs. The average workweek at the time of the Civil War was sixty-eight hours; by the turn of the century, it had been reduced to sixty hours; the ten-hour day and the six-day workweek typical of about three-quarters of a century ago have today been generally replaced by the standard eight-hour day, five days weekly. Thus, within the past hundred years, average persons have gained nearly thirty additional hours of free time weekly for use in activities of their own choosing. Indications are that the workweek will be further reduced in the future [11,14]. Both young and elderly people have even greater amounts of spare time. Technological advances foster the possibility of earlier retirement for older people and prolong the economic immaturity of the young. Along with the advantages in such developments are hazards resulting from enforced idleness.

In addition to shortening the workweek, technological progress has broadened opportunities for extended vacation periods. This has a strong bearing upon recreation, for more people are increasingly able to develop interests of their own choosing to greater depth, and to travel greater distances to places which have particular appeal.

Those adequately prepared for proper use of increased spare time in the future will benefit greatly in satisfying their creative needs. Many benefits will accrue from various forms of recreational interests and activities. Educational philosophy, of both an informal and a formal nature, and at all academic levels, is responding to this challenge in preparing increasing numbers of individuals for such opportunities.

Improvement in Travel Facilities

There has been a great improvement in methods and facilities for travel. As a result, patterns of both work and play have changed materially. Our horizons, as well as our activities, are much broader than they once were.

The automobile has been the most vital factor in this development. Automobile registrations rose from 4 in 1895 to over 2,000,000 in 1915 and by 1975 numbered over 100,000,000 [9].

The travel radius of the average American family was phenomenally increased by the development of the automobile. Practically overnight, recreational journeys consisting of one-day trips to a picnic ground near the end of a streetcar line were lengthened to weekends spent at points of interest many miles distant. The automobile also made possible extended trips to places which, because of the necessity of expensive, time-consuming rail journeys, had been previously inaccessible to the average citizen.

Development and wider use of motor vehicles by the public and the consequent interest in extended travel were soon followed by improved and additional highways. Today, good roads span the length and breadth of our land. They penetrate to remote nooks and crannies and, except in rare instances, are usable throughout the year.

The development and improvement of various types of aircraft and the increasing diversity of sophisticated recreation equipment promise even greater impact on future recreational travel habits [11]. Such developments have positive as well as negative implications, but those that provide easier access to remote backcountry and other relatively inaccessible locations threaten the overuse of such areas and the destruction of their environmental and related values.

Change in Attitude toward Recreation

General public attitudes toward work and recreation also have undergone a change. Work simply for work's sake is no longer a primary criterion of the full life for increasing numbers of people. But during the formative years of our country the philosophy of the times regarded recreation, per se, as wasteful of time and effort—in effect, not respectable. In New England, particularly, recreation simply for personal enjoyment was severely frowned upon.

As an indication of the early American attitude toward recreation, witness the policy of Cokesbury College, as noted in the "Methodist Discipline" in 1792: "The students shall be indulged with nothing which the world calls play. Let this rule be observed with the strictest nicety; for those who play when they are young, will play when they are old."[2]

SUMMARY

Although recreation means many things to many people, it involves spare-time interests and activities which embody personal choice and enjoyment. Constructive use of spare time is important to the well-being of the individual, the community, and the nation, since the growth of an individual is determined as much by how spare time is occupied as by how required workday tasks are performed.

Spare time and leisure are not necessarily synonymous. Leisure, which results in maximum benefit to the individual through free choice of interests and activities, demands the exercise of responsibility in that choice, in positive use of spare time.

Technological progress has developed an essentially urban pattern of life in the United States, raised our general standard of living, increased our spare time, and expanded and improved our transportation facilities. Public attitude toward the relation of work and leisure also has been greatly modified. These facts, together with the growth and changing composition of our population, indicate that the future will witness a growing importance of recreation as a form of leisure. This, in turn, will prompt greater recognition of the fact that abilities necessary to realization of the benefits of recreational opportunities should be developed in the maximum number of people. In addition, there will be increasing pressure to maintain environmental quality basic to many interests and activities; and there will be increasing

---

[2] Methodist Episcopal Church, "The Doctrines and Discipline of the Methodist Episcopal Church in America," Parry Hall, Philadelphia, 1792, p.68.

use of existing recreational lands and facilities and continued demand for additions to such resources, properly distributed in accordance with need, in quantity, quality, and variety.

SELECTED REFERENCES

1 Brightbill, Charles K.: "The Challenge of Leisure," Prentice-Hall, Englewood Cliffs, N.J., 1960.

2 Clawson, Marion: How Much Leisure, Now and in the Future? In James C. Charlesworth (ed.), "Leisure in America: Blessing or Curse?" Monograph 4, American Academy of Political and Social Science, Philadelphia, 1964.

3 Clawson, Marion, and Jack L. Knetsch: "Economics of Outdoor Recreation," Resources for the Future, Johns Hopkins, Baltimore, 1966.

4 de Grazia, Sebastian: "Of Time, Work and Leisure," Doubleday, Garden City, N.Y., 1962.

5 Harden, Garrett: The Tragedy of the Commons, *Science*, vol. 162, no. 3859, pp. 1243–1248, Dec. 13, 1968.

6 Huizinga, Johann: "Homo Ludens: A Study of the Play Element in Culture," trans. by R. F. C. Hull, Beacon Press, Boston, 1955.

7 Jensen, Clayne R.: "Outdoor Recreation in America: Trends, Problems and Opportunities," 2nd ed., Burgess Pub. Co., Minneapolis, 1973.

7a Keller, Barbara A.: Leisure Education: Pathway to a Better Life, *Parks and Recreation*, vol. 11, no. 1, January 1976.

8 Menninger, W. D.: Recreation and Mental Health, *Recreation*, vol. 42, no. 8, November 1948.

8a Mobley, Tony A.: Philosophical Thought, *Parks and Recreation*, vol. 11, no. 7, July 1976.

9 Motor Vehicle Manufacturers Assn.: "Motor Vehicle Facts and Figures, 1976," Detroit, 1975.

10 Sarnoff, David: The Fabulous Future, *Fortune*, vol. 51, no. 1, pp. 82–83, January 1955.

11 Sharpe, Grant W.: Forest Recreation: A Look at the Year 2000 A.D., *Proceedings of the Society of American Foresters Meeting*, Detroit, Oct. 24–28, 1965, Washington, 1966.

12 Tolley, William P.: The American Heritage of Leisure, *Proceedings of the National Conference on Professional Education for Outdoor Recreation*, pp. 146–151, Syracuse, N.Y., 1964.

13 U.S. Department of Commerce, Bureau of the Census: "Statistical Abstracts of the United States, 1977," U.S. Government Printing Office, Washington, 1977.

14 U.S. Department of the Interior, National Park Service: "A Study of the Park and Recreation Problems of the United States," U.S. Government Printing Office, Washington, 1941.

15 U.S. Department of the Interior: "The Population Challenge," Conservation Yearbook No. 2, U.S. Government Printing Office, Washington, 1966.

16 Vogt, William: "People! Challenge to Survival," Sloane, New York, 1960.

17 Wrenn, C. G., and D. L. Harley: "Time on Their Hands: A Report on Leisure, Recreation, and Young People," prepared for the American Youth Commission, American Council on Education, Washington, 1941.

Chapter 2

Wild Lands and Recreation

Recreation may be broadly related to specific interests and activities favored by different individuals, or to the locale where those interests and activities are pursued. Recreationists may be spectators or participants. The locale may be indoors or outdoors. Outdoor recreation may be subdivided according to the basic types of lands involved, as "wild lands," typified by dispersed or extensive activities, or "developed lands," typified by concentrated or intensive activities.

As considered in this text, wild lands are natural or largely unmodified. Their physical development is minimized, limited to small sites, or completely lacking; and pursuit and enjoyment of their recreational opportunities depends largely upon protection of basic environmental conditions.

Wild lands are usually located some distance from population centers, and some are rather inaccessible. They may or may not be specifically designed for recreation: thus, privately owned lands used primarily for production of agricultural or forest crops are included here with lands of more truly wild or natural character. They are essentially undeveloped; further, most recreational values typical of such lands (hunting, fishing, greenbelts) are more closely related to wild than to developed lands.

This book also places historical and archeological areas in the same category with wild lands even though they normally lack important natural interests. They are so considered because of their unique historical or archeological character and because they are often under the same administrative authority as certain wild lands. For instance, many areas of this type, as well as wild lands, are administered by the National Park Service.

The primary concern here is outdoor recreation on wild lands, as previously defined. Outdoor recreation on developed lands, such as municipal parks and playgrounds and related high-density areas, has a different basis and is a specialized field of recreation in its own right. Except where specifically related to broad outdoor recreation problems or to recreation on wild lands, recreation on developed areas is not within the sphere of this book.

RELATION OF WILD AND DEVELOPED RECREATIONAL AREAS

Basically, the focus of recreation on wild lands is on environment; it is *resource-oriented* whereas that of developed lands is *activity-oriented.*

Few outdoor recreational interests and activities are unique to wild lands. Because of the esthetic value of wild lands, they are often selected for many forms of recreation that could be conducted elsewhere. For instance, satisfactions derived from a picnic in a city park are largely social; a picnic in a more natural wild-land setting offers scope for more varied enjoyment.

On developed recreational lands the major emphasis is on providing physical conditions and facilities necessary to featured activities (sports, group interests, engineered or "manicured" surroundings). While care is exercised in maintaining an attractive setting, retention of natural conditions is a minor concern. Some developed recreational areas have resulted from rehabilitation of land on which natural conditions have been completely destroyed; in other cases natural conditions may be sufficiently distinctive to warrant preservation.

Developed recreational areas are usually within or in proximity to population centers. Being readily accessible, they provide opportunities for a wide variety of beneficial interests and activities for large numbers of people. They can be utilized easily for short periods by people with limited free time, and in most cases they are well-adapted to recreational interests and activities and physical developments which are often inappropriate on wild lands. Thus, they are important to perpetuation of unique or fragile wild lands (national parks, wilderness), since much of the demand for activities and development often inappropriate on wild lands can be satisfied on developed areas having less important natural interests.

Admittedly, the distinction between developed and wild recreational lands is not sharply defined; there are many gradations. Some developed recreation areas include sizeable natural sections. Conversely, portions of larger wild-land recreation areas (national parks and forests, many state parks) absorb heavy public use. These limited sections are often highly developed; however, such sites include only a small percentage of the essentially undeveloped areas of which they are a part.

Ambiguity of Terms

The term "wild lands" is (except for historical and archeological areas) generally used in reference to lands as defined in the first paragraph of this chapter, despite certain ambiguities. Outdoor recreation, as a widely accepted profession, is relatively new, thus many general terms are not precisely defined. Lack of clear recreational terminology creates ambiguities which often cause misunderstanding and hamper constructive communication between professionals and the public, and sometimes between professionals themselves. This interferes with the most effective planning and public use of recreational land of all types.

The term "wilderness" is subject to different interpretations, due to wide variations in individual background and outdoor experience. The term "park" creates even greater confusion. It has many connotations, including neighborhood playground park, city park, county park, regional park, state park, tree-farm park, industrial park, national park—even ball park.[1] It should be obvious that there are differences in the purposes of these parks regardless of the similarity of their basic nomenclature, and that objectives of their management and public use vary accordingly. Until recreation terminology is standardized and made specific, students must rely upon the instructor's broader knowledge and understanding to clarify the ambiguities of many terms in general current usage.

VALUES OF RECREATION ON WILD LANDS

Wild lands offer excellent opportunities for health-giving, leisure-time pursuits which can expand individual horizons. Recreation in natural surroundings on wild lands provides for development of physical skills as well as intellectual and cultural interests [9].

To a large extent individuals engaged in recreation on wild lands are on their own; their enjoyment is greatly dependent upon personal resources. They must, in a limited sense, meet the physical demands of the outdoors as their forefathers did, and the degree of their success is a reflection of personal vigor and self-reliance. Similarly, recreation on wild lands challenges personal intellect and cultural resources; it offers opportunity to develop ability to perceive and understand significant interests (geological, biological, historical, archeological) inherent in such areas. In some cases

[1] The senior author recalls his consternation when, during early years of employment in a national park, people occasionally confused his association there with a baseball park of similar name in a nearby city. Even today sports broadcasters, referring to the power of some prodigious batter, occasionally exclaim, "He can hit a ball out of any park, including Yellowstone!" One wonders if such statements, though facetious, reveal a lack of public understanding of the difference between types of parks.

maximum recreational benefits are derived only from a combination of physical and intellectual capabilities.

Physical Values

Physical values of recreation on wild lands come primarily from such activities as picnicking, camping, fishing, hunting, hiking, mountain climbing, riding, skiing, boating and swimming. Physical pleasures are not the only rewards of such activities. For instance, picnicking and camping in company with people of similar interests contribute to social pleasures; activities which vary from normal pursuits (mountain climbing, skiing) involve a spirit of adventure and test ability to recognize and surmount inherent hazards; and to many who enjoy fishing, a full creel is one of the rewards of a fishing trip to a region of scenic splendor.

Intellectual and Cultural Values

Intellectual and cultural values are derived from such interests as photography, painting, handicrafts, nature study, research, understanding archeological or historical interests, and even meditation. Often spiritual uplift accompanies a recreational experience in a dramatically beautiful wild-land setting. These activities, however, in addition to being enjoyed for themselves are often rewarding physically. The photographer or artist who climbs a mountain or journeys off the beaten track to obtain a particular picture, or the naturalist or scientist who exerts great effort in seeking a particular specimen, frequently develops a high degree of physical skill. In such cases, however, necessary physical activity is a means to an end rather than an end in itself.

DISTRIBUTION OF WILD-LAND RECREATIONAL AREAS

Wild lands have long been important in outdoor recreation. Informally, their use for a wide variety of interests and activities (hunting and fishing) has been traditional, and for over 100 years formally designated recreational wild lands (national and state parks, forests, and related areas) have been part of the American scene.

Initially, however, these formally designated areas were not well integrated. They were not established as a result of a carefully conceived plan. Further, there was little recognition of the complementary functions of developed recreational lands and recreation on wild land.

Just as early municipal parks came into being as a result of readily recognizable local requirements, most early wild-land recreational areas were established largely because of the energy, enthusiasm, and perseverance of perceptive individuals who recognized the value of protecting bits of the significant American scene, as a result of pressures from similarly interested groups, or because of a happy coincidence of conditions at the time of their establishment. For instance, it is doubtful if some of our national parks, national monuments, state parks, or wilderness areas would exist today had they not been set aside at a time when they were relatively more remote and consequently less important as a source of raw materials for industry than they are today; or had they not been championed by farsighted employees of land-managing agencies, public-spirited citizens, or organized groups concerned with preserving outdoor interests [8,13].

Initially, satisfying growing public demand for all types of outdoor recreation was characterized by expediency. Insufficient attention was given to provision, adequate dispersal, and coordination of both wild and developed recreational areas required to meet the need. The nature and extent of varied outdoor recreational demands were also incompletely understood. Further, little thought was given to the allocation of different types of areas for recreational interests and activities most appropriate to perpetuation of environmental conditions basic to outdoor recreational values, including environmentally interesting, recreational areas readily accessible to residents of crowded urban centers. In some sections of the country recreational areas were extensive and diverse; other regions not only lacked some types of recreational lands but, as a result of earlier extensive exploitation, possessed too little space which could be readily designated for such purposes [13]. For instance, most of the larger and better-known, strongly resource-oriented national parks and forests were established in the West. Of even greater significance, only a fraction of our seacoast was retained in public ownership, developed, or was capable of being developed, for public recreation [19–21].

This unbalanced opportunity for recreation often resulted in public pressure which prompted forms of recreation not adapted to certain areas, resulting in deterioration of their significant and fragile values. The distressing over-development and huge crowds found in parts of certain national parks is a case in point. Further, recreation was not generally regarded as an important resource of those lands utilized for production or raw materials for industry; their recreational potential was often damaged by excessive exploitation. As a result, environmental quality and dependent recreational values have suffered severely in many places.

These conditions showed the need for careful planning of both current and future recreational uses of wild lands. It became evident that wild and developed recreational lands had many complementary functions and that both types were required in greater number and variety, located in relation to need, to accommodate public demand for diverse recreation [13]. It became evident also that recreational and other land uses should be consistent with the nature of environment and that the natural resources on lands where such activities were in the public interest should be utilized in accordance with the perpetuation of all basic land values [14,22,23]. Certain types of uses, recreational and otherwise, are compatible with one another; others are not. Only enlightened and perceptive planning and management, which adequately consider public recreational demands consistent with perpetuation of environmental quality, foster proper diversity of recreational and other uses important to widest possible public interests and requirements.

Since publication of the findings of the Outdoor Recreation Resources Review Commission in 1962 [13], steps have been taken to alleviate problems relative to public recreational use of wild lands. However, much land primarily valuable for outdoor recreation had already been preempted by other forms of use, and the task of restoring its recreational potential had become herculean in scope, made extremely difficult by tremendous cost, the nature of existing landownership patterns, and technical difficulties.

COMPETITION IN USE OF WILD LAND

Recreational values of wild land are variously affected by most activities. For instance, industrial development and the growth of large urban centers have resulted in invasion of open space as well as in the pollution of streams, lakes, and ocean beaches. Private acquisition of choice recreational sites, particularly on lake and ocean shores, has eliminated a large part of such land from the possibility of general public use; on such high-premium recreational lands, the needs of the masses should be given precedence over the desires of the few.

Methods of harvesting timber and handling live stock grazing which ignore their impact on the environment affect scenic values. Such ill-advised actions may also have far-reaching adverse effects on environmental relationships through acceleration of upland erosion and silting of streams. Indiscriminate drainage of swamps and marshes greatly affects the numbers of migratory waterfowl, and the settlement and cultivation of marginal farmlands often lead to the disappearance of interesting birds and mammals.

Controversies have developed over construction of dams and resultant formation of artificial lakes [11,12]. True, such features provide many recreational benefits in addition to their primary functions (hydroelectric power, irrigation), especially where other opportunities for water-based activities are lacking. However, if original values of affected lands and waters are ignored, recreational interests of equal or even greater importance may be destroyed by flooding of distinctive historical, archeological, biological, geological or scenic features. Biological requirements of fishes must also be considered. Construction of dams should provide for continuance of periodic upstream movement of migratory species; otherwise such species may be seriously reduced in number or, in some cases, even eliminated. It is also important to recognize that large artificial lakes formed behind dams may raise water temperatures beyond the limit of tolerance for certain species.

It should be emphasized that these pages hold no brief for recreational management of wild lands at the expense of total exclusion of other uses of land which are vital to modern life. However, it is in the public interest that in each specific case all aspects of human need must be carefully investigated before final decisions are made as to the type and character of most advantageous land use. Lands clearly most valuable for different forms of recreation, especially those typified by fragile or significant values (national parks, wilderness areas), should be so designated. On multipurpose lands utilization of resources, including recreation, should be coordinated wherever possible. No longer can we afford to act hastily or without due consideration for the future and correct mistakes of ill-advised action later. Too often such mistakes are irreparable.

Competitive Recreational Uses of Wild Lands

Many recreational uses of wild lands are themselves incompatible, for people of various recreation interests visualize different possibilities on identical areas. A few examples follow.

Hunters and those who wish merely to observe, study, and photograph wildlife are rarely in agreement on the paramount values of an area. Fishing enthusiasts are often at loggerheads with water-skiers on the same waters. Skiers who demand elaborate lifts and related facilities and those who champion the natural winter scene as a site for enjoyment of this sport are rarely in accord. Many people regard the expanding use of powerboats, trail bikes, and off-road vehicles, aircraft, and, in winter, snowmobiles for reaching outlying points of interest as a distressing disruption of the quiet and solitude of the outdoors. Campers and picnickers have different objectives; thus, separate sites are desirable for accommodation of these activities. In campgrounds, groups equipped with tents and those with trailers or auto campers have different requirements. And those who desire ready access by road to remote regions, and comfortable or at least convenient, accommodations when they get there, differ from wilderness enthusiasts in point of view. Such differences of opinion, resulting from absence of uniformity in general recreational objectives, as well as from an incomplete understanding of the overall problems involved, highlight many difficulties pertaining to the acquisition, planning, development, management, and public use and enjoyment of recreational areas.

MAINTENANCE OF ENVIRONMENTAL QUALITY

It is important to recognize that benefits of outdoor recreation depend upon much more than availability of specifically designated lands (parks, forests, wildlife reserves, wilderness areas). Such specifically designated areas are vital to public outdoor recreation, but the maintenance and perpetuation of the quality of our *total* environment is equally important [14,22,23]. In fact, in the long view, as inevitable urban expansion continues and as remaining wild lands increasingly come under more intensive management, it is likely that maintenance of the interest and beauty of our total environment will be more important than the amount of acreage in specifically designated recreational lands. There must be greater public interest in the necessity of adjusting to rather than dominating the environment.

It is expected that environmental interest and beauty will be maintained in designated wild-land recreational areas, but lands beyond the boundaries of such areas should also be utilized in a way to retain their attractiveness. For instance, well-cared-for farm and forest lands, though managed for commercial objectives and never used or intended for use for any form of recreation, have an important recreational function. They provide attractive open space or greenbelts in the vicinity of towns and cities, and bordering highways and related transportation facilities; in that manner they are related to recreational interests and overall recreational land programs. In short, recreational workers should not gauge the success of their efforts merely by the number and type of specific recreational areas established, the number of picnic areas or campsites and related facilities provided, or the miles of trails or roads developed. They should also be vitally interested in the maintenance of overall environmental quality, both without as well as within areas with which they are specifically concerned.

NEED FOR QUALIFIED WILD-LAND RECREATIONAL LEADERSHIP

Professionally educated, enlightened, perceptive, enthusiastic leadership is the key to proper coordination of the recreational picture in the United States. These qualities are as important to "grass roots" workers concerned with detailed management as to higher echelon employees who make major policy decisions. Such leadership promotes economy of operation, perpetuation of recreational interests, an understanding of public recreational needs, interests, attitudes and actions, as well as maximum enjoyment and benefits of a recreational experience.

If maximum recreational value is to be provided at minimum cost, varied public recreational services of diverse areas should fit like pieces of a jigsaw puzzle. In that manner recreational interests and activities inappropriate to certain lands, and unnecessary duplication of services on contiguous areas within specific regions, can be advantageously eliminated. All types of recreational areas, ranging from small municipal neighborhood playgrounds to distant, more extensive national parks and wilderness areas, are interrelated; each provides opportunity for specific kinds of recreational interests and activities.

Both the nature and the environmental associations of such areas differ; understanding these factors is important in allocating to different land those uses which are most conducive to the perpetuation of their recreational values. If follows that wild-land recreational workers should be aware of, and interested in, the problems and progress of their contemporaries in municipal, county, and other more highly developed recreational lands, and vice versa.

The sizable investment in lands used solely and specifically for recreation today is, in itself, sufficient reason for qualified professional leadership in recreational land management. Without such leadership the recreational values inherent in those lands will not be properly maintained and the investment will be largely nullified. In addition, since the character of public use of recreational areas, as well as the cost of maintenance, is largely determined by the nature and plan of necessary physical facilities (roads, trails, campgrounds), such features must be carefully considered by personnel who not only are qualified in design and construction but are also aware of the relation of such facilities to resultant public use and the impact of such use upon the environment. Also, since recreation is of varying importance on multipurpose lands, those concerned with management of such lands should understand their relation to recreation so that this resource may be properly coordinated with other values. Further, future expansion of recreational opportunities calls for careful advance planning, guided by an understanding of the reasons for recreational demand and the different types of recreational areas suited to prospective users. Thus, public recreational requirements may be anticipated and provision made for them. For instance, before rising costs make it impossible, areas suitable for recreation, and still unused for other purposes, should be acquired.

Many of the more difficult and frustrating problems of recreational land management are people-related. Leadership is also required in development of public responsibility in the use of recreational areas. It should also promote understanding of the reasons underlying official policies and regulations which guide such use. Official policies, usually based upon the long-term view of maintaining current recreational values for continued use in the future, sometimes seem unduly restrictive to individuals and groups having special interests. Such individuals and groups should recognize the logic of a long-term viewpoint and that they show willingness to cooperate with others who have different points of view, even to making certain sacrifices. Uncontrolled recreational use of wild land is no longer acceptable. We may not like it, but in the future individual preferences will have to be increasingly subordinated to consideration for others.

Further, leisure-time interests of modern individuals are largely conditioned by an essentially urban life style. Though increase in urban living has accelerated public interest in environmental protection and wild-land recreation, urban people are often unfamiliar with the outdoors. Consequently they lack self-reliance and understanding of wild lands, which may cause annoying or even serious difficulties. Today many people must learn how to conduct themselves in the outdoors before they can expect to use and enjoy its opportunities fully without damaging basic values. Assuming that one is physically able, maximum safety and personal enjoyment of varied recreational activities on wild land come only with an understanding of the interests and hazards involved. For instance, competent skiers recognize the signs of potentially dangerous avalanche areas; good hunters exercise caution in handling their weapons; and a knowledge of native plants and animals, or an understanding of geological processes, enhances the pleasures of a visit to the mountains. Interpretive programs foster the latter in many areas.

Knowledge and understanding of a natural environment also foster good outdoor manners. Such awareness encourages participation in perpetuating the beauty of unspoiled surroundings; this is extremely important because outdoor recreational values are not inexhaustible and, in many cases, are very fragile. Careless treatment, whether by design or ignorance, reduces the worth of an area. Most people know of formerly attractive places ruined by thoughtless acts or deliberate vandalism.

Finally, since recreation bases its appeal primarily on "fun" and freedom of choice of activities, and since human beings are creatures of habit, recreational interests and outlook are often circumscribed by individual background. Many people take advantage only of most readily available opportunities which demand minimum personal effort. They may not only ignore opportunity to broaden their perspective through recreation but may, on occasion, even resist such opportunities. Only experienced, subtle, and perceptive direction can jog such people from self-imposed routine which, in some cases, may not be in keeping with the primary purpose of an area. A story (which may or may not be true) illustrates a lack of understanding of the primary purpose of national parks on the part of a group of young men. Arriving in such an area for the first time they immediately sought the public dance hall. On being informed that such a facility did not exist in that area they exclaimed, "What do you expect people to do here anyway, just look at the scenery?"

PROFESSIONAL EDUCATION IN RECREATION

Professional education in recreation [1,3-5,7,9,10,16-18] has developed along two principal lines, owing largely to historical differences in recreational use of different types of land. Each of these educational philosophies still retains a degree of autonomy, but unification of principal objectives, particularly in basic fundamentals relevant to similar needs and problems, typifies many recreation curricula today.

Many educational institutions have long provided curricula in recreation, incorporated in departments of physical education for both men and women. Such curricula are adapted to students with a primary goal of employment in high-density recreational areas, such as in municipal and county parks and playgounds, where emphasis is on sports and related activities. Such programs, weak in the natural sciences, are not well-adapted to recreational management of wild lands. However, some institutions now incorporate such programs in a broader curriculum which gives greater attention to both natural and social science under a Department of Recreation and Park Administration.

Ⅹ Professional education in recreational management of *wild* lands, instituted in a meager fashion as early as the 1920s, has greatly changed and expanded. Early curricula were basically slanted toward resource management; little, if any, attention was given to people-related aspects of wild land recreational management, a deficiency readily recognized by pioneers in that field. The growth of public interest in environmental maintenance and the phenomenal increase in public recreational use of wild lands soon indicated the need for greater breadth in curricula designed for students of wild-land recreational management. Both undergraduate and graduate programs of that nature are now offered by colleges and universities in various parts of the country.[2]

At most institutions offering programs in recreational management of wild lands the undergraduate curriculum aims at development of a broad educational background with strong emphasis on the natural and social sciences, together with exposure to fundamental recreational management techniques. Considerable emphasis is also placed on proper use of English, necessary to communication of ideas, as well as upon mathematics which is basic to engineering and statistical analysis in planning and development of wild-land recreational areas. Lower division years are devoted to the basic courses in the natural and social sciences. Upper division courses build upon this foundation. In addition, upper division students are given a basic introduction to technical skills important in recreational land management procedures, including land planning, policy determination, and development and operation of facilities and services.

Graduate programs are designed primarily for individuals who demonstrate potential for upper echelons of management or for a career in research, teaching, or some particular specialty. Such programs are generally

---

[2] These are often related to colleges of forestry, forest resources or natural resources. Though forestry has been challenged as a logical base for such programs, it is natural that forestry and recreational management of wild lands attract young people with similar interests. Both fields of interest are based upon understanding of biological laws pertinent to plants and animals in relation to environment. The basic interests of many wild-land recreational areas are closely related to their forest cover. In addition, basic forestry education emphasizes protection, land survey and planning, trail and road construction, and related activities which are also important in recreational land management. The close affinity of forestry and recreational management of wild lands is further emphasized by the fact that many professional foresters are engaged in various types of recreational work. Many have made notable contributions to the recreational management of wild lands and some, like Aldo Leopold and Robert Marshall, are recognized as pioneer leaders in this area.

related to individual requirements. They may place emphasis on either the social (people-related) or natural science (resource) approach to wild-land recreational management. They may be developed within a formalized recreational land management department or along with other relevant disciplines, such as sociology, economics, geography, architecture or landscape architecture, law or political science, or the natural sciences (e.g., botany, zoology, geology).

SUMMARY

Wild-land recreational areas are resource-oriented, typified by largely unmodified conditions and dispersed or extensive activities. Major management concerns include maintenance of environmental conditions and guidance of public recreational use to enhance varied recreational experiences. By contrast, highly developed and more readily accessible recreational areas such as municipal and county parks are activity-oriented, typified by concentrated or intensive activities. They are a distinct specialty and are not emphasized in this text except where directly related to recreation on wild lands.

Despite certain ambiguities, agricultural and managed forest lands are included here with more truly natural wild lands; they are essentially undeveloped and recreational activities provided are closely related to activities on certain wild lands. Historical and archeological areas are also included with wild lands, due to their close relation because of their unique qualities and, often similar administrative relationships.

Today wild-land recreational areas are recognized as important for a variety of stimulating physical, intellectual and cultural interests and activities. However, most of the original wild-land park and related recreation areas were established because of the energy and persistence of perceptive individuals or groups at a time when such areas were less valuable as sources of raw materials, or when they were relatively more remote. Further, expediency characterized early efforts to provide and develop wildland recreational areas. Most resource-oriented parks and forests were established on public lands in the West, while the population was, and is, concentrated primarily in the Eastern United States. There was also little early recognition of the important relationship between highly developed, readily accessible recreational areas and those on more remote wild lands; this has resulted in some inappropriate developments on certain wild lands which have become well established in the public mind and which have caused problems.

Initially, recreation was not generally regarded as an important function of wild lands utilized for raw material production. As a result, with increased interest in wild-land recreation, numerous conflicts developed between resource-extraction and recreation-use of land. Increased recreational use of wild land also prompted an increasing number of conflicts between groups of recreationists having special interests. Such conflicts can be solved only by perceptive planning which recognizes the degree of compatibility of specific recreational activities.

This chapter also notes the importance of esthetically pleasing, well-managed forests and farmlands which, though not directly used for recreation, function as greenbelts about cities and towns and enhance the interest of our total environment. This chapter also cautions that the public will have to accept an increasing degree of regimentation of all types of recreational activities on wild land so that the maximum number of people may share in resultant benefits.

Finally, increasing use of wild land for recreation has prompted an increase in professionally oriented, academic curricula at numerous colleges and universities on both the undergraduate and graduate levels in a diversity of fields relevant to wild-land recreation. The goal of such educational efforts is to provide necessary qualified leadership in recreational planning and management.

SELECTED REFERENCES

1 Brightbill, Charles K.: Education for Recreation Leadership, *Proceedings on the National Conference on Professional Education for Outdoor Recreation*, Syracuse, N.Y., 1964.
2 Clawson, Marion: "Land and Water for Recreation," Rand-McNally, Chicago, 1963.
3 Clawson, Marion, and Jack L. Knetsch: "Economics of Outdoor Recreation," Resources for the Future, Johns Hopkins, Baltimore, 1966.
4 Crane, Lyle E.: Education in Outdoor Recreation, *Proceedings of the National Conference on Outdoor Recreation Research*, Ann Arbor, Mich., 1963.
5 Dana, Samuel T.: "Education and Outdoor Recreation," U.S. Department of the Interior, Bureau of Outdoor Recreation, U.S. Government Printing Office, Washington, 1968.
6 Fischer, D. W., and others: "Land and Leisure," Maaroufa Press, Chicago, 1974.
7 Floyd, J. Whitney: Forest and Wildlife Education for Outdoor Recreation, *Proceedings of the National Conference on Professional Education for Outdoor Recreation*, Syracuse, N.Y., 1964.
8 Hendee, John C., Richard P. Gale, and Joseph Harry: Conservationists, Politics, and Democracy, *Journal of Soil and Water Conservation*, vol. 24, no. 6, November-December 1969.
9 Jensen, Clayne R.: "Outdoor Recreation in America: Trends, Problems, and Opportunities," 2nd ed., Burgess Pub. Co., Minneapolis, 1973.
10 LaGasse, Alfred B., and Walter L. Cook: Historical Development of Professional Education Programs for Outdoor Recreation, *Proceedings of the National Conference on Professional Education for Outdoor Recreation*, Syracuse, N.Y., 1964.

11 Moser, Don: Dig They Must, The Army Engineers, Securing Allies and Ac-
    quiring Enemies, *Smithsonian Magazine*, vol. 7, no. 9, pp. 40–51, December
    1976.
12 Moser, Don: Mangrove Island Is Reprieved by Army Engineers, *Smithsonian
    Magazine*, vol. 7, no. 10, pp. 68–77, January 1977.
13 Outdoor Recreation Resources Review Commission: "Outdoor Recreation for
    America: A Report to the President and to the Congress by the ORRRC," U.S.
    Government Printing Office, Washington, 1962.
14 President's Council on Recreation and Natural Beauty: "From Sea to Shining
    Sea," U.S. Government Printing Office, Washington, 1968.
15 Sharpe, Grant W., Clare W. Hendee and Shirley W. Allen: "Introduction to
    Forestry," 4th ed., McGraw-Hill, 1976.
16 Smith, Julian W.: Leadership Preparation for Outdoor Recreation, *Proceedings
    of the National Conference on Professional Education for Outdoor Recreation*,
    Syracuse, N.Y., 1964.
17 Smith, Julian W., and others: "Outdoor Education," 2nd ed., Prentice-Hall,
    Englewood Cliffs, N.J., 1972.
17a Stein, Thomas A., and Roger A. Lancaster: Professional Preparation, *Parks and
    Recreation.* vol. ll. no. 7. July 1976.
18 Underhill, A. H.: "Outdoor Education—Training and Research," Bureau of
    Outdoor Recreation, U.S. Government Printing Office, Washington, 1967.
19 U.S. Department of the Interior, National Park Service: "A Report on Our
    Vanishing Shoreline," Washington, 1958.
20 U.S. Department of the Interior, National Park Service: "Our Fourth Shore,
    Great Lakes Shoreline Recreational Survey," Washington, 1959.
21 U.S. Department of the Interior, National Park Service: "Pacific Coast Recrea-
    tion Area Survey," Washington, 1959.
22 U.S. Department of the Interior: "The Race for Inner Space," U.S. Govern-
    ment Printing Office, Washington, 1964.
23 U.S. Department of the Interior: "The Quest for Quality," Conservation Year-
    book No. 1, U.S. Government Printing Office, Washington, 1965.

Yellowstone National Park, first area of its kind, was established in 1872. Changes in recreational use of wild lands since that time embody much more than the attire of visitors, such as that of this group at Handkerchief Pool in 1903. *(National Park Service.)*

Section Two

Evolution of Recreational Land Use

Initial Interests in Recreational Land Values

Recreational values have always been present in the outdoors, but only in recent times have steps been taken to manage, preserve, and utilize them on a continuing basis.

The history of recreational use of wild lands, outlined in this and the following two chapters, notes significant developments over many years. This historical outline is important since the upsurge of public interest in recreation in recent decades has prompted increased concern for perpetuation of recreational land values. This increased interest has also exposed both negative and positive effects of policies and directions still affecting today's programs. Understanding of historic actions may promote solutions to many of today's recreational land management problems. The historical record revealed here will help present-day recreation leaders to recognize the reasons underlying earlier developments and to build upon the successes and profit from the failures of their pioneer counterparts.

EARLIEST RECORDED RECREATIONAL LANDS

In one guise or another, tracts of land have been reserved for park and recreation purposes since time immemorial. The earliest of these were established by the nobility, primarily for personal pleasure or self-aggrandizement. The concept of establishing such areas for general public use, though existing in early periods of recorded history, did not assume importance until the nineteenth century.

In hunting one finds a close affinity with primitive and modern concepts of outdoor recreation. To primitive peoples hunting was a means of sustaining life rather than recreation; they recognized their dependence upon a continuing supply of wild game and developed certain rules by which the taking of that game was guided. The modern science of wildlife management, the keystone of good hunting and fishing and an important aspect of recreation on wild lands, has evolved from practices that date from antiquity [7,13].

The first parks on record, featuring woodlands, vineyards, and other vegetation, and interspersed with trails and ponds, date back to 2500 B.C. in ancient Babylonia and Sumer in western Asia. Similarly, parklands were not uncommon during the heyday of Assyria, Persia, Greece, and Rome [4,6]. Some of these were designated as private hunting preserves, a practice that was continued during medieval times by European nobility.

In particular, wild land for modern recreation has a close relation to areas of this type in Great Britain. In feudal England, where a forest was more important as a source of game than of timber, hunting by the nobility, greatly extended by William the Conqueror and later Norman kings, was not modified until after the adoption of the Magna Charta in 1215 [7,13].

Today most of those medieval English preserves are but historical memories, but two areas exist as modern survivals of that period. Both the Forest of Dean, west of Gloucester [8], and the New Forest, near Southampton [9], can trace their ancestry directly to the Norman period and earlier.[1]

During the Renaissance, lavish private formal gardens became the vogue on the European continent. This fashion, originating in northern Italy, continued to the latter part of the eighteenth century, with Versailles, just outside Paris, and Schönbrunn, near Vienna, being among the more noted examples. Development of English estates, however, though affected by such interest on the Continent, generally followed a more natural rather than a highly formal pattern [4, 6].

While attention to recreation was largely in the interests of privileged classes during ancient and medieval times, the needs of the general public

---

[1] In 1087 the New Forest was decreed by William the Conqueror to be his royal domain, thus giving rise to its name, which has persisted to the present time. Today, by the slow processes of history, this area has become the common heritage of all Englishmen, administered by the British Forestry Commission for grazing, timber production, and public recreation. Its boundaries embrace 144 square miles of forest, meadow, and moor, of which about 100 square miles is publicly owned crown land. The Forestry Commission, principal administrative agency of this and similar areas in England, is a direct descendant of the lord wardens appointed by the medieval kings to preserve their personal domain, and the principal administrative officer of the New Forest is still known by the ancient title of deputy surveyor [9].

were not completely ignored. Public parks are known to have existed in the twelfth century B.C. in certain cities of what are now Sri Lanka (Ceylon) and India [4,6]. Ancient Greece and Rome made provision for certain types of public recreational needs, and by the end of the thirteenth century, public squares and, later, areas suited for games and various athletic contests came into existence in many parts of Europe [4,6].

By the nineteenth century, many nations of the world began to adopt more democratic principles, largely as a result of the effects of the American and French Revolutions. Thus, restricted private parks and hunting preserves were made increasingly available to the general populace [4,6].

Eventually many such areas which formerly had been the sole property of wealthy or powerful individuals came under state control with provision for general public access and use. For example, the many public parks which are such an attractive feature of modern metropolitan London once were, like the more distant and extensive Forest of Dean and the New Forest, the personal property of the Crown [4,6].

Establishment of specific areas of wild land primarily for preservation and public understanding of varied significant interests (geological, biological, archeological, historical) and enjoyment of scenic and related outdoor recreational values (sight-seeing, hiking, climbing, camping, boating, fishing, hunting) is generally conceded to have followed the initial steps taken in the United States toward the end of the nineteenth century. Today this concept of land use is widely recognized throughout the world. Over 100 nations have established national parks and various types of related reserves for preservation of significant interests and for public enjoyment (see Chapter 17).

RECREATION AND THE AMERICAN CONSERVATION MOVEMENT

In the United States the current extensive and growing interest in the recreational use of wild land is commonly regarded as having evolved from our general interest in the regulation of forests, wildlife, soils, water, and similar natural resources. However, the record indicates that this is not entirely the case. True, until recent years, progress in the conservation of other more tangible land values has been more obvious; but rather than being incidental to the broad conservation movement, interest in recreational value of wild land was one of several principal motive forces if not the primary one. Evidence of this is the fact that the first extensive areas of wild land to be reserved for public benefit were dedicated to an outdoor recreational objective. The Yosemite Grant (1864), Yellowstone National Park (1872), and the Niagara Falls Reservation (1885) came into being well in advance of our national and state forests, federal and state wildlife reserves and refuges, and similar areas of specifically dedicated public lands important to varied objectives of modern American conservation practices.

There were, of course, earlier manifestations of public interest in the regulation of natural resources in the United States. However, establishment of the Yosemite Grant, Yellowstone National Park, and the Niagara Falls Reservation served largely in preparing public opinion for acceptance of more complete conservation principles involving the perpetuation of scenic, environmental, and recreational resources of wild land.

The American conservation movement was marked by many important early milestones. Among the most noteworthy were restrictive colonial laws relating to game and timber, the passage of the Great Ponds Act by the Massachusetts Bay Colony, the origination and initial development of municipal parks, the reservation of lands surrounding the mineral springs in the Ouachita Mountains of Arkansas, and the birth of the national park concept. The latter involved the first suggestion of a national park and the establishment of the Yosemite Grant, the first area of wild land set aside specifically for public recreational use.

Early Reservation of Wild Land for Public Benefit

The Great Ponds Act, passed by the Massachusetts Bay Colony in 1641, was the first important milestone in the reservation of wild land for the public benefit. As such it has a direct relation with outdoor recreation.

The act decreed that about two thousand bodies of water, each exceeding 10 acres in size and collectively amounting to an area of approximately 90,000 acres, were to remain as a public resource forever open to the public for "fishing and fowling." With the passing of time, the Great Ponds lost much of their earlier utilitarian value and became more important and most generally used for recreational purposes. In 1923, when this trend from the original concept was questioned, the attorney general of Massachusetts ruled that the Great Ponds Act, permitting public access to, and use of, these waters, was still valid even though the character of public use had changed [14].

The second major milestone in the history of American conservation, as it relates to outdoor recreation on wild land, occurred in 1832, when Congress passed an act reserving four sections of land in the Ouachita Mountains of Arkansas "for the future disposal of the United States" [20, 23,24]. The act stated further that this reservation "shall not be entered, located, or appropriated, for any other purpose whatever" [20]. This area included a number of hot mineral springs whose waters were thus reserved for posterity and removed from the danger of private monopoly and exploitation.

Although the Hot Springs Reservation was not established because of its recreational values, these assumed increasing importance in later years. As a result, the hot springs area was incorporated into the National Park System in 1921 as Hot Springs National Park [22,24].

Early Municipal Parks in the United States

The common, or green, typical of many New England towns has its roots in the American colonial period, and although such areas were established for reasons other than recreation, their recreational values eventually assumed a dominant role as the communities grew. One of the most noteworthy examples of such early municipal public areas is the Boston Common, established in 1634, which has served the citizens of Boston for over 300 years [4,19].

Recognition of the need for open spaces in town planning was expressed in somewhat similar fashion in other sections of the United States during its formative period. In accordance with Spanish custom, a public square, or plaza, was reserved in the development of most early Spanish settlements in America [21]. In 1682 William Penn reserved a number of tracts for public use within the city of Philadelphia [4,11,21]. James Edward Oglethorpe was guided by related ideas in developing the city of Savannah, Georgia, in 1733 [4,21], and open areas were provided for by Major Pierre Charles L'Enfant in planning Washington, D.C., in 1791 [4]. Other early examples of public open spaces include a bowling green in New Amsterdam, forerunner of New York City, in 1732; the site of old Fort Dearborn in Chicago, in 1839 [4]; and public squares reserved in the initial planning of Salt Lake City by Brigham Young, in 1847 [21]. Additionally, beginning in the third decade of the past century a number of rural scenic cemeteries were developed. They were not uncommonly used about that time for picnicking and related types of outdoor activities. Mount Auburn, the first of such areas, was established near Boston in 1831 [11].

Central Park in New York is one of the most significant of municipal parks in the United States. Established in 1853,[2] it was the first large area acquired largely by purchase of land by a municipality exclusively for public recreational use. Its early administration, planning, and development were largely directed by Frederick Law Olmsted, who from 1864 to 1866 played a major role in the establishment and early administration of the Yosemite Grant.[3]

BIRTH OF THE NATIONAL PARK CONCEPT

As previously stated, the reservation of wild land for recreational purposes was a potent force in the modern American conservation movement. Since

[2] Central Park, the outgrowth of numerous earlier suggestions for a large public park on Manhattan Island, was first proposed by a group of prominent citizens in 1850. In 1853 the state legislature authorized its establishment and the purchase of necessary lands; land acquisition was begun late in the same year [1,4,15].

[3] Olmsted was appointed superintendent of Central Park in 1857. In 1858 the design for improvement of the area proposed by Olmsted and Calvert Vaux was approved by the park commissioners; in general outline, this plan served as a guide to subsequent development [1,4,15]. Olmsted's connection with the Yosemite Grant occurred during the period when he was manager of General Fremont's Mariposa Estate in California [2,16,17].

the establishment of national parks figured prominently in such affairs, the birth date of the national park concept is highly important.

First Proposal of a National Park

In 1833, the influential and widely circulated *New York Daily Commercial Advertiser* published a series of letters by George Catlin,[4] explorer and artist, who had visited the Indian country of the upper Missouri in 1832 [11]. Catlin's experiences prompted his interest in the American Indian and caused him to ponder ways and means of preserving segments of native interests for the future. One of his letters included this significant observation:

> . . . and what a splendid contemplation too, when one (who has traveled these realms and can duly appreciate them) imagines them as they might in the future be seen (by some protective policy of government) preserved in their pristine beauty and wildness, in a magnificent park, where the world could see for ages to come, the native Indian in his classic attire, galloping his wild horse amid the fleeting herds of elks and buffalos. What a specimen for America to preserve for her refined citizens and the world, in future ages. A nations park, containing man and beast, in all the wild and freshness of their nature's beauty. I would ask no other monument to my memory, nor any other enrollment of my name amongst the famous dead, than the reputation of having been the founder of such an institution [3].

This statement is highly significant in that it antedates by more than three decades the establishment of the first area of wild land for public benefit primarily because of recreational values (Yosemite Grant, 1864), and by nearly forty years the establishment of the first national park (Yellowstone, 1872). It is a reflection of the change from negative American attitudes toward nature, which began early in the eighteenth century. This change in attitude resulted in large measure from poets, writers, and artists whose works extolled nature's beauties, thus making the interests of the outdoors more meaningful [11]. In Catlin's remarks one observes the dawn of an awareness of the esthetic and cultural qualities inherent in significant segments of typical, primitive America and the need for their preservation. In a somewhat similar vein Thoreau also expressed the growing interest in protection of wild places about the middle of the past century [11]. Such ideas, firmly linked with the establishment of national parks, were also important in the designation of other types of wild land for various outdoor recreational purposes.

The Yosemite Grant

The Yosemite Grant, established in 1864, was the first extensive area of wild land to be set aside primarily for public recreation. Although the federal government did not assume administrative authority for the Yosemite

---

[4] Catlin's letters, together with his drawings, were later published in book form [3].

Grant at the time of its establishment, and did not recognize its responsibility in that direction, interest in the unique character of the Yosemite Valley and the nearby Mariposa Grove of Big Trees[5] prompted it to entrust these parts of the public domain to the state of California "upon the express conditions that the premises shall be held for public use, resort, and recreation; shall be inalienable for all time. . . . " [16,20][6]

The bill concerning the Yosemite Grant was introduced into Congress on March 28, 1864, by Senator John Conness of California, who stated that its purpose was:

> . . . to commit them [Yosemite Valley and the Mariposa Grove of Big Trees] to the care of the authorities of that State for their constant preservation, that they may be exposed to public view, and that they may be used and preserved for the benefit of mankind. . . . The plan [of preservation] comes from gentlemen of fortune, of taste, and of refinement. . . . The bill prepared by the commissioner of the General Land Office, who takes a great interest in the preservation both of Yosemite Valley and the Big Trees Grove [16].[7]

It was passed by the Senate on May 17, passed by the House on June 29, and signed by President Abraham Lincoln on July 1, 1864 [16,17].

This was a memorable event, especially when one considers that it occurred during the Civil War, one of the darkest periods of our history. It is also significant that the language of the bill establishing the Yosemite

---

[5] Commonly known as giant sequoia (*Sequoia gigantea*); some authorities consider this tree a single species in a distinct genus—*Sequoiadendron giganteum*.

[6] The first civilized men to see the valley were American Trappers, members of the Walker expedition, who viewed it from the north rim in the fall of 1833, while laboriously journeying westward across the Sierra Nevada [5,16]. In March, 1851, the valley was first entered by the Mariposa Battalion, a group of American citizen-soldiers organized to put down an Indian uprising that followed the discovery of gold in California [16]. The recalcitrant Yosemites, for whom the Mariposa Battalion named the valley, were pursued to this point.

The first "tourist party" visited Yosemite Valley in June, 1855 [16]. This journey was prompted by accounts of the earlier military expeditions which appeared in San Francisco newspapers. One of these accounts mentioned a spectacular waterfall of prodigious height. James M. Hutchings, then publishing the *California Magazine* in San Francisco, became intrigued with the possibility of describing such a spectacle in his publication; with several companions, including an artist and two Indian guides, he made the long horseback journey into the Sierra and "spent five glorious days in scenic banqueting" in the valley [10,16]. As a result of publicity given Yosemite Valley by Hutchings, interest in the area quickly developed. Soon, various well-known publications of the period began extolling the interests of the area, and prominent writers, artists, photographers, and public figures added their praise.

Coincident with developing interest in Yosemite Valley was the discovery of several groves of giant sequoia on the western slope of the Sierra, including the one located a few miles south of Yosemite Valley. In 1857 and 1858, the *Atlantic Monthly* and *Harper's Weekly* began agitating for the preservation of these groves [11].

Thus the idea of preserving significant areas in their natural state for the enjoyment of present and future generations began to take form. Further, by 1864, there was need for immediate positive action; as part of the public domain Yosemite Valley was subject to entry, and several units of it had already been acquired by private individuals. The establishment of the Yosemite Grant gave priority to public rights in the area and, after considerable litigation, claimants to certain lands in the valley were satisfied with a financial settlement [12,16].

[7] Also see *Congressional Globe*, May 14, 1864, p. 2301.

Grant paralleled the intent of later national parks. Further, Frederick Law Olmsted, one of the planners and an early administrator of Central Park in New York City, as previously noted, was one of those who supported the establishment of the Yosemite Grant; he also served as one of its original commissioners [2,16].[8]

EARLY COMMERCIAL RECREATIONAL FACILITIES

One should not overlook the significance of early interest in general recreational travel and commercial recreational facilities in the outdoors [11]. This interest was, naturally, first manifested in the East. Accommodations for visitors were available at Franconia Notch in the White Mountains as early as 1820, and a hotel, later considerably enlarged in response to public patronage, was built in the Catskills in 1825. These were among the earliest visitor accommodations in out-of-the-way places, although a number of health resorts and more readily accessible beach locations on the Atlantic had been utilized by the public for some time. Following the opening of the Erie Canal, in 1827, canal-boats offering sleeping and eating facilities began making trips through New York State to Lake Ontario. For more than a decade this mode of travel was in high favor. Soon thereafter, travel to outlying areas was extended by early railroads of the Eastern seaboard region. Thus, early public interest in the recreational values of wild land preceded the first official actions concerning the perpetuation of them.

These early recreational facilities were the seeds from which our modern, diversified, and extensive "tourist industry" has grown. Slowly, as communities in various parts of the United States developed and achieved a sense of permanence, and as travel facilities improved, public recreational interest in distant places expanded.

SUMMARY

The recreational use of land dates from antiquity. Origins of such use can be traced to ancient parks and related areas of the Middle East and parts of southern Asia. Later such use was manifested in early Greece and Rome, eventually spreading to other sections of Europe during feudal times and the Renaissance.

Although there were exceptions, such lands were initially established by the nobility for their personal pleasure and prestige. Through different periods of history they assumed different forms, according to the mode of the times, such as sites set aside for games and athletic contests, hunting preserves, and formal gardens.

---

[8] Olmsted had left New York City a few years earlier to undertake the management of the Mariposa Estate, a large tract of land owned by General Fremont and located in the foothill region near Yosemite [16,17]. Primarily because of his experience in landscape architecture and park planning, Olmsted assumed the major responsibility of the early administration of the Yosemite Grant; he served as its original custodian [2].

Table 3-1 Chronological Highlights of Wildland Recreation in the United States

1634: Boston Common (eventual Boston city park) established.

1641: Great Ponds Act passed by Massachusetts Bay Colony.

1820: Early commercial resort hotel established in White Mountains, New Hampshire.

1832: Hot Springs Reservation, Arkansas, established.

1833: Initial proposal of a "nations park" by George Catlin.

1853: Central Park, New York City, established.

1858: Mount Vernon, Virginia, acquired by Mount Vernon Ladies Association.

1864: Yosemite Grant (initial state park) ceded to California by Federal Government.

1872: Yellowstone National Park established.

1875: American Forestry Association formed.

1876: Dr. Franklin B. Hough appointed Forestry Agent in Department of Agriculture.

1881: Division of Forestry formed in Department of Agriculture.

1891: Forest Reserve Act passed; Yellowstone Timberland Reserve (first of eventual national forests) established; initially under jurisdiction of Department of the Interior.

1892: Sierra Club formed by John Muir.

1895: Initial county park established in Essex County, New Jersey.

1903: Initial wildlife reserve (Pelican Island, Florida) established.

1905: U.S. Forest Service formed in Department of Agriculture; forest reserves transferred from Department of the Interior; Gifford Pinchot first Chief of the Forest Service.

1906: Antiquities Act passed (authorized establishment of national monuments); Yosemite Grant re-ceded to Federal government and incorporated into Yosemite National Park (est. 1890).

1908: National Conservation Conference of Governors convenes; President Theodore Roosevelt and Gifford Pinchot, Chief of the Forest Service, were leaders in discussions.

1913: Hetch Hetchy Dam, Yosemite National Park, authorized; apex of Muir-Pinchot controversy.

1916: National Park Service established in Department of the Interior; Stephen T. Mather named first director.

1918: Recreational values of national forests investigated by F. A. Waugh.

1921: National Conference on State Parks initiated by Stephen T. Mather.

1922: Initial funds provided officially for recreation on national forests.

1924: National Conference on Outdoor Recreation convenes (initial effort for national recreation planning); Gila Primitive Area, New Mexico, designated by Forest Service, largely through efforts of Aldo Leopold.

1925: Initial official recreation policy formulated by Forest Service for national forests.

1926: Restoration of Williamsburg, Virginia, begun; Recreation and Public Purposes Act passed, providing for recreational use of public domain lands.

1929: National Wildlife Refuge System initiated; Forest Service designates Primitive Areas (L-20 regulation) on national forests.

1930–1942: Depression years; federal emergency work programs (WPA, CCC, PWA, NYA) developed.

1933: Tennessee Valley Authority Act passed; recreational use of TVA projects authorized.

1939: Wilderness regulations (U-1, U-2, U-3) formulated by Forest Service.

1941: Tree-Farm program and Tree-farm Parks initiated in State of Washington.

1944: Flood Control Act passed; authorized recreation on Corps of Engineer projects.

1941–1945: World War II; federal emergency work programs and wildland recreation curtailed.

1956: Mission 66 program initiated by National Park Service.

1958: Operation Outdoors program initiated by Forest Service.

1958–1962: Outdoor Recreation Resources Review Commission develops report, a catalyst for national recreational planning.

1960: Multiple Use Sustained Yield Act (re national forests) passed.

1962: Bureau of Outdoor Recreation established in Department of the Interior.

1964: Wilderness Act passed, authorized establishment of National Wilderness Preservation System; Land and Water Conservation Fund Act passed; Public Land Law Review initiated.

1965: Recreation on Bureau of Reclamation reservoirs liberalized and expanded.

1969: National Environmental Policy Act (re Federal lands) passed.

1974: Forest and Rangeland Renewable Resources Planning Act passed.

1975: Eastern Wilderness Act passed.

1976: National Forest Management Act passed; Federal Land Policy and Management Act (Bureau of Land Management organic act) passed.

Eventually, as democratic principles gradually replaced earlier autocratic systems of government, many of these areas were made increasingly available to the general public. Some surviving remnants of these early European areas are now well-known public parks and reserves.

Establishment of wild lands for public recreational use was one of the important aspects of the American conservation movement, which began to take form during the latter part of the nineteenth century, and which also involved protection of forests, wildlife, and related natural resources. Earliest manifestations of public interest in such matters included the reservation of the Great Ponds by the Massachusetts Bay Colony in 1641, establishment of the Hot Springs Reservation in the Ouachita Mountains of Arkansas in 1832, and the birth of the national park concept—including the first proposal of a national park in 1833 and the establishment of the Yosemite Grant in 1864. The Yosemite Grant, forerunner of Yosemite National Park, was the first area of wild land set aside specifically for public recreational use.

Establishment of public areas by pioneer communities during the American colonial period is closely related to concepts of public recreational use of wild lands. Though recreation was but one of the initial values of such early public areas, recreational uses expanded and eventually became dominant as these communities grew in size. They were the basis of our present municipal park systems. One of the most noteworthy municipal parks is Central Park in New York City, which dates from 1853. Its early administration, planning, and development were largely in the hands of Frederick Law Olmsted, who later supported establishment of the Yosemite Grant, was one of its original commissioners, and served as its original custodian.

Olmsted was a most competent land-use planner. He understood the separation of land uses and natural scenery. Some of his development principles for Yosemite Valley are still in effect today.

However, public interest in the recreational values of wild lands preceded recognition of official responsibility in the protection of these values. The first commercial accommodations necessary for recreational use of wild lands were provided in the Northeast as early as the 1820s. Later expansion of such facilities, together with early development of relatively comfortable means of travel, were the nuclei of our present important "travel industry."

SELECTED REFERENCES

1 Anonymous: "An Outline History of Central Park," City of New York, Department of Parks, n.d. (Mimeographed.)
2 Brockman, C. Frank: Principal Administrative Officers of Yosemite: Frederick Law Olmsted, *Yosemite Nature Notes*, vol. 25, no. 9, pp. 106–110, September 1946.

3 Catlin, George: "The Manners, Customs, and Condition of the North American Indians," London, 1841, vol. 1, pp. 261–262.
4 Doell, Charles E., and Gerald B. Fitzgerald: "A Brief History of Parks and Recreation in the United States," Athletic Institute, Chicago, 1954.
5 Farquahar, Francis W.: Walker's Discovery of Yosemite, *Sierra Club Bulletin*, vol. 27, no. 4, pp. 35–49, August 1942.
6 Gotheim, Marie Luise: "A History of Garden Art" (Walter P. Wright, ed.; translation by Laura Archer-Hind), 2 vols., Dent, London, Dutton, New York, 1928.
7 Graham, E. H.: "The Land and Wildlife," Oxford, New York, 1947.
8 Great Britain, Forestry Commission: "Forest of Dean: National Forest Park Guides," His Majesty's Stationery Office, London, 1947.
9 Great Britain, Forestry Commission: "New Forest: Forestry Commission Guide," Her Majesty's Stationery Office, London, 1951. (Reprinted 1952.)
10 Hutchings, James M.: "In the Heart of the Sierras," Pacific Press, Oakland, Calif., 1886.
11 Huth, Hans: "Nature and the American," University of California Press, Berkeley, 1957.
12 Ise, John: "Our National Park Policy," Johns Hopkins, Baltimore, 1961.
13 Leopold, Aldo: "Game Management," Scribner, New York, 1947.
14 Nelson, Beatrice: "State Recreation," National Conference on State Parks, Washington, 1928.
15 Reed, Henry Hope, and Sophia Duckworth: "Central Park: A History and a Guide," Potter, New York, 1967.
16 Russell, Carl P.: "100 Years in Yosemite," University of California Press, Berkeley, 1947.
17 Sax, Joseph L.: America's National Parks—Their Principles, Purposes, and Prospects, *Special Supplement to Natural History Magazine*, October 1976.
18 Sharpe, Grant W., Clare W. Hendee, and Shirley W. Allen: "Introduction to Forestry," 4th. ed., McGraw-Hill, 1976.
19 State Street Trust Co.: "State Street: A Brief Account of a Boston Way," Boston, 1906.
20 Tolson, Hillary A.: "Laws Relating to the National Park Service, the National Parks and Monuments," U.S. Government Printing Office, Washington, 1933.
21 U.S. Department of the Interior, Bureau of Labor Statistics: "Park Recreation Areas in the United States," Miscellaneous Publication No. 462, U.S. Government Printing Office, Washington, 1928.
22 U.S. Department of the Interior, National Park Service: "Annual Report of the Superintendent of National Parks to the Secretary of the Interior for the Fiscal Year Ended June 30, 1916," U.S. Government Printing Office, Washington, 1916.
23 U.S. Department of the Interior, National Park Service: "Hot Springs National Park, Arkansas," U.S. Government Printing Office, Washington, 1950.
24 U.S. Department of the Interior, National Park Service: "Index of the National Park System," U.S. Government Printing Office, Washington, 1977.

Growth of Interest in Recreational Use of Wild Land

Public awareness of the need for all aspects of conservation developed greatly between the establishment of the Yosemite Grant, in 1864, and 1900. During that period our first five national parks, as well as initial state parks, were established. In addition, a number of states formed forestry commissions and state forests, the first federal forest reserves (now known as national forests) were formed, and the nucleus of the U.S. Forest Service evolved. Also important during those years was the establishment of two agencies which were later merged to form the U.S. Fish and Wildlife Service, which administers our National Wildlife Refuge System.

The momentum developed during this period continued beyond the turn of the century and, despite resistance and occasional reverses, lent its force to the expansion and refinement of the entire program of natural-resource and environmental conservation in the United States. A significant feature of such developments was the increase in number and type of areas of wild land to serve the growing demand for recreation.

DEVELOPMENT OF THE NATIONAL PARK SYSTEM

The National Park System had its genesis in the establishment of the early national parks and monuments. The first area officially designated as a national park was Yellowstone. Claims are sometimes made that the National Park System originated with the establishment of the Hot Springs Reservation in 1832 or with the establishment of the Yosemite Grant in 1864 since both were later given national park status. However, the national park concept had not fully matured at the time those earlier reservations were established, and they were not officially designated as national parks.

The First National Park

Yellowstone National Park, established March 1, 1872 [17,18,26,30,50], was the first national park in the United States, as well as in the world. Though it was antedated by several reserves—Hot Springs, 1832; Fontainebleau, near Paris, France, 1853; Yosemite Grant, 1864—establishment of Yellowstone National Park introduced the dramatic new term "national park," which gave emphasis to conservation and crystallized interest in later establishment of other national parks in the United States and throughout the world.

The history of events leading to the establishment of Yellowstone National Park began with the first exploration of that region by John Colter, a member of the Lewis and Clark expedition, in 1807 and 1808 [8,13].[1] Other adventurers followed in Colter's footsteps.[2] All told unbelievable stories of the Yellowstone area when they returned to civilization. These stories eventually aroused official curiosity, resulting in a number of expeditions to the region.[3]

The most significant exploration of the Yellowstone was conducted in 1870 by a group of nine prominent Montana citizens, led by Henry D. Washburn and Nathaniel P. Langford, with a military escort of five cavalrymen under the command of Lieutenant G. C. Doane. Our first national park resulted from the efforts of this group. The suggestion of a national

[1] Colter had become interested in the upper Missouri region during the expedition's westward trek to the Pacific in 1805. In 1806, upon the expedition's return to the Missouri, he was released at his own request in order to explore that area. He discovered the geysers and other evidences of hydrothermal activity in the Yellowstone, but his reports of these phenomena were received by the outside world with derision. As a result, the Yellowstone country was known for many years as "Colter's Hell" [8,13].

[2] Joseph Meek, one of a number of "mountain men" engaged in the fur trade, visited Yellowstone in 1829; Warren A. Ferris, clerk of the American Fur Company, penetrated the area on several occasions in the 1830s and 1840s; and James Bridger, fur trader and "mountain man," made numerous visits to the Yellowstone previous to 1850. Like Colter, all these early explorers told of the wonders which they had observed, only to be met with public skepticism. Bridger embellished accounts of his observations with the wildest fancies of his imagination, and his tall tales of Yellowstone have earned him a unique place in the folklore of the early American West [8,13].

[3] In 1859 and 1860, a government expedition under the command of Captain W. F. Raynolds skirted, but unfortunately never entered, the area now included in the park. In September 1869, the Folsom-Cook-Peterson expedition spent a month in the Yellowstone area, during which time many of its wonders were seen. Folsom's account of that trip appeared in the *Western Monthly*, a Chicago publication, in July 1870. The experience of this group greatly influenced later expeditions; in fact, there is evidence that the idea of a national park was first suggested by Folsom [8,13].

park is credited to Cornelius Hedges, a lawyer from Helena, Montana, during a discussion about their campfire at the junction of the Firehole and Gibbon Rivers, their last camp in what is now Yellowstone National Park, concerning what to do with the results of the expedition. The area was in public domain at that time; anyone had the privilege of establishing a claim in accordance with the law governing such action and eventually gaining ownership of desired property. Supposedly, Hedges proposed that the group forgo personal claims and favor establishment of a national park forever to be protected and available to all the people. His suggestion is said to have met with general favor [13,18,26].

However, there is some doubt as to the authenticity of this oft-told tale. It is derived from a statement made by Langford some years later. Others also claimed to have made such a suggestion; and there is evidence that the idea of Yellowstone National Park was influenced by the language of the bill establishing the Yosemite Grant in 1864. Nevertheless, the Washburn-Langford-Doane expedition was primarily responsible for the establishment of the first national park.

After returning to Helena, Langford took steps to achieve the establishment of Yellowstone National Park. The aid of William H. Clagett, newly elected delegate to Congress from Montana, was enlisted. Later, in Washington, Clagett and Langford drew up the Yellowstone bill, which was introduced into the House by Clagett on December 18, 1871 [8,13].

During the summer of 1871, two government parties made additional studies of the Yellowstone region, one under the leadership of Dr. F. V. Hayden, United States geologist, who became an ardent supporter of the proposed park [8,13]. In the Hayden party was W. H. Jackson, pioneer photographer, who made a remarkably fine series of Yellowstone photographs, samples of which were placed in the hands of all senators and congressmen by Dr. Hayden. Following a favorable opinion by the Secretary of the Interior, in 1872 the Yellowstone bill was adopted by the House on January 30, passed by the Senate on February 27, and signed by President Grant on March 1 [8,13,17,30].

Other Early National Parks

In 1890, Sequoia, General Grant (incorporated into Kings Canyon National Park in 1940), and Yosemite National Parks[4] were established [17,50].

---

[4] Sequoia and General Grant National Parks owe their existence largely to the efforts of George W. Stewart, editor of the *Visalia Delta* [17,26]. Beginning in 1879, in cooperation with a group of public-spirited citizens, Stewart conducted an active campaign for the preservation of those areas which contain extensive representative stands of giant sequoia.

Yosemite National Park is a monument to John Muir. Muir arrived in Yosemite in 1868 [54]. For several years, he lived and worked in Yosemite Valley and the adjacent Sierra Nevada area, studying that region and observing its despoliation. His enthusiasm and knowledge, gained through personal investigation, soon brought him into national prominence as a writer.

In the case of Yosemite, federal parklands surrounded the state-controlled Yosemite Grant, which was not receded to the federal government until 1906 [17,26,50]. Just before the turn of the century, on March 2, 1899, Mt. Rainier National Park,[5] the fifth of these areas, came into being [17, 22,50].

The Antiquities Act

The Antiquities Act, passed June 8, 1906, marked another important milestone in the development of the National Park System. On that date the Act for the Preservation of American Antiquities, introduced into Congress by Representative John F. Lacey, received the signature of President Theodore Roosevelt and became law [17,26,50]. This act empowered the President of the United States to set aside, as national monuments, areas of federally controlled land containing historic landmarks, historic or prehistoric structures, or other objects of historic or scientific interest.

The Antiquities Act is designed to protect and preserve such interests for the benefit of future as well as present generations; it is similar in general purpose to legislation establishing national parks, except that Presidential proclamation rather than congressional action is usually required.[6] It had the support of numerous archeologists, historians, and scientists who had recognized the need for such action as a result of gross vandalism at many significant unprotected sites. Within one year after passage of the Antiquities Act, five of our present series of more than fourscore national monuments had been established.[7]

A number of national parks[8] were originally national monuments [50]. In those cases, the areas were protected until legislation necessary for their redefinition as national parks could be prepared and passed by Congress.

His first article appeared in the *Sacramento Record-Union* on Feb. 2, 1876 [25]. Later writings, based upon a hiking trip south from Yosemite in 1875, emphasized the need for preserving the magnificent groves of giant sequoia; these articles aided Stewart and his associates in their efforts to establish Sequoia and General Grant National Parks. Muir attracted the interest of Robert Underwood, editor of *Century Magazine*, and in 1889 he became a regular contributor to that publication [26,54]. His work was to influence thousands of people on matters pertaining to the preservation and wise use of our natural resources.

[5] The establishment of Mt. Rainier National Park resulted from the combined efforts of the National Geographic Society, the American Association for the Advancement of Science, the Geographical Society of America, the Sierra Club, and the Appalachian Mountain Club [17,22]. Although the original bill, introduced into Congress by Senator Watson Squire of the state of Washington in 1894, did not receive favorable action, a revised bill passed both houses of Congress in 1899 and, on Mar. 2 of that year, was signed by President McKinley.

[6] A number of national monuments have been established by congressional action, representing exceptions to normal procedure.

[7] Devils Tower, Wyoming, Sept. 24, 1906; El Morro, New Mexico, Dec. 8, 1906; Montezuma Castle, Arizona, Dec. 8, 1906; Petrified Forest, Arizona, Dec. 8, 1906; Chaco Canyon, New Mexico, Mar. 11, 1907. Casa Grande National Monument, established Mar. 2, 1889, was administered as a national park until Aug. 3, 1918, when it was changed to national monument status [46].

[8] Carlsbad Caverns, Grand Canyon, Olympic, Zion, Bryce, Petrified Forest.

Although an area receives more secure protection as a national park than as a national monument, considerable time is often required before the support of a majority of the members of Congress can be obtained for the establishment of a national park. In such cases there is danger that efforts may become mired in a morass of legal and political technicalities. Further, forewarned by public interest in an area, those having selfish interest may take advantage of the time lag, legally establish themselves, and destroy, or at least greatly modify, the unique character of the area in question. Since establishment of a national monument usually involves action by but one man—the President—it can be accomplished with greater dispatch. Although national monuments can be decreased or increased in area by Presidential proclamation, only congressional action can eliminate them. Thus, although the protection given these areas is not so absolute as that given national parks, it renders them inviolate as long as they retain a satisfactory area or, as has been desirable in several cases, until they are redefined by congressional action as national parks.

National Park Service Formed

The National Park Act, passed by Congress in 1916 and signed by President Woodrow Wilson on August 25 of that year, coordinated the administration of the national parks then in existence, as well as that of certain national monuments, under a central, specialized authority and laid down certain basic tenets for their proper management and use [17,25,26,30, 45,46,50].

Early Difficulties in National Park Administration Establishment of the National Park Service was prompted by numerous difficulties in national park administration which developed as the number of parks increased [17,26]. The difficulties were manifested almost immediately after the establishment of Yellowstone National Park in 1872, for in the designation of that area Congress made no provision for financial support of an adequate program of administration or protection, or for legal authority to enforce rules and regulations. These important considerations were also largely neglected in the establishment of many later national parks. As a result, there developed a disjointed relation between various national parks, and the lack of a cohesive administrative authority threatened to undermine the concept upon which the parks had been founded and to impair the public services they were intended to render.

During the first five years of the existence of Yellowstone National Park, N. P. Langford served as superintendent without remuneration. The protection of wildlife in Yellowstone National Park was generally ignored during its early years; not until 1894, after a particularly flagrant violation involving hunting in the park, did Congress provide for formal law enforcement or define park offenses and specific penalties. Meanwhile, many applications for leases and concessions of various kinds were received from people who failed to understand national park objectives, and some of the early superintendents who followed Langford not only lacked appreciation of the basic concept of the national park idea but even became unwisely involved in irregular practices in operating facilities for visitors. This untenable situation eventually prompted action. In 1883 a bill was passed by Congress permitting the Secretary of the Interior to request the War Department to assign troops to Yellowstone National Park for the purpose of patrolling the area. Soon thereafter, such a request was made, and from 1886 to 1918, units of cavalry protected Yellowstone National Park; their commanding officers served as acting superintendents. This period also witnessed the construction of the park's basic highway system by the Corps of Engineers [8,17,26].

From 1901 to 1914, Sequoia, General Grant (incorporated into Kings Canyon National Park, 1940) and Yosemite National Parks also were protected by the United States Cavalry [14,17,25]. As in the case of Yellowstone, the officers who served as acting superintendents left an outstanding record of achievement.

For a number of years several national parks, such as Mt. Rainier National Park in the state of Washington [17], and many national monuments which were adjacent to, or surrounded by, national forests were administered by the U.S. Forest Service. In such cases the forest supervisor also acted as the principal administrative officer of the national park or national monument.

Such irregular divisions of responsibility in the field had a counterpart in the lack of unified authority in the office of the Department of the Interior in Washington, D.C. There, responsibility for the national parks was assigned to various officials of the Department who handled such matters in addition to their regular duties [17,26].

Early Suggestions for a National Parks Bureau   A bureau of national parks was first suggested by Dr. Horace McFarland, president of the American Civic Association, and Charles Evans Hughes, governor of New York, during the National Conservation Conference of Governors in 1908 [17,26]. Although nothing tangible resulted from the suggestion, McFarland, with the backing of the American Civic Association, continued to work toward that goal. The U.S. Forest Service, which the dynamic Gifford Pinchot had welded into a coordinated whole in 1905, served as his example. In 1910, McFarland found official support in Secretary of the Interior Richard A. Ballinger, who, in his report to the President that same year, advocated a national parks bureau with an adequate qualified staff [26].

In 1911, Walter L. Fisher became Secretary of the Interior. He had a deep interest in the national parks and, backed by the railroads and the American Automobile Association, he called a meeting of national park officials and other interested individuals in Yellowstone National Park [26].

A similar conference was held in Yosemite National Park in 1912. Thus, for the first time, friends and officials of the national parks joined in a discussion of common problems; on both occasions a national parks bureau was advocated. These meetings had the personal blessing of President Taft, who, in a speech before the American Civic Association in 1911, stated that he was keenly aware of the unsatisfactory administrative status of the national parks [26].

During this period, W. B. Aker, an assistant attorney in the Department of the Interior, served as liaison officer for the national parks in addition to other duties [17,26]. Although he was required to concern himself with only the fiscal affairs of the national parks, he was sincerely interested in all aspects of national park matters. He rendered a service far greater than could normally have been expected from anyone in a similar position.

By 1912, the need for a national parks bureau was so obvious that on February 2 President Taft sent a special message to Congress in which he stated:

> I earnestly recommend the establishment of a Bureau of National Parks. Such legislation is essential to the proper management of these wonderful manifestations of nature. . . . The first step in that direction is the establishment of a responsible bureau, which shall take upon itself the burden of supervising the parks and of making recommendations as to the best method of improving their accessibility and usefulness [26].

Although Congress failed to take action on the President's suggestion, the idea continued to ferment. In 1913, Franklin Lane became Secretary of the Interior, and, in lieu of a national parks bureau, he broadened the responsibilities of the position of assistant to the secretary and gave that post to Adolph C. Miller, professor of economics at the University of California. Miller, to whom specific responsibility for the national parks was delegated, supervised work on appropriate bills relative to the establishment of a national parks bureau; in addition, he set up the framework for better correlation between national parks then in existence by appointing Mark Daniels as superintendent of national parks[26].

Before Miller had completed six months of service, he was "drafted" by President Wilson for a post concerned with the Federal Reserve Act [26]. Daniels continued as superintendent of national parks, but the problem of finding a suitable replacement for Miller was not solved until the following year. At that time Secretary Lane received a letter of complaint about the administration of the national parks, signed by Stephen T. Mather. Lane knew this man well. He was a friend and former classmate at the University of California, a successful Chicago businessman who had been making regular summer pilgrimages into the western mountains for years, and a member of the Sierra Club of California, the Prairie Club of Chicago, and the

American Civic Association. Lane asked Mather to assume responsibility for the administration of the national parks and, at a considerable financial sacrifice, Mather accepted. On June 21, 1915 [17,26], he was sworn in as assistant to the secretary. Horace Albright, who had come to Washington with Miller the previous year, was assigned to work with Mather [17,26]. These two men continued in close association from that day until the time of Mather's resignation in 1929.

Passage of the National Park Service Act   Soon after his appointment as assistant to the secretary, Stephen T. Mather vigorously attacked the problem of establishing a bureau of national parks. With the help of Horace Albright he enlisted the aid of Congressman William Kent and a group of men[9] who were vitally interested in the national parks. This group worked cooperatively to prepare a park service bill which was finally passed by both the House and the Senate. On August 25, 1916, the act establishing the National Park Service was signed by President Woodrow Wilson [17,26,30]. Stephen T. Mather was named Director of the fledgling bureau.

Mather was a strong, dedicated leader who attracted supporters, and was able to organize a loyal and competent staff to operate the National Park Service. Wealthy in his own right, he invested his own funds for worthy park projects which he personally inspected whenever possible. Though interested in the preservation of parks as natural preserves, he also felt the need for roads and adequate hotel developments in the parks to encourage travel and thus gain support from the automobile and railroad traveler. He was also concerned for the education of the visitor and encouraged the establishment of interpretive services in the National Park System.

Aided by his able assistant, Horace Albright, who followed him as Director from 1929 to 1933, Mather's philosophy and policies persisted for many years in the National Park Service. His influence was crucial in the development of the National Park Service and established a pattern for strong agency growth and personnel loyalty. The orientation of the service has been primarily toward the national seasonal visitor rather than the local community. This is different from the Forest Service position, which has been toward the local community.

At the time of its establishment the National Park Service was given jurisdiction over fifteen national parks then in existence,[10] as well as twen-

---

[9] John Raker, Dr. Horace McFarland, Frederick Law Olmsted, Robert S. Yard, Robert B. Marshall, Enos Mills, Henry A. Barker, Richard E. Watrous, and Gilbert Grosvenor.

[10] National parks under the jurisdiction of the National Park Service upon its establishment on Aug. 25, 1916, were Casa Grande Ruin (established 1889), Crater Lake (established 1902), General Grant (established 1890), Glacier (established 1910), Hawaii (established Aug. 1, 1916), Lassen Volcanic (established Aug. 9, 1916), Mesa Verde (established 1906), Mt. Rainier (established 1899), Platt (established 1906), Rocky Mountain (established 1915), Sequoia (established 1890), Sullys Hill (established 1904), Wind Cave (established 1903), Yellowstone (established 1872), and Yosemite (established 1890) [45].

ty-one national monuments [45]. Since that time the National Park Service has greatly expanded in size, diversity of areas, and responsibilities. The number of national parks and national monuments has increased, and additional legislation has provided for the inclusion of other types of areas within the National Park System.[11] By 1937, growing complexity of the National Park System prompted establishment of several regional offices for purposes of decentralized administration [50].

EARLY INTEREST IN FOREST CONSERVATION

As early as 1867 the states of Michigan and Wisconsin formed fact-finding committees for the purpose of studying and reporting upon the destruction of their forest resources. Similar action was taken by Maine in 1869 and,

---

In addition to the aforementioned national parks, the Hot Springs Reservation was also placed under National Park Service administration. [45].

Casa Grande Ruin, established Mar. 2, 1889, was reclassified as a national monument on Aug. 3, 1918 [47]. Sullys Hill National Park was abolished and turned over to the Biological Survey, now the U.S. Fish and Wildlife Service, for a game preserve on Mar. 3, 1931 [47]. General Grant National Park was incorporated into Kings Canyon National Park upon the establishment of that area on Mar. 4, 1940 [50].

[11] The act of Feb. 21, 1925, provided for the acquisition of lands, through donations, in the southern Appalachian Mountains and Mammoth Cave regions of Kentucky for national parks. Previously, national parks and national monuments had been set aside from public lands. Following authorization by Congress in 1926, the act eventually resulted in the establishment of Great Smoky Mountains, Mammoth Cave, and Shenandoah National Parks, supplementing Acadia, first national park in the eastern United States [49].

The act of Mar. 3, 1933, provided for an executive order consolidating all national parks and national monuments, national military parks, national battlefield parks and sites, certain national cemeteries, national memorials, and the national capital parks under the administration of the National Park Service. Previously, some of the aforementioned areas had been administered by the War Department, U.S. Forest Service, and other federal agencies [49,50].

The Historic Sites Act of Aug. 21, 1935, provided for the establishment and protection of national historic sites, as well as a wide range of relevant historical programs [49,50].

The Park, Parkways and Recreation Area Study Act of June 23, 1936, authorized studies related to development of the National Park System, including areas having primary recreational interests [49].

The act of June 30, 1936, provided for the administration and maintenance of the Blue Ridge Parkway by the National Park Service, thus introducing the concept of the rural parkway into the National Park System [49].

The act of Aug. 17, 1937, established Cape Hatteras National Seashore, first area of its type in the National Park System [49].

The act of Aug. 7, 1946, provided the National Park Service with authority to administer recreation on areas under jurisdiction of other federal agencies. This resulted in cooperative agreements with the Bureau of Reclamation and other federal agencies for administration of recreation on such areas as Lake Mead and Glen Canyon National Recreation Areas [49,50].

The act of Aug. 7, 1961, authorizing the establishment of Cape Cod National Seashore, provided for the use of appropriated funds at the outset for the purchase of lands for park use. Previously such areas had been established by setting aside public lands, or through initial donations of land to the federal government by public or private interests [49].

Several acts in 1972 (P.L. 92-589; P.L. 92-692) and 1975 (P.L. 93-555) provided for inclusion of National Recreation Areas near large cities (San Francisco, New York, Cleveland) in the National Park System [44].

within a few years, by a number of other Eastern states. By 1885, the states of New York, California, Colorado, and Ohio had formed forestry commissions.[12]

The first tangible interest in forest conservation by the federal government was manifested in 1876, when Dr. Franklin B. Hough was appointed as a forestry agent in the Department of Agriculture. Hough's appointment, resulting from official interest in an address he gave at the annual meeting of the American Association for the Advancement of Science in 1873, was the seed from which the U.S. Forest Service grew [16,27,29]. Today this agency administers the important recreational resources of the national forests as part of its multiple-use program.

DEVELOPMENT OF THE U.S. FOREST SERVICE

By 1881, as a result of the activities of Franklin B. Hough and supporters of his program, federal interest in forestry broadened [16,27]. In that year the Division of Forestry was established in the Department of Agriculture; its purpose was purely advisory. It was not until 1891 that the first federally controlled forest, known as the Yellowstone Timberland Reserve, was established from the public domain. For more than a decade, the administration of this and other early reserves was vested in the General Land Office of the Department of the Interior. The completely separate Division of Forestry, elevated to the status of a bureau in 1901, continued to serve in an advisory capacity in their management. It was 1905 before the federal forest reserves were placed under the control of federal foresters of the Bureau of Forestry; soon thereafter the names Bureau of Forestry and forest reserve were changed, respectively to U.S. Forest Service and national forest—designations by which they are known today.

The amalgamation of federal foresters and federal forest lands under a unified administration and the organization of the U.S. Forest Service in approximately its present form resulted largely from the efforts of Gifford Pinchot, charismatic early forestry leader.

Pinchot, who had become affiliated with the Division of Forestry during the early stages of its development, was placed in charge of its activities in 1898 [27] and immediately instituted a militant campaign to correlate federal forestry activities. When these efforts bore fruit in 1905, he continued as chief of the U.S. Forest Service,[13] greatly strengthening this bureau and surrounding himself with loyal associates. He received the cooperation

[12] Initial forestry commissions in California, Colorado, and Ohio soon became inoperative; thus, New York has the distinction of having the oldest record of official state forestry activities [16,27].

[13] Although Pinchot resigned as chief of the U.S. Forest Service during the administration of President William Howard Taft as a result of a controversy with Secretary of the Interior Ballinger over public-land-management questions, he organized the U.S. Forest Service along fundamental lines which continued to guide the programs of his successors [16,27]

of President Theodore Roosevelt, whose interest in various phases of natural-resource conservation was manifested in many ways. President Roosevelt called a conference of political, business, and scientific leaders in 1908 to consider broadly interrelated problems concerning the conservation of natural resources. This conference, known as the National Conservation Conference of Governors [16,27], had far-reaching effects. It was responsible for extensive additions to the national forests, the establishment of many state conservation commissions, and a National Conservation Commission, appointed by the President with Pinchot as chairman [16,27]. This commission developed an inventory of the nation's natural resources and suggested plans for their proper use. However, recreational land values were ignored.

Early proponents of forest conservation did not consider recreation as an important natural resource of forest land. The establishment of forest reserves and, later, the organization of the U.S. Forest Service were motivated by interest in the sustained yield of other values such as timber, forage, and water. Orientation was toward local economics and needs for forest products.

For many years the two major aspects of natural-resource conservation, one concerned with the preservation of significant or scenically beautiful areas in parks and the other with the proper use of more tangible assets in forest reserves, were considered as separate entities with little in common and largely incompatible. Nevertheless, as will be noted later, legislation, by which the original forest reserves were established, provided for eventual broadening of the program of multiple use of national forest resources to include recreation.

DEVELOPMENT OF RECREATIONAL USE OF NATIONAL FORESTS

In addition to being an important source of timber, forage, and other tangible natural resources, national forests today are vital units in our outdoor recreational program. The U.S. Forest Service has developed the recreational potential of areas in its charge as one of several important values of the national forests, and it has coordinated such recreational uses with those of other important recreational lands. But the current extensive recreational use of national forests was not typical of the first years of the forest conservation movement in the United States. Early foresters could not envisage today's great public interest in the recreational values of the national forests; at that time, few people did. There was little to indicate the eventual need for our present extensive system of varied outdoor recreational areas. Consequently, although a few forestry leaders began calling attention to growing public interest in, and use of, national forests for outdoor recreation about 1910, official U.S. Forest Service recognition of recreation as a valid national forest resource did not develop for more than a decade. Further, for many years many foresters exhibited a negative attitude toward such use.

The reasons for this early negative attitude are not difficult to understand. In their formative period the national forests were largely undeveloped: their boundaries were not clearly defined; the nature and abundance of their varied natural resources were not fully inventoried or understood; road and trail development was meager; and, when it existed, the technical training of limited personnel was largely based upon European standards which had to be reevaluated to meet American conditions. These and related difficulties were slowly corrected as appropriations increased and as experience developed.

In addition, early American forestry education emphasized technical matters pertaining to the production, harvesting, and utilization of tangible forest products. Recreation, which it neglected, posed problems of a very different and more intangible kind.

The early negative attitude of foresters toward recreation was further influenced by unfortunate personality clashes between forestry leaders and exponents of complete preservation, mostly relative to controversies over jurisdiction of certain lands.[14]

Although interest in other values of forest land prompted the establishment of the first federal forest reserves, early legislation relative to these areas can be interpreted as providing for public recreational use. The act of June 4, 1897,[15] which outlined the broad policy of management for the forest reserves, included the following provisions [39]:

> He [the Secretary] may make such rules and regulations and establish such service as will insure the objects of such reservations, namely, to regulate their occupancy and use and to preserve the forests thereon from destruction. . . . Nor shall anything herein prohibit any person from entering upon such forest reservations for all proper and lawful purposes . . . . Provided, that such persons comply with the rules and regulations covering such forest reservations.

The act of February 28, 1899,[16] opened the door still wider for the public utilization of recreational values in the national forests, as indicated in this passage [39]:

---

[14] One of the earliest of the controversies involved the damming and subsequent flooding of Hetch Hetchy Valley in Yosemite National Park, a struggle which began about the turn of the century, when the city of San Francisco became interested in reservoir sites in the Sierra Nevada as a source of water for her expanding population [26,54]. Gifford Pinchot, chief of the U.S. Forest Service, favored the development of the Hetch Hetchy project. He was opposed by a group led by John Muir, famous writer, naturalist, and founder of the Sierra Club. The issue was not resolved until 1908, when access to the Hetch Hetchy Valley was granted to the city of San Francisco [25]. Construction of the dam and development of the reservoir resulted.

Later, a number of areas which qualified for national park status were withdrawn from the national forests and placed under a separate administration as national parks [26]. Several of these transfers evoked bitter debate over the priority of land use; these disagreements further embittered foresters, delaying their recognition of recreation as a valid forest resource.

[15] 30 Stat. 35; 16 U.S.C. 551; and 30 Stat. 36; 16 U.S.C. 482.

[16] 30 Stat. 908; 16 U.S.C. 495.

The Secretary of the Interior . . . hereby is authorized, under such rules and regulations as he from time to time may make, to enter or lease to responsible persons or corporations applying therefore suitable spaces and portions of ground near, or adjacent to, mineral, medicinal, or other springs, within any forest reserves established within the United States, or hereafter to be established, and where the public is accustomed or desires to frequent, for health or pleasure, for the purpose of erecting upon such leased ground sanitoriums or hotels, to be opened for the reception of the public.

It should be pointed out that the early negative attitude toward recreation on national forest lands was not shared by all Forest Service employees and members of the forestry profession. Many, notably Aldo Leopold, Robert Marshall, and Arthur Carhart, were responsible for many advances in recreational use of national forest lands which are of primary importance today. In particular, both Leopold[17] and Marshall[18] were exponents of wilderness. The nuclei of our National Wilderness Preservation System were the primitive, wilderness, and wild areas of the national forests,[19] administratively designated by the U.S. Forest Service.

One of the first employees of the U.S. Forest Service to publicly recognize the recreational values of the national forests, and the trends of public interest in them, was Treadwell Cleveland, Jr.. In an article "National Forests as Recreation Grounds," published in 1910 by the American Academy of Political and Social Science, Philadelphia, Cleveland made this statement [10,21]:

Fortunately, the object for which the National Forests were created and are maintained, will guarantee the permanence of their resources and will bring about their fullest development for every use . . . .

So great is the value of national forest area for recreation, and so certain is this value to increase with the growth of the country, and the shrinkage of the wilderness, that even if the forest resources of wood and water were not to be required by the civilization of the future, many of the forests ought certainly to be preserved, in the interest of national health and well-being, for recreation use alone.

Recognition of the recreational values of the national forests at the highest level is noted for the first time in this excerpt from the annual report of Henry Solon Graves, chief of the U.S. Forest Service, for the fiscal year ending June 30, 1912 [32]:

[17] See *Journal of Forestry*, vol. 46, no. 8, pp. 605-606, August, 1948.
[18] See *Journal of Forestry*, vol. 38, no. 1, pp. 61-62, January, 1940; also *The Living Wilderness*, vol. 16, no. 38, pp.10-23, Autumn, 1951.
[19] First of these areas was the Gila Primitive Area in the Gila National Forest of New Mexico, designated in 1924 largely through Leopold's efforts; a portion was reclassified as a wilderness area in 1953. The Bob Marshall Wilderness Area in the Flathead and Lewis and Clark National Forests of Montana memorializes Marshall's efforts.

With the construction of new roads and trails the forests are visited more and more for recreation purposes, and in consequence the demand is growing rapidly for sites on which summer camps, cottages, and hotels may be located. In some of the most accessible and desirable locations the land has been divided into suitable lots of from 1 to 5 acres to accommodate as many visitors as possible. The regulations of this department for handling this class of business seem to be entirely satisfactory. Permits are issued promptly and on conditions with which permittees willingly comply.

Some objection is heard to the fact that the permit is revocable in the discretion of the department. If occupancy of lots wanted for summer camps, cottages, and hotels for a period of years could be authorized, more substantial buildings than are now being erected would probably be put up.

Less than three years later, the act of March 4, 1915, authorized the Secretary of Agriculture to issue, for periods not exceeding thirty years, permits to responsible citizens for sites, not to exceed 5 acres needed for recreation and public convenience [39].

Increasing use of national forests for recreation prompted this statement from Chief Forester Graves in his report for the fiscal year ending June 30, 1917 [33]:

The use of some of the National Forests for recreation purposes is growing to such importance as to be one of the major activities. Upon the Angeles National Forest permits for 814 residences, 26 hotels, and 28 summer resorts were in force at the end of the fiscal year.

It is believed that the use of National Forests along this line, as shown by the foregoing figures, represents only a promising beginning of the development which is to follow.

In 1918, the U.S. Forest Service employed F. A. Waugh to make a five months' field investigation of the recreational values of national forest lands [21]. Waugh's recommendations were outlined in a small booklet, "Recreation Uses on the National Forests," published by the U.S. Government Printing Office in 1918 [53]. This was the first official Forest Service study of recreation; it is important in that it recognized recreation as one of the major uses of the national forests. Recreation, however, was not given specific financial support by the U.S. Forest Service until 1922. Previous to that year limited recreational facilities had been provided without special allotments for that purpose, largely as a matter of expediency and primarily as a means of protecting public health and property. Since the number of people using the national forests for recreation was constantly increasing, such procedure could not continue indefinitely; as a result, annual reports of the Chief Forester began urging official recognition of recreation as a valid resource of the national forests. An excerpt from the report for the fiscal year ending June 30, 1920, follows:

As an important use, it [recreation] bids fair to rank third among the major services performed by the National Forests, with only timber production and stream flow regulation taking precedence of it [34].

The act of May 11, 1922 (Agricultural Appropriation bill), provided $10,000 for recreational development in the national forests [21], a sum largely earmarked for improvement of existing campgrounds. That meager appropriation, infinitesimal by present-day standards, is significant in that it was the first tangible support given to recreational use of the national forests. It initiated a trend which soon established recreation as a recognized national forest resource, along with timber, forage, water, and related values. Today, recreation is regarded as of dominant importance on many national forests.

Even in its early stages, development of an active recreational program on national forest lands was recognized as advantageous to forestry as well as to the general public. In an article published in the *Ames Forester* in 1922, Robert G. Schreck of the U.S. Forest Service made this statement regarding recreational development in the national forests [21]:

> The recreational movement in the National Forests has done what years of propaganda could never have accomplished. For years the Forest Officers have tried to interest the public in their work and the great necessity for adequate fire protection.
> The insertion of recreation into our Forests has [accomplished] and is accomplishing more for the interest of conservation than any other method resorted to. It has not only converted the local people to fire protection, game preservation, and reforestation, but it is acting as a stimulant to increase and arouse interest in the good things that the U.S. Forest Service stands for.

Col. William B. Greeley, chief forester of the U.S. Forest Service from 1920 to 1928, included these paragraphs in his reports for the fiscal years ending June 30, 1924 and 1925:

> The coordination of outdoor recreation with timber production is wholly germane to the practice of forestry, and is an essential part of any sound plan of national forest administration [37].

> Recreation use, under proper safeguards and supervision, is wholly compatible with timber production and watershed protection and may properly be planned for in systematic forest management [38].

Thus, as implied by Colonel Greeley's words, increasing recreational use of the national forests prompted the U.S. Forest Service to prepare, for the first time, a formal policy to guide the development of such activities. Formulated in 1925 by E. A. Sherman, associate forester, this policy [28] has since been greatly expanded.

Today the importance of recreation as a national forest resource is indicated by the fact that all levels of the U.S. Forest Service organization include recreation specialists with varying degrees of authority and responsibility. Further, though the act of June 4, 1897, which outlined the initial broad management policy of the forest reserves, failed to mention recreation specifically, it was supplemented by the Multiple Use Act of 1960 (P.L. 86-517), which stated that "the national forests are established and shall be administered for outdoor recreation, range, timber, watershed, and wildlife and fish purposes." Recreation was thus recognized, officially, as having importance comparable to that of other national forest resources. Provisions of this act were further defined and strengthened by passage of the Forest and Rangeland Renewable Resources Planning Act (P.L. 93-378) in 1974 and the National Forest Management Act (P.L. 94-588) in 1976.

GROWTH OF RECREATIONAL IMPORTANCE OF BLM LANDS

The Bureau of Land Management (BLM) of the Department of the Interior was formed in 1946 by consolidation of the General Land Office and the Grazing Service.[20] BLM administers over 450 million acres (182 million hectares) of natural resource lands. That area is the remaining portion of the original public domain which, at one time, exceeded 1.8 billion acres (729 million hectares).

Lands administered by the Bureau of Land Management have long been used for unorganized forms of outdoor recreation (hunting and fishing—subject to state laws, hiking, camping, picnicking, and related activities). In addition, large areas have been transferred to other public agencies which directly provide for many types of recreational opportunity (national parks and forests, wildlife refuges).

In 1926, as a result of passage of the Recreation and Public Purposes Act (P.L. 69-386), recreation was officially recognized as a resource along

---

[20] The General Land Office was established in 1812 to survey and, as authorized by various land laws, to dispose of the public domain in ways conducive to development of the country; it also maintained records of public land transfers and subsequent ownership of such lands. The Grazing Service, established in 1934 by the Taylor Grazing Act (P.L. 74-482), facilitated more orderly management of livestock grazing on about 176 million acres (71,280 million hectares) of public rangeland. The Bureau of Land Management also inherited responsibility for multipurpose management of about 2.6 million acres (over 1 million hectares) of forest land in western Oregon by authority of the Oregon and California Sustained Yield Forestry Act of 1937 (P.L. 75-405). These O & C lands included public-land grants to the Oregon and California Railroad Co. to aid in construction of a railroad, and to the state of Oregon to aid in the construction of the Coos Bay Military Wagon Road. Terms of these grants were not fulfilled, and lands involved were reconveyed to the federal government [9,40].

More than 1 billion acres (405 million hectares) of the original public domain have been disposed of since 1781. This includes over 300 million acres (121.5 million hectares) by cash sale and miscellaneous methods; 287 million acres (116 million hectares) granted or sold to homesteaders; 300 million acres (121.5 million hectares) granted to states for support of schools, colleges and universities, and public projects; 94 million acres (38 million hectares) granted to certain railroads; 61 million acres (24.7 million hectares) given as military bounties; 34 million acres (13.7 million hectares) in settlement of private claims; and 34 million acres (13.7 million hectares) granted or sold under the Timber Culture Act and related legislation.

with forage, timber, minerals and related values. Many states, counties, municipalities, and nonprofit organizations have obtained land for recreation under provisions of this act, together with related land laws and their subsequent amendments.[21] Recreation values of BLM lands, together with policies of their management and use, received strong emphasis in the Federal Land Policy and Management Act of 1976 (P.L. 94-579), commonly known as the BLM Organic Act [19,31].

A mimeographed statement issued by the Secretary of the Interior, April 16, 1958, outlined the first specific, official recreational land-use policy for lands under BLM jurisdiction. In 1960 recreational facilities were first constructed by BLM on O & C lands in western Oregon. By 1963 a separate recreational staff was formed to undertake planning and development of recreational resources and to administer recreational management of BLM lands (see Chapter 10).

WILDLIFE CONSERVATION DEVELOPMENTS PERTINENT TO RECREATION

Federal wildlife conservation programs, gradually expanded and improved over many years, make significant contributions to public outdoor recreation. Though hunters and fishermen are the major beneficiaries of such programs, the benefits are by no means limited to those groups. Recreationists interested primarily in observing or photographing wildlife also are favored.[22]

U.S. Fish and Wildlife Service

The history of tangible steps toward the conservation of native wildlife species in the United States by the federal government covers over 100 years, dating from 1871, when Congress passed the act establishing the Commission of Fish and Fisheries [6], predecessor of the Bureau of Fisheries of the Department of Commerce. In 1886 Congress passed another act, establishing the Division of Economic Ornithology and Mammalogy, later the Bureau of Biological Survey of the Department of Agriculture [6]. Al-

---

[21] Includes the Taylor Grazing Act of 1934 (P.L. 73-482), O & C Sustained Yield Forestry Act of 1937 (P.L. 75-405), Small Tract Act of 1938 (P.L. 75-577), Classification and Multiple Use Act of 1964 (P.L. 88-607), and Public Land Sale Act of 1964 (P.L. 88-608).

[22] Several significant legislative acts have been passed in the interest of wildlife protection and management. The Lacey Act, passed in 1900 [6,12], was designed to halt indiscriminate slaughter of native birds and mammals. In 1918, following the ratification in 1916 of a treaty between the United States and Great Britain relative to the protection of birds migrating between the United States and Canada, the Migratory Bird Treaty Act was passed. This act was later amended to fulfill requirements of a migratory-bird treaty with Mexico, ratified in 1937 [6,7,12].

Other legislation includes the Migratory Bird Hunting Stamp Act of 1934, as amended, and the Federal Aid in Wildlife Restoration Act of 1937 [6]. The former provided for the annual purchase of a duck stamp by all migratory-bird hunters for the purpose of financing research in waterfowl management, as well as for the acquisition of waterfowl sanctuaries; the latter levied an excise tax on hunting arms and ammunition for the purpose of developing a special fund to be used in aiding the state in various wildlife projects.

though these two federal agencies were originally concerned only with research and investigation, their scope in later years was gradually broadened to encompass the protection and management of native fishes and wildlife. In 1939 the Bureau of Fisheries of the Department of Commerce and the Bureau of Biological Survey of the Department of Agriculture were transferred to the Department of the Interior, and in 1940, by authority of the Reorganization Act of 1933, amalgamated into one organization known as the Fish and Wildlife Service. The diversified program of the Fish and Wildlife Service is highly important to recreational use of wild lands. In particular, this bureau manages our extensive National Wildlife Refuge System.

National Wildlife Refuge System

The federal program of wildlife refuge acquisition and development originated in 1903, when the Pelican Island National Wildlife Refuge, a 5-acre area on the east coast of Florida, was established by Executive order of President Theodore Roosevelt. It protects a favorite nesting site of the brown pelican [6]. However, the federal program of wildlife refuge acquisition and development first assumed major importance in 1929 when the Migratory Bird Conservation Act was passed [6]. This act was the cornerstone of the National Wildlife Refuge System (see Chapter 10).

National wildlife refuges, game ranges, and fish hatcheries, though established for conservation of wildlife and their environments, are increasingly utilized by the general public for outdoor recreation, particularly wildlife-oriented recreation. Such use, provided that it is compatible with the primary wildlife purposes of such areas, was authorized in 1962. In addition, acquisition of limited areas of adjacent lands for necessary recreational development, where such development on refuges may have adverse effects on fish and wildlife populations, or on management operations, was also authorized.[23]

RECREATIONAL USE OF FEDERAL RECLAMATION PROJECTS

Projects developed by the Tennessee Valley Authority, the Bureau of Reclamation, and the Corps of Engineers, primarily for irrigation, hydroelectric power, municipal and industrial water supply, flood control, improvement of navigation, and related purposes, began to assume major importance for recreation in the 1930s.[24] Today recreation is officially recognized as one of many benefits of these multipurpose projects (see Chapter 10).

[23] Act of Sept. 29, 1962 (P.L. 87-714), as amended (16 U.S.C. 460 (b)-460 (k) (4).

[24] The Tennessee Valley Authority, established in 1933, gave early recognition to the development of the recreation resources along the TVA reservoir system. The Bureau of Reclamation was established in 1902; the Corps of Engineers, established in 1802, was engaged in nonmilitary engineering and construction before enactment of the first Rivers and Harbors Act in 1924. In due course, these latter two agencies began developing the recreation resources of their reservoirs, primarily in response to public demand.

Current recreational policies of these three agencies, founded upon various legislative acts, are basically similar. They lean strongly toward indirect rather than direct development and management of recreational potential, usually providing recreational land to other public, and, in some instances, private interests. In some cases they transfer recreational respon-sibilities to other public agencies more directly concerned with, or having longer experience in, recreational management.

Tennessee Valley Authority

Authorization for development of the recreational potential of TVA projects is contained in the Tennessee Valley Authority Act of 1933 (P.L. 73-17) and Executive Order No. 616, June 8, 1933. This act provided for transfer, lease, or sale of lands having recognized recreational potential to other federal as well as state and local agencies and, under certain condi-tions, to private organizations and individuals. Between 1933 and 1937 TVA also developed several recreation demonstration areas in cooperation with the National Park Service and the Civilian Conservation Corps to stimulate the interest of public and private agencies in the recreational potential of TVA developments.

Later, broadening of TVA recreational policy involved direct devel-opment and management of the recreational and environmental potential of a 170,000-acre (68,850 hectare) area known as Land Between the Lakes, as well as development of basic recreational facilities at selected reservoir sites. The Land Between the Lakes project was initiated by TVA in 1959 and received Executive approval in 1963. The Public Works Appropriation Act of 1964 (P.L. 88-511) provided funds for initial planning, land acquisi-tion, and development at Land Between the Lakes; and the first facilities were available to the public in June of the same year. Development of basic facilities at TVA reservoir public use areas began in 1969 to ensure the general public a means of safe, sanitary, and convenient access to TVA lakes and shorelines.

Bureau of Reclamation

Since 1934, matters relevant to the protection and management of fish and wildlife resources of the Bureau of Reclamation reservoirs and contiguous lands have been handled by the Fish and Wildlife Service, or comparable state agencies, by authority of the Fish and Wildlife Coordination Act of 1934 (P.L. 121), as amended. The Bureau of Reclamation usually transfers responsibilities for recreational development and management of Bureau of Reclamation projects to other federal agencies, or comparable state or local interests, largely through cooperative agreement pursuant to this bureau's authority for appropriate utilization of project resources, the Reclamation Act of 1902 (P.L. 161), as amended.

Prior to 1965, recreation development on new projects was included in project plans only as specifically provided for by Congress in individual project-authorizing acts. However, the Federal Water Project Recreation

Act of 1965 (P.L. 89-72) provided general authority for recreation on new developments and limited authority to develop and expand recreational opportunities on existing projects.

Corps of Engineers

Authority for recreational development and public use of recreational opportunities on projects developed by this agency is contained primarily in the Flood Control Act of 1944 (P.L. 534), as amended. In addition, protection and management of fish and wildlife resources of Corps of Engineering projects, like those of the Bureau of Reclamation, are handled by the Fish and Wildlife Service, or comparable state agencies, by authority of the Fish and Wildlife Coordination Act of 1934, as amended.

DEVELOPMENT OF STATE PARK SYSTEMS

Establishment of the Yosemite Grant in 1864 initiated the concept of the reservation of wild land for recreational use. Since the federal government entrusted this area to the care of the state of California, and since it was so administered for about forty years, it was also the first state park. Thus, the state parks have a longer history than any other type of wild-land recreational area.

Though the Yosemite Grant was receded to the federal government and incorporated into Yosemite National Park (established 1890) in 1906, a number of early state parks were established before the turn of the century. The movement to preserve an area surrounding Niagara Falls, initiated in 1867, achieved success in 1885, when the Niagara Falls Reservation was dedicated [15,23]. The year 1885 also witnessed the transfer of an obsolete military reservation on Mackinac Island from the federal government to the state of Michigan; previously this area had had a brief existence as a national military park [17,23,26]. Minnesota established the first portion of Itasca State Park in 1891; two historical areas were also established by that state about the same time—Birch Coulee in 1893 and Camp Release in 1889 [23].

Also, in 1885 the state Legislature of New York established the Adirondack Forest Preserve. Since cutting of timber was forbidden in that area in 1897 and on state lands in the Catskills in 1899, both the Adirondack and Catskill areas assumed the essential character of state parks. The famous Palisades Interstate Park of New York and New Jersey had its origin in 1895, when the first lands of the area were acquired [23].

However, despite its early beginning the state park movement did not begin to attract significant attention until 1921, several years after establishment of the National Park Service. Establishment of the National Park Service and resultant development and improvement of areas in its charge soon drew public interest and attention to these areas, resulting in constantly increasing numbers of visitors. It became evident that the term "national park" embodied commercial magic, which was reflected in the economy of adjacent communities. A veritable flood of proposals for the establishment of additional national parks developed; many of these proposed areas, largely sponsored by biased interests, were unworthy of national park status. In 1916 alone, sixteen areas were proposed for inclusion in the National Park System [26,45].

Stephen T. Mather, director of the National Park Service, was aware of the danger of diluting national park standards through the addition of areas lacking in outstanding, nationally significant features, and he recognized that many areas other than national parks possessed recreational values which were needed and would be increasingly valuable in later years. He diverted the pressure for additional national parks into proper channels by calling a conference of interested parties for the purpose of planning the extension and development of state park systems [26].

Des Moines, Iowa, was selected as the convention site and about two hundred delegates from twenty-five states gathered there in January 1921. As a result, a permanent organization known as the National Conference on State Parks was formed [23,26]. Since that time this body[25] has met annually to discuss common state park problems and to further common interests. Much of the progress in the development of state parks stems from activities of this organization. Today, each of the fifty states has a state park system. The number of individual state parks has greatly increased. They are more adequately financed, and they are better administered. In addition, state forests, fish and wildlife areas, reservoirs, areas contiguous to state highways, and related state lands are increasingly used for recreation (see Chapter 11).

MUNICIPAL, COUNTY AND REGIONAL RECREATIONAL AREAS

Though establishment of Central Park in New York City (see Chapter 3) was followed by increased interest in municipal parks elsewhere, such interest developed slowly. By 1877 only twenty of our larger cities had municipal parks and by 1892 only a hundred cities had made provision for them. Extension of municipal parks was more rapid after the turn of the century, paralleling early growth of public interest in natural-resource conservation and recreational use of wild lands. Between 1902 and 1926 the number of cities with municipal parks more than doubled, from nearly 800 to almost 1,700 [51].

Expansion of municipal park systems, in turn, led to development of parkways, as well as to the acquisition of municipally owned and administered park areas outside city limits. As early as the 1920s the park systems of both Phoenix, Arizona, and Denver, Colorado, included outlying recreational areas of that kind [51].

---

[25] Name changed in 1974 to National Society for Park Resources.

The nature and philosophy of municipal park management have changed over the years. Initially conceived as sylvan open spaces primarily for passive diversion (often highlighted by signs warning visitors to "Keep off the Grass"), municipal park systems have become increasingly important as centers of more active interests, ranging from team sports to nature study and various cultural activities. Today, modern city park systems provide a variety of areas for diverse recreational activities [41,44]

County parks also have a long history. The county park movement originated in Essex County, New Jersey, in 1895 [51]; however, only a few areas of that kind were established prior to 1920. Today many county park systems supplement those operated by municipalities and, through the National Association of Counties, a forum is available for an exchange of ideas and discussion of mutual problems [44].

A more recent development has been the growth of independent regional, district or metropolitan park authorities which administer recreational lands in several adjoining counties, usually near large cities. They provide recreational opportunities for residents of the area included and are particularly important in eastern United States.

As noted more completely in Chapter 11, provision of readily accessible recreational opportunities near where most people live and work has become increasingly important in recent years. There is a critical need for areas that can be readily utilized by the growing number of urbanites, especially those who reside in crowded urban cores. In addition to the increasing amount of free time available to many people today, the situation is rendered even more acute by the energy crisis, which gives promise of being with us in the future. For this and other reasons many people find it necessary today to confine their recreational activities to areas close to home.

A study conducted jointly by the Bureau of Outdoor Recreation (reconstituted as the Heritage Conservation and Recreation Service. 1978) and the National Park Service, completed in 1976, was directed toward improvement of urban recreation. The purpose of this study was to determine open space requirements of urban centers, to indicate what needed to be done, and to note who should be responsible for meeting urban recreational needs. Cities and counties obviously have the pivotal role but the Federal government has also been drawn into certain urban recreational programs. Both the Gateway National Recreation Area in the outer harbor area of New York and the Golden Gate National Recreation Area in the San Francisco Bay region were established in 1972. In 1975 the Cuyahoga Valley National Recreation Area was established near Cleveland, Ohio. Lands in these areas have been acquired and will be developed, operated and maintained as parts of the National Park System [44].

PUBLIC RECREATIONAL USE OF PRIVATE LANDS

Recreational functions of private lands today are quite different from those of pioneer mountain and beach resorts mentioned in Chapter 3. Baroque hostelries where people formerly spent entire annual vacations have been replaced by operations geared to more rapid visitor turnover and the "tourist industry" has become important to the economy of many parts of the country. Varied commercial recreational facilities and services have been developed within and enroute to wild-land recreational areas. On many privately owned lands and waters certain types of recreation are compatible with the primary purpose of producing food, timber, electricity and related needs; in some instances provision of recreational opportunities on such areas adds to their financial return. In addition, private enterprise has become increasingly involved in development and sale of specialized recreation equipment.

As public recreational interests and activities reacted to changes in the American life-style, the recreational values of private lands and waters have become generally recognized as of great importance. It has been recognized that satisfying rapidly growing public recreational demands requires a cooperative effort by both private and public interests; that governmental agencies cannot be expected to shoulder that responsibility alone [43].

The profit motive, though important in public recreational use of certain private areas, is not always a primary objective. Increasingly, many areas serving varied recreational purposes have been acquired or otherwise controlled by public-spirited individuals and different types of nonprofit organizations, including youth, religious, and civic groups; educational, scientific, or historical institutions; and outdoor, conservation, hunting and fishing clubs. In some cases initiation of such activities antedates the turn of the century. Commercial aspects of such operations are usually confined to minimum charges to defray costs of operation and maintenance. Occasionally recreational use of such lands requires an organization membership, but membership requirements are so liberal that, in effect, these areas are essentially public in character.[26]

---

[26] A list of such organizations is found in the *Conservation Directory, 1975*, 21st ed., published by the National Wildlife Federation.

Noteworthy examples include the Appalachian Mountain Club, organized 1876; Audubon Society, established 1886; Sierra Club, organized in 1892; Mazama Club, organized 1894; Mountaineers, organized 1906; and the Nature Conservancy. The latter organization was initiated in 1917 by a group of scientists within the Ecological Society of America; it was incorporated in 1951 as a nonprofit corporation under the laws of the District of Columbia.

The Mount Vernon Ladies Association, organized in 1858, owns the plantation home of George and Martha Washington. The first 200 acres (40.5 hectares) were purchased in 1858; this was later increased to 481 acres (195 hectares). Originally run-down, it was subsequently restored by the association which maintains this beautiful historic shrine by means of visitor fees.

Restoration of the Colonial city of Williamsburg was begun in 1926 with funds provided by John D. Rockefeller, Jr. It includes a 130-acre (52.6 hectares) restored area with more than 500 buildings and 84 acres (34 hectares) of gardens and greens representative of this city during the eighteenth century, when it was the capital of Virginia, at the time of Washington, Jefferson, Patrick Henry, and other American patriots.

Public Recreation on Agricultural Lands

Privately owned farms and ranches offer increasing opportunity for a variety of commercial recreational services and facilities [43]. Dude ranching in the West dates from the early 1900s. Vacation farms, a recent variation of that activity, are increasingly important in more densely populated regions, particularly in the East. Where there is sufficient demand, other types of recreational opportunities may be offered to the public on a commercial basis. Charging for hunting priveleges on farms and ranches, as well as for fishing in ponds and lakes on such areas, is now a common practice.

In some parts of the country management of agricultural land primarily for revenue derived from hunting leases to specific groups or organizations is rapidly expanding. In such instances maintenance of suitable environmental conditions and adequate stocking of game and fish are often based on scientific wildlife management techniques carried on by landowners with the assistance of government experts. Further, commercial picnic areas, campgrounds, and trailor parks; vacation cottages; various types of sports areas; and even nature study areas are increasing on agricultural land that has attractive terrain and related features.

Expansion in recreational use of agricultural land created the need for assistance to landowners desirous of entering this field of activity. An early step in this direction was the Food and Agriculture Act of 1962 (P.L. 87-703) and the subsequent Food and Agriculture Act of 1965 (P.L. 89-321), provisions of which enabled various agencies of the U.S. Department of Agriculture, in its Rural Areas Development Program, to offer such assistance.[27]

Public Recreation on Private Industrial Lands

Since the 1920s the number of large land-owning industrial firms permitting certain types of public recreation on lands under their control has been slowly but steadily growing [43]. Though initially such activities were considered merely a public relations gesture, they are becoming more firmly established as part of general company policy. The growth of such activities on private industrial forest lands is most noteworthy.

Since the primary interest of industrial forest land owners is the production of successive crops of timber, anything that might interfere with this objective was initially viewed with disfavor. Hunting and fishing were condoned on such areas for many years, but even these informal activities were not encouraged until recently. In fact, insofar as it was possible, some owners attempted to prohibit such use largely because of possible vandalism, owner liability responsibilities in case of accidents, and cost. However, with time, this attitude was gradually tempered by broader recognition of owner-land-stewardship responsibility. All forms of long-term multiple-use

[27] Principal agencies involved include the Soil Conservation Service, Agricultural Stabilization and Conservation Service, and Farmers Home Administration [41,43].

benefits now receive more adequate consideration than formerly, including watershed protection, soil stabilization, wildlife management, and, most recently, maintenance of environmental interests and provision for varied public outdoor recreational activities. This attitude of the forest industry was prompted largely by growing public interest in the recreational potential of such lands and the concomitant opportunity for improving the industry's public image, which had suffered as a result of earlier destructive logging practices. By the 1930s a number of the larger industrial forest land owners had begun to develop cooperative programs, whereby company personnel aided in the controlled use of their lands for hunting, fishing, berry picking, and similar activities that did not require specially developed facilities. Many company logging roads were opened to public use at specified times and under specified conditions, area maps were provided to help travelers find recreational objectives and, in some cases, regularly manned information stations were maintained at strategic points to aid visitors. Eventually, these informal cooperative ventures were broadened to include development of public facilities for picnicking, camping and related activities. Certain companies also established specifically designated tree-farm parks and, in some instances, initiated fairly sophisticated forest recreational use policies administered by special recreational personnel.

Initiation of the Tree Farm Program in the State of Washington in 1941 gave momentum to public recreational use of privately owned forest lands. The tree-farm concept, aimed at protection and management of such lands for sustained production of forest products and other benefits and services spread rapidly to a national level, sponsored by the American Forest Institute.[28] The first tree-farm park was also established in the State of Washington in 1941 [5]. Following World War II other tree-farm parks were established elsewhere in the Pacific Northwest and, eventually, in other parts of the country [43].

Growth of public recreational use of industrial forest lands prompted the American Forest Institute to undertake the first survey of the nature and extent of that use in 1956. Additional surveys from 1960 to 1968 [1-4] indicated the expanding and changing character of public recreational use of these lands as well as continuing cooperation of industrial forest land owners (see Chapter 12). The future of this voluntary program depends upon the responsibility of recreationalists who use these lands as guests, as well as the solution of some still unsolved problems relative to the cost of providing and maintaining recreational opportunities and facilities.

SUMMARY

The decades following the establishment of the Yosemite Grant in 1864 and extending well into the twentieth century were characterized by many significant developments in recreational land use. Yellowstone National Park, established in 1872, was followed by the designation of other early national

[28] Name changed from American Forest Products Industries in 1968.

parks, as well as other types of areas now included in the National Park System. Difficulties in independent administration of early national parks eventually resulted in the establishment of the National Park Service in 1916.

Other important developments led to the establishment of the U.S. Forest Service. In the case of both the National Park Service and the Forest Service, we see the role of strong, dominant leaders initiating programs and long-range policy directions. Mather, of the Park Service, was concerned for the preservation and public use of parks; Pinchot, of the Forest Service, established a pattern of forest use for production with recreational values in a secondary role. Broadening of the recreational policy of the U.S. Forest Service, officially initiated in 1925, eventually resulted in recreation being legally recognized as one of the major resources of the national forests.

By the 1930s recreational use of federal reclamation projects was becoming increasingly apparent. As a result, the Tennessee Valley Authority, the Bureau of Reclamation, and the Corps of Engineers formulated policies to develop adequate recreational opportunities on areas under their respective jurisdictions. Today recreation is recognized as one of several important resources on these multipurpose projects.

The period since 1945 has been characterized by the growing recreational importance of lands administered by the Bureau of Land Management, as well as lands of the U.S. Fish and Wildlife Service. The National Wildlife Refuge System dates from the establishment of the Pelican Island National Wildlife Refuge in 1903.

State park establishment, begun before the turn of the century, received a strong assist from the National Park Service, resulting in the establishment of the National Conference on State Parks (now known as National Society for Park Resources) in 1921. In time, as public demand developed, state parks systems were formed in each of the fifty states. In addition, other types of state lands were increasingly used for recreation. Further development of municipal park systems, dating from the establishment of Central Park in New York City in 1853, as well as county and regional or district parks, dating from 1895, paralleled expanding interest in recreational value of federal and state lands.

Increasing public demand for recreational opportunity also emphasized the importance of private lands for public recreation. Many individual private landowners began developing their lands for public use, often on a commercial basis, and by 1962 legal authorization was provided whereby federal agencies could offer technical and financial assistance in such development. Of particular importance was the increasing willingness of industrial forest landowners to permit public recreational use of their lands, culminating in tree-farm parks, the first of which was established in 1941.

SELECTED REFERENCES

1   American Forest Institute: "Public Outdoor Recreation: Results of a Survey by American Forest Institute, 1968," Washington, 1968.

2 American Forest Products Industries: "Forest Industry Recreation Survey," Washington, 1958 (mimeographed).

3 American Forest Products Industries: "Recreation on Forest Industry Lands, Results of a Survey by AFPI, 1960," Washington, 1960.

4 American Forest Products Industries: "Comparison of 1960 and 1962 Survey Results of 87 Selected Companies: Recreation," Washington, n.d. (dittoed).

5 Billings, Frederick: Public Parks on Private Property, *Planning and Civic Comment,* vol. 22, no. 4, December 1956.

6 Butcher, Devereux: "Seeing America's Wildlife in Our National Refuges," Devin-Adair, New York, 1955.

7 Carson, Rachel: "Guarding Our Wildlife Resources" (Conservation in Action, No. 5), Fish and Wildlife Service, U.S. Department of the Interior, Washington, 1948.

8 Chittenden, J. M.: "Yellowstone National Park" (Rev. by Eleanor Chittenden Cress and Isabelle Story), Stanford University Press, Stanford, California, 1954.

9 Clawson, Marion: "Man and Land in the United States," University of Nebraska Press, Lincoln, 1964.

10 Cleveland, Treadwell: National Forests as Recreation Grounds, *Annals of the American Academy of Political and Social Science,* vol. 35, no. 2, March, 1910.

11 Doell, Charles E., and Gerald B. Fitzgerald: "A Brief History of Parks and Recreation in the United States," Athletic Institute, Chicago, 1954.

12 Gabrielson, Ira A.: "Wildlife Management," Macmillan, New York, 1951.

13 Haines, Aubrey L.: "Yellowstone National Park—Its Exploration and Establishment," U.S. Government Printing Office, Washington,1974.

14 Hampton, H. Duane: The Army in the National Parks, *Journal of Forest History,* vol 10, no. 3, October 1966.

15 Huth, Hans: "Nature and the American," University of California Press, Berkeley, 1957.

16 Ise, John: "The United States Forest Policy," Yale University Press, New Haven, 1920.

17 Ise, John: "Our National Park Policy," Johns Hopkins, Baltimore, 1961.

18 Langford, N. P.: "The Discovery of Yellowstone National Park, 1870," J. E. Haynes, St. Paul, 1923.

19 LeMaster, Dennis C.: The BLM Organic Act, *Journal of Forestry,* vol. 75, no. 2, February 1977.

20 McGuire, John R.: National Forest Policy and the 94th Congress, *Journal of Forestry,* vol. 74, no. 12, December 1976.

21 Maughan, Kenneth O.: "Recreation Development in the National Forests," Technical Publication No. 45, N.Y. State College of Forestry, Syracuse University, Syracuse, 1934.

22 Meany, E. S.: "Mount Rainier: A Record of Exploration," Macmillan, New York, 1916.

23 Nelson, Beatrice: "State Recreation," National Conference on State Parks, Washington, 1928.

24 Pinchot, Gifford: "The Fight for Conservation," University of Washington Press, Seattle, 1967 (originally published by Doubleday Page and Co., 1910).

25 Russell, Carl P.: "100 Years in Yosemite," University of California Press, Berkeley, 1947.

26   Shankland, Robert: "Steve Mather of the National Parks," Knopf, New York, 1951.
27   Sharpe, Grant W., Clare W. Hendee and Shirley W. Allen: "Introduction to Forestry," McGraw-Hill, New York, 1976.
28   Sherman, E. A.: "Outdoor Recreation on the National Forests," U.S. Forest Service, Washington, May 25, 1925 (mimeographed).
29   Steen, Harold K.: "The U.S. Forest Service: A History," University of Washington Press, Seattle, 1976.
30   Tolson, Hillary A.: "Laws Relating to the National Park Service, the National Parks and Monuments," U.S. Government Printing Office, Washington, 1953.
31   U.S. Congress: "Federal Land Policy and Management Act of 1976," (P.L. 94-576), U.S. Government Printing Office, Washington, 1976.
32   U.S. Department of Agriculture, Forest Service: "Report of the Forester for 1912," Washington, 1912.
33   U.S. Department of Agriculture, Forest Service: "Report of the Forester," Washington, 1917.
34   U.S. Department of Agriculture, Forest Service: "Report of the Forester," Washington, 1920.
35   U.S. Department of Agriculture, Forest Service: "Report of the Forester," Washington, 1921.
36   U.S. Department of Agriculture, Forest Service: "Report of the Forester," Washington, 1922.
37   U.S. Department of Agriculture, Forest Service: "Report of the Forester," Washington, 1924.
38   U.S. Department of Agriculture, Forest Service: "Report of the Forester," Washington, 1925.
39   U.S. Department of Agriculture, Forest Service: "The Principal Laws Relating to Forest Service Activities" (Agric. Handbook 453), U.S. Government Printing Office, Washington, 1974.
40   U.S. Department of the Interior, Bureau of Land Management: "Public Land Statistics, 1975," U.S. Government Printing Office, Washington, 1975.
41   U.S. Department of the Interior, Bureau of Outdoor Recreation: "Federal Assistance in Outdoor Recreation," U.S. Government Printing Office, Washington, 1970.
42   U.S. Department of the Interior, Bureau of Outdoor Recreation: "The Bureau of Outdoor Recreation—Federal Focal Point for Outdoor America," U.S. Government Printing Office, Washington, 1975.
43   U.S. Department of the Interior, Bureau of Outdoor Recreation: *Outdoor Recreation Action, Spring 1975*, U.S. Government Printing Office, Washington, 1975.
44   U.S. Department of the Interior, Bureau of Outdoor Recreation: *Outdoor Recreation Action, Fall 1976*, U.S. Government Printing Office, Washington, 1976.
45   U.S. Department of the Interior, National Park Service: "Annual Report of the Superintendent of National Parks to the Secretary of the Interior for the Fiscal Year Ended June 30, 1916." U.S. Government Printing Office, Washington, 1916.
46   U.S. Department of the Interior, National Park Service: "Annual Report of the Director of the National Park Service to the Secretary of the Interior for the

Fiscal Year Ended June 30, 1917," U.S. Government Printing Office, Washington, 1917.

47 U.S. Department of the Interior, National Park Service: "Annual Report of the Director of the National Park Service to the Secretary of the Interior for the Fiscal Year Ended June 30, 1918," U.S. Government Printing Office, Washington, 1918.

48 U.S. Department of the Interior, National Park Service: "Annual Report of the Director of the National Park Service to the Secretary of the Interior for the Fiscal Year Ended June 30, 1931," U.S. Government Printing Office, Washington, 1931.

49 U.S. Department of the Interior, National Park Service: "Road to the Future," n.p., 1964.

50 U.S. Department of the Interior, National Park Service: "Index of the National Park System and Affiliated Areas As of June 30, 1977," U.S. Government Printing Office, Washington, 1977.

51 U.S. Department of Labor, Bureau of Labor Statistics: "Park Recreation Areas in the United States," Misc. Pub. No. 462, U.S. Government Printing Office, Washington, 1928.

52 Van Doran, Carlton S., and Louis Hodges: "America's Park and Recreation Heritage—A Chronology," U.S. Government Printing Office, Washington, 1975.

53 Waugh, F. A.: "Recreation Uses on the National Forests," U.S. Government Printing Office, Washington, 1918.

54 Wolfe, Linnie M.: "Son of the Wilderness: The Life of John Muir," Knopf, New York, 1947.

Evolving Programs and Concepts of Wild-Land Recreation

Many current concepts of wild-land recreation and perpetuation of environmental quality originated in earlier years. The conditions which brought them about were recognized, in incipient stages of their development, by numerous persons who tried to stir interest in prompt, timely action; though minor successes were occasionally scored, their efforts were generally abortive. A "climate" necessary for general wide-scale acceptance and implementation of their proposals had not yet developed. But by the mid-fifties conditions had changed noticeably, and within a decade values inherent in the importance of ecological relationships in perpetuation of environmental quality and wildland recreation were recognized and became "fashionable." As a result, many early recommendations were eventually accepted and activated; in some instances resultant programs exceeded initial expectations.

One of the earliest indications of these changes was the recognition of the need for national recreational land planning. In turn, this was followed by important developments that made recreational use of wild lands and environmental protection become important national issues.

SIGNIFICANT EVENTS IN NATIONAL RECREATIONAL
LAND PLANNING

The Outdoor Recreation Resources Review Commission, which functioned from 1958 until shortly after the publication of its report in 1962, was a catalyst in the development of public interest in comprehensive national recreational land planning and a major factor in implementing positive action toward that goal. Recommendations of this commission also prompted broader actions concerning perpetuation of environmental interest and quality.

However, national recreational land planning did not develop suddenly. Interest in coordinated recreational land planning on a national level began in 1924, when the President appointed a Committee on Outdoor Recreation[1] to coordinate widely separated viewpoints and interests of various federal, state, and local agencies in formulating a national recreational policy to serve as a guide for future action. To assist the committee in considering all aspects of this problem, the first National Conference on Outdoor Recreation was held in Washington May 22-24, 1924. Numerous public and private recreational leaders attended, and an executive committee and various advisory councils were appointed to undertake aspects of the task. An emerging national recreational plan, resulting from work during intervening years, was reviewed at the second National Conference on Outdoor Recreation, held in Washington January 20-21, 1926. One result of these meetings was a report on Recreational Resources of Federal Lands, by a Joint Committee of the American Forestry Association and the National Parks Association under auspices of the National Conference on Outdoor Recreation, issued in 1928. This effort, ahead of the times, unfortunately was not productive of anything permanent [1,2,3].

Planning for proper development and use of natural resources, including recreation, was implemented during the Depression by various emergency agencies. In particular, the National Planning Board was established to advise and assist the Public Works Administration in coordination of efforts between federal, state, and local governments. Its report, submitted to the President in 1934, led to its reorganization as the National Resources Board with broader responsibilities, including development of a "program and plan of procedure dealing with physical, social, governmental, and economic aspects of public policy for the development and use of land, water, and other national resources and such related subjects as may from

---

[1] The committee consisted of John Wingate Weeks, Secretary of War and author of the Weeks Act for the conservation of Eastern forests; Hubert Work, Secretary of the Interior, in charge of the National Parks System, reclamation projects, Indian reservations, and public lands; Henry Cantwell Wallace, Secretary of Agriculture, in charge of the national forests and wild life sanctuaries; Herbert Hoover, Secretary of Commerce, in charge of the Bureau of Fisheries; James J. Davis, Secretary of Labor; and Franklin Roosevelt, Assistant Secretary of the Navy, Executive Chairman.

time to time be referred to the Board by the President." Various reports of the National Resources Board led to the creation of the National Resources Committee on June 14, 1935, which was expected to have more permanent status. It developed considerable information on natural resources but ceased to function when the United States entered World War II [6,21].

Recreation Gains during Depression Years

Recreation, historically regarded in America as incidental to the business of living, did not begin to evolve as a modern concept until the Depression of the 1930s. Before then the meager financial support of recreation areas and programs seriously limited the number of competent employees attracted to this line of work. Many who chose recreation as a career did so out of dedication to an idea, rather than because of opportunity for personal recognition or financial gain. In particular, appropriations for early national and state parks and national forest recreation areas were so limited that maintenance of even basic standards was difficult; achievement of that goal often demanded some measure of personal sacrifice.

Although the Depression materially affected the economic and social climate of the nation, it was a boon to recreation. Faced with the possibility of serious problems resulting from widespread unemployment, Congress passed various laws to initiate a number of emergency works programs [6,21]. Agencies such as the Public Works Administration (PWA), Civilian Conservation Corps (CCC), Works Progress Administration (WPA), and National Youth Administration (NYA),[2] though sometimes ridiculed for worker inefficiency, nevertheless contributed greatly in many ways to the expansion and improvement of recreational facilities and opportunities. Activities in which these agencies were involved included reforestation; prevention and suppression of forest fires and outbreaks of destructive forest insects and diseases; research and publication of research results; improvement of interpretive exhibits; construction of equipment for proper housing of scientific collections; erosion and flood control; improvement and expansion of trails, campgrounds and picnic areas, water systems, sanitary facilities, and related needs often inadequately dealt with in recreational areas of that time. Many employees of these emergency agencies were highly qualified specialists who normally might not have been attracted to this field of activity. Though lacking in specialized abilities, the great majority, usually young people, benefited from trained leadership in development of particular skills or interests, as well as from the opportunity to engage in productive work. Some continued their association with the various organizations served by these emergency agencies after the Depression, and a number eventually rose to high places of authority.

---

[2] The high point in activities of various emergency agencies was approximately 1935. By 1942 all had been phased out, as their need was diminished by improved economic conditions and as the United States became deeply involved in World War II.

The Depression also brought to the fore simple inexpensive pleasures, largely ignored in more affluent times. During Depression years recreational values were less likely to be rated on the basis of cost; increasing numbers of visitors to recreational areas discovered recreational interests that they had previously ignored or overlooked, and which could be enjoyed with minimum expenditure. Further, to an increasing degree Americans began to appreciate that environmental interest and beauty had practical values, that such values were worth protecting, and that their protection depended largely on carefully conceived long-range planning and the exercise of personal responsibility. Recreation as a logical part of life, as well as a profession, was on the way to coming of age.

Also during the Depression years, a number of recreation demonstration areas were developed by the National Park Service as examples of what might be accomplished for public benefit through most appropriate recreational use of certain types of wild lands. Some of these recreation demonstration areas were later incorporated into several state park systems.

Mission 66 and Operation Outdoors

Later noteworthy recreational planning activities were related to the Mission 66 program of the National Park Service [29], initiated in 1956, and the Operation Outdoors program of the U.S. Forest Service, initiated in 1958 [20]. Principal objectives of these programs were the rehabilitation, improvement, and modernization of recreational facilities in National Park Service areas and national forests, which had deteriorated badly during the years of World War II and were inadequate to meet the demands of rapidly increasing numbers of visitors.

NATIONAL OUTDOOR RECREATION RESOURCES REVIEW COMMISSION

This commission was established [9] by authority of the Outdoor Recreation Resources Review Act (P.L. 85-470), approved June 28, 1958.[3] It represented the most tangible effort on a national level toward the study, planning, and coordination of varied public recreational needs and resources so

---

[3] The commission consisted of four members of the Senate Committee on Interior and Insular Affairs, appointed by the President of the Senate; four members of the House Committee on Interior and Insular Affairs, appointed by the President, who were "known to be informed about and concerned with the preservation and development of outdoor recreation resources and opportunities and experienced in resource conservation planning of multiple resource uses." One of the latter was appointed by the President as chairman of the commission.

The Outdoor Recreation Resources Review Act also made provision for an executive secretary and necessary personnel, as well as an advisory council to work with the commission in carrying out the purposes of the act. The advisory council consisted of liaison officers appointed by various federal and independent agencies with a direct interest and responsibility in various phases of outdoor recreation, together with twenty-five additional members representing major geographical areas and group interests, appointed by the commission.

that future as well as present Americans could be assured of outdoor recreational opportunities of adequate quality, quantity, type, and distribution.

The commission's report was published and presented to the President and the Congress in January, 1962 [9]. It was based upon twenty-seven specific published studies carried out by the commission staff and certain qualified outside contractors. The report included recommendations of the commission, consisting of a national outdoor recreation policy; guidelines for management of outdoor recreation resources; expansion, modification, and intensification of existing programs to meet increasing needs; establishment of a special bureau in the federal government to oversee such activities; and a federal grants-in-aid program to states.

ESTABLISHMENT AND LATER MODIFICATION OF THE BUREAU OF OUTDOOR RECREATION

Two significant results of recommendations by the National Outdoor Recreation Resources Review Commission were establishment of the Bureau of Outdoor Recreation in the Department of the Interior,[4] April 2, 1962 [26], and passage of the Land and Water Conservation Fund Act (P.L. 88-578), September 19, 1964 [23].

The Bureau of Outdoor Recreation provided leadership in planning and coordination of outdoor recreation programs sponsored by various public agencies and private land owners. The related legislation provided a fund for financing needed extensions of outdoor recreational opportunities.

In January 1978, by order of the Secretary of the Interior, the Bureau of Outdoor Recreation was superseded by a new agency designated as the Heritage Conservation and Recreation Service [29a,29b]. This new agency assumed some of the original responsibilities of the Bureau of Outdoor Recreation. In addition, certain responsibilities of BOR were transferred to the National Park Service, and vice versa. Relevant matters concerning these changes are outlined in Chapter 7.

ESTABLISHMENT OF THE NATIONAL WILDERNESS PRESERVATION SYSTEM

On September 3, 1964, the President signed the Wilderness Act (P.L. 88-577), thus establishing the National Wilderness Preservation System [7,11, 12,26]. Efforts toward this end, initiated by the Sierra Club and the Wilderness Society in the late 1940s, had resulted in the introduction of the first of a series of wilderness bills[5] into the Eighty-fourth Congress, second

---

[4] Established by order of the Secretary of the Interior; the Bureau's Organic Act (P.L. 88-29) was passed by Congress and signed by the President on May 28, 1963 [26].

[5] S. 4013—Humphrey and others, June 7, 1956; H.R. 11703—Saylor, June 11, 1956; H.R. 11751—Metcalf, June 13, 1956; H.R. 11791—Reuss, June 14, 1956; H.R. 11806—Miller, June 18, 1956.

session, in June, 1956. No action was taken on any of these original proposals. During the following eight years several variations of them were considered by Congress, and numerous hearings on their merits were held in various parts of the country. The hearings evoked considerable, often bitter, controversy and debate, and none of the early bills received congressional approval. Eventually reasonable compromises were developed on major points of contention.[6] Although the compromises were not completely acceptable to everyone concerned, the legislation thus developed represents one of the more significant milestones in the history of recreational use of wild lands.

Basically the Wilderness Act provides maximum possible permanent statutory protection of natural qualities typical of certain undeveloped, roadless federal lands with a minimum contiguous area of 5,000 acres (2,025 hectares). Wilderness areas, designated by Congress and approved by the President, cannot be modified except by congressional action. However, administrative responsibility for these lands is the same as before passage of the act; in addition, provisions were made for continuation of certain well-established activities and prior rights.

The Wilderness bill provided for the immediate inclusion of fifty-four existing wilderness and wild areas,[7] as well as the Boundary Waters Canoe Area,[8] within the national forests, aggregating 9,139,721 acres (3,702,000 hectares). It provided also for a ten-year study period to determine suitability or unsuitability for wilderness use of primitive areas[9] within the national forests, roadless portions of national parks and monuments, and similar undeveloped sections of national wildlife refuges and game ranges. Units of federal land in these latter categories are considered separately and, following completion of necessary study and public hearings on the nature of recommended disposition and management, may be added, in whole or part, to the National Wilderness Preservation System.

Since passage of the Wilderness Act studies have been completed on certain areas not initially included in the National Wilderness Preservation System, resulting in establishment of additional wilderness areas in the national forests of the West. Subsequently, the "Eastern Wilderness Act" (P.L. 93-622) was passed and became law, January 3, 1975. Except for smaller size limitations on areas involved, its provisions are basically similar to the earlier 1964 act. As a result, certain roadless portions of the national forests east of the Great Plains have been officially designated as wilderness areas. The "Eastern Wilderness Act" also provided for study of other undeveloped sections in eastern national forests for possible designation as wil-

---

[6] Bill S. 4 was passed by the Senate, Apr. 9, 1963, and H.R. 9070 by the House, July 30, 1964.

[7] Previously administratively designated under USFS regulations U-1 and U-2.

[8] Previously classified as the Superior Roadless Area.

[9] Previously administratively designated under USFS regulation L-20.

derness and recommended similar action for certain lands within eastern
areas of the National Wildlife Refuge System and the National Park System[10] [19].

PUBLIC LAND LAW REVIEW COMMISSION

Since our land laws were developed over many years as a result of independent action at various sessions of Congress in response to timely needs, they
were not always properly related to one another. The expanding importance
of varied benefits of wild lands, highlighted by controversies over different
proposals of use, indicated that there was great need for better coordination
of the objectives of the various land laws and the manner of their administration. The Act Establishing the Public Land Law Review Commission
(P.L. 88-606), which became law on September 19, 1964, was intended to
serve as a step toward this goal [13].

The Commission[11] was directed to (1) review the relation of existing
public land laws; (2) determine the adequacy of the public land laws to
meet current and future needs in providing maximum general public benefits; (3) identify and evaluate the division of administrative responsibility
among various agencies of the federal government concerned with the public lands and public land laws; and (4) determine whether and to what
extent revisions are necessary in the public land laws and relevant rules and
regulations. Further, the Commission was directed to submit a report at a
specified time[12] to the President and the Congress recommending both
administrative and legislative actions which should be taken to assure "that
the public lands of the United States shall be (a) retained and managed or
(b) disposed of, all in a manner to provide the maximum benefit for the
general public."

Several thousand public land laws were in effect at the time this act
was passed.

---

[10] Act of October 19, 1976 (P.L. 94-577) designated as wilderness sixteen units in the
National Wildlife Refuge System and three units within the national forests; it also designated
eight wilderness study areas within the national forests. The Act of October 21, 1976 (P.L.
94-567) designated as wilderness certain lands within thirteen units of the National Park System and revised boundaries of three of these thirteen areas.

[11] Though similar studies of our land laws were made in 1879, 1903, and 1930, the
Commission was the first of these four groups to be composed of members of Congress [32]. It
had nineteen members, consisting of six members from the Senate Committee on Interior and
Insular Affairs, a like number from the House Committee on Interior and Insular Affairs (in
each case equally divided between majority and minority parties), six members who were
appointed by the President (not to include officers of federal agencies), and the nineteenth
member and chairman of the Commission, who was elected by the other eighteen members.

The bill provided also for a full-time staff director, together with necessary personnel to
carry out routine assigned tasks, as well as an advisory council to assist the Commission. The
advisory council consisted of liaison officers from various interested federal departments and
agencies, together with twenty-five members appointed by the Commission who represented
various major citizen groups interested in public land law problems. Further, each governor
was requested to designate a representative to work with the Commission and the advisory
council.

[12] Original date of Dec. 31, 1968, was later extended.

The Commission's report, *One Third of the Nation's Land,* was presented to the President and the Congress in June, 1970 [10]. The report was based on data from public meetings held throughout the country and the results of thirty-three research studies related to the Commission's investigation.

The Commission made 137 specific recommendations, including the need for basic revisions in the land laws so that, in the future, lands disposed of would be only those lands where nonfederal ownership benefit to the general public would be maximum.

To improve recreational land use, recommendations were made concerning the role of the Bureau of Outdoor Recreation (as previously noted, superseded by the Heritage Conservation and Recreation Service, January 1978) in national and state recreation planning, changes in the Land and Water Conservation Fund Act, the need for recreation user fees, federal responsibility for public accommodations on federal public lands. Unique public land areas of national significance were to be identified and protected, and guidelines were to be established for minimizing conflicting land uses on public lands. Private enterprise was to be encouraged to play a greater role in development and management of intensive recreation use on public lands not designated for concessionaire development. Further it was recommended that Congress provide guidelines for managing public land resources for recreation, revising the classification system suggested by the Outdoor Recreation Resources Review Commission (see Chapter 7). The need for rights-of-way across private lands to provide access to public land and limits on federal recreation land acquisition policy was indicated [10].

Since the Commission was concerned with all public land laws, there were of course overlaps between recreation recommendations and those for other land uses. Although specific legislation has not been enacted to adopt these recommendations in total, many subsequent changes in agency policy and regulations reflect the intent of PLLRC recommendations. Passage of the National Environmental Policy Act (1969), Forest Management Act (1976), and the Federal Land Policy and Management Act (1976) also incorporated many of the ideas advanced by the PLLRC.

ADDITIONAL EVENTS IMPORTANT IN WILD-LAND RECREATION

Over many years other federal agencies, as well as commissions and related official bodies, have become involved, directly or indirectly, in outdoor recreation [24,25,26]. In some instances their activities have been authorized by specific laws, in others by extension of agency policy in response to public demand. In addition, certain significant legislative acts have recently been passed by Congress and have received Presidential approval.

Miscellaneous Federal Agencies and Related Official Bodies

Some of the more important federal organizations with varied responsibilities relative to recreational land use are noted in following paragraphs.

Federal Highway Administration   This agency of the Department of Transportation was formerly known as the Bureau of Public Roads. For many years it has cooperated with the National Park Service, Forest Service, and other federal agencies in the construction of roads in various areas of federal land [24]. By authority of the Federal-Aid Highway Act of 1958 (P.L. 85-899), as amended, this agency is also responsible for federal aid to states in the construction of the National System of Interstate and Defense Highways; it also cooperates with state highway departments in the development of access routes, subsidiary roads, and related highway services, including safety rest areas and parking places at scenic, historic, and related points of interest along highways. Further, scenic aspects of roads and parkways are subject to provisions of the Highway Beautification Act of 1965 (P.L. 89-285) and the Department of Transportation Act of 1966 (P.L. 89-670), as amended, as well as to consideration by the Environmental Quality Council and the Citizens Advisory Committee on Environmental Quality [18,24,26].

Indian Reservations[13]   These lands have considerable outdoor recreational potential, but the Indians have traditionally been reluctant to permit any use, including recreational use, which might impinge upon the independent owner status of these reservations. However, by 1960 tribal councils of a number of Indian Reservations, recognizing general public interest in such areas as a source of employment and income opportunity for reservation residents, have sponsored various kinds of recreation developments (24). These activities, outlined in Chapter 12, have been encouraged by the Bureau of Indian Affairs.

Environmental Quality Council and Citizens Advisory Committee on Environmental Quality[14]   These two agencies were established May 29, 1969 by Executive Order No. 11492 [26,30]. They are concerned with all aspects of recreation and natural beauty. They review recreation and natu-

---

[13] Tribal Indian Reservations are Indian property and, thus, private rather than public land. Such land is held in trust for the Indians by the federal government, with management and basic conservation principles supervised by the Bureau of Indian Affairs of the Department of the Interior, subject to consent of the Indian owners.

[14] Superseded the Recreational Advisory Council and Citizens Advisory Committee, established May 4, 1966 by Executive Order No. 11278, which had similar responsibilities. Change in names indicates growing awareness that outdoor recreational interests are related to and dependent upon environmental quality. The Council is a Cabinet-level policy advisory body. The Citizens Advisory Committee is composed of members selected by the President for their interest in outdoor recreation and natural beauty.

ral beauty plans and programs of federal agencies and make recommendations to the President on matters relevant to recreational policy. They were
also empowered to conduct studies in related fields and to encourage and
assist federal agencies in coordinating their recreational programs effectively.

Environmental Protection Agency Established December 2, 1970, this
agency fosters effective action at all levels of government, as well as of
private interests, on behalf of all environmental matters. Since its responsibilities extend beyond those related simply to recreation it serves as the
public's advocate for maintenance of a livable environment.

Soil Conservation Service Assistance of private land owners in development of recreational potentials of agricultural land by this agency of the
Department of Agriculture is briefly noted in Chapter 4 (p. 65).

Other Significant Legislation
The Endangered Species Act of 1966 (P.L. 91-135) provided for protection
and propagation of native species of fish and wildlife that are threatened
with extinction. It was supplemented by the Endangered Species Act of
1973 (P.L. 93-205) which provides similar protection for native plant species. The Estuary Act of 1968 (P.L. 90-454) authorized the Secretary of the
Interior, in cooperation with the states, to conduct an inventory and examination of the nation's estuaries and their natural resources [14]. The Wild
and Scenic Rivers Act of 1968 (P.L. 90-542), as amended, provided for the
designation of certain largely natural, free-flowing major streams as compo-
nents of a National Wild and Scenic River System [15,28]. The National
Trails System Act of 1968 [P.L. 90-543], as amended, designated the Appalachian and Pacific Crest Trails as initial units in a proposed National
Trails System [16,27].

The National Environmental Policy Act of 1969 (P.L. 91-190) was
signed by the President on January 1, 1970. This act declared a national
policy concerning productive and enjoyable harmony between people and
the environment, prevention of environmental damage, and better understanding of natural resource ecology; it also established a three-member
Council on Environmental Quality [17,18,25].

Recreation is also considered in provisions of the Federal Water Pollution Control Act Amendments of 1972 (P.L. 92-500). Section 404c provides
that the Army Corps of Engineers issue permits for discharge of dredged or
fill material into navigable waters at specified sites—including authority to
deny such permission where such action will have an unacceptable adverse
effect on recreation areas.

The Alaska Native Claims Settlement Act of 1971 (P.L. 92-203) is
destined to have considerable impact on the reservation of wild-land recreation areas in Alaska [26]. In addition to granting native Alaskans title to
certain areas, this act authorized consideration of new national parks, wildlife refuges, wild and scenic rivers, and similar areas. Key federal lands

were withdrawn from development until December 19, 1978, ending Congressional action establishing such areas. This affects the extent of land in Alaska administered by the National Park Service, the Fish and Wildlife Service, the Bureau of Land Management and the Forest Service. Congress did not act in time, but seventeen areas aggregating 56 million acres (22,680,000 hectares) were designated as national monuments by Presidential proclamation. Most were added to the National Park system. A final solution depends upon future developments.

CONSERVATION ORGANIZATIONS AND LAND-USE CONFLICTS

From the beginning, the designation of wild lands for recreation prompted inevitable resistance from exponents of more utilitarian land uses. Such controversies have continued to the present time and they will undoubtedly typify future years.

One of the earliest of such controversies involved John Muir and the Sierra Club in their unsuccessful effort to save the Hetch Hetchy Valley in Yosemite National Park from development as a reservoir (p. 53). The American Forestry Association[15] has long been concerned with wise use of forest land, including use for recreation. The National Parks Association[16] has championed national park establishment and preservation; it also cooperated with the American Forestry Association during the 1920s in the initial, though unsuccessful, efforts to develop a national recreational land-use program (p. 72). Later, the Wilderness Society and Sierra Club spearheaded the long fight which finally resulted in the establishment of our National Wilderness Preservation System (pp. 75–77). These and many similar organizations, both national and local in scope and working alone or in coalition, played prominent roles in many other land-use disagreements related to recreation and environmental protection and preservation.

Conservation organizations [8] exert significant impact on recreational land-use policy and management. Many are more politically effective than professional or scientific societies with either similar or opposing views which may also be involved in land-use conflicts. All land managers encounter such organizations; their work will be more effective if they understand the nature of membership, goals, organizational structure, and administrative procedures of such groups.[17]

[15] Founded 1875; oldest of our conservation organizations.

[16] Now known as the National Parks and Conservation Association. Its interests have been expanded to include broader environmental concerns due to interrelationships of national park problems with overcrowding, multiple-use planning, and pollution.

[17] Influential conservation organizations with preservationist objectives include the Sierra Club, Wilderness Society, National Audubon Society, Nature Conservancy, Save the Redwoods League, Friends of the Earth, Alaska Conservation Society, Alaska Coalition, Defenders of Wildlife, and Federation of Western Outdoor Clubs. Those of more localized influence include the Olympic National Park Associates and North Cascades Conservation Council, both of the Pacific Northwest. Because of varied interpretations of "conservation" many related organizations (ski, off-road vehicle and various outdoor sports clubs) emphasize the utilitarian aspects of recreation, usually favoring their particular interests. They frequently offer opposition to preservationist groups.

GENERAL COMMENTS AND CONCEPTS

At this point it may be helpful to the reader to bring major points together and focus on where we are. In the preface an organization framework was introduced, showing interrelationships of the parts of the book. We have seen that given more nonwork time, mobility, and income, plus changing attitudes and a taste for the outdoors, more urban people are seeking outdoor recreation in forests, parks, and other nonurban wild lands. A relationship has been shown between the manager of the recreation lands, the environmental resource, and the user. The role of interpretation as a catalyst has only been alluded to—so far.

This history of outdoor recreational use of wild lands has been closely associated with development of resource conservation, particularly forest resources. Many of our great public parks and recreation areas are in the West, and the protection of these areas has required long and difficult struggles by inspired leaders, groups, and individuals. Planning thus far has not always been broadly conceived to include the interests of the visitor as well as those of the manager-planner. In an earlier period of much land, a small population, and slow transportation, individual rights in land use could more easily be gratified. Today this is no longer the case. Research should provide insights for better planning and management.

The development of both the National Park System and the U.S. Forest Service were explained and elaborated upon. We found that recreation land-use policies of the two agencies are quite different. The National Park Service is more nationally oriented, possibly due to the emphasis on seasonal visitation, from great distances. Management policy is toward protection and preservation of the natural environment while encouraging public use. These contradictory objectives add great difficulty in national park administration.

The Forest Service has a generally utilitarian policy toward its regular multiple-use forest lands, emphasizing support of local economies around or within national forests. Yet in the management of wilderness, Forest Service policy is perhaps more preservationist and limiting to development than that of National Parks.

The outline of significant events since the 1930s in this chapter provides insight for the future of recreational land management. Our growing, urbanized society provides the clientele for our varied recreational lands. On public and to some extent on private lands, consent of the people is necessary to area perpetuation. It will be essential for land managers to try to understand the goals and behavior of recreation visitors and to make certain recreation visitors understand managerial operation—as is emphasized in Chapter 6.

Visitors will view the recreation area manager and other visitors, by their own standards, not by those of the manager. Yet they may be directed by careful planning and adequate communication. Individual differences of age and sex also figure in visitor variance. Social class differences in taste, interests, and occupational roles have an effect on leisure patterns. Access to most of our big parks requires automobile use and often segments of leisure time not readily available to all. Are we perhaps too road-oriented?

Activities enjoyed in youth or with the family group may well persist into adult life, though it is also possible to learn new skills by observation and the enjoyment of others with whom we identify. Inferences as to motivation are difficult, but for some, as the mountain climber, uncertainty of outcome is important. For others, freedom from responsibility and minimal risks are thought to be part of a recreation camping experience. People visit areas for many reasons, varying along a continuum from social reasons, as enjoying the contact with others in the campground, to environmental reasons, as experiencing the beauty of nature. Interpretation can be useful in generating environmental interest, but will be more difficult with urban-oriented visitors unless it is stimulating and pleasurable. How could the manager use interpretation effectively?

A study of wilderness visitors in the Pacific Northwest found that post-college-educated users had more wilderness-purist attitudes and that more urban-bred people were wilderness purists than small-town or rurally raised respondents. In another study of campers in national forest and national park car campgrounds and backcountry, urban-bred people were found to be stronger differentiators of environments than rural-raised interviewees. Urban wilderness users preferred National Park Service backcountry to Forest Service wilderness.

Is it possible that support for wilderness and protected environments of parks will come largely from educated city dwellers? There are of course more urban than rural people, but what of the views of the city dweller generally? Why would people prefer National Park backcountry to Forest Service wilderness? What of the differences in agency policy and the range of recreation land-types?

An Evolutionary Hypothesis for Two Bureaus

Perhaps the historic agency development of the U.S. Forest Service and the National Park Service as described earlier may be used to give insights into present-day manager-visitor relationships in the use of wild-land environments for recreation. Anthony Downs, in "Inside Bureaucracy" [5], states that bureaus may be formed from existing bureaus by split-offs generated by zealots or charismatic leaders.[18] Both agencies were formed this way with Pinchot and Mather as the leaders. They dominated their small bureaus, selecting their associates carefully, pushing for their own forms of land management, obtaining bureau support from Presidents, congressmen, other political leaders, and businessmen outside the agency. We might call this the *inception stage*. The national forests and the national parks had the personal attention of leaders whose policies could be directly applied to

[18] Anthony Downs. "Inside Bureaucracy," Boston, Little, Brown, a Rand Corporation Research Study, p. 6. Copyright 1966, 1967 by the Rand Corporation.

field areas and to all personnel. Loyalty to the great leader was a hallmark of these agencies, morale was high, and they could usually rely on support of conservation organizations such as the American Forestry Association or the National Parks Association (and in Forester Pinchot's case, the Society of American Foresters, of which he was a founder). With much land and few resource users, inconsistencies in management or otherwise competitive uses were not so obvious as they are today. Demand for National Forest products was limited and locally oriented. Large National Park hotels served the life-style of most of the visitors and park supporters. Acquisition of new lands was an important agency function.

With the loss of Pinchot and Mather, leadership was passed to loyal lieutenants who carried on the founders' policies and successfully expanded the bureaus in the *planning, or organization, stage.* With the growth of the organization, the contact with individual forests by the Chief of the Forest Service, and parks by the Director of the National Park Service, decreased. More emphasis went into building the organization structure (regional organizations). Master planning, procedure manuals, and the like became important. In addition new functions were added (Emergency Conservation Work in the 1930s), and the types of resource users and visitors served expanded. Competition among resource users increased. Outside groups became more critical of agency policy.

As they grew the agencies began competing with each other, due partly to different concepts of land-use management and the desire to create national parks out of national forests (e.g., Kings Canyon National Park, California; Olympic National Park, Washington). Also the agencies' emphasis shifted more toward timber production in the U.S. Forest Service and toward development for mass public use in the U.S. National Park Service (e.g., Mission 66). Today we seem to be in the *mass use—development stage,* in which organizations are very large with more administrative officers, and resource-management problems and allocation among competing clients are very complex. The initial goals of the agencies have been expanded to cover more resource uses (e.g., Multiple Use Act, 1960, together with later refinements for the U.S. Forest Service). Within the agencies the leaders are further removed from field problems by complex organizational frameworks, and the orientation of men of ambition is toward the position above them rather than to the resource-management tasks. At the same time, from the recreation point of view, both bureaus face increasing numbers of visitors with increasingly complex characteristics and interests. Contact with organizations that once provided a great deal of support becomes more difficult and criticism of agency policy more frequent. Internal criticism of agency policy by staff is not encouraged.

This is just one point of view, and the reader is encouraged to study the organizational development in groups or bureaus of his knowledge to see if parallels exist. With as much diversity of areas, resource uses, types of visitors and groups, and with the need for flexible planning to provide a range of opportunities, how can bureaus in the mass use—development stage be adequately responsive to such variation? At least today's leaders usually are not so definite and specific in policy dictation as were the great founders of these organizations.

SUMMARY

Current concepts of wild-land recreation and perpetuation of environmental quality evolved over many years; early efforts to speed up this process met with little success. Development of a national recreational plan was attempted as early as 1924, and during Depression years in the 1930s efforts were made to bring about better coordination of recreational uses of different types of public lands. The Depression was responsible also for modifications in public attitude toward recreation on wild lands, which favored later development of improved policies and programs.

Progress was halted during World War II, but conditions afterwards, together with the population explosion and economic and social changes, brought increasing numbers of people to all types of recreational lands. The number of wild-land recreational areas and their facilities, which had deteriorated during the war years, was inadequate to meet accelerating demand.

Outdoor recreation became a major issue in 1958, when the Outdoor Recreation Resources Review Commission was established. The report of the Commission, published in January 1962, included recommendations for recreational land planning which were acted upon shortly afterwards. The Bureau of Outdoor Recreation was soon established—later to be superseded by the Heritage Conservation and Recreation Service, January 1978. In 1965, passage of the Land and Water Conservation Fund Act made possible cooperation between the federal government, the states, and their political subdivisions on matters pertaining to outdoor recreation. In addition, the concept of a National Wilderness Preservation System, which had been a highly controversial matter for more than a decade, became reality on September 3, 1964, when the President signed the Wilderness Act. The Public Land Law Review Commission was also established in 1964; during its several years of activity it made numerous recommendations that have been reflected in later land laws and policies of various land management agencies relevant to wild-land recreation.

Other significant events since the 1960s included liberalization of public recreational use of Indian reservations, establishment of the Environmental Protection Agency, and passage of additional noteworthy legislation. In addition, provisions of the Alaska Native Claims Settlement Act of 1971 indicate that extensive additions to various types of wild land reservations in Alaska can be expected in the future. Reference is also made to the numerous land-use controversies that have typified the many years since public interest in recreational values of wild land became generally evident, and of the important role played by numerous conservation organizations in those controversies.

SELECTED REFERENCES

1 Anonymous: For a National Outdoor Recreation Policy, *National Parks Bulletin,* no. 29, Apr. 30, 1924.
2 Anonymous: Organizing Recreation, *National Parks Bulletin,* vol. 7, no. 47, January 1926.
3 Anonymous: Recreation Resources of Federal Lands, *American Forests,* vol. 14, no. 418, October 1928.
4 Clawson, Marion: "The Federal Lands Since 1956—Recent Trends in Use and Management," Resources for the Future, Johns Hopkins, Baltimore, 1967.
5 Downs, Anthony: "Inside Bureaucracy," Little, Brown, Boston, 1967.
6 Ise, John: "Our National Park Policy," Johns Hopkins, Baltimore, 1961.
7 Nash, Roderick: "Wilderness and the American Mind," Yale University Press, New Haven, 1967.
8 National Wildlife Federation: "Conservation Directory, 1976," Washington, 1976.
9 Outdoor Recreation Resources Review Commission: "Outdoor Recreation for America: A Report to the President and to the Congress by the ORRRC," U.S. Government Printing Office, Washington, 1968.
10 Public Land Law Review Commission: "One Third of the Nation's Land," U.S. Government Printing Office, Washington, 1970.
11 U.S. Congress: "An Act to Establish a National Wilderness Preservation System for the Permanent Good of the Whole People, and for other Purposes," (P.L. 88-577), 88th Cong., S.4, Sept. 3, 1964.
12 U.S. Congress: "National Wilderness Preservation System: Message from the President of the United States," 89th Cong. 1st Sess., H.R. 79, Feb. 8, 1965.
13 U.S. Congress, Committee on Interior and Insular Affairs: "Objectives, Functions and Operations of the Public Land Law Review Commission," Committee Print No. 21, 89th Cong., 2nd Sess., U.S. Government Printing Office, Washington, 1966.
14 U.S. Congress: "Estuary Act" (P.L. 90-454), 90th Cong., H.R. 25, Aug. 3, 1968.
15 U.S. Congress: "Wild and Scenic Rivers Act," (P.L. 90-542), 90th Cong., S. 119, Oct. 2, 1968.
16 U.S. Congress: "National Trails System Act," (P.L. 90-543), 90th Cong. S. 827, Oct. 2, 1968.
17 U.S. Congress: "National Environmental Policy Act of 1969," 91st Cong., 1st Sess., Senate Calendar No. 287, Report No. 91-296, U.S. Government Printing Office, Washington, 1969.
18 U.S. Congress: "An Act to Establish a National Policy for the Environment, to Provide for the Establishment of a Council on Environmental Quality, and for Other Purposes," (P.L. 91-190), 91st Cong., S. 1075, Jan. 1, 1970.
19 U.S. Congress: "An Act To Further the Purposes of the Wilderness Act by Designating Certain Acquired Lands for Inclusion in the National Wilderness Preservation System, To Provide for the Study of Certain Additional Lands for Such Inclusion, and for Other Purposes" (Eastern Wilderness Act), (P.L. 93-622), 93rd Cong., S. 3433, Jan. 3, 1975. U.S. Government Printing Office, Washington, 1975.

20 U.S. Department of Agriculture, Forest Service: "Operation Outdoors," U.S. Government Printing Office, Washington, 1957.
21 U.S. Department of the Interior: "Back of the Buffalo Seal," U.S. Government Printing Office, Washington, 1936.
22 U.S. Department of the Interior, Bureau of Land Management: Public Land Commissions, Our Public Lands, vol. 17, no. 2, Summer 1967.
23 U.S. Department of the Interior, Bureau of Outdoor Recreation: "Land and Water Conservation Fund Act, as Amended," U.S. Government Printing Office, Washington, 1968.
24 U.S. Department of the Interior, Bureau of Outdoor Recreation: "Federal Outdoor Recreation Programs," U.S. Government Printing Office, Washington, 1968.
25 U.S. Department of the Interior, Bureau of Outdoor Recreation: "Administrative and Legislative Directives to the Bureau of Outdoor Recreation," U.S. Government Printing Office, 1975.
26 U.S. Department of the Interior, Bureau of Outdoor Recreation: "The Bureau of Outdoor Recreation: Focal Point for Outdoor America," U.S. Government Printing Office, Washington, 1975.
27 U.S. Department of the Interior, Bureau of Outdoor Recreation: *Outdoor Recreation Action, Winter 1976,* U.S. Government Printing Office, Washington, 1976.
28 U.S. Department of the Interior, Bureau of Outdoor Recreation: *Outdoor Recreation Action, Spring 1977,* U.S. Government Printing Office, Washington, 1977.
29 U.S. Department of the Interior, National Park Service: "Mission 66 in Action," n.p., n.d.
29a U.S. Department of the Interior: Citizens, States Invited to Share in Selecting Historic and Natural Sites for Preservation, Press Release (mimeo.), Jan. 23, 1978.
29b U.S. Department of the Interior: "The National Heritage Program" Washington, D.C., January 1978.
30 U.S. Government: Executive Order No. 11278—Establishing a President's Council and a Committee on Recreation and Natural Beauty, *Federal Register,* vol. 31, no. 87, May 5, 1966.

Camping in a wild-land recreational area is rewarded by pleasant social as well as environmental experiences; Ratcliff Lake, Davey Crockett National Forest, Texas (Class II, General Recreational Area). *(U.S. Forest Service; Robert E. Hintz, July 1966.)*

Section Three

People-Relationships

The Recreation Visitor: Motivation, Behavior, Impact[1]

Wild-land recreation means many forms of *interaction* between people and wild-land environments. People have an impact on environments, and vice versa. Adequate management therefore requires more than the direct protection, renewal, or development of wild-land recreational resources. It requires also that human behavior be influenced, channeled, or regulated. Its proper goals cannot be attained without some guidance from those disciplines which contribute to our knowledge of human behavior.

This chapter is intended as an introduction to the basic insights available from the fields of knowledge pertaining to the behavior of human beings. But no one chapter can take the place of thorough training in university courses in the several disciplines which provide these insights. The principal emphasis here is sociological and social-psychological, but the comparable importance of other social sciences is acknowledged and should be kept in mind.

[1] Prepared by William R. Catton, Jr., Professor of Sociology at Washington State University, Pullman, Washington.

IMPORTANCE OF INSIGHTS FROM SOCIAL SCIENCE

There are economic and political aspects of wild-land recreation, e.g., allocation of resources, material and financial, to this use in competition with other uses, and allocation of regulative authority to one agency or another. These issues call for insights from economics and political science. Adequate understanding of people's desires, interests, motivations, habits, and any potential there may be for modifying any of these, calls for insights from psychology, especially social psychology. Sociology, too, can contribute knowledge on such matters, as well as some understanding of probable trends in the composition of the wild-land recreation clientele, tendencies among wild-land recreationists toward depreciative or deviant uses of recreation resources, and knowledge of the social factors influencing public preferences among alternative management policies.

Sociological knowledge is needed also regarding pertinent organizational processes, both in the bureaucratic agencies responsible for recreational wild lands and in the numerous voluntary associations which exert pressure upon them from time to time.

SELF-FULFILLING EXPECTATIONS

As the human habitat fills up with people, more people become frustrated in more ways and on more occasions. Their wrath seeks *available* targets, often without sufficient concern, as social psychologists have noted, as to whether availability reflects culpability [15,26,32]. City fire fighters, for example, have sometimes been stoned, shot at, and verbally abused while battling flames in American urban ghettos. "It's frustrating," said one member of the Los Angeles Fire Department, "to be despised by the very people you're trying so hard to help."

Under modern conditions, wild-land protection could similarly become a thankless task. If the devoted efforts of management personnel go unacknowledged and the best-intentioned decisions of officials in protective agencies are consistently depreciated for falling short of the ideal, eventually the result could be serious demoralization rather than the reinforcement required if the achievements of such agencies are ever to approach perfection.

If the nature and source of the threat to wild-land recreation areas are misperceived, interested parties may try to "defend" these areas by actions which actually endanger them. Unjustly abusing their humanly imperfect guardians would be one example of an action that could have this unintended effect. The classic illustration of such "self-fulfilling expectations" was offered by Robert K. Merton, Columbia University sociologist. He cited the example of a bank's failing because of panic efforts of depositors to withdraw funds in response to unfounded (but believed) rumors of the bank's insolvency [33].

In much the same manner, those who wish to ensure the preservation of wild areas for the enjoyment of future generations probably contribute inadvertently to their erosion and desecration. Now that large numbers of people have the time and the affluence and the desire to seek their recreation in such environments, these areas *need* protection more than ever before. Resource-management agencies can provide this protection only if the vast majority of their personnel at all levels have the proper training and experience and are truly dedicated to the task. Essential dedication can be undermined by excessive, uninformed, or unsympathetic criticism from a public which misunderstands the causes of past deterioration of our wild areas.

This unwanted outcome might result from a kind of organizational attrition. Any such management agency as, for example, the National Park Service, is more than a group of high-minded individuals. Of necessity it is also a government bureau with a formal structure. It is dependent for funds and authority on a politically oriented Congress that is beholden to a constituency it more often conceives as reluctant taxpayers than as devotees of nature. Organizational constraints can sometimes run counter to the values of the organization's own personnel [1,18]. When this happens, the relationship between the organization and its clients may help determine whether noble values or more mundane influences will prevail. Many persons in the Park Service are alert to and would welcome any concrete indications of public support for the ideals of wild-land preservation. Their performance of organizational duties can benefit from a "watchdog" function carried on by various voluntary associations like the Sierra Club, the Wilderness Society, or the National Parks and Conservation Association. But if *excessive, carping* criticism seemed to be all they got from the conservation-minded citizens from whom they would tend to expect gratitude and moral support, the result could be that the most conscientious members of the service would become demoralized and would resign. Their places would then tend to be filled by less devoted, more bureaucratic-minded mercenaries, for whom park protection tasks would increasingly be seen as a job, not as a calling. The self-fulfilling expectation would thus have operated at the organizational level, changing the composition of an agency's personnel in the direction of an initially inaccurate image, making the organization more nearly as nonidealistic as it was wrongly thought to be.

But this same social-psychological tendency, the "self-fulfilling expectation," can also be used for positive goals. It is the principle that is implicit in the common practice of campground managers who try to reduce the amount of littering by frequent and thorough collection of trash. It is understood that litter on the ground invites more litter; people who experience (and thus expect) a messy environment tend to behave in ways that keep it messy, but people who experience (and thus expect) neat surroundings tend to behave in ways that preserve neatness.

The prominent placement of a visitor register book, where visitors are obviously expected to leave their mark, is likewise commonly used as a means of minimizing defacement of public facilities and natural features.

The principle of self-fulfilling expectations has been described and illustrated here, not because it is the most important idea in social science, but because it is one that has no parallel in such disciplines as botany, zoology, or geology. Processes of geological uplift and erosion cannot be influenced by a mountain's "expectation" as to its eventual height and contours, and even the flora and fauna of a wild area hardly can be imagined to influence the eventual composition of their community by "expectations" about it which could in some way influence their symbioses and their distribution. Even among human beings by no means all expectations bring about behavior that fulfills those expectations. The instances cited here are simply intended to indicate that distinctive processes do occur among humans and give rise to distinctive principles discovered by social science research. Many social science ideas are useful to wild-land recreation management. Other important ideas include insights into human personality traits, into the nature and functioning of human societies, and organizations and groups, and into sources of human variety.

BASIC SOCIOLOGICAL PRINCIPLES

Sociological Perspective

Because guidance and control of human behavior is an inevitable part of recreational management of wild lands—to ensure protection and proper use—it is essential that basic sociological principles be included in the knowledge with which resource managers are equipped.

Modern sociology starts from the premise that human beings get to be what they are from their experiences in groups, and can do things collectively and as socially nurtured beings which they could not do otherwise. The seemingly infinite variety of social encounters and social situations can actually be reduced to a finite set of categories. The probable behavior in any given class of encounters is predictable, in principle, partly by taking into account the web of group memberships in which people are involved [10,20,41].

Norms, Ethnocentrism, Culture

In ongoing groups, norms develop. Groups impose sanctions to minimize the deviation of their members' behavior from the norms. Members also comply with group norms as a result of internalizing them in a socialization process. "Socialization" is a term sociologists use to refer to the process whereby attitudes, habits, skills, and social standards of judgment are transmitted to people through their group involvements and their interactions with other human beings [4l].

From birth onward, each human being undergoes a socialization process which links that person to groups and to society. In this process each of us acquires a personality, including the ability to speak and think. It is also in this process that we acquire our many other skills, our unique personal constellation of attitudes, and even our conception of ourselves. Socialization is a lifelong process, and each person is both a product of it and an agent engaged in socializing others whenever he or she interacts [50].

In most societies, the principal context for early socialization is the family. The family not only links generation to generation by providing for care and training of children; it also regulates sexual behavior and reproduction, provides role models, and affords the satisfactions of intimate group life which tend to ensure its continuation. But family functions and family structure change as society changes. Family systems vary markedly from one society to another, and each people tends to regard its accustomed forms as normal and natural. "Ethnocentrism" refers to the universal human tendency to evaluate the behavior of other groups not by their standards but by the standards of one's own group. Ethnocentrism is a fact of life that can be important to all persons whose professions require them to try to redirect any aspect of human behavior. It is a natural result of the fact that human personalities are social products. People have ethnocentric tendencies in regard to all sectors of life [41].

The kinds of norms which will prevail in any given group, community, or society will depend in part on its relation to a physical and biological as well as social environment. Through many different processes human beings adapt themselves to the conditions of life set by their environments. Not all norms arise out of ecological adaptation, but norms that require ecologically probable behavior can be more readily enforced than those which require ecologically improbable behavior. For example, in a campground where parking stalls are physically too small to accommodate two cars, or are laid out slightly below the grade level, or are bounded by a neat row of logs, the environment-protecting rule of "one party per campsite" will require little overt enforcement. If the rule is instead communicated only verbally, by leaflet, or by sign, not by physical circumstance, its enforcement may be difficult or impossible in periods of peak use. Much environmental damage may then ensue.

Despite apparent ecological constraints on human behavior, human beings do differ from other species in that their behavior *can be* extensively shaped by normative considerations as well as by nonnormative circumstance. One of the key concepts of sociology and anthropology is "culture." This term refers to a system of socially acquired and socially transmitted standards of judgment, belief, and conduct. Differences among cultures have much to do with bringing about differences in the actions and expectations of people in different nations or regions.

Communication and Organization

Human society and culture are possible because of the unparalleled capacity of the human race for communication through the use of language. But language shapes as well as permits perception and thought. It links person to person and gives one an extensive social heritage in addition to a biological heritage. Social heritage is, of course, much less fixed than biological heritage, and it provides a human being with many niches (rather than just one) in the ecosystems in which one is involved.

Organization extends human capabilities. People in organizations which are structurally similar, tend to show similar attitudes and behavior in spite of differences in organizational goals or in their individual personalities. Large-scale pursuit of complex technical goals tends to foster the establishment of a type of formal organization approximating what is called bureaucracy. Sociologists use the term "bureaucracy" in a descriptive, not a derogatory, sense. In this objective sense, bureaucracy involves a clear-cut division of labor, a clear hierarchy of administrative authority, explicit rules and circumscribed role expectations, a detached and impersonal approach to all tasks, and assignment of personnel to positions according to technical qualifications. Real organizations fall short of the bureaucratic model because people holding positions in them (who have experienced socialization in more intimate group contexts) tend to resist depersonalization of themselves and their interactions.

Society is a self-perpetuating system. Social organization is inherently resistant to change. But social changes do occur. Innovative behavior, not easily distinguished immediately from deviant behavior, results from imperfect socialization which bestows skills but does not preclude unconventional applications thereof. Rates of innovation vary in different times and different social settings. Rates of acceptance of innovations depend on their perceived utility. How useful an innovation will be thought to be may in turn depend on such factors as the prestige of the source, the prestige of previous adopters, generalized social resistance or receptivity to novelty, perceived compatibility of the innovation with (or adaptability to) pre-existing culture patterns, and past experience with change.

Disorganization

Disorganization of a society can cause deviant acts by its members. Changes in a society's scale of values, inconsistencies in its normative prescriptions and expectations, impediments to the application of sanctions, and prevalent anticipations of nonconformity, all tend to facilitate deviant behavior. Societal tolerance limits are subject to change. Behavior regarded as deviant at one time may subsequently become the accepted standard of the group, and vice versa. The incidence of deviant acts depends in part on the availability of opportunities. Insofar as wild-land recreation tends to isolate people from surveillance by others, it affords such opportunities. Activities considered deviant by the larger society may be fostered by deviant normative subsystems and by illicit organization. The population categories most involved in wild-land recreation have tended to be the ones least involved in such deviant subcultures or illicit organizations.

Voluntary Associations

In urbanized society, most people interact in a segmental (only partially involved) way with others—except within families or intimate groups of friends, which sociologists call "primary groups." This segmentalism of urban life has fostered the development of assorted voluntary associations which engage in activities that vary from highly consummatory to highly instrumental. Many of these organizations serve their members as partial and occasional substitutes for the decreasingly common primary group experience. Some provide certification of status and rank of their members in an occupational specialty or some other significant category in the larger community. This function stands out in societies with large populations and extensive occupational specialization. Some voluntary associations, called "social movements," engage in concerted efforts to change attitudes, behavior, or social relationships in a larger society.

Various outdoor activity clubs, organized to facilitate their members' interest in skiing, hiking, camping, boating, etc., constitute clear examples of *consummatory* voluntary associations. Conservationist organizations, on the other hand, tend to be more *instrumental* and may be regarded as social movements since they expressly seek to influence public policies. Such groups as the Society of American Foresters and other professional organizations perform—among numerous other functions—the public certification of status and rank.

Human Differences

One fact the manager of wild-land recreation resources must always keep in mind is that people are not all alike. Many human differences are socially produced; other differences are socially endowed with meanings not inherent in their biological origins. Age and sex are universal dimensions of social differentiation, but they are differently used in different societies. Other readily visible differences (such as race) are often but not uniformly taken into account in the patterning of human interactions. Social differentiation provides the basis for elaborating organization. If all humans were alike, there could hardly be any of the complex organizations by which we accomplish complex tasks. Variation is thus a useful fact of human life, but it is also a source of many problems. In both respects awareness of it is important in wild-land recreation planning and management.

SOCIAL STRATIFICATION AND RECREATION

Recreation and social stratification are dynamically interrelated. Existing patterns of social differentiation, both vertical and horizontal, as well as changes in these patterns through time, may be a partial cause of some variations in recreational activity [28]. In other contexts, however, recreational behavior may be seen as the independent variable, making its own contribution to an ever-evolving system of social differentiation and strati-

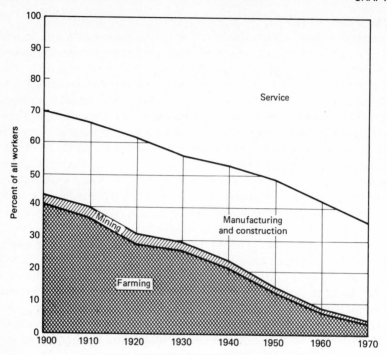

Figure 6-1 Changing pattern of work among U.S. working population.

fication. And in some situations, stratification may be more appropriately viewed as a *control* variable, rather than as either cause or effect.

Stratification as Cause

Social classes still differ in their relative access to recreational opportunities despite the undeniable changes of the past century. In many American cities, for example, the share of recreational land located in the lowest-income parts of the city is even less than the share of personal income received by the residents of those areas. Conversely, the share of recreational land located in the higher-income sections is even more generous than the share of monetary wealth. Consequently, urban blacks lack proportionate access to public parks, owing indirectly to discriminatory employment and residential segregation [11].

Free admission to public parks in the United States does not much offset the disadvantage of the poor. In crowded cities where poor people are concentrated there are proportionately fewer public parks than in wealthier and suburban areas. Moreover, access to most state parks, or national parks and national forests, depends on automobile ownership and ability to afford travel costs. Admission fees, if any, are a negligible fraction of the total cost of access to such places [45].

It is not only in differential access to recreation sites that stratification affects leisure behavior. Tastes, desires, and interests are also stratified, presumably as a result of unlike socialization experiences [12,22]. As the occupational structure of a nation's economy changes, the way that nation's people will perceive the natural environment may change as a consequence. From Figure 6-1 it is apparent that a sharply declining proportion of Americans are employed in occupations which would tend to define the land chiefly as a source of *materials*. Conversely, there has been a marked increase in the proportion who can earn their living by rendering some service (rather than by growing things or making things). It is probably easier for people in such nonextractive and nonfabricating roles to regard land as a locale for having experiences. In short, American labor-force trends are consistent with the trend toward redefining the natural environment as a source of desired experiences rather than a source of desired things.

There are evident links between occupational milieu and behavior outside the occupational role. Both the work situation and the nature of the work, together with influences from occupational categories clearly differentiate the leisure behavior of occupational categories [21]. The extent to which recreation is commercialized varies for different social strata. One study found that the percentage of respondents who reported that they devoted most of their leisure time to commercial-type activities was highest in the lowest occupational prestige level [12].

There are occupational differences in the probability of moonlighting, or holding a second job. Several million workers in the United States hold a second job more or less regularly. Many of these moonlighters are self-employed in one of their jobs—farming, a profession, a small business. Men are more likely than employed women to hold two jobs, especially in the 25 to 54 age bracket. In some occupations, moonlighting is especially prevalent, e.g., among members of the police or fire forces [14].

One survey technique that has been used to investigate leisure-time *interests* (as distinct from situationally conditioned leisure-time *activities*) has been to ask people what they would do with one or two hypothetical extra hours per day. Response patterns commonly reflect occupational differences or other types of stratification. In one such study, the modal response of the highest occupational prestige level was that the extra hours would be devoted to reading or studying. (It may be inferred, therefore, that people in the higher level occupations will tend to have greater appreciation of the natural values of wild lands—their geological, biological, institutional, and archeological characteristics.)

Such people may put less emphasis than others upon recreational values resulting from physical development of the areas. These people, mostly in the professions, were less inclined than any other level to sleep, rest, relax, or loaf in the extra time. None of them said they would use it for television viewing. More people on this level than on any other said they would devote the extra time to working at their jobs. In contrast, for the lowest occupational prestige level, the most common response was that the hours would be used to sleep, relax, rest, or loaf. This lowest level was also more inclined than any other to use the extra time for watching TV.

It has been suggested that leisure time can be best used only if some of it is *invested* in preparation for subsequent leisure activities [47]. More gratifying experiences can be had later if some present leisure is used to cultivate interests and skills. But social strata apparently differ in their recognition of this relationship between present and future. Ability and willingness to defer gratification are learned traits [2] and are unequally acquired by members of different social classes.

Differential receptivity to educational recreation may partly explain the existence of a socioeconomic gradient in certain forms of outdoor recreation. The more or less steady increase in recreational use of wild lands may be partly due to the parallel rise in educational attainment of the general population. Various studies [3,23] have found that some 60 percent or more of the visitors to wilderness areas are drawn from the top 10 percent of the population (in terms of educational attainment). Wilderness recreation has grown at conspicuously faster rates than other types of outdoor recreation. There is some evidence to suggest that the educational upgrading of the population has contributed to this growth [24]. Educated people are mentally equipped to derive esthetic and intellectual satisfactions from contacts with primeval nature to a greater extent than are the less educated.

Some leisure activities have had elite origins and have later become comparably widespread among lower strata, too. Such downward diffusion often depends on technological progress, which can reduce the expense involved in the activity. It is not always possible, however, to disentangle the effects of such progress from whatever universal tendency there may be for lower strata to emulate the behavior of higher strata as much as circumstances allow.

By the middle of the nineteenth century, travel was becoming quite feasible for the wealthy as a form of recreation. Turnpikes, canals, and railroads had been built, the steamboat had developed, and all these afforded geographic mobility to those with money. Construction of summer resorts was one result. At first Easterners constituted the principal clientele. Westerners with social aspirations soon joined their Eastern counterparts, and every summer Southern plantation owners too, came north to the resorts of New England and the Mid-Atlantic coast. By 1890, there were numerous middle-class summer hotels, and the downward diffusion was well under way [16].

Automobiles, in the first few years after their introduction, cost almost as much to maintain and operate for a year as to buy. In 1907, the president of Princeton University, Woodrow Wilson, warned that automobiles were giving workers and farmers direct glimpses of the "arrogance of wealth" and thus spreading socialistic feelings. But even before World War I, owning and operating automobiles ceased to be such an exclusive avocation. Their diffusion downward through the social hierarchy continued through and beyond the war. As cars became cheaper to buy and to use, and as highways improved and became more abundant, country people gained increased access to urban leisure-time opportunities, and city people regained access to the country. This new mobility was so significant for both groups that gasoline sales remained remarkably steady right through the Great Depression when renewed poverty exacted many sacrifices. Nor has the rise of gasoline prices in the 1970s curtailed use.

Stratification as Effect

Recreation has become a growth industry [46]. Provision of facilities and conditions required by various recreational activities sustains an assortment of ranked and coordinated occupations. When hundreds of thousands took up skiing, for example, the manufacturing and selling of skiing equipment and clothing became substantial businesses. Jobs arose for builders and operators of ski resorts. Early entrants in such a boom have unusual opportunities for upward social mobility. As such a new industry expands, it exerts growing pressure for reallocation of public lands for a new recreational use.

Patterns of recreational behavior can thus be the change-producing variable, and labor-force structure can be, to some extent, a dependent variable. It has been suggested that "the way leisure is used affects a culture as much as or more than the 'productive' work of that culture" [13]. In many instances a large industry has provided the means for pursuit of fun, and society has never again been the same [42]. Widespread diffusion of automobile ownership through the population of the United States, for example, led to patterns of vacation travel which fostered construction of new forms of tourist accommodation. In the 1930s, in the Western states, the forerunner of the motel came into being—clusters of overnight frame cabins, usually without private plumbing at first, and sometimes even requiring tourists to provide their own bedding. Before long, the signs at the side of the road began using the word "modern" as a euphemistic intimation that a group of these cabins had inside plumbing. By the 1960s the erstwhile "cabin camp" had evolved into more or less luxurious motels in which tiled bathrooms and carpeting were ubiquitous and television and swimming pools nearly so. Attractive restaurants were often part of the premises, too [16].

In 1900 the summer-resort business was small. It catered mostly to the wealthy. Half a century later there was a massive "vacation industry" catering in many ways to a much broader clientele. There are many communities whose economic base consists mainly of the expenditures of tourists and vacationists. Such business is actively sought by some communities as the answer to local economic problems.

In the future, some leisure-dependent occupations or communities or industries will expand and some will contract. Others will merely hold steady. Which will do which may depend upon, among other things, the form in which additional increments of leisure are attained. If the working *day* is shortened, city parks may be affected, but this increase in leisure would have little direct impact on most state parks, or national parks and forests. It would thus have little impact on the tourist industry. If the working *week* is shortened, gasoline sales are likely to rise, and campground construction within a hundred-mile radius of each large city is likely to boom. If *annual* vacations are lengthened or made more numerous, overseas airlines will do increased business, but so will winter resorts and the builders of summer homes. Campgrounds hundreds of miles from major urban agglomerations will be inundated.

It is a fact of considerable importance that a large fraction of the labor force work in occupations directly or indirectly dependent upon the outdoor recreational expenditures of others, e.g., the automobile complex, producers and distributors of camping, skiing, fishing, hunting, and mountaineering equipment.

Stratification as Control Variable

The amount of leisure time per capita in a society and the way it is distributed among various activities depend partly on the way the population is distributed among different phases of the life cycle [39] and among different occupations. In America, agricultural employment has declined markedly, and this has contributed to the increase in per capita leisure. Increased longevity—making for more years spent in retirement—has also been important. Increased participation of women in the labor force has partially offset these trends by reducing the average per capita leisure. But married female employment has augmented the financial ability of families to make choices regarding the use of whatever nonworking time their members do have [13]. Projection of probable future trends in such matters has become a fairly routine task for demographers, and it will be of increasing importance to agencies and persons managing recreational wild lands.

The actual growth of leisure cannot be accurately seen without considering changes in the social structure. Some major changes have confused the picture. Since 1850, leisure has increased more in the manufacturing and mining industries than elsewhere. Agricultural leisure did not increase appreciably until the twentieth century. Most of its increase came after 1940. But millions of people left agriculture in the meantime, and went into urban occupations. So the mean leisure per capita in the whole population was more conspicuously changed than in most occupations considered alone. Self-employed persons, civil servants, professionals, and executives have experienced little or no increase in leisure. The fastest recent drop in hours of work per week has been in low-ranked jobs. Here there is also often a period of some weeks of unwanted leisure (unemployment) each year [49]. For lower-ranked occupations, leisure is often unstable, unpredictable, and intermittent. For elite occupations, it tends to be bunched and predictable. Its use varies accordingly.

MOTIVATIONS AND WILD-LAND RECREATION NORMS

People are likely to acquire appetites for the recreational activities in which they had the most abundant and gratifying experience as they were growing up [29]. There are intergenerational continuities in recreation preferences. Any recreational activity that is typically engaged in together by the members of a family may be expected to persist into the next generation—if its enjoyment has been shared in common. Recreational values may be learned in childhood. According to the psychological "law of effect," the probability of any behavior in a given situation depends on the consequences which have followed similar acts in the past in similar situations [27]. Human beings, however, more than other creatures, can learn by observation and "vicarious reinforcement." We can learn to value recreational activities which have been *rewarding to others,* even if we ourselves have rarely experienced them, provided the others are persons with whom we identify.

One can observe a parent taking the family up a wilderness trail on a summer weekend, but one cannot directly observe the values that cause that individual to do it. It is possible to infer motivation in various ways. One might go to that destination, see what the place is like, and infer that the parent went there in order to be in that kind of place. Or one might watch or ask what the parent does upon arrival and infer that this trail user went there for the opportunity to do those things. Or one might go and look at the place the parent came from and infer that this individual went into the wilderness to get away from that place. Or one might watch or ask what the parent does in the former place, and infer that the trip into the wilderness was undertaken in order to escape doing those things.

Motivations are inferential constructs; they cannot be directly observed. One might ask the trail user some questions, and one answer might be, "I like to hike up this trail because . . ." Those words might be *assumed* to have some causal connection with the visitor's nonverbal behavior [31]. But it would be important to realize that without further evidence one couldn't really be sure whether the visitor's verbalized reasons motivated the hiking behavior or whether the hiking behavior motivated the visitor's verbalized *rationalization* [38].

Thus, there is a need to be tentative in what is said about the motivations of recreational users of wild lands. It is important to be as meticulous and precise as possible in stating the observational facts upon which motivational inferences are to be based [8].

To draw some boundaries around this inferential process, consider two extremes: first, the ardent mountain climber and, second, the sedentary camper who spends the weekend with family, dog, transistor radio, ice chest filled with beer or soft drinks, and the trailer, relaxing in a forest recreation facility within 50 or 100 miles of the city in which that person lives and works.

The Quest for Uncertainty

Mountaineering has been studied as a way of gaining insight into recreational motivations [17]. Mountain climbing can hardly be attributed to the ordinary *instrumental* motivation that presumably characterizes the rational activities of the world of work; there are rather obvious reasons for *not* climbing a mountain, such as fatigue and danger. People do it in increasing numbers, even so.

The American expedition which Emerson studied as a climbing member was attempting to climb Mt. Everest from two different approaches— the Southeast Ridge, which had been climbed before, and the West Ridge, by which the summit had never been reached. At the end of each day, Emerson had each member of the expedition write in a diary a subjective estimate of the likelihood of success by each route. Each climber also wrote each evening what activities the climber wanted to perform next day. From these activity statements Emerson derived a measure of task motivation strength.

He compared day-to-day variations of an individual's responses, and he compared the responses of the West Ridge party with the responses of the party climbing the conventional Southeast Ridge. Both comparisons showed that if success seemed highly probable, *or* if failure seemed highly probable, then motivation was reduced! When there was genuine uncertainty as to whether the party would succeed or fail, then motivation was high. Communications between climbers tended to fall into a pattern which had the effect of *fostering* uncertainty about end results. If success began to seem assured to one climber, other companions would begin to point out ominous signs. If failure began to seem inevitable, a climber's partners began asserting grounds for optimism.

The *fun* obtained from mountain climbing is in carrying on the task in the face of doubt as to whether the summit will be reached or will prove unattainable. The summit of a mountain defines a problem. A problem which has never yet been solved may not be soluble; but it may not be known to be insoluble. First ascents are especially valued because a summit which has never been reached may not be reachable; but it is not known to be unreachable. However, a mountain which *has* been previously climbed, or a puzzle which has been solved many times, does not thereby lose all its value. For any given individual it may remain uncertain whether *that particular individual* can climb that mountain or solve that puzzle.

Group norms emerge even in recreation. In other realms of behavior, norms may have other functions, but in recreation they perform the function of preserving uncertainty. In mountaineering, for example, climbers shun equipment which makes the climb too easy. The legitimacy of carrying oxygen in climbing Everest has come to be questioned. The former uncertainty as to whether Everest could be climbed by a human being has thus been escalated (in response to its affirmative resolution) into the next higher uncertainty: can a human being climb it without oxygen?

Generalizing, it may be suggested that one important type of value underlying the recreational use of wilderness by its *average* devotee appears sometimes to be the mystery it holds. It presents puzzles to be solved. The visitor implicitly asks by entering the wilderness, "How well can I do with limited resources?" The challenge lies not merely in coping *physically* with the uncertainties posed by the environment, but also in coping with its intellectual problems. Norms arise which prescribe patterns of behavior perceived by the recreationist as germane to this value. Some of these norms may incidentally help protect the environment, but there is no guarantee that protection of fragile environments and enhancement of user fun can always be fostered by the *same* norms. The user's quest for uncertainty may sometimes but not always be a force for ecological balance. Moreover, it is not the only source of user norms.

The Quest for Freedom from Responsibility

Another sociologist has provided some clues to the motivations implicit in wild-land recreation by studying depreciative behavior in forest campgrounds [6]. It seems to be commonly believed both by recreationists and by campground managers that there are no thieves among campers. Accordingly, expensive equipment is left unguarded, often out in the open, and cars and trailers are often left unlocked and unattended. Implicit norms arise prescribing this casual style of campground living. Both the expectation that theft is unlikely and the tendency not to report it when it does occur probably are indicative of major motivations for camping. Camping may be motivated to a considerable extent by the desire to participate in a way of life that is thought to be free from such urban irritations.

Campbell and his associates noted instances of theft ranging from the teenage pilfering of beer and carbonated beverages from campers' ice chests to the systematic looting of locked automobiles. It was found that campers who had been victims of campground theft were stubbornly reluctant to redefine the campground as anything but a crime-free environment. Not all campground damage is done, as imagined, by noncamping vandals who invade the campground for malicious purposes. Children of camping families, representing a broad segment of the camping public, it was found, also are involved, partly because camping parents seem to define the campground naïvely as a hazard-free and invulnerable environment.

As Figure 6-2 clearly shows, the composition of the population by which children are socialized underwent marked change between 1940 and 1970. For each child under fifteen years of age in the United States in 1970 there was about 0.62 person in the parents' age bracket (over twenty-five but under forty). In 1940 this ratio had been 0.95, and it had fallen to 0.65

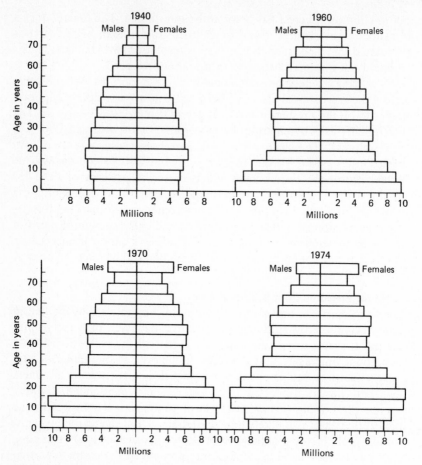

Figure 6-2 Age and sex composition of the U.S. population.

by 1960. Thus the children of 1960 and 1970 were being socialized more by interaction with age-mates and less by interaction with people of their parents' generation. Even without the further effects of urbanization, affluence, and television, this change alone should have been expected to produce a rise in deviant behavior among the youths and young adults of the late 1960s and the 1970s. By 1974 the parent-age/child-age ratio was starting to rise again; it was 0.76. But note that the number of persons in the high-crime age brackets (the fourth and fifth bars from the bottom) had increased.

Upon arriving in a campground, many parents readily cast off the burden of supervising their children. The chance to attain temporary freedom appears to be one motive for camping. Many problems arise under such circumstances from the activities of people who are often ignorant or ill-informed as to the consequences of their actions in the campground. It is an environment whose requirements they do not fully understand. They thus become temporarily and inadvertently inconsiderate. When firewood is scarce, for example, they may simply obtain it from an adjacent campsite (which amounts to unwitting theft from another camper) or by chopping down an available tree with little or no recognition of the number of growing years required for its replacement. Campers unaware of the danger to tinder-dry forests often build fires outside designated fireplaces, without meaning to be arsonists. The fun value of fire play underlies a whole series of ecologically inappropriate norms insofar as it leads the pleasure-seeking visitor to regard a campfire as a rightful prerogative to be enjoyed by whatever means.

To understand the behavior of campers, it must be remembered that the campground is an environment whose requirements are not fully comprehended by many of its users. The naïve quest for short-run solutions to one's own immediate problems, in simple pursuit of fun and in ignorance of the long-run ramifications for others or for the environment, apparently underlies much depreciative behavior in campgrounds. One important motivation for camping seems to be the desire to escape the usual necessity for considering the consequence of one's actions. Campgrounds are thought to be environments which permit such abrogation of responsibility.

In cities, privacy is created in public places by walls of indifference toward the strangers one encounters so constantly. The anonymity which creates privacy also frees the individual from responsibility for controlling others' behavior [34]. This releases time and energy for performing other tasks. The norm of noninvolvement has been transferred from cities to the public campground. Campers may be observed passively standing by as their neighbor or their neighbor's child violates campground law, damages facilities, or creates a public nuisance. It may be tentatively inferred from this that part of the camper's motivation in coming to the campground was to be among strangers in a live-and-let-live atmosphere. Moreover, the campground is thought by such visitors to be a setting in which the privacy thus gained entails minimal risks. Accordingly, some of the innocently antisocial behavior of children might be curbed by locating campgrounds in places where there is just enough of an obvious physical hazard (such as a small gorge with a rushing stream in its bottom) to prevent the camper from discontinuing his parental surveillance the moment he and his children arrive.

Increased volume of recreational use of wild lands makes formal and explicit rules increasingly necessary. Rules that may be essential for protecting the recreational resource often conflict with behavior patterns that were established in the days of low-density camping. This is a cogent example of what sociologists have come to call "cultural lag"—stress that occurs when interconnected parts of a culture change at different rates of speed [37].

Campground rules which interfere with what campers apparently regard as an inherent right to have an enjoyable time are likely to be violated. These people are at play, and, in play, rules are made to keep the fun going. So a rule which interferes with fun tends to be seen as no rule at all. Users of various kinds of motorized equipment that are taboo in a wilderness setting (because they not only destroy tranquility but can seriously damage fragile ecosystems) simply do not accept their exclusion from such areas.

Some Dimensions of Variation

Two polar opposites of motivation have thus been delineated and yet shown to be related—the mountaineer's quest for uncertainty and the urbanized camper's quest for privacy, freedom of association, and freedom from responsibility for the consequences of one's actions. Several ways in which motivations for recreational *travel* vary may next be considered [7].

First, in response to the question, "What was the chief purpose of your trip?" tourists' answers may vary between specificity and diffuseness. Some people who received a questionnaire after visiting Mt. Rainier National Park indicated a very *specific* wish to camp in a particular spot in the park. On the other hand, one family from Illinois wrote, "To see the West and visit relatives." Their motivation was *diffuse*, and their visit to Mt. Ranier was hardly attributable to the specific features of the natural environment in that park [48]. In addition to Mt. Rainier, their trip had included six other national parks. Such visitors appear to be truly motivated at least in part by *environmental* attractions but in a very general way rather than by the precise attributes of a particular locale.

Second, some people visit national or state parks or forests quite incidentally to their travels to visit relatives, urban centers, world's fairs, etc. Variation in this regard can be attributed to a motivational dimension of qualitative *similarity* or *diversity* of goals. A family from a suburb of Portland, Oregon, said after visiting Mt. Rainier, "We have never visited any other national park because of a habit over past years of spending our brief vacation times visiting relatives and friends. There are several national parks that we would very much like to see and we plan to make up for lost time in future years by visiting them. Especially interested in Grand Canyon, Crater Lake, Yosemite, Bryce Canyon, Glacier, Rocky Mountain, and Zion." These people already had formed latent preferences among national parks, even though they had never visited any, having been deterred by qualitatively different vacation destinations—friends' and relatives' homes. An incidental visit to one national park *with relatives* had evidently broken a barrier for them.

Third, people who do deliberately go into wild-land recreation areas as destinations vary along a continuum of *social* versus *environmental* interests. For many campers, camping appears to be more motivated by social than environmental concerns. Their activities are primarily oriented to other campers rather than to attributes of the natural environment [25]. Rules designed to protect the environment or even to protect its visitors from its hazards are often not comprehended and are ignored if they interfere with social pleasures. Interpretive facilities and activities are similarly ignored and remain ineffective, unless perceived as an arena for pleasurable social encounters. People can change, however, given time. Outdoor recreationists whose interests are initially more social than environmental may acquire an increasing orientation to the environment through repeated exposure to it, particularly if reinforced by stimulating interpretive experiences [19] and by involvement in an organization (such as the Sierra Club) that combines consummatory and instrumental concerns. Perhaps even more important, a socially oriented visitor may occasionally come under the primary group influence of another visitor who is more environment-oriented. The latter may pass on a personalized version of the lessons learned from the more formal interpretive sources [5].

A fourth type of variation in travel motivation pertains to spatial locations of travel destinations relative to the traveler's point of origin. The traveler is more likely to visit two destinations on the same trip if the two lie roughly in the same compass direction from home, so that one can serve as a stepping-stone en route to the other [7]. The typical itinerary of the national park visitor appears to be an elongated oval or crescent. Such itineraries generally include one or more other parks en route to or from the most remote park visited. This proclivity for multidestination itineraries results in the fact that a wild-land recreation site is likely to be more often visited if it is near another such site. Numbers of visits also increase in proportion to the recreation site's proximity to a population center, of course.

Attitude Differences by Urban versus Rural Upbringing

Urban living implies a life-style in which there is a diversity of both things and activities. Sociologists have developed two opposite views of the value orientations likely to be fostered by urbanization. One view holds that persons brought up in cities have their sensitivity to environmental diversity dulled and degraded and thus should be more likely than those not socialized in cities to carry over into their wild-land recreation activities an expectation of doing urban things. The other view implies just the opposite, that *wilderness purist* value orientations would be more common among city-raised people because they are more sensitive and discriminating than those socialized in nonurban surroundings.

In a study designed to test whether urban upbringing increases or decreases sensitivity to wilderness values, a psychometric scale was devised to measure attitudes ranging between *wilderness purism* (a desire to adapt one's habits to the environment rather than adapting the environment to one's habits) and *urbanism* (imposing urban apparatus and activities upon wild-land recreation environments). Over 1,300 wilderness area users who responded to a questionnaire containing this scale were categorized by their responses as "urbanists," "neutralists," "weak wildernists," "moderate wildernists," or "strong wildernists." Most persons in the sample tended to have wildernist attitudes, of course, but even these users of wilderness areas varied appreciably in the intensity of this value orientation [24].

The questionnaire asked respondents whether they had been brought up mainly in a city, a small town, or a rural area. Only 6.3 percent of the city-bred respondents had urbanist or neutralist attitudes, compared with 8.3 percent of those raised in small towns, and 11.4 percent of those who grew up in the country. Of those brought up in a city, 67 percent were moderate or strong wildernists, compared with 59.6 percent of those raised in small towns, and 53.1 percent of those from rural backgrounds.

Holding an urbanist value orientation and applying it in wilderness environments apparently goes with a lower level of attained education than does adherence to wildernist value orientations. Strong wildernists constituted 13.3 percent of those respondents who had not completed high school, 15.9 percent of those who were high school graduates, 19.6 percent of those with some college education, 27.2 percent of those who were college graduates, and 28.7 percent of those with postcollege education.

COMPETITION, OVERUSE, CARRYING CAPACITY

As indicated in previous chapters, public demand for wild-land recreation opportunities has taken on large porportions. One result of the boom in recreational use of wild lands has been increased frequency of confrontations between incompatible uses [9]. Antagonistic relations between different types of wild-land recreationists can arise when volume of use increases markedly in relation to space available. The interests of those who seek solitude, and those who wish to enjoy the wild attributes of more or less primeval environments may clash with the interests of persons whose pleasures depend on extensive artificial facilities, use of motorized equipment, etc. Resource managers may find themselves in a cross-fire from which there is no easy escape.

As has been suggested by two investigators who studied one such clash of interests, the emotion generated in confrontations between recreationists who enjoy using off-road vehicles and other recreationists who prefer self-propelled forms of mobility such as hiking or canoeing "is much more intense than a simple difference in choice of outdoor pursuit would seem to warrant." The reason appears to be that one's chosen recreation activity serves as a symbolic means of identification with a cultural group. At a public hearing one of these researchers "heard proponents of ORVs refer to their opponents as 'long-haired unemployed hippies' and 'elitist millionaires.' The same group often refer to themselves as 'patriotic,' 'family people,' or 'hard-working middle-class citizens.' The ORV user has often been stereotyped as 'lower-class, uneducated and consumer oriented'" [30].

Research in Minnesota in 1971 showed there were real differences between the environmental attitudes of a sample of cross-crountry skiers and a sample of snowmobilers. The two samples differed significantly in their responses to each of nine statements that had environmental implications but were not directly pertinent to the recreational preferences of either group. For example, in response to the statement, "We need the Alaskan oil pipeline in spite of possible environmental hazards," 27.6 percent of snowmobilers but only 8.2 percent of cross-country skiers said they agreed or strongly agreed. At the same time, 13.7 percent of the snowmobilers but only 4.6 percent of the cross-country skiers agreed or strongly agreed that "Development of the SST should have been continued in spite of possible environmental effects because it means more jobs and a boost to the economy" [30].

Using another set of statements to measure differential understanding of or sympathy toward the idea that distinct areas have to be provided for different recreational uses, the research found the ski touring sample much more in agreement than the snowmobiler sample with access-restriction and use-regulation as means of maintaining environments [30]. Attitude differences between different user groups may thus be a factor that has to be taken into account by resource managers.

Visitor satisfaction with the recreational experience may be impaired, however, not just by competition from users with incompatibly *different* recreational desires and habits, but also by excessive encounters with other visitors who may be intent on doing the *same* kind of thing. Seekers of solitude, when numerous, can impede each other's pursuit of happiness. Recognition of this fact by managers of wild lands, especially as they have been confronted with public resistance to proposals for restricting access to overused areas, has led to many studies of "recreational carrying capacity" [43,44].

Initial assumptions underlying such inquiry were overly simplistic. Ideals of wild-land recreation were presumed to have evolved from experience in a time when vast tracts of wilderness were available to small numbers of visitors—whose entry into such areas therefore afforded them solitude, enabling them to perceive without interference the grandeur of the environment, resulting almost inevitably in a thrilling kind of recreational experience (see Figure 6-3). In contrast, by extrapolation of recent episodes of heavy use, it was easy to view the future in terms of hordes of humanity invading ever-diminishing tracts of wild land, encountering therein many competing users, feeling the congestion of the area acutely, and coming out frustrated.

For some visitors to some areas, now and in future years, just that kind of frustration may indeed occur. But for many it will not be the usual experience, because the relations between numbers and the quality of the recreational adventure is not that simple or direct. This became evident during the course of rather elaborate studies designed to ascertain the recreational carrying capacity of the Grand Canyon for visitors floating through it aboard rafts on the Colorado River [35,36]. During periods when visitor density varied so much that the maximum density was almost twelve times

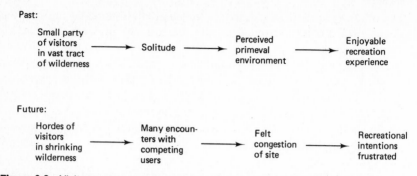

Figure 6-3 Visitor numbers and recreation pleasure (oversimplified models).

the minimum, visitors' ratings of the satisfaction derived from their river trip hardly showed any correlation with perceived crowding. Moreover, perceived crowding was unrelated to number of contacts with other parties on the river, and barely related to number of contacts with other parties at various attraction sites in the canyon.

The lack of correlation between such variables appeared to be due in part to the fact that for 90 percent of the visitors on the rafts this was their first Grand Canyon river-running trip; hence they had no prior experience to provide a comparative frame of reference for interpreting a given number of contacts on this trip as "crowding." But it was also discovered that there were various behavioral adaptations by which crowding (e.g., competition for beach campsites) was avoided when anticipated by the trip leaders. On the basis of such findings, a considerably more elaborate model appears necessary (see Figure 6-4). As we shall see in a moment, the additional features of this model may indicate to the imaginative manager of recreational wild lands additional ways of protecting the resource from impairment by overuse, and ways of enhancing the recreation experience, or at least protecting it from degradation.

It must be remembered, first of all, that the left-hand term in Figure 6-4 "recreation visitor density," is a *variable*; there can be many degrees of density between the two extremes envisaged at the beginning of the two hypothetical causal chains in Figure 6-3. Second, it must be remembered that most wild-land recreation is a *social* activity; people enter wild-land areas not as isolated individuals but as members of groups (e.g., families, or small numbers of close friends), and their enjoyment is affected by the presence of these companions as truly as by the absence of strangers. It is also affected, presumably, by salient features of the natural environment. But two intervening variables may influence the extent to which the wild-land recreationist's experience becomes mainly an unpleasant effort to contend with crowds of non-acquaintances or becomes instead a gratifying encounter with nature, shared with chosen co-enthusiasts: (1) trails, shelters, facilities, signs, and other developments provided by the resource-management agency may help to channel visitor activities, minimizing the unwanted encounters and facilitating the desired ones; (2) by choice or by chance, visitors may adjust their activities so that distractions and congestion are avoided even though they exist in the area.

Again, there are several variables that intervene between the visitor's actual encounters with nature and with other human beings and the *perceptions* thereof: (1) visitors to recreation sites differ from each other in many ways, and they perceive their experiences partly in accord with their various personal tendencies; (2) as members of different groups, and as products of different cultures or subcultures, with different past experiences, they bring with them into the wild-land setting different norms and expectations; (3) different recreationists bring and use different equipment; (4) different groups of visitors interact differently.

As long as the issues of recreational carrying capacity are conceived in terms resembling the oversimplified model shown in Figure 6-3, recreation resource management agencies faced with excessive use pressure appear to have no recourse other than restricting admissions to an area if they wish to ensure that those who do enter will have continuing opportunities for "a quality experience."

But the more detailed model shown in Figure 6-4 suggests several other management options which may be used (sometimes instead of, sometimes in conjunction with, restriction of access). There is the option of protective development. Its most obvious form may consist of the routing of trails, or the placement of signs and facilities to encourage appreciative and non-destructive contact with natural features and avert unnecessary congestion.

In Glacier National Park, for example, when crowds from a newly opened Visitor Center at Logan Pass began to spread out onto fragile alpine meadows in the vicinity, their urge to walk was protectively channeled by construction of a slightly elevated boardwalk. Although it was controversial because it was itself a defacement of the natural scene, the boardwalk was a type of development that afforded gratifying visual contact with the meadow but prevented trampling of alpine vegetation, soil compaction, and erosion. It meant that the effective carrying capacity of the meadow was raised to the pedestrian traffic capacity of the boardwalk [44].

There is the option of encouraging or even requiring density-compensating behavioral adjustments, such as requiring one-way traffic on a loop trail so that most parties using the trail encounter only one or two others immediately behind them or ahead of them. With two-way traffic, each party encounters all parties going the opposite way during the time it takes them to travel the length of the trail. Recent efforts to reverse previous trends and discourage use of brightly colored tents, are an effort to make each party of campers more unobtrusive, thereby enabling backcountry visitors to experience wilderness with less conspicuous human intrusion.

Recreation visitor characteristics (social class, occupation, etc.) may not be subject to much change by resource managers' efforts. But there is the option of trying to instill environmentally nondestructive norms, and appreciative rather than consumptive expectations, through programs of protective interpretation.

There is the option of influencing (or even regulating) the equipment brought into an area by recreation visitors, or at least influencing or regulating its use once it has entered the area. Campground "quiet hours" would be one simple example, when visitors are expected to turn off radios, refrain from pounding tent stakes, not run generators on their trailers, etc. One can feel less crowded in an area with dozens of others, who either have no noisy gear or are circumspect in using it, than in an area shared with perhaps one other party, if that party happens to be continually revving up an unmuffled motor or continually watching a portable TV set on high volume.

As the foregoing paragraphs imply, human adaptability is remarkable. But it is not infinite. The several options by which enlightened resource management may augment recreational carrying capacity do *not* mean that people may be jammed without limit into any given area to have a good time.

Some aspects of the carrying capacity issue seem obvious, and not all are controllable by resource managers. The number of encounters with other humans will presumably depend on natural characteristics of the site as well as on the ratio of visitors to area. For example, as there is a decrease in the density of cover (in wilderness near timberline) a given number of persons in a given space tend to become more visible to each other. Thus for psychological reasons as well as ecological, high-country recreation areas may be expected to have lower carrying capacity than low-land forests [4].

In addition to the sheer visibility of other humans (whom the visitor did not come to see), wear and tear on the natural features of a recreation

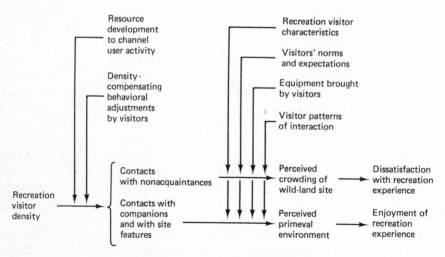

Figure 6-4 A model of visitor density effects and mitigating factors.

site will tend to be greater, the greater the number of visitors; wear and tear beyond the site's natural recuperative powers indicates, of course, that the carrying capacity of the site has been exceeded.

Finally, there *are* ecological constraints. After all the social adaptations implied in Figure 6-4 have been considered and perhaps implemented, there remain botanical, zoological, hydrologic, sanitary, edaphic, topographic, and spatial limits to face up to. There are limits that ultimately cannot be transcended except at the cost of impairing the capacity of a wild-land environment to continue providing the kinds of human experience for which it is being managed.

Without the insights provided by the inquiries of social scientists, as sampled in this chapter, human reactions to such limits could be easily misunderstood. Such misunderstanding—either by members of management agencies or by members of their publics—would almost always reduce the effectiveness of wild-land management *and* the pleasure of the recreation visitor.

SELECTED REFERENCES

1 Blau, Peter M.: "Bureaucracy in Modern Society" Random House, New York, 1956.
2 Bredemeier, Harry C., and Richard M. Stephenson: "The Analysis of Social Systems," Holt, New York, 1962.
3 Burdge, Rabel: Levels of Occupational Prestige and Leisure Activity, *Journal of Leisure Research,* vol. 1, pp. 262–274, Summer 1969.
4 Bury, Richard L.: Recreation Carrying Capacity—Hypothesis or Reality? *Parks & Recreation,* vol. 11, no. 1, pp. 22–25, 56–58, January 1976.
5 Caldwell, Paul, Jr.: "America's Camping Book," rev. ed., Scribner, New York, 1976.
6 Campbell, Frederick L., John C. Hendee, and Roger Clark: Law and Order in Public Parks, *Parks and Recreation,* vol. 3, pp. 28–31, 51–55, October 1968.
7 Catton, William R., Jr.: Intervening Opportunities: Barriers or Stepping Stones? *Pacific Sociological Review,* vol. 8, pp. 75–81, Fall 1965.
8 Catton, William R., Jr.: "From Animistic to Naturalistic Sociology," McGraw-Hill, New York, 1966.
9 Catton, William R., Jr.: The Wildland Recreation Boom and Sociology, *Pacific Sociological Review,* vol. 14, pp. 339–359, July 1971.
10 Cheek, Neil H., Jr., and William R. Burch, Jr.: "The Social Organization of Leisure in Human Society," Harper & Row, New York, 1976.
11 Cheek, Neil H., Jr., Donald R. Field, and Rabel J. Burdge, "Leisure and Recreation Places," Ann Arbor Science Publishers Inc., Ann Arbor, Mich., 1976.
12 Clarke, Alfred C.: The Use of Leisure and Its Relation to Levels of Occupational Prestige, *American Sociological Review,* vol. 21, pp. 301–307, June 1956.
13 Clawson, Marion: How Much Leisure, Now and in the Future? in James C. Charlesworth (ed.), "Leisure in America: Blessing or Curse?" American Academy of Political and Social Science, Philadelphia, 1964.

14 Clawson, Marion, and Jack L. Knetsch: "Economics of Outdoor Recreation," Johns Hopkins, Baltimore, 1966.

15 Dollard, John, Neal Miller, Leonard Doob, O. H. Mowrer, and R. R. Sears: "Frustration and Aggression," Yale University Press, New Haven, 1939.

16 Dulles, Foster Rhea: "A History of Recreation: America Learns to Play," 2nd ed., Appleton-Century-Crofts, New York, 1965.

17 Emerson, Richard M.: "Games: Rules, Outcomes and Motivation," paper presented to AAAS Symposium: Psychology and Sociology of Sport, Dallas, December 1968.

18 Etzioni, Amitai: "Modern Organizations," Prentice-Hall, Englewood Cliffs, N.J., 1964.

19 Faich, R. G., and Richard P. Gale, The Environmental Movement: From Recreation to Politics, *Pacific Sociological Review*, vol. 14, pp. 270–287, July 1971.

20 Faris, Robert E. L. (ed.): "Handbook of Modern Sociology," Rand McNally, Chicago, 1964.

21 Gerstl, Joel E.: Leisure, Taste and Occupational Milieu, *Social Problems*, vol. 9, pp. 56–68, Summer 1961.

22 Harry, Joseph: Work and Leisure: Situational Attitudes, *Pacific Sociological Review*, vol. 14, pp. 301–309, July 1971.

23 Harry, Joseph, Richard P. Gale, and John C. Hendee: Conservation: An Upper-Middle Class Social Movement, *Journal of Leisure Research*, vol. 1, pp. 246–254, 1969.

24 Hendee, John C., William R. Catton, Jr., Larry D. Marlow, and C. Frank Brockman: "Wilderness Users in the Pacific Northwest: Their Characteristics, Values, and Management Preferences," U.S. Forest Service, Pacific Northwest Forest and Range Experiment Station, Research Paper PNW-61, Portland, Ore., 1968.

25 Hendee, John C., and Frederick L. Campbell: Social Aspects of Outdoor Recreation: The Developed Campground, *Trends in Parks and Recreation*, vol. 6, pp. 13–16, October 1969.

26 Henry, Andrew F., and James F. Short: "Suicide and Homicide: Some Economic, Sociological, and Psychological Aspects of Aggression," Free Press, New York, 1954.

27 Hill, Winfred F.: Learning Theory and the Acquisition of Values, *Psychological Review*, vol. 67, pp. 317–331, October 1960.

28 Kando, Thomas M. and Worth C. Summers: The Impact of Work on Leisure: Toward a Paradigm and Research Strategy, *Pacific Sociological Review*, vol. 14, pp. 310–327, July 1971.

29 Kelly, John R.: Socialization Toward Leisure: A Developmental Approach, *Journal of Leisure Research*, vol, 6, pp. 181–193, Summer 1974.

30 Knopp, Timothy B., and John D. Tyger: A Study of Conflict in Recreational Land Use: Snowmobiling vs. Ski-Touring, *Journal of Leisure Research*, vol. 5, pp. 6–17, Summer 1973.

31 Lundberg, George A.: The Natural Science Trend in Sociology *American Journal of Sociology*, vol. 61, pp. 191–202, November 1955.

32 Maier, Norman R. F.: "Frustration: A Study of Behavior without a Goal," McGraw-Hill, New York, 1949.

33 Merton, Robert K.: "Social Theory and Social Structure," enlarged ed., Free Press, New York, 1968.

34 Milgram, Stanley: The Experience of Living in Cities, *Science,* vol. 167, pp. 1461–1468, Mar. 13, 1970.

35 Nielson, Joyce McCarl: Crowding Models, Stress, and Wilderness, *Mass Emergencies,* vol. 1, pp. 249–260, 1976.

36 Nielson, Joyce McCarl, Bo Shelby, and J. Eugene Haas: Sociological Carrying Capacity and the Last Settler Syndrome, *Pacific Sociological Review,* vol 20, pp. 568–581, October 1977.

37 Ogburn, William F.: Cultural Lag as Theory, *Sociology and Social Research,* vol. 41, pp. 167–174, January-February 1951.

38 Pareto, Vilfredo: "The Mind and Society," Harcourt, Brace & World, New York, 1935.

39 Rapoport, Rhona, and Robert N. Rapoport: "Leisure and the Family Life Cycle," Routledge and Kegan Paul, London, 1975.

40 Reissman, Leonard: Class, Leisure and Social Participation, *American Sociological Review,* vol. 19, pp. 76–84, February 1954.

41 Robertson, Ian: "Sociology," Worth, New York, 1977.

42 Soule, George: The Economics of Leisure, *Annals of the American Academy of Political and Social Science,* vol. 313, pp. 16–24, September 1956.

43 Stankey, George H., and David W. Lime: "Recreation Carrying Capacity: An Annotated Bibliography," U.S. Forest Service, General Technical Report INT-3, Intermountain Forest and Range Experiment Station, Ogden, Utah, 1973.

44 Stottlemeyer, Robert: Estimating Carrying Capacity for the National Parks, in Betty van der Smissen (compiler), "Indicators of Change in the Recreation Environment—A National Research Symposium," College of Physical Education and Recreation, The Pennsylvania State University, State College, Pa., pp. 359–372, 1975.

45 Vaux, H. J., Jr.: The Distribution of Income among Wilderness Users, *Journal of Leisure Research,* vol. 7, pp. 29–37, 1975.

46 Vickerman, R. W.: "The Economics of Leisure and Recreation," Macmillan, London, 1975.

47 Weiss, Paul: A Philosophical Definition of Leisure, in James C. Charlesworth (ed.), "Leisure in America: Blessing or Curse?" American Academy of Political and Social Science, Philadelphia, 1964.

48 Wicker, Allan W., and Sandra L. Kirmeyer: What the Rangers Think, *Parks & Recreation,* vol. 11, pp. 28–30, 42–43, October 1976.

49 Wilensky, Harold L.: The Uneven Distribution of Leisure: The Impact of Economic Growth on "Free Time," *Social Problems,* vol. 9, pp. 32–56, Summer 1961.

50 Yoesting, Dean R., and Dan L. Burkhead: Significance of Childhood Recreation Experience on Adult Leisure Behaviour: An Exploratory analysis, *Journal of Leisure Research,* vol. 5, pp. 25–36, 1973.

Glacier National Park, Montana, contains examples of a Class IV, Unique Natural Area, because of its geological significance and diversified plant and animal life. *(National Park Service.)*

Section Four

Recreational Resources

Resource Types, Classification; The Heritage Conservation and Recreation Service

The term "resource" has a variety of connotations, depending on numerous factors, including personal points of view. This applies to recreational resources as dealt with in this text.

DEFINITION OF "RESOURCE"

The dictionary defines a resource as something that lies ready for use.[1] Resources may be intangible (cultural, intellectual, esthetic) or tangible (financial, natural), but they must be valuable in satisfying or providing for some human requirement. Their value varies with time, place, and individual preference. Many things considered as valuable resources today were not so regarded in the past; what may be highly valuable in one place may not be so elsewhere; and, for various reasons, things having great value to some people are often of little consequence to others. Resource values depend upon current desires or requirements; their importance is generally in inverse ratio to their abundance or availability. Scarcity enhances their value, confirming the truth of the old adage that one rarely worries about the water until the well goes dry.

[1] "Webster's New World Dictionary of the American Language" (College Edition), World Publishing Co., Cleveland, 1959.

121

Interest in conservation developed after much wanton destruction of natural resources (forests, forage, soils, wildlife). Clean air and water, as well as environmental interest and beauty, were taken for granted until pollution, litter, or poorly planned or ill-advised development had caused deterioration of formerly attractive landscapes. Interest in the establishment of new parks and related reserves has grown with increased urbanization, reduced open space, and overcrowding of existing areas. Public support for establishing protected areas, necessitating certain sacrifices and costs, developed only after serious depletion of some assets brought realization of the worth of those that remained.

KNOWLEDGE AS A RECREATIONAL RESOURCE

Knowledge as a resource is not a widely held concept. However, when knowledge is defined as *understanding,* a clear perception of fact or truth, its role as a resource becomes apparent. It is included here in that context because of the great effect informed opinion can have on land use, including use of various types of land having diverse recreational values.

As noted in previous chapters, though many types of land, both public and private, embody numerous recreational values, none of these areas, because of differences in character and location are suited to all kinds of recreational use. It has also been emphasized that individuals view recreational opportunities in the outdoors from varied, highly personalized perspectives. Many recreational problems stem from differences in points of view over, or misunderstanding of, the most advantageous use of land—including recreational land uses. Anyone who has worked in a recreational area, on a one-to-one basis with people, can testify to this.

As defined above, knowledge of factors which determine the nature of most logical land uses, recreational as well as utilitarian, is important to maintenance of the productivity and esthetic qualities of lands and waters. The degree of public understanding of economic, social, and environmental relationships involved bears strongly upon land management decisions which affect both present and future generations. Such knowledge can be considered a resource just as timber, water, electric power, and minerals are considered resources.

Knowledge as an important recreational resource depends upon individual background, education, and experience with particular reference to the following:

(1) *Awareness of the importance of recreation, especially outdoor recreation, and the inherent benefits to individuals and society.*

As noted in Chapter 1, new avenues of meaningful interests can be explored and developed through recreation.

(2) *Understanding the relationship between areas having recreational as opposed to utilitarian functions.*

Most lands have particular values of one kind or another. These relate to provision of various utilitarian needs, different types of recreational opportunity, or perpetuation of interest and beauty of the natural scene which enhances quality of life. Satisfying society's diverse requirements demands balance in land use which involves different kinds of both multipurpose and single-use lands. Development of this balance depends upon public understanding of various factors (scientific, economic, social, political) which determine the most advantageous uses and interrelationships of specific land areas.

3 Understanding relationships of areas having different recreational functions.

Even single-purpose recreational lands differ widely in character. Understanding potential strengths and weaknesses of various areas emphasizes their most appropriate uses, whether intensive or dispersed. Coordination of single-purpose recreational areas (even their different parts, if extensive) having different recreational values maximizes recreational opportunities. Areas ranging from small neighborhood playgrounds to those of extensive size may be involved. Coordination also enhances the quality of recreational experiences by separating conflicting recreational uses; minimizes impairment of significant or fragile features; and nurtures perpetuation of recreational opportunities.

4 Understanding geological, biological, archeological, and historical associations.

Most people will derive greater enjoyment from a recreational experience, particularly on wild lands, if they understand how scenic features are formed; if they can identify plants and animals and understand environmental associations; or if historical and archeological relationships are recognized. Such knowledge also enhances appreciation of recreational values, thus prompting responsibility for their care. It also develops understanding of the outdoors which promotes ability to recognize and avoid hazards.

All levels of formal education, supplemented by numerous informal educational programs, seek to develop such insight. Examples of informal programs include those sponsored by youth groups; organizations concerned with the elderly, disadvantaged or handicapped; museums and related institutions; and outdoor and conservation associations. Informal education is also a basic purpose of interpretive programs, now recognized as important in management of many types of recreational areas. Public relations efforts aimed at developing good citizenship in the care and protection of natural resources (Smokey the Bear; Howdy Raccoon) have similar objectives.

LAND AS A RECREATIONAL RESOURCE

Many types of lands are adapted to different kinds and combinations of recreational use. Readily accessible, highly developed areas such as municipal parks and playgrounds receive only limited consideration in this book. However, their vital recreational functions and their highly important relation to more natural wildland recreational areas should be recognized. By providing easily accessible recreational opportunities for large numbers of people, they help relieve pressure for recreational development and activities not attuned to the character of certain other areas, especially more natural wild lands.

Efficient coordination of different types of land, adapted to various forms of recreation, provides maximum recreational opportunity with the least impact upon over-all environment. It also minimizes duplication of services, thus favoring economic operation within specific areas.

For example, at one time there was considerable pressure for installation of permanent ski lifts in certain subalpine areas in Mount Rainier National Park. These proposals were viewed with disfavor by the National Park Service because of the impact such unsightly structures would have on the scenic magnificence of that unique national park. The National Park Service viewpoint was not prompted by indifference to the need or value of such ski lifts; they objected because of the inappropriate character of such lifts in a significant national park.

This problem was solved by cooperation of the Forest Service. Under careful supervision, to minimize impact on the environment, the Forest Service permitted development of several highly satisfactory and popular ski areas on nearby, less significant sections of national forests in the Washington Cascades. Thus, both groups of recreationists were accommodated; those whose interests related largely to enjoyment of the pristine scene, and those who found satisfaction as part of larger crowds with opportunity of obtaining the maximum number of exhilarating down-hill runs with minimum climbing effort.

It follows that planning and coordinating recreational opportunities of various lands must consider quality as well as quantity of recreational experiences. As emphasized by the Outdoor Recreation Resources Review Commission [2], "the problem is not one of total acres but of *effective* acres."

Administrative Responsibilities For Recreational Lands

Most recreational land important for various forms of recreation is administered by public agencies (federal,[2] state, county, municipal, and district or regional park authorities). However, considerable amounts of land owned and operated for various purposes by private enterprise are increasingly important for recreation. The functions and relationships of recreational lands, with particular emphasis on wild lands, are discussed in Chapters 8 through 12. In addition, numerous other agencies, commissions, boards,

---

[2] Most federal land management agencies important to recreation are in the Department of the Interior [Chaps. 8-10]. The most notable exception is the U.S. Forest Service which has been in the Department of Agriculture since the turn of the century. For many years, during numerous administrations, there have been abortive attempts to unify such agencies under a single Department of Natural Resources, a title informally adopted by the Department of the Interior. This matter shows signs of heating up again as revision of this text progresses. Only time will tell if establishment of such a department will materialize, or if interest in it will subside once more.

and related organizations have varying responsibilities for recreation, though they do not administer land. The Heritage Conservation and Recreation Service, most important of these, is discussed later in this chapter.

BASIC CLASSIFICATION OF RECREATION LANDS

The Outdoor Recreation Resources Review Commission, in "Outdoor Recreation for America" [2], suggested a system for classifying outdoor recreation resources that would provide a common framework for management and recreation zoning that could be applied nationally. Six broad area classes were outlined with the concept that particular types of resources and areas would be managed for definite uses or combinations of uses.

Subsequently, the Bureau of Outdoor Recreation[3] adopted the classification system to provide uniformity in nationwide and state agency planning. The BOR was concerned with the lack of consistency in systems developed by various states throughout the United States and adopted the six-class system recognizing that any one park or recreation area may have combinations of capability-use characteristics.

Table 7-1 shows the six classes and their characteristics of location, general types of recreation development activities, and physical features. There are, of course, problems in application since different agencies have differing land-use patterns upon which the classes are imposed. For example, class III, natural environment areas, on national forest lands is applied to mixed recreation and production lands, while national park class III lands are not open to resource production. Size of class units is also a problem, and there are other complications which the reader is asked to consider based upon land-policy objectives developed so far in this text.

In addition, individual states have developed classification systems related to area designation. For instance, Minnesota state planners have proposed the use of such classes as state park, state recreation area, state riverway, and related types of areas. Nonetheless, the foregoing classification system provides a convenient means of viewing recreation resource-management considerations for analytical purposes. We will use it later in presenting a management framework.

HERITAGE CONSERVATION AND RECREATION SERVICE

As noted in Chapter 5, this agency was established by order of the Secretary of the Interior, January 25, 1978 [8,9].

The Heritage Conservation and Recreation Service is not a land management agency. It serves as a federal focal point for planning, evaluation, and coordinating the protection and preservation of the nation's cultural

---

[3] As noted later in this chapter, the Bureau of Outdoor Recreation was reconstructed in 1978 under the name of Heritage Conservation and Recreation Service (HCRS), with certain changes and additions in responsibilities.

Table 7-1 Suggested Basic Recreational Land Classes[a]

Classes	Location	Developments	Recreation activities	Physical characteristics
I High-density recreation areas	Urban but may be in nat'l parks	Intensive; exclusively for recreation	Activity-oriented sports, games, etc.	Attractive; natural or man-made
II General outdoor recreation areas	More remote than I, usually	Less intensive than I, but picnic, campgrounds, man-made facilities including hotels, stores, ski areas, etc.	Extensive; fishing, water sports, games, etc.	Attractive; natural to man-made
III Natural environment areas	More remote than I or II; largest acreage class	Limited—roads, trails, camping, picnic facilities; multiple-use management	Related to natural environment; hiking, camping, boating, hunting, etc.	Natural; attractive settings; varied landforms, lakes, etc.
IV Unique natural areas	Any place features found	Very limited; walks, trails, etc.	Study of natural features, sight-seeing	Outstanding natural features, scenic, scientific, geologic; part of a larger unit usually
V Primitive areas	V-A—where established under Wilderness Act; V-B—usually remote from cities	None to limited trails; usually no motor equipment	Wilderness hiking, camping, etc.	Natural, wild; *undeveloped*; away from civilization
IV Historic and cultural sites	Where sites exist	Limited—walks, interpretive centers, etc.	Sightseeing, study of sites	Associated with historic, cultural interests; national, state, local

[a] Adapted from USDI, "Bureau of Outdoor Recreation Manual, part 241, Nationwide Plan, 1966" and ORPRC. "Outdoor Recreation for America," 1962

and natural heritage, and helps provide adequate recreation opportunities for everyone. It is a reconstruction of the Bureau of Outdoor Recreation, [4] resulting in only slight modification of BOR recreational functions with additional responsibilities for a newly inaugurated National Heritage Program [8,10]. Thus, the Heritage Conservation and Recreation Service has a broader national commitment than the former Bureau of Outdoor Recreation. It is concerned with the protection and utilization of both recreational and heritage (natural, cultural, historical) resources, and development of intergovernmental and private sector capabilities to fulfill that commitment.

BOR Functions Incorporated into HCRS

The Heritage Conservation and Recreation Service inherited certain functions of the Bureau of Outdoor Recreation and has incorporated them into its expanded programs. It has responsibility for (8):

1 *Administering the Land and Water Conservation Fund.* This fund, by authority of the Land and Water Conservation Fund Act (P.L. 88-578), as amended, provides matching grants to states for planning, acquisition, and development of public outdoor recreation areas, and money to federal agencies for acquiring nationally significant lands and waters.[5]

2 *Reviewing applications for National Recreation Trail designations.*

3 *Land and water resource planning.* BOR was a leader in recreation resource planning through its role in Statewide Comprehensive Outdoor Recreation Plans;[6] by providing recreation planning input to land and water related resource projects; conducting studies of special resource areas; and reviewing proposals for federally assisted transportation projects. The HCRS has assumed the leadership for most of these programs.

4 *Nationwide Outdoor Recreation Planning.* The first Nationwide Outdoor Recreation Plan was developed by BOR. It was published in 1973 as *Outdoor Recreation:A Legacy for America.* (This plan, by law, must be updated every five years.) It provides a basis for establishing the roles and responsibilities of all levels of government, and the private sector, in meeting outdoor recreational needs [4].

5 *Coordinating federal outdoor recreation programs.* HCRS evaluates and monitors programs of federal agencies contributing to or affecting outdoor recreation.

6 *Transferring surplus federal real property.* HCRS arranges for transfers of surplus federal lands to state and local governments for park and

---

[4] The Bureau of Outdoor Recreation was established in the Department of the Interior by order of the Secretary of the Interior on April 2, 1962. Its "Organic Act" (P.L. 88-29) was passed by Congress and signed by the President in May 1963.

[5] Grants are allocated to states and federal agencies on a percentage basis. The Land and Water Conservation Fund [3] is composed of revenues from the sale of federal surplus real property, the federal motor boat fuels tax, and Outer Continental Shelf mineral receipts.

[6] Before a state can qualify for money from the Land and Water Conservation Fund, it must have a Statewide Comprehensive Outdoor Recreation Plan approved by HCRS.

recreation purposes; such transfers are accomplished by HCRS, working with the General Services Administration.

7 *Recreational technical assistance.* HCRS provides technical assistance to recreation suppliers and users; publishes technical papers' and booklets; and maintains a clearing house of recreation-related information and a referral system to other sources of competence.

8 *Environmental reviews.* HCRS prepares environmental impact statements and reviews the recreation and heritage program aspects of statements prepared by other agencies to ensure that proposed actions will not reduce or destroy existing or potential outdoor recreation opportunities or heritage resources.

Exchange of Functions

As part of the overall National Heritage Program the responsibilites of the Office of Archeology and Historic Preservation—the National Natural Landmarks Program, the National Register of Historic Places, and the Historic Preservation Grants Program—all formerly handled by the National Park Service, have been transferred to the Heritage Conservation and Recreation Service. The National Park Service will be conducting the congressionally authorized studies of rivers and trails being considered for inclusion in the National Wild and Scenic Rivers or National Trails Systems. Previously, these studies had been done by the Bureau of Outdoor Recreation. The National Park Service has also assumed the former Bureau's responsibility for the recreation aspects of federal water project implementation studies required by the Federal Water Project Recreation Act. The National Park Service will continue to administer the several hundred areas which make up the National Park System.

Additional Responsibilities

The Heritage Conservation and Recreation Service is coordinating the development of, and will be the federal administrator for, the new National Heritage Program [8,10].[7]

Development of the National Heritage Program is intended to result from a strong partnership among all levels of government, private organizations, and individual citizens. Such an approach reaches to "grass roots" levels. Numerous conservation groups, historical societies, community and cultural organizations, and local governments have long worked for heritage preservation, though from their own points of view. Similarly, various agencies of both state and federal governments have shown great concern for environmental values by enacting laws for their preservation. However, such activities have not been well coordinated, nor have they fulfilled all

---

[7] The National Heritage Program was initiated by the President's Environmental Message of May, 1977. Subsequently, the Secretary of the Interior formed a National Heritage Task Force and, after a six months' effort, basic elements of the National Heritage Program were produced. At the time of this text revision, development of the National Heritage Program was still in the beginning stage; details are expected to unfurl as provisions of their implementation, including necessary legislation, are established.

needs. Additional natural, cultural, and historical aspects of the American heritage should be evaluated, with a view to possible protection, before they are irrevocably lost. The Heritage Conservation and Recreation Service provides leadership for necessary expanded, voluntary activities on the part of individuals, organizations, and appropriate government agencies.

Organization of the Heritage Conservation and Recreation Service

Organization of HCRS is similar to the former Bureau of Outdoor Recreation. Headquarters, with offices of the Director and staff, are located in Washington, D.C. There are seven regional offices, together with an Alaska Area Office, which supervise HCRS activities within specific sections of the country.[8]

SUMMARY

Resources may be tangible (natural, financial) or intangible (intellectual, cultural, esthetic). Their value varies with time, place, availability, and individual preference. Scarcity enhances their value. Knowledge, in the light of understanding, as a clear perception of fact, is considered an important resource here. It is directly related to informed public opinion which is basic to understanding of different land values, including designation of areas for various outdoor recreational uses and the nature of public recreational activities on such areas.

Land is a much more evident recreational resource. Different types of land are adapted to various kinds of recreational interests and activities. Maximum recreational opportunity can be provided with minimum impact upon the environment and with maximum economy of operation by relating types of recreation to those areas best able to accomodate them.

Six basic classes of recreational land, based upon capability-use characteristics, are useful in land-use analysis and planning. Most land used for recreation is administered by public agencies but many kinds of privately owned lands are also used for recreation. In addition, a number of agencies are involved with outdoor recreation, though they do not directly administer land. Most important of these is the Heritage Conservation and Recreation Service.

---

[8] Regions with location of headquarters are: *Northwest,* Seattle, Wash. (Idaho, Oregon, Washington); *Pacific Southwest,* San Francisco, Calif. (Arizona, California, Nevada, Hawaii, Guam, American Samoa); *Mid-Continent,* Denver, Colo. (Colorado, Iowa, Kansas, Missouri, Montana, Nebraska, North and South Dakota, Utah, Wyoming); *South-Central,* Albuquerque, N.M. (Arkansas, Louisiana, New Mexico, Oklahoma, Texas); *Lake-Central,* Ann Arbor, Mich. (Illinois, Indiana, Michigan, Minnesota, Ohio, Wisconsin); *Southeast,* Atlanta, Ga. (Alabama, Florida, Georgia, Kentucky, Mississippi, North and South Carolina, Tennessee, Puerto Rico, Virgin Islands); *Northeast,* Philadelphia, Pa. (Connecticut, Delaware, Maine, Maryland, Massachusetts, New Hampshire, New Jersey, New York, Pennsylvania, Rhode Island, Vermont, Virginia, West Virginia, District of Columbia). Headquarters of the Alaska Area Office is at Anchorage, Alaska.

The Heritage Conservation and Recreation Service, formed in the Department of the Interior in 1978, represents a reconstruction of the Bureau of Outdoor Recreation. It administers most programs originally handled by the Bureau of Outdoor Recreation and, in addition, has significant new responsibilities. The latter include the National Heritage Program, officially announced in January 1978. At the time this text was being revised the National Heritage Program was still in the beginning stage; its various aspects will develop as authorized by necessary legislation. This program was designed to coordinate and expand efforts at all levels of government, and efforts of private organizations and individuals, in the preservation of examples of the American heritage (natural, cultural, historical).

SELECTED REFERENCES

1   Clawson, Marion: "Land and Water for Recreation: Opportunities, Problems and Policies," Rand McNally, Chicago, 1963.
2   Outdoor Recreation Resources Review Commission: "Outdoor Recreation for America: A Report to the President and to the Congress by the ORRRC," U.S. Government Printing Office, Washington, 1962.
3   U.S. Department of the Interior, Bureau of Outdoor Recreation: "Land and Water Conservation Fund Act, as Amended," U.S. Government Printing Office, Washington, 1968.
4   U.S. Department of the Interior, Bureau of Outdoor Recreation: "Outdoor Recreation: A Legacy for America," U.S. Government Printing Office, Washington, 1973.
5   U.S. Department of the Interior, Bureau of Outdoor Recreation: "Administrative and Legislative Directives to the Bureau of Outdoor Recreation," U.S. Government Printing Office, Washington, 1975.
6   U.S. Department of the Interior, Bureau of Outdoor Recreation: "The Bureau of Outdoor Recreation—A Focal Point for Outdoor America," U.S. Government Printing Office, Washington, 1975.
7   U.S. Department of the Interior, Bureau of Outdoor Recreation: "Cooperative Management for Recreation," n.p., n.d.
8   U.S. Department of the Interior: Establishment of a Heritage Conservation and Recreation Service; Order No. 3017, Office of the Secretary of the Interior, Jan. 25, 1978.
9   U.S. Department of the Interior: Citizens, States Invited to Share in Selecting Historic and Natural Sites for Preservation, mimeographed press release, Jan. 23, 1978.
10 U.S. Department of the Interior: "The National Heritage Program," Washington, D.C., January 1978.

Chapter 8

The National Park System

The National Park Service, a bureau in the U.S. Department of the Interior, is charged with the administration of national parks and related areas by authority of the act that established it. This act, passed by Congress and signed by President Woodrow Wilson on August 25, 1916, was designed to unify the administration of the national parks and national monuments then under the jurisdiction of the Department of the Interior. It stated that [11]:

> The service thus established shall promote and regulate the use of the Federal areas known as national parks, monuments, and reservations hereinafter specified by such means and measures as conform to the fundamental purpose of said parks, monuments, and reservations, which purpose is to conserve the scenery and the natural and historic objects and the wild life therein and to provide for the enjoyment of the same in such manner and by such means as will leave them unimpaired for the enjoyment of future generations.

EXTENT AND DIVERSITY OF THE NATIONAL PARK SYSTEM

The National Park Service administers several hundred areas of diverse sizes and types, widely distributed about the country, having an aggregate area of approximately 31 million acres (12.5 million hectares) in 1977 (Table 8-1). National parks, although best known and having the greatest aggregate acreage and greatest travel, are only a part of the National Park System. Also included are a variety of other significant areas (national monuments and various types of parks and sites of historical interest), together with certain other lands which embody high-quality scenic or recreational values whose protection is in the national interest.

LEGAL STATUS OF AREAS IN THE NATIONAL PARK SYSTEM

This diversity, coupled with various names applied to these lands, occasionally leads to some confusion as to the relation of various types of areas. Differences in name do not imply degrees of importance, significance, or size. Each unit in the National Park System has specific interests; each is

Table 8-1 Summary of the National Park System, June 30, 1977[a]

Classification	Number	Acres	Hectares
National Parks	37	15,619,634.31	6,335,951,90
National Monuments	82	9,880,980.09	4,001,496.94
National Preserves	2	654,550.00	265,092.75
National Lakeshores	4	196,678.92	79,661.96
National Rivers[b]	6	373,684.91	150,342.39
National Seashores	10	595,211.45	241,060.64
National Historic Sites	53	15,050.19	6,095.33
National Memorial Park	1	70,408.64	28,515.50
National Memorials	22	6,019.08	2,437.73
National Military Parks	11	34,425.28	13,942.24
National Battlefield Parks	3	6,685.18	2,707.50
National Battlefields	8	6,611.20	2,677.54
National Battlefield Sites	2	1,801.00	769.50
National Cemeteries[c]		1,616.35	654.62
National Historical Parks	18	78,502.19	31,793.39
National Recreation Areas	16	3,493,112.51	1,414,710.58
National Parkways	4	159,060.07	64,419.33
National Scenic Trail	1	52,034.25	21,073.87
Parks (other)[d]	10	31,896.48	12,918.07
National Capital Parks[e]	1	5,374.20	2,176.65
White House	1	18.07	7.32
National Mall	1	146.35	59.24
National Visitor Center	1	18.01	8.14
	294	31,283,518.73	12,669,824.96

[a]National Park System subject to change. Proposals of Alaska Native Claims Settlement Act, when completed, are expected to more than double the size of the National Park System (see pp. 80–81).

[b]Includes Wild and Scenic Rivers and Riverways.

[c]Includes Administrative Sites. Administered in conjunction with associated National Park System units; not listed separately.

[d]Parks without national designation.

[e]One system of about 350 units within the District of Columbia, Maryland, Virginia, and West Virginia.

Source: "Index of the National Park System and Affiliated Areas as of June 30, 1977," U.S. Government Printing Office, Washington, 1977.

nationally important in its own right. Size is a distinguishing characteristic of most, but not all, national parks, and of many national monuments. Two national monuments (Katmai and Glacier Bay, in Alaska) are both larger than the largest national park, Yellowstone National Park.

These areas differ primarily in the method of their establishment; in short, their legal status. The following paragraphs summarize the basic differences among the principal classifications [18]:

1 *National parks* are established only by specific act of Congress; likewise, enlargement or reduction of national parks is possible only by act of Congress.

2 *National monuments.* Most areas in this category have been established by Presidential proclamation, by authority of the Act for the Preservation of American Antiquities, which became law on June 8, 1906. The Antiquities act authorized the President to set aside, as national monuments, federal lands and waters which contain historic landmarks, historic or prehistoric structures, and other objects of historic or scientific interest. National monuments may be enlarged or reduced in size by Presidential proclamation, but only Congress can abolish them. A major result of the proclamation power was its success in setting aside vast areas of nationally significant lands and waters until Congress saw fit to make them national parks. Several national monuments have been reclassified as national parks. Congress may establish national monuments and did so in 1968 in authorizing Biscayne National Monument, Florida. Most national monuments, however, are the result of proclamation.

3 *National military parks, national battlefield parks and sites, national memorials and cemeteries, many national monuments, and the national capital parks* were originally administered by various government agencies. On June 10, 1933, these areas were consolidated under National Park Service administration by authority of the Reorganization Act, which became law earlier in the same year.

4 *National historic sites.* The Historic Sites Act of August 21, 1935, provided for the establishment of national historic sites to be protected and preserved for public inspiration and enjoyment.

5 *Related scenic and recreational areas.* More recent legislation has been prompted by growing public interest in outdoor recreation and the need for environmental protection. Such legislation has provided legal basis for the acquisition or designation of various national seashores, national parkways, national recreation areas, and related protected lands.[1] Most of

---

[1] *The Park, Parkway and Recreation Study Act, June 23, 1936,* authorized the National Park Service to conduct studies of park, parkway, and recreational area programs. Subsequently, the concept of national rural parkways was embodied in the *act of June 30, 1936,* providing for national park administration of the Blue Ridge Parkway. Cape Hatteras National Seashore, first area of its type, was established by the *act of Aug. 17, 1937,* thus paving the way for formation of similar areas under national park administration. Of particular importance in this respect was the *act of Aug. 7, 1961,* authorizing the establishment of Cape Cod National Seashore, including the use of appropriated funds for the purchase of large areas of land for public park purposes; previously, most National Park Service areas had resulted from designation of existing public lands, or from lands donated to the federal government for such

these areas (national parkways, national seashores, national lakeshores, and some national scenic riverways) have been placed under administration of the National Park Service; some national recreation areas are administered jointly with other agencies by interbureau agreement.

ORGANIZATION OF THE NATIONAL PARK SERVICE

The National Park Service organization includes a headquarters staff in Washington, D.C., nine regional offices, several field offices, one planning and service center, two training centers, and personnel in each of the various national parks, monuments, historic sites, and related areas.

The principal administrative officer of the National Park Service is the Director, who is responsible to the Secretary of the Interior. Each of the nine regional offices is in the charge of a Regional Director, who supervises National Park Service activities within a given region[2] and reports to the Director of the National Park Service in Washington, D.C. Each of the national parks, monuments, historic sites, and related areas is administered by a Superintendent who reports to the Regional Director.

The national headquarters in Washington consists of the offices of the Director, a Deputy Director, several Associate Directors and Assistant Directors, and other "key" headquarters administrative and policy-making personnel with their supporting staff who, at various levels, are responsible for different aspects of National Park Service activities and interests. Such activities and interests, organized under such basic categories as legislation, administration, operations, and professional services, are greatly diversified. They reflect the expanding importance and increasing responsibilities of the National Park Service in matters concerned with the protection, preservation, interpretation, and public use of National Park Service areas, as well as in cooperative efforts of the National Park Service with organizations of similar character concerned with national parks and equivalent reserves in other parts of the world.

An Assistant Solicitor, in charge of legal matters, is a member of the staff of the Solicitor of the Department of the Interior but attends, or is represented at, meetings of the staff of the Director of the National Park Service.

---

purposes by private or other public interests. The *Surplus Property Act of 1944,* as amended, authorized the National Park Service to cooperate with the General Services Administration in investigating surplus properties for public park and recreation purposes. The *act of Aug. 7, 1946,* provided for administration of recreational aspects of areas under jurisdiction of other federal agencies. As a result, cooperative agreements were developed between the National Park Service and the Bureau of Reclamation relative to provision for adequate public recreational use of certain reclamation projects, designed as recreation areas. Included are Lake Mead National Recreation Area, Arizona-Nevada; Glen Canyon Recreation Area, Arizona-Utah; and Coulee Dam Recreation Area, Washington. Although Flaming Gorge Recreation Area, Wyoming-Utah, began under joint National Park Service-Forest Service administration, full responsibility was transferred to the Forest Service in 1968.

[2] Names and headquarters of National Park Service regions (Fig. 8-1) are *North Atlantic,* Boston, Mass.; *Mid-Atlantic,* Philadelphia, Pa.; *National Capital Parks,* Washington, D.C.; *Southeast,* Atlanta, Ga.; *Midwest,* Omaha, Neb.; *Rocky Mountain,* Denver, Colo.; *Southwest,* Santa Fe, N.M.; *Western,* San Francisco, Calif.; *Pacific Northwest,* Seattle, Wash.

Regional offices are somewhat similarly organized. The Director of each region has a Deputy Director, several Associate Directors, and a staff of administrative and professional employees concerned with specific National Park Service activities within the region.

Various national parks, monuments, historic sites, and related areas complete the National Park Service organization. In each case the Superintendent is responsible for all matters pertaining to proper management and administration of a particular area, including general supervision of all planning and development therein.

The size and complexity of the staff in each unit of the National Park System are dependent upon the character of the area. The more complex organizations are divided into several principal departments: protection—under supervision of the Chief Park Ranger or, in some cases, Chief of Operations; fiscal, or varied business functions—in the charge of the Administrative Officer (in large areas) or the Administrative Assistant (in small areas); interpretation—supervised by the Chief of Interpretation; and maintenance—in charge of the Chief of Maintenance. The staff of some larger parks may also have a Sanitary Engineer who supervises matters relative to local public health; in addition, an officer of the Public Health Service is assigned to each Regional Office of the National Park Service. A few national parks also have a Park Landscape Architect, who is advisory to the Superintendent.

ADMINISTRATIVE POLICIES OF THE NATIONAL PARK SERVICE

The policy of the National Park Service was first defined approximately 1½ years after establishment of the agency in a letter dated May 13, 1918, signed by Secretary of the Interior Franklin Lane and addressed to Director Stephen T. Mather. The Secretary listed the following broad principles of national park management [3,16]:

> First, that the national parks must be maintained in absolutely unimpaired form for the use of future generations as well as those of our own time; second, that they are set apart for the use, observation, health, and pleasure of the people; and third, that the national interest must dictate all decisions affecting public or private enterprise in the parks.

A more detailed official statement of national park policy, prepared in conjunction with others interested in national park affairs, by Louis C. Crampton, special attorney for the Secretary of the Interior, was incorporated in the annual report of the Director of the National Park Service for the fiscal year ended June 30, 1931 [15]. Among the seventeen items emphasized in this policy statement were the following:

1 Supreme examples of scenic, scientific, or historic features, sufficient to justify national interest in their preservation, should characterize the greatly varied areas of the National Park System.

Figure 8-1 The National Park System: Distribution of areas and regional organization, 1977. *(National Park Service.)*

2 The twofold purpose of these areas is enjoyment and use by the present generation together with preservation unspoiled for the future—specifically these areas should be "spared the vandalism of improvement"; present use should not result in impairment of interests for the future.

3 Education (public understanding of significant interests typical of various areas) and inspiration are major aspects of use and enjoyment of the National Park System; recreation in its narrower sense ("having a good time") is a proper incidental use but exotic forms of amusement should not be encouraged, nor should anything that conflicts with or weakens enjoyment of inherent values be permitted.

4 Natural resources of these areas (forests, wildlife) should be considered from a noncommercial objective, emphasizing primitive or natural, rather than artificial, conditions.

5 Necessary developments (roads, buildings) should be in harmony with the environment, and their intrusion should be held to the absolute minimum.

6 The public welfare and best interests of park visitors should be considered in provision of necessary facilities and services, as well as in respect to federal control of land and federal jurisdiction over rules and regulations within boundaries of various areas.

Current Policy of the National Park Service

Since formulation of initial administrative policies for the National Park System, acts of Congress and Executive orders have greatly expanded the responsibilities and duties of the National Park Service. As a result, initial primary emphasis upon preservation of natural conditions was not relevant to certain more recently added areas which, by their nature and purpose, were noteworthy for other important values. In particular, National Recreational Areas, and to a lesser degree areas of simple scenic quality (National Parkways), had already been variously modified; moreover, their significant features, where they existed, were of secondary importance. Further, public interest in and use of such areas emphasized activities and related necessary developments which often necessitated further environmental modification, even though such modification would not seriously impair their scenic attractiveness. Even significant archeological and historical areas demand managerial procedures different from areas of truly natural character. Archeological and historical interests relate primarily to activities of earlier peoples; hence natural conditions in such areas are usually modified in some degree.

Modern management of areas of the National Park System also has to consider recent and probable future technological innovations, as well as changes in social and economic conditions. These factors have been, and will continue to be, reflected in public recreational interests and demands, and consequent impact of rapidly accelerating use of all types of areas within the National Park System.

Despite changes, largely reflections of increased public use of areas in the National Park System, basic National Park Service policies have been fairly consistent. This is particularly true of natural areas (many national parks and monuments), archeological areas, and historical areas. Concepts initially defined in 1918 and expanded in 1931 have been adapted to specific management requirements of areas in each of the various classifications (Table 8-1). These recognize that planned, orderly, harmonious development required to serve visitors will have to be based upon minimum needs in each case, utilizing results of research as well as latest management techniques. Management aimed at maintaining such areas "absolutely unimpaired" for the "use, observation, health, and pleasure of the people" is a difficult if not impossible task.

National Park Service policy also indicates the necessity of maintaining large sections of wilderness in natural areas [17]. In addition, emphasis is placed upon development of public understanding of significant interests as a principal adjunct of public enjoyment and protection of areas, particularly those of natural, archeological, and historical character. Further, expansion of the National Park System, cooperation with other organizations having similar objectives (both at home and abroad), and continued upgrading of personnel are features of National Park Service policy.

An extension of National Park Service policy, with reference to national recreation areas, occurred in 1972. In that year Gateway National Recreation Area was established in the outer harbor of New York City (P.L. 92-592) and Golden Gate National Recreation Area was established in the San Francisco Bay region (P.L. 92-589). They were followed by creation of the Cuyahoga Valley National Recreation Area near Cleveland in 1975 (P.L. 93-555). All these national recreation areas are administered by the National Park Service. This indicates increasing Federal interest in provision of readily accessible recreational opportunities for residents of large urban centers [13]. Some people object to this trend in National Park Service policy. They feel that urban recreation is the responsibility of some other authority; that money and effort involved should be applied to other areas in the National Park System, particularly those of unique natural quality.

This emphasis on urban recreation by the National Park Service reflects agency evolution as noted in Chapter 5. A point made by Anthony Downs in "Inside Bureaucracy" is that "as bureaus grow older the breadth of functions they serve increases".[3]

RELATION OF NATIONAL PARK SYSTEM TO OTHER RECREATIONAL LANDS

Although the bill establishing Yellowstone National Park referred to that area as a "pleasuring ground," and although national parks are often referred to as outdoor playgrounds, the basic concept upon which most Na-

[3] Anthony Downs: "Inside Bureaucracy," Boston, Little Brown, a Rand Corporation Research Study, p. 264. Copyright by the Rand Corporation, 1967.

tional Park Service areas were established, and upon which they are administered, differs greatly from that of other recreational lands. This is indicated in foregoing statements of National Park Service policy.

Many areas of the National Park System are, in essence, "outdoor museums." Included are natural (many national parks and monuments), archeological, and historical areas. They may have spectacular scenery but scenic beauty is not the only criterion for their existence. The high value of their significant features requires maximum protection; and greatest value from a visit to such areas comes from understanding of the great truths of natural and human history which they portray. Though they vary widely in specific features their fundamental significance qualifies them for basically similar management philosophy under the same administration. Obviously, management and public use of such unique recreational lands must be guided by criteria that are quite different from other types of recreational areas, both within and without the National Park System.

Administration of such areas according to an outdoor-museum concept, however, does not rule out the possibility of fun and enjoyment; it seeks to guide related outdoor recreational interests and activities into channels which are in keeping with their outdoor-museum character. Further, it favors concentration of other types of outdoor recreational interests and activities not acceptable in national parks and related significant areas on lands of recreation value which are better able to accommodate them. Most people realize that commercial exploitation of natural resources cannot be condoned in areas of unique, significant quality. However, it is not as generally recognized that development of recreational facilities, or encouragement of recreational activities, that are at variance with preservation of unique, often fragile, interests is damaging and undesirable in significant recreation areas.

The term "outdoor museum," now widely recognized, was first introduced by Robert Sterling Yard of the National Parks Association. He made the following statement in an article published in the *Scientific Monthly* of April, 1923 [24]:

> The primary use may be described sufficiently for present purposes by calling a national park a museum. Our national parks system is a national museum. Its purpose is to preserve forever, "for the use and enjoyment of the people," certain areas of extraordinary scenic magnificence in a condition of primitive nature. Its recreational value is also very great, but recreation is not distinctive of this system. Our national reservations are also recreational. Our national forest, set apart for scientific commercial utilization, is very highly recreational. The function which alone distinguishes the national parks system from the national forest is the museum function made possible only by the parks' complete conservation.

Earlier statements about the national parks, although they did not use the term "outdoor museum," suggested that concept. In his "Diary of the

Washburn Expedition to the Yellowstone and Firehole Rivers in the Year 1870," N. P. Langford states that [5]:

> . . . amid the canyon and the falls, the boiling springs and sulphur mountain, and, above all, the mud volcano and the geysers of the Yellowstone, your memory becomes filled and clogged with objects new in experience, wonderful in extent, and possessing unlimited grandeur and beauty. It is a new phase in the natural world; a fresh exhibition of the handiwork of the Great Architect; and, while you see and wonder, you seem to need an additional sense, fully to comprehend and believe.

The fiscal year ending June 30, 1916, marked the publication of the first annual report on the national parks. The following statement was included in this report [14]:

> Clearly they are not designated solely for the purpose of supplying recreational grounds. The fostering of recreation purely as such is more properly the function of the city, county, and state parks, and there should be a clear distinction between the character of such parks and national parks.

SOME SIGNIFICANT INTERESTS OF THE NATIONAL PARK SYSTEM

The National Park System embodies a national resource of tremendous importance and value. It will retain its value only so long as its various areas are protected and used in a manner that respects their significant qualities.

Areas of the National Park System offer many dramatic, inspirational examples of the results of geological processes which have shaped the face of our land. The geysers and hot springs of Yellowstone National Park and the waterfalls and monumental granite cliffs of Yosemite National Park become more rewarding if the reasons for their existence are understood. Grand Canyon National Park is viewed in its true perspective when something is known of the manner by which the great canyon of the Colorado River was formed. The geological history of Mount Rainier, a huge volcanic cone and dominant feature of Mount Rainier National Park, as well as Crater Lake in Crater Lake National Park, and Mauna Loa and Kilauea in Hawaii Volcanoes National Park, imply the power of nature in one of its wildest moods. Glacier National Park, despite its name, is exceeded in number and extent of glaciers by a number of other areas of the National Park System; but its faceted peaks, broad U-shaped valleys, and spectacular lakes attest to the erosive power of extensive glaciers that once typified that region.

Significant plant and animal life and related intricate ecological associations characterize many areas. Everglades National Park offers a spectacular array of subtropical avifauna. The giant saguaro cactus, typical of Saguaro National Monument, is a familiar desert trademark. Spectacular migrations of caribou, as noted in Mount McKinley National Park, symbolize biological associations of the far north. The dramatic spectacle of the regular evening flight of countless bats from the bat cave in Carlsbad Caverns National Park becomes meaningful when one understands the nature, habits, and environmental requirements of those creatures. A knowledge of factors which contributed to the great size and age, even the very existence in modern times, of the giant sequoias adds zest to a visit to Sequoia National Park.

Numerous archeological areas of the National Park System exhibit significant evidences of former civilizations. Mesa Verde National Park is but one example of such areas; it may be truly enjoyed if one views its cliff dwellings from the perspective of former inhabitants. Effigy Mounds National Monument and the unique remains of prehistoric mounds and villages in Ocmulgee National Monument offer opportunity to obtain additional insight into the life of earlier peoples.

Equally important are those areas which are related to historical events which have shaped the development of our nation. Visits to El Moro, Fort McHenry, Fort Sumter, Custer Battlefield, Scotts Bluff, and Homestead National Monuments; Shiloh and Gettysburg National Military Parks, and Independence Hall National Historical Park lift American history from the pages of a book. Understanding the impact of events that took place in such areas develops an appreciation of our American heritage, as well as of pride in the hardihood and valor of our American forebears.

Visitors will enjoy most areas of the National Park System to a greater degree if they understand the significance of the varied features, if they *see* rather than merely look at them. This can be an educational experience from which elements of compulsion, often typical of general learning processes, are absent. Development of such understanding is the major objective of National Park Service interpretive programs.

The foregoing paragraphs barely touch the many meaningful interests of National Park Service areas. However, since much has been written about such matters this limited treatment should serve the purpose of this text. Readers are urged to consult any one of a number of good, readily available books which elaborate on the significance of various areas of the National Park System. A few of these are noted in this chapter's list of references [1,9,10,19].

PUBLIC USE OF THE NATIONAL PARK SYSTEM

Interest in the National Park System is reflected in the phenomenal public use of these areas. With the exception of a relatively few periods, such as during the years of World War II (1942-1945) the number of visitors has mounted constantly. In 1904, when the first accurate records were kept, there were 120,690 visits. By 1920, only four years after establishment of the National Park Service, the number of visits exceeded 1,000,000. Even dur-

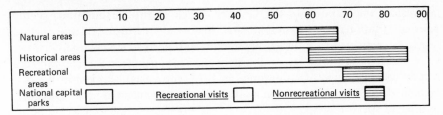

Figure 8-2   Visits to the National Park System, by management category, 1975 (calendar year). *(Source: "Public Use of the National Park System, Calendar Year Report, 1975," U.S. Government Printing Office, Washington, 1976.)*

ing depression years of the 1930s the number of visits continued to mount, reaching over 21,000,000 in 1941. By 1964 the number of visits had passed 100,000,000 and seven years later the 200,000,000 mark had been exceeded. In 1977 the total number of visits for all areas of the National Park System was more than 262,000,000.

The relative public appeal of the various categories of areas that exist within the National Park System in recent years is indicated quite clearly in a breakdown of data for the 1975 calendar year (Figure 8-2). For that period, natural areas reported a total of 66,836,500 visits (11,506,200 noted as nonrecreational[4]); historical areas, a total of 86,038,800 visits (27,057,200 nonrecreational[4]); recreational areas, a total of 79,485,500 visits (9,894,900 nonrecreational[4]); and the National Capital Parks, a total of 6,484,000 visits.

SUMMARY

Lands administered by the National Park Service, aggregating over 31 million acres (over 12.5 million hectares) include several hundred areas of varying types, ranging from small historical sites to extensive tracts of land. Designations of various types of areas in the National Park System are often incorrectly interpreted as being indicative of the degree of relative importance, significance, or size. However, their basic differences are largely in their legal status, for all were established according to certain procedures defined by federal laws.

The National Park Service is a bureau in the Department of the Interior. The basic administrative structure of this organization consists of the headquarters in Washington D.C., a number of Regional Offices strategically located with reference to National Park Service areas of somewhat similar character, and various field offices and specific units of the Service. The principal administrative officer is the Director, who is responsible to the Secretary of the Interior. Each Regional Office is headed by a Regional

---

[4] Visits prompted by reasons other than specific interest in features of the area, such as business or driving through.

Director, who reports to the Director. Each of the various units of the Service (national parks, monuments, historical, recreational, and related areas) is managed by a Superintendent, who reports to a Regional Director.

Current administrative policies of the National Park Service, founded upon basic principles first outlined in 1916, upon establishment of the National Park Service, have been adapted to the management of various categories of specific areas.

National Park Service policy for management of both natural and historical (including prehistory) areas provides for public use and enjoyment, consistent with minimum disturbance of natural or historical values. Management of national recreational areas favors active recreational activities and interests in an attractive setting, without destroying pleasant surroundings upon which such interests and activities depend. Several national recreational areas administered by the National Park Service are located near large cities.

Within the National Park System are outstanding examples of the geological, biological, archeological, and historical interests of our country. Selection of these areas for inclusion in this system is predicated upon their national significance in a particular field of interest and the dramatic, inspirational manner in which that interest is portrayed. Thus, in essence, most National Park Service areas are "outdoor museums," important because of their vital contribution to American culture and education. Maximum enjoyment of these areas, including "having a good time," is derived through understanding of their many significant interests. In that sense, they serve a somewhat different purpose from any other important recreational lands lacking in national significance.

Public use of the National Park System has grown phenomenally since 1904. More than 262,000,000 visits were reported for all types of areas in 1977.

SELECTED REFERENCES

1 Butcher, Devereaux: "Exploring Our National Parks and Monuments," (7th edition, revised) Gambit, Boston, 1976.
2 Cameron, Jenks: The National Park Service: Its History, Activities and Organization, *Service Monographs of the U.S. Government*, no. 11, Institute for Government Research, Appleton-Century-Crofts, New York, 1922.
3 Crampton, L. C.: "Early History of Yellowstone National Park and its Relation to National Park Policies," U.S. Government Printing Office, Washington, 1932.
4 Downs, Anthony: "Inside Bureaucracy," Little, Brown, Boston, 1967.
5 Langford, N. P.: "The Discovery of Yellowstone National Park, 1870," J. E. Haynes, St. Paul, Minn., 1923.
6 Merriam, John C.: The Meaning of National Parks, *National Parks Bulletin*, vol. 10, no. 57, November 1929.

7   National Park Service and U.S. Forest Service "The National Parks and the National Forests, Their Purposes and Management," U.S. Government Printing Office, Washington, 1975.

8   Sax, Joseph L.: "America's National Parks: Their Principles, Purposes, and Prospects," Special Supplement to *Natural History Magazine,* October 1976.

9   Tilden, Freeman: "The National Parks: What They Mean to You and Me," Knopf, New York, 1954.

10 Tilden, Freeman: "The National Parks," Knopf, New York, 1968.

11 Tolson, Hillary: "Laws Relating to the National Park Service, the National Parks and Monuments," U.S. Government Printing Office, Washington, 1933.

12 U.S. Department of the Interior: Secretary Hickel Announces Policy Guidelines for National Park System, Washington, June 22, 1969. (Mimeographed press release)

13 U.S. Department of the Interior, Bureau of Outdoor Recreation: "Outdoor Recreation Action," Report No. 41, Fall 1976, U.S. Government Printing Office, Washington, 1976.

14 U.S. Department of the Interior, National Park Service: "Annual Report of the Superintendent of National Parks to the Secretary of the Interior for the Fiscal Year Ended June 30, 1916," U.S. Government Printing Office, Washington, 1916.

15 U.S. Department of the Interior, National Park Service: "Annual Report of the Director of the National Park Service to the Secretary of the Interior for the Fiscal Year Ended June 30, 1932," U.S. Government Printing Office, Washington, 1932.

16 U.S. Department of the Interior, National Park Service: "Our Heritage: A Plan for its Protection and Use, Mission 66," Washington, n.d.

17 U.S. Department of the Interior, National Park Service: "The National Park Wilderness," Washington, n.d.

18 U.S. Department of the Interior, National Park Service: "Road to the Future," n.p., 1964.

19 U.S. Department of the Interior, National Park Service: "Index of the National Park System," U.S. Government Printing Office, Washington, 1977.

20 U.S. Department of the Interior, National Park Service: "Administrative Policies for Natural Areas of the National Park System," U.S. Government Printing Office, Washington, August 1968.

21 U.S. Department of the Interior, National Park Service: "Administrative Policies for Recreational Areas of the National Park System," U.S. Government Printing Office, Washington, August 1968.

22 U.S. Department of the Interior, National Park Service: "Administrative Policies for Historical Areas of the National Park System," U.S. Government Printing Office, Washington, August 1968.

23 U.S. Department of the Interior, National Park Service: "Public Use of the National Parks; a Statistical Report (various periods)," Washington, v.d.

24 Yard, Robert S.: Historical Basis of National Park Standards, *National Parks Bulletin,* vol. 10, no. 57, November 1929.

National Forests as Recreational Areas

A wide variety of recreational opportunities is available on lands of the National Forest System, administered by the Forest Service. As noted in Chapter 4, the Forest Service was established as a bureau in the Department of Agriculture in 1905.

THE NATIONAL FOREST SYSTEM

The Forest Service administers over 187 million acres (76 million hectares) of land. Most of this area is occupied by 154 national forests; the remainder comprises 19 national grasslands (over 3.8 million acres; 1.5 million hectares) and other miscellaneous areas (about 2.4 million acres; 960,000 hectares). Varying portions of the National Forest System lie in forty-four states, Puerto Rico, and the Virgin Islands. About 88 percent of these lands are in the West, including Alaska(Figure 9-1).

The Forest Service does not control all land within the boundaries of national forests and grasslands. Intermixed with Forest Service lands are[1]

---

[1] In addition, certain areas administered by the National Park Service are partly or completely surrounded by national forest lands; in most cases these were formed by withdrawal and reclassification of former national forest lands by various federal legislative acts. Among such areas are Bryce Canyon, Crater Lake, Glacier, Grand Canyon, Kings Canyon, Lassen Volcanic, Mt. Rainier, Olympic, Rocky Mountain and North Cascades National Parks; Cedar Breaks, Chiricahua, Devils Postpile, Gila Cliff Dwellings, Great Sand Dunes,

approximately 38.7 million acres (15.7 million hectares) of state, private, and other nonfederal lands. The fragmentary ownership pattern typical of some areas of the National Forest System stems largely from early homestead and mining laws, together with federal grants from the public domain to certain states (for schools and other purposes) and railroads (to encourage Western development) and repurchase of lands in the Weeks Law forest of the East. To alleviate resultant administrative difficulties, and particularly to favor public interest through improved management of all resources of the national forests and grasslands, the Forest Service, wherever feasible, consolidates its control within boundaries of various units by a continuing program of land exchange and purchase.[2]

LEGAL STATUS OF NATIONAL FORESTS

National forests are based upon the act of March 3, 1891, which authorized the President to reserve, by proclamation, certain lands from the public domain and to designate such lands as forest reserves. The act provided [10]:

> That the President of the United States may, from time to time, set apart and reserve, in any State or Territory having public land bearing forests, any part of the public lands wholly or in part covered with timber or undergrowth, whether of commercial value or not, as public reservations, and the President shall, by public proclamation, declare the establishment of such reservations and the limits thereof.

The primary purpose of this act was to effect a general revision of various laws concerning disposition of public lands, which had sometimes been characterized by irregular practices. The act contained twenty-four sections, the twenty-fourth providing for the establishment of forest reserves. Authority of the President to establish national forests from public lands, by proclamation, was withdrawn by Congress in 1907, largely because of Western opposition to such action. Other forests were created pursuant to the Weeks Law of March 1, 1911, as amended. The national grasslands are a result of the Bankhead-Jones Act of July 22, 1937, as amended. The National Forest Management Act of 1976 (P.L. 94-588) gave statutory status to the National Forest System. Thus the system lands could be returned to public domain only by an Act of Congress.

ORGANIZATION OF THE FOREST SERVICE

The Forest Service is organized in regional, decentralized form, permitting wide latitudes in authority for Regional Foresters, Forest Supervisors, and

---

Lava Beds, Montezuma Castle, Saguaro, Sunset Crater, Timpanogos Cave, Tonto, Tuzigoot, and Walnut Canyon National Monuments.

[2] Many exchange and purchase units include land with important recreational values.

Figure 9-1 Distribution of the national forests and regional organization of the Forest Service. *(U.S. Forest Service.)*

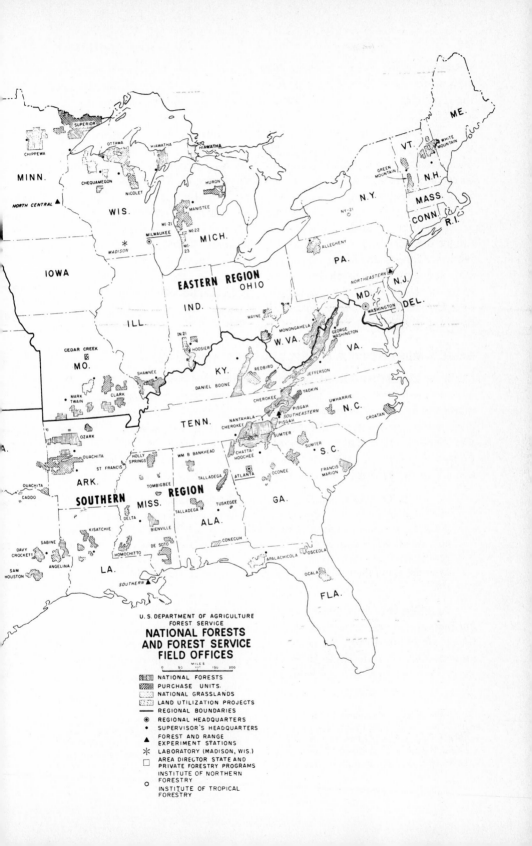

U.S. DEPARTMENT OF AGRICULTURE
FOREST SERVICE

NATIONAL FORESTS
AND FOREST SERVICE
FIELD OFFICES

MILES
0   50   100   150   200

NATIONAL FORESTS
PURCHASE UNITS
NATIONAL GRASSLANDS
LAND UTILIZATION PROJECTS
REGIONAL BOUNDARIES
REGIONAL HEADQUARTERS
SUPERVISOR'S HEADQUARTERS
FOREST AND RANGE
EXPERIMENT STATIONS
LABORATORY (MADISON, WIS.)
AREA DIRECTOR STATE AND
PRIVATE FORESTRY PROGRAMS
INSTITUTE OF NORTHERN
FORESTRY
INSTITUTE OF TROPICAL
FORESTRY

District Rangers. Within a framework of broad national and regional policies, professional managers at different organizational levels make the on-the-ground decisions which guide the management of the national forests and grasslands.

The headquarters organization, in Washington, D.C., consists of the Chief and staff, various units of which are concerned with forest activities on a national level, including forest research and cooperative federal-state forest management programs for nonfederal lands. The National Forest System is divided into nine regions,[3] each in the charge of a Regional Forester, who with staff has regional responsibilities. Within each region are a number of national forests which, in turn, are composed of several ranger districts, averaging about 225,000 acres (91,055 hectares) in area. National forests are in the charge of a Forest Supervisor, who is aided by staff assistants responsible for various activities on the forests. Ranger districts, the basic administrative units of the Forest Service, are in the charge of a District Ranger, who, with staff assistants, directs and supervises all district activities.

BASIC FOREST SERVICE POLICY AND RESPONSIBILITIES

Multiple use and sustained yield for maximum, long-term public benefit have been a fundamental policy of the Forest Service in the protection, management, and development of national forest resources for timber, outdoor recreation, water, wildlife and fish, and forage purposes. This concept was clearly defined in Secretary of Agriculture James Wilson's letter of February 1, 1906, shortly after the establishment of the Forest Service, to Chief Forester Gifford Pinchot. An excerpt from that document follows [5]:

> . . . In the administration of the National Forests it must be clearly borne in mind that all land is to be devoted to its most productive use for the permanent good of the whole people, and not for the temporary benefit of individuals or companies. All resources of the National Forests are for use . . . and where conflicting interests must be reconciled the question will always be decided from the standpoint of the greatest good for the greatest number in the long run. . . .

Actually, this principle was inherent in the act of June 4, 1897, which outlined management policies of the initial forest reserves, even before the formation of the Forest Service. Provisions of this act, together with later amendments, as reflections of the wishes of the people in management of the national forests, are the basis of Forest Service administration policy.

---

[3] Names and headquarters of the nine regions of the Forest Service are *Northern*, Missoula, Mont.; *Rocky Mountain*, Denver, Colo.; *Southwestern*, Albuquerque, N. Mex.; *Intermountain*, Ogden, Utah; *California*, San Francisco, Calif.; *Pacific Northwest*, Portland, Ore.; *Southern*, Atlanta Ga.; *Eastern*, Milwaukee, Wisc.; and *Alaska*, Juneau, Alaska. (The former Lake States region has been incorporated into the Eastern region.) Also see Fig. 9-1.

Current procedures adhere to statutory directives of the Multiple Use—Sustained Yield Act of 1960 (P.L. 86-517), of particular interest because it specifically mentions recreation as a national forest resource.

The authorization of certain uses of the national forests, such as mining, generation and distribution of electric power, highway construction, and defense needs, is the responsibility of other departments and agencies but is closely coordinated with the Forest Service. Management of fish and wildlife, including establishment of hunting and fishing regulations and enforcement of game laws are state responsibilities under a policy of joint federal and state jurisdiction. Management of the fish and wildlife habitat is the responsibility of the Forest Service.

In addition to responsibilities relative to the administration of the National Forest System, the Forest Service conducts a forest research and a cooperative forest management program. Its research program deals with all aspects of the protection, management, and development of forest and related wild-land resources—including recreation—as well as the utilization and marketing of resultant products. Research is conducted at eight forest and range experiment stations, the Forest Products Laboratory at Madison, Wisconsin, the Institute of Northern Forestry, at Fairbanks, Alaska, and the Institute of Tropical Forestry in Puerto Rico, under the direction of the directors of those units. The Forest Service also administers a program of grant and contract research for universities and others. The Cooperative Forest Management Program of the Forest Service seeks to have other federal, state, and private landowners apply multiple use-sustained yield forest management to their forest lands.

RECREATIONAL POLICY OF THE FOREST SERVICE

The importance of recreation in national forest administration varies according to the management situation in various sections of the country. It may differ from one national forest to another. All national forest lands have some recreational value, but this aspect of their management is given a greater degree of importance on some areas than on others; on a number of national forests, recreation receives the most emphasis, but all resource uses receive equal consideration in development of management plans.

Basic Forest Service recreational policy emphasizes (1) integration of recreation with all other uses of national forests by careful and coordinated resource management, and by designation of specific areas for certain types of recreation not compatible with other national forest uses; (2) maintenance and perpetuation of an attractive and appropriate environment for forest recreation, with emphasis on spaciousness, including preservation of rare and fragile flora, fauna, and other features; (3) major attention to the interests of the general public, rather than those of special groups or individuals; (4) participant rather than spectator activities, favoring those requiring a minimum of cost, special equipment, and ability; (5) minimum restrictions on users, consistent with protection of environment, public health and safety, and rights of others; and (6) cooperation with other agencies and organizations, both public and private, in the most economical development of a wide range of complementary recreational opportunities in a given locality.

An attempt is made to provide a spectrum of recreation opportunities and experience levels from developed to wilderness lands with almost no improvements. Under the terms of the Forest and Rangeland Renewable Resources Planning Act of 1974 (P.L. 93-378) the Forest Service plans to emphasize dispersed recreation rather than activities at developed sites [12].

The "Forest Service Manual" describes these basic policies in greater detail as follows [13,14]:

Coordination:
 1 The Recreation resources of the National Forests will be managed in conjunction with all the other forest resources under the principles of multiple use. This does not mean that specific areas may not be devoted principally to recreation. In general, however, over any area large enough to be classified as an administrative unit, such as a ranger district, recreation use will take its place with grazing, mining, water storage, timber production, and other uses.
 2 The recreation developments on the National Forests are planned to complement those available on other private and public lands.

For example, National Forest recreation developments in the vicinity of National Parks and along park approach roads will be planned in consultation with the National Park Service in relation to developments in National Parks—the objective being to obtain coordination between the two Services as far as practicable so that developments on the two types of areas may complement each other.
 3 In planning the development of the recreation resource and the necessary adjustments with other uses, the viewpoints of interest groups will be considered.

Preservation of the Natural and the Primitive:
 4 One of the distinctive characteristics of forest recreation is that it is enjoyed in a nearly natural environment. Every effort will be made to preserve this quality and the atmosphere of spaciousness in the planning and development of recreation opportunities.

Further than this, suitable provision will be made for the establishment of areas which will preserve primitive conditions of transportation or vegetation, and where possible, a combination of the two.

Developments:
 5 The Forest Service will develop or permit the development of such facilities as will aid in the enjoyment of those types of recreation appropriate to the forest. It will especially discourage developments which tend to introduce urbanization into the forest.
 6 The Forest Service will install or permit the installation of facilities only to the extent required to serve public needs so as to keep to a minimum the introduction of artificial developments in the forest environment.

7 The basic objective in designing National Forest developments is to have them perform their intended function and at the same time harmonize as much as possible with the natural environment.

8 Preference will be given to recreation developments which emphasize opportunities for participant rather than spectator enjoyment of forest recreation activities.

9 When Federal funds are expended on recreation developments, the objective should be to provide recreation opportunities for relatively large numbers of people and not for the exclusive use of individuals or small groups. The determination of priorities in the expenditure of funds under this policy requires consideration both of the quantity and quality of recreation enjoyment made possible by a development. It also requires that any development should be considered in relation to other developments so that a well-balanced system of recreation facilities will be provided.

Use:

10 The recreation use of the National Forest will be handled with the fewest possible restrictions on users, consistent with the protection of the forest against damage, the observance of essential sanitary and safety measures, and the prevention of actions by individuals or groups which unduly interfere with the enjoyment of others.

11 Uses which require exclusive private occupancy have a proper place in the National Forests, but will be granted only where it appears certain that the desired areas will not be needed for more general public uses. In determining the public need, future as well as present requirements must be considered and the estimates of future needs should be liberal.

12 Charges will be made at public recreation areas for special services such as (1) charcoal, (2) electricity, (3) checking clothes, renting suits and towels, (4) boat rental, (5) use of ski tows and lifts, (6) hot showers (if artificially heated), and (7) any special services of similar character.

13 Permit fees for resorts, services, and summer homes will be based on the fair value of the land, as determined by the rental charges for comparable privately owned land, with due allowance for all differences between the conditions associated with the use of public and private land.

RECREATION PLANNING AND ADMINISTRATION OF THE NATIONAL FORESTS

Recreation values of the national forests generally receive equal consideration with the other resource values. Their planning, development, use, and maintenance are handled, in varying detail and degrees of responsibility, at all levels of the Forest Service organization from the office of the Chief to that of the District Ranger.

Fundamental policies of national forest recreation use, on the national level, are established by the Chief as authorized by the Secretary of Agriculture, subject to provisions of legislation passed by Congress and to Executive directives. Planning objectives set forth in state recreation plans and the plans of others are also considered in preparing recreation plans for the National Forest System.

The recreational resource planning unit in the National Forest System is the recreation management composite. This is a geographical area usually consisting of a complex of recreation-developed sites and dispersed areas that have sufficiently strong interrelations to require further amplification of the national forest plan. Management composites are made only for situations with significant use and enjoyment.

Basis for Recreation Plans

The national forest recreation plans are guides for further management actions. As such, they are an assemblage of current management objectives and policies with the necessary descriptive material and factual data for understanding the situation and for arriving at decisions as to the best courses of action to meet the objectives. Plans are continuously monitored and updated as necessary to reflect changes by the following factors [13,14]:

   1 *Current recreation resources of the forests.* These are listed in an inventory of varied recreational values of the forest and include a determination of specific areas best suited to different types of recreation use. In addition, the human capacity for each type of recreation use, as well as for each type of recreation area, is estimated, and an outline of recreation developments in the vicinity, other than those on the forests, is prepared.

   2 *Constraints on recreation use on the forests.* Consideration is given to other needs that can be supplied by the forests, which may receive emphasis equal to or greater than that of recreation (forage, water supply, timber, fish and wildlife habitat, and other resources).

   3 *The potential recreation demand of the area or region of which the forest is a part.* Future public recreation needs and their relation to national forest management are important in planning. Factors such as present and probable population trends, technological developments affecting recreation, and probable trends in private and public recreation development must be carefully weighed in arriving at decisions.

In consideration of the foregoing factors, various areas selected for recreation development are allocated on the basis of their particular value or combination of values to specific types of recreation activity. The current status of such areas is indicated on the recreation base map as "developed and in use" or "reserved for future development." In the latter case, areas scheduled for immediate future development are separated from lands to be held in reserve.

Actual development of each recreation area, as provided for in the recreation plan, is preceded by the preparation of action lists and detailed tract plans showing the location and design of all improvements, together with necessary specifications. Such plans are prepared by landscape architects in the Regional Forester's office or the Supervisor's office, upon the advice of the Forest Supervisor or District Ranger.

DISTINCTION BETWEEN NATIONAL FORESTS AND NATIONAL PARKS [16]

Since national forests and national parks often have common characteristics (forests, scenic beauty), and since both receive heavy recreation use, the basic purposes served by these two types of public land often appear to be similar. Therefore, distinctive differences in their recreation functions and management objectives are not always clearly understood.

National forests are basically utilitarian. With few exceptions (oil, gas, minerals, and wilderness), their resources are renewable and, in the multiple use-sustained yield concept of management, can be periodically harvested and reestablished on the same land. Outdoor recreation activities in the national forests are integrated with the management of other resources. Included are those lands which are compatible with the production of timber, those requiring development for the accommodation of large crowds, and in addition, those which demand solitude, such as wilderness. This relatively liberal recreation policy is possible in national forests because of their extensive area and physiographic variation, plus the action taken to coordinate uses and to disperse users over wide areas.

By contrast, national parks, as well as many other areas of the National Park System, are managed as outdoor museums. The highly significant and often fragile character of the features in these areas demands a more restrictive policy of recreational use. Preservation of their highly significant natural, scientific, and inspirational qualities is a basic concern. Thus, in national parks public hunting is not permitted; timber and other resources are not utilized commercially; and certain recreation activities and facilities are not included.

Both these philosophies of wild-land management, concerned with different aspects of conservation, fulfill vital and specific needs. Properly coordinated, they supplement one another in the provision of a wide variety of highly necessary public benefits and services.

RECREATIONAL RESOURCES OF THE NATIONAL FORESTS[1,8,9]

Diversity of outdoor recreation opportunities, in all seasons, is one of the principal characteristics of the national forests. Somewhere in their vast acreage climbers, hikers, riders, skiers, canoeists, or boaters find varied opportunities to test their skill or stamina. There are also outlets for the interests of both amateur and professional photographers, artists, naturalists, and historians. And those who merely seek a scenic drive, a picnic, a visit to a lake, or similar casual relaxation in a pleasant environment can also be rewarded. Since hunting and fishing are permitted in the national forests, subject to state laws and regulations, these areas play a vital role in such forms of outdoor recreation. Through its Wildlife Management Staff Unit, the Forest Service works closely with state fish and game departments on lands under its jurisdiction.

National forests include most types of North American forest environment with their related plants and animals. Included are varied coniferous forests of the West, coniferous-broadleaved forests in the Lake States and southern Appalachians, and, to the south, subtropical and a medley of tropical regions. Some of these forest regions are noted for seasonal beauty of flowers or fall foliage. National forests also include the largest specimens of many native North American tree species. Arboreal communities of particular interest receive special protection. For example, the Ancient Bristlecone Pine Botanic Area in the Inyo National Forest, California, includes America's oldest living vegetation.

More than one-third of the big game population of the United States, as well as many small mammals and numerous species of birds, inhabit the national forests. They are managed to maintain an adequate population-environment balance.

Equally diverse are facilities to aid visitors in enjoyment of national forest recreation opportunities. These range from a variety of readily accessible, developed sites to remote wildernesses [1,7] completely lacking in modern conveniences. The concept of wilderness and primitive areas of the national forests originated with the establishment in 1924, by administrative order, of the Gila Primitive Area in New Mexico. With passage of the Wilderness Act in 1964, fifty-four then-classified areas were incorporated into our National Wilderness Preservation System.

Numerous opportunities are available to serve almost every personal interest, with due consideration of available time, physical condition, family responsibilities, or financial status. In addition to many federal, state, and county highways which serve the national forests, there are many miles of forest development roads open to the public.[4] Roads in the national forests offer scenic views or panoramas, or provide access to points from which journeys into remote areas by trail, on foot or on horseback may be initiated. The thousands of miles of trails in the national forests include substantial portions of the famous Appalachian Trail in the East and the Pacific Crest Trail in the Far West. A wide choice in picnicking or camping experience is possible in numerous picnic areas and campgrounds strategically located along both main highways and remote byways. More sophisticated accommodations include modern motels or hotels, as well as "rustic" cabins or lodges and dude ranches, in equally varied accessible or remote

[4] Under certain conditions, such as periods of extreme fire hazard, closures may be invoked.

locations. Establishment of organized camps by youth, church, and other groups offers opportunities for group activities.

COORDINATION OF USE OF NATIONAL FOREST LANDS

To effect proper coordination of the most logical uses of the national forests, lands are grouped under a zoning approach. Generalized and special zones, as needed, are utilized. They include:

1 Water influence zones: areas for existing or anticipated significant public outdoor recreational occupancy, use, and enjoyment along streams and rivers and around lakes, reservoirs, and other bodies of water; areas in which uses and activities are oriented to overwater travel and outdoor recreation.

2 Travel influence zones: areas for existing or anticipated significant public outdoor recreational occupancy, use, and enjoyment along existing and planned overland routes of travel; areas in and around existing or planned developed recreation sites.

3 Special management zones: areas formally designated by the Congress, Secretary of Agriculture, Chief of the Forest Service, or Regional Forester.

4 Other management zones: developed as necessary to meet the needs of the resources, topography, types of present and proposed use, and access.

The foregoing classification is based on careful resource inventory and appraisal which must necessarily consider a wide variety of interrelated factors. Among the more important of such considerations are the physical characteristics and quality of sites suited to different types of recreation, trends in recreation needs and interests, present and future demand and degree of use, development costs, and relative importance of recreation and other national forest uses.

Developed and Dispersed Recreation Uses

Recreation use of the national forests is characterized by two phases—developed sites and dispersed.

Intensive recreation use activities require facilities and developments for the comfort and convenience of users or to protect the environment. To accommodate these activities, the Forest Service provides developed sites. These include observation sites, camp and picnic grounds, playground park and sport sites, swimming and boating sites, organization camps, commercial public service sites, winter sports sites, recreation residence sites, and visitor centers.

The dispersed phase is characterized by relatively low-density use, well distributed over broad expanses of land and/or water. It encompasses the entire land and water resource base not included in the developed phase. Development in support of the dispersed phase typically consists of roads, trails, parking places, and rather simple facilities designed more for protection of the environment than for the convenience of the user.

National forest lands that are primarily valuable as developed sites are designated on recreational plans. The establishment, development, and coordination of such necessary public recreational facilities, carried out with due regard for the maintenance of varied recreational interests, public health, and safety, are determined by District Rangers, Forest Supervisors, and Regional Foresters under broad authority granted by the Chief.

Practically all national forest lands are open and available to the public for some type of outdoor recreation. Many recreation uses are thoroughly compatible with scientific management of other resources. Some recreation activities are favored by such management; for instance, hunting is improved by proper timber harvest, which enhances the habitat for deer and certain other game animals. However, certain interests and activities are of such nature, or enjoy such wide popularity, that maximum recreation use and enjoyment, as well as environmental protection and proper relation of recreation with other forest uses, are achieved by designating specific areas for them. Various experience levels ranging from primitive to modern are currently recognized in national forest recreation management (see Table 9-1). Integrated environmental treatment and facility designs are a part of the planning processes. Thus, the national forests offer a range of opportunities for recreation experiences providing a high degree of personal challenge and privacy and minimum development, as well as areas having recreation potential for larger crowds, which can be most advantageously realized by maximum development (Table 9-1).

Recreation land classifications recommended in the report of the Outdoor Recreation Resources Review Commission[5] [2] are, in general, applicable to various types of areas on the national forests which are specifically designated for different recreation interests and activities.

Brief comments on various types of specifically designated areas, recognized by the Forest Service as offering special recreation opportunities, follow. Recommended classifications are indicated by roman numerals in parentheses [13].

Wildernesses and Primitive Areas (V). Prior to enactment of the Wilderness Act of 1964 (P.L. 88-577), the national forests contained four kinds of areas specifically designated for wilderness purposes: *primitive, wil-*

---

[5] The classes are I, High-density; II, General; III, Natural; IV, Unique; V, Primitive; and VI, Historic and Cultural Sites (see Chapter 7).

derness, wild, and *canoe areas.*[6] The first category was retained, at least pending further study, but the Wilderness Act provided for the immediate inclusion of the last three categories as wildernesses in the National Wilderness Preservation System.

In 1976 the national forests contained 92 wildernesses with an aggregate area of 12.6 million acres (9 million hectares), and 17 primitive areas aggregating over 3 million acres (1.2 million hectares).

Except for the Boundary Waters Canoe Area in Minnesota, the Great Gulf Wilderness in New Hampshire, and the Linville Gorge Wilderness in North Carolina, all the designated Forest Service wildernesses and primitive areas were initially in the West. Among the largest of these are: Mazatzal Wilderness, Arizona (205,346 acres; 83,165 hectares); John Muir Wilderness, California (504,263 acres; 203,227 hectares); Salmon Trinity Alps Primitive Area, California (285,756 acres; 115,731 hectares); Weminusha Wilderness, Colorado (400,907 acres; 162,367 hectares); Idaho Primitive Area, Idaho (1,232,744 acres; 499,261 hectares); Selway-Bitterroot Wilderness, Idaho-Montana (1,243,659 acres; 503,682 hectares); Bob Marshall Wilderness, Montana (950,000 acres; 384,750 hectares); Gila Wilderness, New Mexico (433,916 acres; 175,736 hectares); Eagle Cap Wilderness, Ore-

---

[6] *Primitive areas.* Designated modified, or eliminated by the Chief Forester, under regulation L-20, adopted in 1930. Under this regulation, seventy-three primitive areas were established by 1939; some were later redesignated as wilderness areas under the more restrictive regulation U-1. Primitive areas still in existence retain this classification until determined otherwise by Congress.

Wilderness areas. Designated, modified, or eliminated by the Secretary of Agriculture, upon recommendation of the Chief Forester, under regulation U-1, which replaced L-20 in 1939. Regulation U-1 stipulated that wilderness areas were to have a minimum area of 100,000 acres (40,500 hectares); it also provided a greater degree of protection to wilderness qualities than did regulation L-20.

Wild areas. Designated, modified, or eliminated by the Chief Forester, under regulation U-2 also adopted in 1939. Regulation U-2 stipulated that the same protective restrictions applicable to wilderness areas applied to wild areas, although their size was smaller (5,000 to 100,000 acres; 2,025 to 40,500 hectares).

Canoe areas. Designated, modified, or eliminated by the Secretary of Agriculture under regulation U-3, adopted in 1930. Regulation U-3 provided for maintenance of the natural quality of such areas in the vicinity of streams, lakes, and portages without unnecessary restrictions on other uses (including timber harvest) at a distance from these key recreational locations. Since passage of the Wilderness Act, "no cut zones" have been extended by the Secretary of Agriculture, upon recommendation of a special citizens review committee, which was formed in 1964. The Boundary Waters Canoe Area is the only one in this category. It is on the Superior National Forest in northern Minnesota, contiguous with Quetico Provincial Park in Ontario, and was formed in 1958 by consolidation of three smaller, earlier, specially designated "roadless areas" (Caribou, Little Indian Sioux, and Superior).

Since the foregoing areas were established by administrative regulation rather than by law, the stability of their boundaries and the protection afforded their wilderness quality was not so permanent as many felt would be desirable. This fact prompted initial interest in federal wilderness legislation in 1955, which, in 1964 culminated in enactment of the Wilderness Act and establishment of the National Wilderness Preservation System. One of the stipulations of the Wilderness Act was that all wilderness, wild, and canoe areas were to be automatically blanketed under its provision as the nucleus of the National Wilderness Preservation System, with administrative authority over these areas remaining with the Forest Service.

Table 9-1 National Forest Levels of Outdoor Recreation Experiences: Associated with Environmental and Activity Considerations

Level	Experience	Environment	Activity
1 Primitive	Recreation opportunities to satisfy basic needs to the maximum extent. Experiences of adventure, challenge, exploration, solitude, and physical achievement, in the absence of controls, important to the user. Opportunity for extreme isolation. A feeling of being a part of nature.	No environmental modification unless absolutely necessary for resource protection. Unmodified natural environment and an absence of man-made developments for comfort or convenience dominates. Only necessary controls applied to users. No motorized access. An environment of spaciousness—seemingly unlimited horizons. Native materials with natural weathering of surfaces.	No man-made furtherance of activity opportunities except indirectly through public safety and resource protection (i.e. trails, trail bridges, signing, and/or the development of primitive type campgrounds). No contemporary activity opportunities. No formal VIS services. High degree of activity skills needed.
2	Recreation opportunities to satisfy basic needs to a near maximum extent as tempered by motorized access. A feeling of achievement for reaching the opportunity through challenging motorized access is important. Few controls evident to the user. Opportunities to socialize with others important although less so than at more primitive experience levels. A feeling of being very close to nature.	Some modification of the natural environment, rustic or rudimentary facilities for comfort and convenience of users are provided. Improvements mostly for protection of the resource. Minimum controls are subtle; sparingly dispersed to minimize contacts with others. Motorized access provided or permitted. Primary access over primitive roads or trails or by experienced boat or aircraft users. Mostly native materials with natural weathering of surfaces.	Slight man-made furtherance of activity opportunities through the placement of primitive type campgrounds, hunter camps, fisherman camps, and/or the dispersion of fundamental type facilities such as stoves, fireplaces, toilets, etc. High activity skill levels required.

	Recreation opportunities	Environment	Man-made furtherance
3 Inter-mediate	Recreation opportunities to satisfy basic needs to an intermediate degree. Controls and regimentation afford a sense of security although some taste of adventure is still important to the user. Opportunities to socialize with others about equal importance as isolation. A feeling of being close to nature.	Natural environment dominates but some modification for comfort and convenience of users. Overstory and ground vegetation moderately modified to improve developed site durability and to provide a sense of privacy. Inconspicuous control of vehicular traffic. Primary access over well-traveled roads or by capable boat or aircraft operators. Mostly native materials with natural color surfaces.	Moderate man-made furtherance of activity opportunities through development of roads, road turn-outs, snowmobile camps, intermediately developed campgrounds and other appropriate types of developed sites. Informal VIS opportunities. Moderate degree of activity skills required.
4	Recreation opportunities to satisfy basic needs to only a moderate degree. Sense of security sought by the user. Regimentation and fairly obvious controls are important. User is aware of opportunity to meet and be with other people; is obviously not isolated. Opportunity to be gregarious within relatively small groups. A feeling of being associated with nature.	Environment is substantially modified. Facilities primarily for comfort and convenience of users. Plant materials usually native but are purposefully situated. Moderate grading of land-forms to maximize usefulness and durability. Traffic controls present and obvious. Access by paved highway or easily negotiated water or air routes. Intermixing of synthetic and native materials.	Considerable man-made furtherance of activity opportunities with a wide range of developed sites provided to facilitate activity participation. VIS services frequently available to extend activity appreciation. Some opportunities to use contemporary activity skills such as snow and water skiing. Moderate degree of activity skill levels suffice.

(Table continued p. 162)

Table 9-1 (*Continued*)

Level	Experience	Environment	Activity
5 Modern	Recreation opportunities to satisfy basic needs to a modest degree. Feeling of security is very important to the user. High degree of opportunity to be gregarious. A feeling of being "next to nature" rather than closely associated with it.	High degree of environmental modification. Many facilities provided for comfort and convenience of users. Overstory ground vegetation and landforms are graded or modified as necessary. Plant materials may be exotic or native. Mowed turf and trimmed hedges not unusual. Privacy often provided by man-made means (walls, structures, screening, etc.). Obvious controls of users for security and resource protection. Access by any appropriate high standard means. A somewhat urbanized environment. Synthetic materials used as needed.	High degree of man-made furtherance of activity opportunities through the placement of a wide selection of developed sites and facilities. Facilities are simple, foolproof and safe, or are operated for the user by an employer, concessionaire, etc. Formal VIS services usually available and a dominant activity. Abundant opportunities for contemporary activities such as snow or water skiing, scuba diving, etc. A learning level for activity skills.

Source: U.S. Forest Service

gon (221,355 acres; 89,641 hectares); High Uintas Primitive Area, Utah (237,177 acres; 90,057 hectares); Glacier Peak Wilderness, Washington (464,471 acres; 188,111 hectares); and Teton Wilderness, Wyoming (563, 500 acres; 282,218 hectares). These are gross areas; those for the primitive areas are subject to change when such lands are classified under the Wilderness Act of 1964. In 1975, Congress designated 16 additional wildernesses in the East with areas ranging from 2,493 to 33,776 acres (1,010 to 13,679 hectares). This was done under the provisions of the act of 1975 (P.L. 63-622), called the Eastern Wilderness Act [4].

Both wildernesses and primitive areas are essentially similar in quality and outdoor recreation value. Modern developments (roads, mechanized transportation, structures) and commercial utilization of natural resources are prohibited or greatly restricted, either by law, as in wildernesses, or by administrative regulation, as in primitive areas. Both types are characterized by expansive, often highly scenic, undisturbed terrain. Those who use these areas must do so "on their own." Travel is on foot, with horses and pack stock, or, in the case of the Boundary Waters Canoe Area, by canoe. Self-reliance, an ability to live with nature, and an understanding of its hazards as well as its interests are necessary for safe and pleasurable use of these undeveloped lands. While the greatest use of wildernesses is for recreational purposes, the 1964 act also provided for scientific, educational, conservation, and historical use.

As their titles imply, there are certain differences between wildernesses and primitive areas,[7] related primarily to the original conditions of their establishment, their current status, and the degree of protection applied. Wildernesses on the national forests are units of the National Wilderness

---

[7] In national forest wilderness, commercial enterprise, structures and installations, roads, and all forms of mechanized transportation are prohibited by provisions of the Wilderness Act, except as specifically permitted and as subject to existing private rights on such lands. The specific exceptions in the Wilderness Act include (1) temporary roads or mechanized access in emergencies concerned with health and safety of visitors, or in the control of forest fire, destructive insects, and disease; (2) prospecting for purposes of obtaining information on resources including minerals after 1983, if carried out in a manner compatible with preservation of wilderness environment; (3) until 1983, location, development, and operation of mining claims, subject to reasonable regulations governing ingress and egress and restoration of the surface as prescribed by the Secretary of Agriculture; (4) investigation, establishment, and maintenance of reservoirs and power plants which are in the public interest, as authorized by the President; (5) grazing of livestock, where such activity was established prior to enactment of the Wilderness Act; (6) fishing and hunting, subject to state laws; (7) continued management of the Boundary Waters Canoe Area in accordance with established Forest Service policy, as authorized by the Secretary of Agriculture.

Primitive areas are administered according to 36 CFR 293.17, in effect at the time the Wilderness Act was passed. Provisions of this regulation are not very far removed from the more severe stipulations of the Wilderness Act; further, great care has always been, and continues to be, exercised by the Forest Service in preventing disturbance of their natural character. Regulations governing primitive areas and the boundaries of the areas were given legal status by the Wilderness Act. All lands within primitive areas must continue to be managed under regulations in effect at the time the Wilderness Act was passed until Congress determines otherwise.

Preservation System. They receive maximum practical protection of their wilderness quality, backed by law, as defined in the Wilderness Act of 1964. Primitive areas are not included in the National Wilderness Preservation System but were given legal status pending a decision by Congress concerning the suitability or nonsuitability of these lands for wildernesses. The Wilderness Act stipulated that, by 1974, all primitive areas on the national forests were to be evaluated as to their suitability or nonsuitability for inclusion, in whole or in part, in the National Wilderness Preservation System.[8] The Forest Service has completed its review and made its recommendations to Congress.

Solitude and a feeling of self-sufficiency, prime ingredients in the appeal of wilderness recreation, are not limited to specifically designated wildernesses and primitive areas. There are extensive undesignated areas for dispersed recreation in the national forests, which provide very challenging recreation experiences. A recent concept is management of certain small, relatively accessible portions of such undesignated lands for limited-access recreation areas. These fulfill the needs of many users, particularly those who lack the necessary time, experience, and physical stamina required in extensive wilderness travel.

Geological, Archeological, and Historical Areas (IV, VI). These areas vary in size but are of sufficient extent to protect and preserve specific interests found on the national forests.

Scenic Areas (IV). Specifically designated lands of this type are characterized by unique or outstanding beauty. Their size varies, and they are often smaller than 5,000 acres (2,025 hectares). They are maintained, as nearly as possible, in an undisturbed condition; hence, development of roads, trails, and other facilities is permitted only to the minimum extent required to make the area accessible.

Observation Sites (I, II, III). The recreation activity of viewing outstanding scenery is normally associated with travel. Where opportunities exist for providing sight-seeing, particularly scenes possessing qualities of beauty or interest which make lasting impressions, the Forest Service develops overlooks or observation sites. These sites usually are turnouts along routes of travel and include parking and sanitation facilities. Some have tables, benches, and stoves to promote picnicking and other day-use activities. The Forest Service maintains more than 437 observation sites.

Winter Sports Areas (II). Recreation use of the national forest is not limited to the summer season. Approximately 225 winter sports areas with

---

[8] The Wilderness Act provided also for similar evaluation of undeveloped portions of lands, with a minimum area of 5,000 acres (2,025 hectares) administered by the National Park Service and the Fish and Wildlife Service, for possible inclusion in the National Wilderness Preservation System.

necessary facilities and services are found in national forests of New England, the Lake states, the Rocky Mountain region, the Southwest, the Cascade area, and the Sierra Nevada region. Although emphasis is placed upon skiing, provisions for other winter sports activities, such as skating, tobogganing, snowmobiling, and snowshoeing, is consistent with the demand for them.

In order to administer this extensive winter sports program, the Forest Service has formulated certain well-defined policies and has established procedures necessary to provide adequate facilities and protect visitors from hazards.

Special facilities for the highly proficient are of secondary importance on national forest winter sports areas; instead the areas are planned for the enjoyment and use of the average participant with specific portions designated for skiers of varying abilities. Such facilities as warming shelters, lunch counters, rope tows, and ski lifts are generally available, and some of the larger and more isolated developments offer regular hotel and meal services. Tows and ski lifts, lunch or meal services, hotel accommodations, and the like are installed and operated by private parties, subject to the full administrative control of the Forest Service. Since national forest objectives under law are different from those for parks, national forest winter sports developments need not be subject to the severe restrictions applicable in National Parks; hence permanent ski lifts of varying types can usually be provided. The Forest Service is mindful of the need for preserving the scenic beauty of areas in its charge, however, and so permanent ski lifts cannot be erected without its permission. Further, hotels for overnight accommodation are not encouraged unless an area lacks such facilities in the immediate vicinity and unless the ski area is located at a distance from population centers.

Qualified Forest Service personnel known as Snow Rangers are stationed at individual winter sports areas to supervise various aspects of these operations. Research in such matters as avalanche hazard removal has been conducted [11], and on areas located along main highways the Forest Service has the cooperation of state highway departments in removing snow from roads and parking areas and of state highway patrols in controlling traffic. Further, the National Ski Patrol cooperates with the Snow Rangers in supervising winter sports activities; this is of particular importance in the rescue of lost or injured skiers and in the provision of competent first aid. In addition, at many winter sports areas on the national forests, ski instruction is provided by instructors certified by the National Ski Association, for beginners and those not yet thoroughly proficient in this outdoor sport.

Organization Camp Areas (II). Facilities (lodging, meal service) necessary for the accommodation of organized groups are developed on organization camp areas. Such areas are specifically designated for development by nonprofit organizations and public agencies, and they are generally used by those who cannot afford expensive accommodations or costly camping equipment. Opportunities of this kind are often favored by such groups as Boy Scouts, Girl Scouts, Campfire Girls, the YMCA, 4-H clubs, churches, and welfare agencies. Administrative control of these areas, allotted on the basis of need, remains within the Forest Service.

Approximately 545 organization camps, most of which are privately owned, operate within the national forests. These units can serve a maximum of about 72,000 people at one time.

Concession Sites (II). Specifically designated areas of this type on national forest land include various public accommodations (hotels, motels, resorts, trailer sites) that are more elaborate than campgrounds and organization camps and are incidental to the enjoyment of the national forests. They also provide for the establishment of related necessary public services (restaurants, stores, gasoline stations, horse and boat liveries).

Facilities of this type must be in keeping with the forest environment and are constructed with private funds, except where essential services cannot otherwise be obtained.[9] Full administrative authority over resort areas is retained by the Forest Service.

Recreation Residence (Summer-home) Sites (II). Units of national forest land which are not needed or suitable for uses of higher priority have been designated on some national forests. On such areas individuals have been permitted to lease lots for summer residences at an annual rate determined by appraisal. Buildings erected conform to Forest Service architectural and construction standards. Over 18,000 summer homes are found in the national forests. The pressures of increasing demands for public-use areas preclude the establishment of additional sites.

National Recreation Areas. A number of areas of this type, characterized by outstanding combinations of outdoor recreational interests and opportunities, have been established by Congress. If they involve national forests, administration is by the Forest Service. The National Forests are also involved in the Wild and Scenic River System of the United States.

PUBLIC RECREATIONAL USE OF THE NATIONAL FORESTS

There has been rapid development of public interest in the diversified recreational advantages offered by the national forests (Table 9-2). Such interest began many years ago, even before the Forest Service gave formal official

---

[9] Two hotels within the national forests, Timberline Lodge in the Mt. Hood National Forest, Oregon, and Magazine Mountain Lodge, in the Ouachita National Forest of Arkansas, were built with federal funds and are owned by the federal government. They are operated by private concessionaires under Forest Service supervision.

Table 9-2 Estimated Outdoor Recreation Use on National Forest System Land in the United States by Type of Activity, 1968 and 1977 (Thousand Recreation Visitor Days)[a]

Activity	1968	1977
Camping	39,214	52,672
Picnicking	6,687	8,317
Recreation travel (mechanized)	36,520	49,325
Boating	3,837	5,940
Water skiing and other water sports	605	803
Swimming and scuba diving	2,855	4,422
Fishing	14,523	16,029
Winter sports	5,676	8,116
Games and team sports	540	1,028
Resort and commercial public service	3,967	4,187
Organization camp use	4,498	3,855
Recreation residence use	8,151	6,826
Hunting	14,049	14,517
Hiking and mountain climbing	4,546	10,258
Horseback riding	2,057	2,884
Gathering forest products	1,283	2,813
Nature studying	850	1,240
Viewing scenery, sports, environment	5,078	7,374
Visitor information	1,780	3,591
Totals	156,716	204,797

[a] Recreation use which aggregates 12 person hours. May entail 1 person for 12 hours, 12 persons for only 1 hour, or any equivalent combination of individual or group use. (U.S. Forest Service)

recognition to recreation as a valid resource of these areas. Use has increased rapidly in recent years, particularly in certain activities, as above comparison of 1968 and 1977 shows. There has been a greater overall increase in activities in dispersed areas than on developed sites.

SUMMARY

The Forest Service, a bureau in the Department of Agriculture, administers over 187 million acres (75.7 million hectares) of land, the major portion of which is included in 154 national forests. Headquarters of the Forest Service, including the office of the Chief is in Washington, D.C. There are nine regions, each in the charge of a Regional Forester. National forests, each administered by a Forest Supervisor, are divided into ranger districts, which are the basic administrative units of the Forest Service. Ranger districts are administered by District Rangers. This decentralized administrative framework permits delegation of authority to varied levels of the Forest Service organization in making decisions concerning uses of national forest lands.

The basic policy of the Forest Service is multiple use and sustained yield for maximum, long-term public benefits in the protection, management, and development of national forest resources for timber, outdoor recreation, water, wildlife, forage, and related values. Forest Service recreation policy emphasizes integration of recreation with other uses of the national forests and the maintenance and perpetuation of an attractive environment for varied forest-oriented outdoor recreational interests and activities. This policy includes preservation of wilderness, rare or fragile flora, fauna, and other features.

Diversity of outdoor recreational interests at all seasons is one of the prinicpal characteristics of the national forests. These reserves embrace large portions of our principal mountain ranges noted for rugged scenic beauty. They also include sections of the Pacific Coast and portions of the lake country of northern Minnesota. And they include most types of North American forest environment with their typical plants and animals. Facilities necessary for public enjoyment of these varied interests include thousands of miles of trails, modern highways and subsidiary roads, and many areas for skiing and related winter sports. There are numerous picnic areas and campgrounds; those which are readily accessible and equipped with modern facilities contrast with more remote, less developed sites. There are also similarly varied hotel and lodge accommodations, usually privately operated. The national forests also include extensive, completely undeveloped primitive areas and wildernesses; the latter are the core of our National Wilderness Preservation System. Development of public interest in the recreational advantages of the national forests began long before the Forest Service gave formal recognition of recreation as a valid national forest resource. From the time when records were first taken, recreational use of the national forests has, in common with other uses of wild lands, grown phenomenally.

Though basically the national forests and the national parks complement each other in providing recreational opportunities, there are also overlaps and areas of competition. Many of the national parks were created from, or are adjacent to, national forests, causing some cases of possible conflicts of interest between the primarily preservationist land-use policy of the National Park Service and the basic utilitarian policy of the Forest Service. Where attempts are made to coordinate planning and management involving both agencies harmonious relationships can develop.

The Forest Service, in its recreation policy, ranges from highly developed areas, involving many recreation and resource uses, to the almost natural wilderness. And there are overlaps in recreational classes. Management of such a spectrum of opportunity areas requires skill, particularly where competitive uses overlap. With the increasing number of visitors, the expanding number of resource producers, and the growing complexity of the organizational structure, the problems of multiple use of the national forests become more difficult. Various interest groups push for their particular interest in hearings and in the media.

SELECTED REFERENCES

1 Freeman, Orville, L., and Michael Frome: "The National Forests of America," Putnam, New York, 1968.

2 Outdoor Recreation Resources Review Commission: "Outdoor Recreation for America: A Report to the President and to the Congress by the ORRRC," U.S. Government Printing Office, Washington, 1962.

3 Steen, Harold K.: "The U.S. Forest Service: A History," University of Washington Press, Seattle, 1976.

4 U.S. Congress: "An Act To Further the Purposes of the Wilderness Act by Designating Certain Acquired Lands for Inclusion in the National Wilderness Preservation System, To Provide for the Study of Certain Additional Lands for Such Inclusion, and for Other Purposes, (P.L. 93-622), 93rd Cong., S. 3433, Jan. 3, 1975," (Eastern Wilderness Act) U.S. Government Printing Office, Washington, 1975.

5 U.S. Department of Agriculture, Forest Service: "Our National Forests," Agricultural Information Bulletin No. 47, U.S. Government Printing Office, Washington, 1951.

6 U.S. Department of Agriculture, Forest Service: "The Work of the U.S. Forest Service," Agriculture Information Bulletin No. 91, U.S. Government Printing Office, Washington, 1952.

7 U.S. Department of Agriculture, Forest Service: "Wilderness," U.S. Government Printing Office, Washington, 1967.

8 U.S. Department of Agriculture, Forest Service: "Outdoor Recreation in the National Forests," Agriculture Information Bulletin No. 301, U.S. Government Printing Office, Washington, 1968.

9 U.S. Department of Agriculture, Forest Service: "National Forest Vacations," (P.A. 1037) U.S. Government Printing Office, Washington, 1973.

10 U.S. Department of Agriculture, Forest Service: "The Principal Laws Relating to Forest Service Activities," (A.H. 453) U.S. Government Printing Office, Washington, 1974.

11 U.S. Department of Agriculture, Forest Service: "Snow Avalanche Handbook" (A.H. 489) U.S. Government Printing Office, Washington, 1976.

12 U.S. Department of Agriculture, Forest Service: "A Summary of a Renewable Resource Assessment and a Recommended Renewable Resource Program," Washington, February 1976.

13 U.S. Department of Agriculture, Forest Service: "Forest Service Manual, National Forest Protection and Management, Recreation, Vol. III," Washington (multilithed).

14 U.S. Department of Agriculture, Forest Service: Forest Service Manual–Title 2300, Recreation Management," Washington (multilithed).

15 U.S. Department of Agriculture, Forest Service: "Report of the Chief of the Forest Service," U.S. Government Printing Office, Washington. v.d.

16 U.S. National Park Service and U.S. Forest Service: "The National Parks and National Forests, Their Purposes and Management," U.S. Government Printing Office, Washington, 1975.

Other Federal
Agencies

Other federal agencies that provide varied outdoor recreational opportunities are the Fish and Wildlife Service, the Bureau of Land Management, and three agencies important in water-based recreation—the Bureau of Reclamation, the Corps of Engineers, and the Tennessee Valley Authority.

FISH AND WILDLIFE SERVICE: ORGANIZATION AND ACTIVITIES

Headquarters of the Fish and Wildlife Service, including the office of the Director, are in Washington, D.C. [19]. There are six regions and the Alaska area office,[1] each supervised by a Regional Director, who reports to the Director. Within each region are various wildlife refuges, fish hatcheries, and wildlife and sport fishery research stations. Field installations, except for those engaged in fundamental sport fishery and wildlife research, report to their own Regional Directors. Those engaged in fundamental research report directly to their Division Chiefs in the Washington, D.C., headquarters.

[1] The six regions are I, *Pacific,* Portland, Oregon; II, *Southwest,* Albuquerque, N.M.; III, *Lake States,* Minneapolis, Minn.; IV, *Southeast,* Atlanta, Ga.; V., *Northeast,* Boston, Mass.; and VI, *Plains States,* Denver, Colo. The *Alaska Area Office* is in Anchorage, Alaska.

Activities of the Fish and Wildlife Service relate to various recreational uses of wild lands; they include:

1   Essential research in fish and wildlife biology and related matters for solution of various sport fish and wildlife problems in the most adequate and economic manner. Research concerns improvement of management techniques; alleviation of animal damage; classification, distribution, and life history studies; prudent use of wildlife resources; pesticides, including surveillance and registration; fish nutrition and disease; endangered species research; wildlife disease studies; and anadromous fisheries work.

2   Management of numerous refuges for mammals, birds, and fishes, together with their environment, to maintain adequate numbers in vigorous condition in typical surroundings, with minimum disruption of other necessary land uses. The extent and quality of wildlife environment in relation to changes attributed to modern technology and land-use pressures, and protection and restoration of rare or vanishing species and their environment are vital concerns of the refuge program.

3   Administration of appropriations provided by laws in the interest of wildlife conservation.[2]

4   Cooperation with other federal agencies, state agencies, and foreign governments on fish and wildlife matters. Such cooperation involves law enforcement; technical wildlife management on projects where wildlife is an important resource, or where developments affect wildlife populations; investigation and importation of foreign wildlife for trial release; training of personnel; management or studies of international faunal resources (migratory birds, fur seal, whale, certain fisheries) as prescribed by treaty or agreement with other nations.

5   Development of public interest in and understanding of the importance of fish and wildlife resources through interpretation, conservation education programs, the mass media, and technical reports and publications.

THE NATIONAL WILDLIFE REFUGE SYSTEM

The National Wildlife Refuge System is the largest and most diversified in the world (Figure 10-1). The aggregate area is over 33 million areas (13,365,000 hectares), with over 380 units ranging in size from a few acres to 9 million acres (3,645,000 hectares). They are in every state except West Virginia, as well as in Puerto Rico and Territorial Islands of the Pacific Ocean. Various areas occur from the Arctic to the tropics and from below sea level to nearly 10,000 feet (3048 meters) in elevation. They include ocean beaches, shoreland and salt marshes, offshore islands, swamps, de-

---

[2] These include the Pittman-Robertson Act, regarding federal aid to states in wildlife restoration; the similar Dingell-Johnson Act, regarding sport fish restoration; and the Wetlands Loan Act and Migratory Bird Hunting Stamp Act, which provide funds for the establishment of flyway refuges.

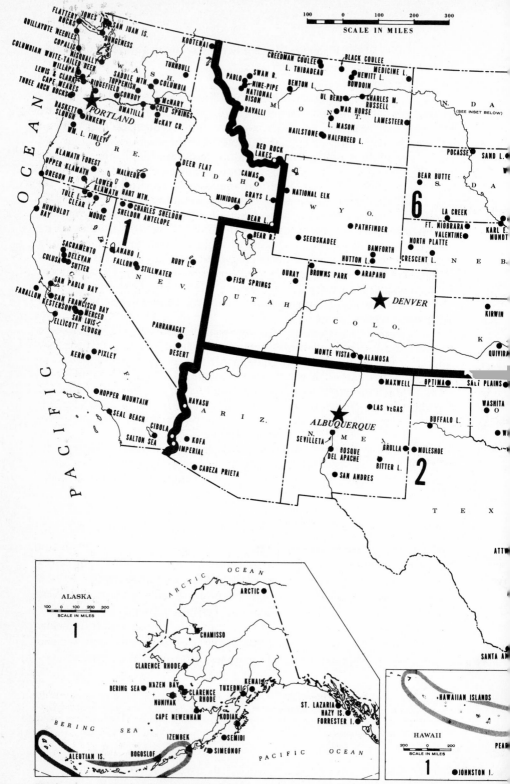

Figure 10-1 National Wildlife Refuge System, 1976. *(U.S. Fish and Wildlife Service.)*

REGIONAL BOUNDARIES

★ REGIONAL OFFICE

serts, prairies, and forests. Within each of these generalized environments are more detailed habitats adapted to particular needs of various species. As a result, faunal interests of these areas are highly significant and noteworthy (Table 10-1). Over 700 of the nearly 800 species of North American birds may be found during at least one season on the National Wildlife Refuges. These lands also provide suitable environment for essentially all North American big-game animals, as well as most smaller mammals and many reptiles. Many refuges provide virtually the only places where some of the rarest of North American wildlife species now exist. All kinds of wildlife are protected on each refuge, but many were established for the protection of one or more unique species, or group of species. No less than 136 units protect one or more endangered species of wildlife.

Many refuges are remote and difficult of access, but others are located close to population centers.[3] About 180 refuges have resident personnel responsible for all operations on the larger area and, many times, for smaller nearby units. Improved means of transportation of equipment has made possible the elimination of duplicate heavy equipment and resulting expensive maintenance.

An increasingly important segment of the National Wildlife Refuge System is the program of waterfowl production areas principally in western Minnesota, North and South Dakota, north-central Nebraska, eastern Montana, and western Wisconsin. These 120 or more units are administered by Wetlands Management District Offices.

Proposals relating to the Alaska Native Claims Settlement Act, when completed, are expected to add to the number of areas and total acreage of the National Wildlife Refuge System (see pp. 80–81).

General Land Management Policy of the National Wildlife Refuge System

Refuges and related lands administered by the Fish and Wildlife Service are managed on a multiple-use basis, consistent with maintenance of desirable wildlife habitat required to support optimum variety and abundance of species. Refuges for migratory waterfowl are not necessarily natural areas. Many have been developed by improving marshes or farmed-out land. Even on some "wild" refuges natural processes are often modified to favor the requirements of certain species. Cultural operations (agricultural crop production, domestic stock grazing, trapping or hunting of surplus animals, timber cutting) may be permitted when in the interest of wildlife populations or the purpose of the area involved. As a result, by-products of refuge

[3] One of the most noteworthy is the Great Swamp National Wildlife Refuge in New Jersey, which is only about an hour's drive from New York City (see Table 10-1).

Table 10-1   Examples of Areas and Interests of the National Wildlife Refuge System[a]

Name	Area (acres; hectares)	Interests
Arctic National Wildlife Range, Alaska	8,900,000 (3,604,500)	Caribou, polar and grizzly bears, Dall sheep, waterfowl, shorebirds
Aleutian Islands, Alaska	2,720,225 (1,103,691)	Sea otters, geese, seabirds, ptarmigans
Cabeza Prieta, Arizona	860,000 (348,300)	Desert bighorns, Sonoran pronghorns, peccaries
Farallon, California	211 (85)	Seabirds, sea lions
Tule Lake, California	37,617 (15,235)	Waterfowl, peregrines, kites
Bombay Hook, Delaware	15,136 (6,142)	Geese, other waterfowl, shorebirds
Loxahatchee, Florida	145,635 (59,482)	Waterfowl, herons, Everglade kites
National Key Deer, Florida	4,406 (1,784)	Key whitetail deer, West Indian birds
Blackbeard Island, Georgia	5,617 (2,275)	Sea turtles, waterfowl, shorebirds
Okefenokee, Georgia	377,548 (152,907)	Alligators, black bears, various birds
Sabine, Louisiana	142,846 (57,853)	Waterfowl, spoonbills, ibises, alligators
Seney, Michigan	95,455 (38,659)	Waterfowl, sandhill cranes, grouse, otters
National Bison Range, Mont.	18,541 (7,509)	Bison, elk, bighorns, deer
Red Rock Lakes, Montana	32,467 (13,149)	Trumpeter swans, moose, grayling
Fort Niobrara, Nebraska	18,667 (7,560)	Bison, Texas longhorns, elk, prarie chickens, sharp-tailed grouse
Desert National Wildlife Range, Nevada	1,588,459 (643,326)	Desert bighorns, mule deer
Brigantine, New Jersey	20,230 (8,193)	Waterfowl, shorebirds, gulls, rails
Great Swamp, New Jersey	5,886 (2,384)	Waterfowl, deer, otter
Malheur, Oregon	181,967 (73,697)	Whistling swans, white pelicans, sage grouse, waterfowl, cranes
Cape Romain, So. Carolina	34,229 (13,863)	Waterfowl, shorebirds, sea turtles, brown pelicans
Santa Ana, Texas	1,980 (802)	Tree ducks, red-billed pigeons, green jays, chachalacas, Mexican birds
Aransas, Texas	90,069 (36,478)	Whooping cranes, shorebirds, water- fowl, roseate spoonbills, deer, turkeys, peccaries
Bear River, Utah	64,895 (26,282)	Waterfowl, shorebirds, muskrats
National Elk Refuge, Wyo.	23,972 (9,709)	Elk, moose, trumpeter swans, sandhill cranes

[a] Unless otherwise noted, areas are National Wildlife Refuges.

Source: "1975 Directory of National Wildlife Refuges," U.S. Department of the Interior, Fish and Wildlife Service, Washington, 1975 (multilithed).

management include income from sale of hay, grazing fees, wildlife-bene-fiting timber operations, sale of pelts of surplus fur-bearing animals, and oil and gas leases.[4]

[4] Section 401, act of June 15, 1935, known as the Revenue-Sharing Act (49 Stat. 383), as amended by the act of Aug. 30, 1964 [78 Stat. 701; 16 U.S.C. 715(s)], calls for payments to the county in which a refuge is located, amounting to three-quarters of 1 percent of the adjusted value of acquired lands, or 25 percent of refuge receipts, at the option of the county.

As stipulated by the Wilderness Act of 1964, refuge lands are being evaluated as to their suitability or nonsuitability for inclusion in the National Wilderness Preservation System; congressional designation has been completed on many areas.

Recreation Policy and Public Use of National Wildlife Refuge System

Recreation on national wildlife refuges is confined almost entirely to wildlife-oriented activities.[5] General recreational activities, services, and facilities suited to large concentrations of people, though appropriate on a few refuges, are not encouraged by the Fish and Wildlife Service. Observation and study of flora and fauna, general sightseeing, fishing, and picnicking are among the principal recreational uses. Camping, however, is generally discouraged, except on specially designated lands sometimes provided for that purpose. Fishing is permitted on many of these areas, and others may occasionally be opened to controlled or managed hunting. Where appropriate, boating and swimming are allowed. A number of refuges feature self-guiding wildlife trails and designated auto tour routes. Wildlife interpretive centers, now available in only a few areas, will be increased in number in the future; these contain exhibits explaining the establishment and operation of refuges and the interests of local animal and plant life. Despite the limitations, recreational use of the National Wildlife Refuge System rose from nearly 3.4 million visits in 1951 to over 32 million visits in 1975. About 82 percent of these visits were wildlife-oriented (54 percent in interpretation included wildlife observations, photography, sightseeing, use of wildlife trails and interpretive facilities; 25 percent fishing; 3 percent hunting). The 18 percent in nonwildlife uses included picnicking (4 percent), boating and water skiing (6 percent), swimming (4 percent), camping (3 percent), and miscellaneous (1 percent).

Adjacent to Okefenokee National Wildlife Refuge a small section of swamp habitat, designated as Okefenokee Swamp Park, is operated by a non-profit organization which has leased land from the state of Georgia. From here boat trips, conducted by licensed guides, may be made for a short distance into the Okefenokee National Wildlife Refuge for the benefit of visitors who wish to experience the feeling of solitude engendered by this interesting area.

National wildlife refuges have a particular appeal to individuals with definite interest in wildlife and related natural history. Hunter's clubs, bird and garden clubs, school and service groups, and professional and scientific societies find them especially attractive. Many refuges are the locale for Christmas Bird Counts, sponsored throughout the country for many years by the National Audubon Society.

[5] Authorized by act of Sept. 29, 1962 (75 Stat. 653), as amended [19 U.S.C. 460(b)-460(k)(4)].

BUREAU OF LAND MANAGEMENT

As noted in Chapter 4, this bureau of the Department of the Interior was formed in 1946 through consolidation of the General Land Office and the Grazing Service. It has jurisdiction over approximately 450 million acres (182,251 million hectares) of land [16], over half of which is in Alaska (Figure 10-2).[6]

General Responsibility and Policy

Varied activities of the Bureau of Land Management are administered under provisions of the Federal Land Policy and Management Act of 1976 (P.L. 94-579), commonly called the BLM Organic Act [12]. This act provides a comprehensive statutory statement of BLM's purpose and authority, together with specifications as to how this agency is to manage lands under its control. A brief summary of its basic provisions follow [8,16]:

1 BLM lands will generally be retained in federal ownership, unless land-use planning, as provided for in the act, indicates that disposal of certain areas will serve the national interest.

2 BLM lands and their resources will be periodically and systematically inventoried; present and future use will be projected through land-use planning and coordinated with planning efforts of other federal and state agencies.

3 Management of BLM lands will be on a multiple use—sustained yield basis, unless otherwise specified by law, recognizing the Nation's need for domestic sources of minerals (including outer continental shelf), food, timber, and fiber.

4 Scientific, scenic, ecological, environmental, historical, archeological, air and atmospheric, and water resources will be protected. Where appropriate, certain areas will be preserved in their natural condition, or managed for the provision of food and habitat for fish, wildlife, and domestic animals, and for outdoor recreation and human occupancy and use.

5 A fair market value will be received from use of BLM lands and their resources unless otherwise provided by statute.

6 Disposal (sale, lease, transfer) and exchange of BLM lands, as well as acquisition of non-federal lands for public purposes, will follow uniform proscribed procedures.

7 States and local governments will be compensated for burdens due to immunity of federal lands from state and local taxation.

Organization of the Bureau of Land Management

Headquarters of the Bureau of Land Management are in Washington, D.C. The principal administrative officer is the Director. The headquarters staff includes various administrative and technical personnel who deal with dif-

---

[6] Under the Alaska Native Claims Settlement Act of 1971 (P.L. 92-203) status of lands in Alaska is rapidly changing.

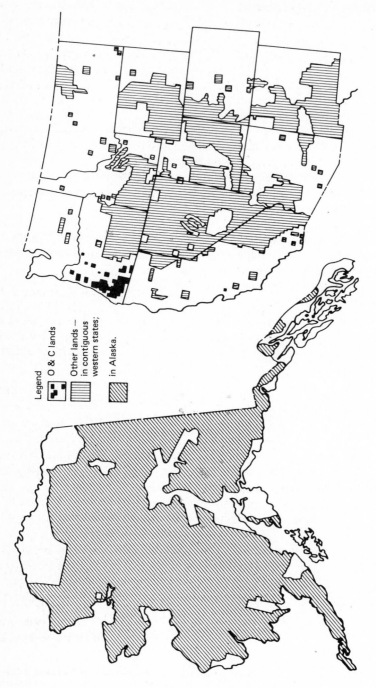

Figure 10-2 Generalized outline of natural resource lands administered by the Bureau of Land Management; status of BLM lands in Alaska is subject to change (see reference to Alaska Native Claims Settlement Act, pp. 80–81). *(Bureau of Land Management.)*

Legend

O & C lands

Other lands — in contiguous western states;

in Alaska.

ferent aspects of the Bureau's far-flung, complex operations (land classification, outdoor recreation, wildlife, minerals, public land survey, forest management, range management, resource conservation, protection, legal matters, administration, and finance). There are twelve state offices,[7] each in charge of a state director and staffed with administrative and technical personnel who deal with various BLM activities in specific areas.

Recreational Resources of BLM Lands

Lands administered by the Bureau of Land Management provide for a multiplicity of outdoor recreational needs and activities. They contain spectacular desert, canyon, and mountain country; noteworthy geological features; river, lake, and ocean frontage; and numerous archeological and historical sites. They may be large expansive areas or small scattered tracts. Large portions of these lands are still generally inaccessible except by the most hardy, resourceful individuals, but some sections are readily reached. In many instances they border routes of recreational travel or are adjacent to national and state parks, national forests, wildlife refuges, and related areas. Occasionally they are near towns and cities.

Among programs in which BLM is involved are those related to development of the National Wilderness Preservation System, National Wild and Scenic River System, and National Trails System, under provisions in relevant acts. BLM has also designated numerous areas where general outdoor recreation is a primary management condition, such as the Red Rock Recreational Area in Nevada [13].

Public Use of BLM Lands

Every year millions of people hunt, fish and camp on BLM lands. In addition, ever-increasing numbers of people are using these areas for hiking, picnicking, float trips, off-road vehicle activity, and other recreational pursuits as well as for solitude and to obtain a primitive area experience.

Recreational use of BLM lands has increased from 9 million visitor days in 1964 to 55 million visitor days in 1974. It is expected to reach 80 million visitor days[8] by 1980.

Summary of BLM Recreational Land-Use Policies [14,15]

Recreation is recognized as an integral part of multiple-use management of BLM lands. Five basic elements are identified:

[7] State offices are located in Anchorage, Alaska; Phoenix, Arizona; Sacramento, California; Denver, Colorado; Boise, Idaho; Billings, Montana; Reno, Nevada; Santa Fe, New Mexico; Portland, Oregon; Salt Lake City, Utah; and Cheyenne, Wyoming. The twelfth office is located at Silver Springs, Maryland. BLM matters in the state of Washington are handled by the Portland office; in North and South Dakota by the Billings office; in Kansas and Nebraska by the Cheyenne office; in Oklahoma by the Santa Fe office; and in other states by the office at Silver Springs.

[8] See Table 9-2 for definition of visitor day.

1 Recreational Resources: natural and cultural resources used by individuals during leisure time which provide a change of pace, a change of social environment, or related satisfactions.

2 Cultural Resources: sites, buildings, structures, objects, or districts that are associated with or representative of people, cultures, or human activities or events; they may be prehistoric, historic, or contemporary.

3 Visual Resources: the composite of land, water, vegetation, animals, structures, and other visible features.

4 Natural History Resources: features of the environment which represent natural phenomena dealing with the development of the earth's surface or the evolution of life and which have scientific values or evoke human interest.

5 Wilderness: management of specific areas of primary primitive value is patterned after criteria defined in the Wilderness Act of 1964 (P.L. 88-577).

In general, the Bureau of Land Management follows the land classification system developed by the Bureau of Outdoor Recreation (see Chapter 7) in correlating its recreational land-use planning with that of other agencies at different levels of government, as well as that of private land owners.

Protection of recreation resources, promotion of visitor safety and welfare, and the enhancement of visitor recreational experience are major considerations of BLM recreation policy. Where necessary, a specific recreation experience will be maintained by determination of a carrying capacity for limitation of numbers of participants using a given land area or engaged in a particular recreation activity. Programs of interpretation and public education are undertaken, where appropriate, to help achieve management and public service objectives.

In areas where BLM has primary responsibility, BLM constructs recreation facilities (trails, roads, campgrounds, picnic areas, interpretive facilities, and related needs) in response to demonstrated management requirements. BLM also maintains recreation facilities at a level that will protect the investment and which will assure achievement of management objectives for visitor recreation experience.

Areas characterized by unique or typical recreation resources, particularly cultural or natural history resources, are managed for protection of such resources; where they are of such significance to warrant long-term protection they are segregated from noncompatible activities and uses. In cases where alteration or destruction of a cultural resource site is unavoidable, all cultural values are salvaged prior to alteration or destruction of their site or setting. Restoration or reconstruction of cultural resources is undertaken only to meet specific recreation resource management objectives, such as interpretation or education. Where compatible with protection objectives, research and investigation of cultural and natural history resources by competent individuals or organizations is permitted, subject to permit or similar controls.

FEDERAL WATER-BASED RECREATIONAL AREAS

The Tennessee Valley Authority, the Bureau of Reclamation, and the Corps of Engineers administer areas consisting of reservoirs and other artificially impounded waters, together with their contiguous lands, resulting largely from construction of dams. These multipurpose projects, developed primarily for irrigation, hydroelectric power, municipal and industrial water supply, flood control, and similar purposes, are extensively used for boating, swimming, water skiing, picnicking, camping, fishing, and hunting. Many people are attracted to these areas also to enjoy their scenic qualities, which are noteworthy in some cases, or to marvel at the engineering aspects of the dams themselves. Since many of these projects are located in arid sections of the West, where there are few natural lakes, or in the Appalachian Southeast, they have a tremenduous effect on outdoor recreation in such regions, including economic benefits.

Tennessee Valley Authority [7,11]

Since its establishment in 1933, the Tennessee Valley Authority has built or acquired 41 reservoirs. These have an aggregate water surface area of over 650,000 acres (263,250 hectares) and a total shoreline of about 11,600 miles (18,676 kilometers). In addition, there are thousands of acres of contiguous lands which either are being used for various types of outdoor recreation or have potential recreational value related to water.

Development of the recreational potential of varied TVA projects has been guided since the start by a carefully formulated recreational policy adapted to principles of broad multiple use. Recreational values of TVA reservoirs and their surrounding lands are carefully examined and assessed for their contribution to the region's development and public recreational use consistent with other TVA requirements. TVA cooperates fully with other public agencies and private holders of recreational areas in the region to assure the greatest possible benefit to the people of the Tennessee Valley and the Nation. Specific features of the general policy follow:

1   TVA observes and records regional and national recreation trends and experiences to assist cooperating public and private agencies in meeting recreation needs.

2   TVA encourages recreation as one of the uses of its reservoirs. Lands acquired by TVA for reservoir purposes become public land, and, unless otherwise utilized, are available for general recreation purposes (hunting, fishing, picnicking, and access to and egress from the waters of

the reservoirs) without charge and without formal instrument of permission.

As a general rule, TVA includes appropriate easements and covenants for these purposes, on behalf of the general public, in deeds for any reservoir shorelands it sells.

Under appropriate conditions, TVA lands are made available for the following specific recreation uses—public parks (federal, state, county, community); group camps; marinas, fishing camps, and boat docks; vacation resorts; summer residences; bathing beaches; scenic protection and preservation; and similar recreation purposes contributing to greater public use and enjoyment of the lakes.

TVA determines which lands are suitable for recreation through analysis of data pertinent to current and future needs. These determinations are made consistent with other TVA program requirements and are coordinated with programs of other public and private agencies.

TVA secures recreation development, management, and operation of reservoir lands lying above designated reservoir levels by other agencies, organizations, and individuals, through appropriate agreements under the Tennessee Valley Authority Act of 1933 (P.L. 73-17), as amended. It also employs methods designed to secure the best qualified operators with due regard to public interests and otherwise to assure equitable treatment among prospective operators or users.

3   TVA participates directly in the development of recreation facilities on its reservoirs and shorelands to serve visitors to TVA dams and powerhouses and to demonstrate the design, construction, and maintenance of facilities for the purpose of furthering development of the regional program.

4   TVA provides consultation, advice, and technical assistance in recreation planning, site improvement and development, initiation of architectural design, sanitation and safety measures, operation and maintenance of recreational enterprises, and the administration of recreation programs to cooperating state agencies, and through these agencies to local public agencies, quasi-public groups, and other organizations and individuals.

5   TVA identifies opportunities to further the recreation program in connection with other activities, such as dam and reservoir construction and the disposal of surplus land.

Effects of TVA Policies   TVA's policies have prompted the establishment of 19 state parks, a number of state wildlife refuges and public shooting areas, and 110 county and municipal parks along the reservoir system. A total of 111 camps have been established along the shoreline by nonprofit organizations and camps. In addition, 310 private marinas and resorts and 21,300 private residences have been developed. TVA has also transferred more than 125,000 acres (50,625 hectares) of land to the National Park Service, Forest Service, and the Fish and Wildlife Service for some form of recreation or wildlife management. Total cumulative investment in recreation and related facilities on TVA lakes exceeded $540,000,000 in 1975.

Also of significance in TVA's current recreation program is the emphasis placed on environmental education; planning for scenic streams, trails, and small wild areas; and development of TVA public use areas along the reservoir system. The agency's environmental education activities demonstrate innovative ways to improve the quality of life and environment of the region and enhance human resource development.

The work on scenic streams encourages public use and enjoyment of Tennessee Valley streams by developing improved access points, coordination of river cleanup projects, and providing accurate information on stream flow and other stream characteristics.

Trail and small wild area activities provide trails and related facilities for walking, hiking, horseback riding, and bicycling access to public lands under TVA management. TVA also identifies, preserves, and makes available for compatible public use, lands that contain interesting and unique natural features.

Development of TVA public use areas, a program initiated in 1969, seeks to ensure current and future generations a means of safe, clean, and convenient access to TVA lakes and shorelands through provision of such basic facilities as picnic tables, launching ramps, beaches, and sanitary facilities.

Land Between the Lakes One of the more noteworthy TVA recreational and educational projects is Land Between the Lakes, involving a 170,000-acre (68,850 hectare) peninsula located between TVA's Kentucky Lake and the Corps of Engineers' Lake Barkley in western Kentucky and Tennessee. The peninsula, about 8 miles (13 kilometers) wide and 40 miles (65 kilometers) long, provides a sufficiently large single-ownership area for a unique demonstration of advantages of multiple-use management, emphasizing development of maximum social and economic benefits for current and future generations. It combines highly varied programs of outdoor recreation, environmental education, and resource management. Development of surrounding areas through cooperation with local and state agencies and individuals is also stressed.

Public Recreational Use of TVA Projects Recreational resources associated with TVA developments are readily accessible to large population centers in the Eastern and Midwestern United States. This has prompted heavy recreational use of TVA reservoirs and contiguous lands. In 1947, when collection of recreation-use data for the entire reservoir system was first undertaken, nearly nine million recreation visits were recorded. Since that time, such use has greatly expanded. In 1975, recreation visits to both public and private areas on TVA lakes were estimated at between 65 and 66 million. Of this total, slightly more than 20 million visits were made to areas owned by TVA. These visits included over two million to Land Between the Lakes, over thirteen million to TVA dam reservation areas, two million to reservoir public-use areas, and three million to reservoir incidential-use areas.

Bureau of Reclamation [17,18]

Reclamation projects developed by this bureau of the Department of the Interior include 264 recreation areas at reservoirs and other features in seventeen Western states. They have an aggregate surface water area of over 1,700,000 acres (688,500 hectares) and a total shoreline of over 12,300 miles (19,803 kilometers), together with contiguous lands aggregating more than 4,000,000 acres (1,620,000 hectares). Public recreational use of these areas has grown rapidly from 1950, when a total of 6 million visitor days was recorded, to 1975 when there were 64.7 million visitor days used.

Jurisdiction relative to the engineering aspects and primary project functions, usually is retained by the Bureau of Reclamation. However, except in certain cases, the Bureau does not assume direct responsibility for development and management of recreation. Though recreation is included in project planning, responsibility for recreational development and management is usually transferred to other federal agencies or comparable state or local interests, largely through cooperative agreement, pursuant to the Bureau's authority (Reclamation Act of 1902, as amended) for appropriate utilization of project resources.[9]

The National Park Service assumes responsibility for recreational development and administration on certain Bureau of Reclamation reservoirs which are included among national recreation areas of the National Park System. Recreational administration on reservoirs within or adjacent to national forests is handled by the Forest Service, and on national wildlife refuges by the Fish and Wildlife Service. Qualified state and local agencies with comparable responsibilities on many reservoirs developed by the Bureau of Reclamation include state park and fish and game departments, regional or county parks, water and irrigation districts, and municipal park and recreation departments or water and irrigation authorities.

Matters relevant to the protection and management of fish and wildlife resources of Bureau of Reclamation reservoirs and contiguous lands are handled by the Fish and Wildlife Service, or comparable state organizations, by authority of the Fish and Wildlife Coordination Act of 1934 (P.L. 121; 73rd Cong., 2nd Sess.), as amended.

---

[9] Prior to 1965, recreation development of new projects was included in project plans only as specifically provided for by Congress in individual project-authorizing acts. However, the Federal Water Project Recreation Act of 1965 (P.L. 89-72) provides general authority for recreation on new developments and limited authority to develop and expand recreational opportunities on existing projects.

In addition to recreational resources of its reservoir areas under organized development and management programs, reclamation development creates significant recreational values in its irrigated project land areas. The total area irrigated on all projects in 1975 was 9,300,000 acres (3,766,500 hectares). The recreational values result primarily from the change from a desert type to an irrigation type of environment for fish and wildlife. Important recreational activities benefiting from this change include upland game bird hunting (primarily pheasants), waterfowl hunting, and fishing.

Corps of Engineers [3-6]

The Civil Works Program of the Army Corps of Engineers contributes to outdoor recreation through nationwide construction, operation and maintenance of reservoirs and stabilizing pools, harbors, and waterways, and the protection and improvement of coastal beaches. The original purposes of these projects were generally to provide navigation, flood control, hydroelectric power, water supply for municipal and industrial use or irrigation. Today, however, recreation is given full consideration in the Corps planning and development in order to provide maximum outdoor recreational potential.

The Corps has developed about 426 recreational areas. Eleven million acres (4,455,000 hectares) of land and water and over 40,000 miles (64,400 kilometers) of shoreline are set aside for public use, with about 2,800 separate sites developed for day-use or overnight camping. The Corps operates and manages more than 32,000 campsites, 24,000 picnic sites, and 450 swimming beaches. Several hundred campsites are set aside for use by groups.

Visitation at Corps lakes has increased from 30 million visits in 1952, the first year data was recorded, to 376 million in 1975. The number of visits exceeds that of any other federal agency.

Authority for recreational development and public use of projects developed by the Corps of Engineers is contained primarily in the Flood Control Act of 1944 (P.L. 534; 78th Cong., 2nd Sess.), as amended, and the Fish and Wildlife Coordination Act of 1934 (P.L. 121; 73rd Cong., 2nd Sess.), as amended. Three other acts pertinent to recreational use of these projects are the Land and Water Conservation Fund Act of 1964 (P.L. 88-578), as amended; the Federal Water Project Act of 1965 (P.L. 89-72), as amended; and provisions of Section 404c of the Federal Water Pollution Control Act Amendments of 1972 (P.L. 92-500).

The Corps of Engineers does not have authority to construct water resources projects primarily for recreation use. It cooperates with other interests—federal, state, and local governmental agencies—in relevant recreational planning, development and administration. Many state parks and related recreation areas have resulted from this practice. Water resources development projects within or adjacent to national forests are planned, developed, and administered in cooperation with the Forest Service. Similar cooperation is carried out with the Fish and Wildlife Service on national wildlife refuges and with state game departments on state wildlife management areas. Management of fish and wildlife is the responsibility of the Fish and Wildlife Service or comparable state agencies. However, when these agencies do not carry out these duties, the Corps of Engineers fulfills that purpose.

Basic facilities necessary to public use, enjoyment, health, and safety are usually constructed by the Corps of Engineers. These include access roads, water supply, sanitary facilities, overlooks, signs, campsites, and picnic areas. Additional developments are provided by cooperating governmental agencies or by nonprofit organizations, which are granted long-term leases without monetary consideration. These agencies are also responsible for recreational administration on such areas. Recreational lands not required for public use may be leased to private individuals or organizations for commercial development, including appropriate services not provided by public agencies under terms negotiated with the Corps of Engineers.

SUMMARY

Various opportunities for outdoor recreation available on lands administered by the National Park Service and the Forest Service are augmented by those on other types of federal lands. National wildlife refuges, administered by the Fish and Wildlife Service; public lands administered by the Bureau of Land Management; and reservoirs and contiguous lands under the jurisdiction of the Bureau of Reclamation, Corps of Engineers, and the Tennessee Valley Authority all provide for appropriate recreational uses, consistent with specific agency policies. In large measure, recreational uses are coordinated with multipurpose management programs designed to fulfill the primary objectives and purposes for which each of these five federal agencies was established.

Recreation on lands of the Fish and Wildlife Service, confined almost entirely to wildlife-oriented activities, relates largely to observation and enjoyment of fauna typical of the diversified National Wildlife Refuge System. The Bureau of Land Management administers varied recreational values of its lands as an integral part of its multiple-use program. It accomplishes that objective in two ways. Under appropriate conditions, by authority of certain land laws, specific areas may be transferred to other agencies at different levels of government, or to private control; or such lands may be retained and managed for recreation directly by BLM. In the latter instance BLM provides and maintains facilities and services necessary to enhancement of visitor recreational experience which are consistent with protection of recreational land values. While recreation is viewed as an important adjunct of reservoirs, together with their contiguous lands, developed by the Tennessee Valley Authority, Bureau of Reclamation, and Corps of Engineers—these agencies view recreation as secondary to the primary purpose of such developments. They usually share recreational responsibilities with other agencies.

SELECTED REFERENCES

1 Carstensen, Vernon (ed.): "The Public Lands: Studies in the History of the Public Domain," University of Wisconsin Press, Madison, 1963.
2 Clawson, Marion: "Man and Land in the United States," University of Nebraska Press, Lincoln, 1964.
3 Corps of Engineers, Department of the Army: Personal communication, Dec. 13, 1976.
4 Corps of Engineers, Department of the Army: "Recreation Statistics, 1974," U.S. Government Printing Office, Washington, 1975.
5 Corps of Engineers, Department of the Army: "The Corps in Perspective since 1775" (Paper presented by Lieut. General J. W. Morris, Chief of Engineers, U.S. Army Corps of Engineers), U.S. Government Printing Office, Washington, 1976.
6 Harrison, Jean: The Corps' Stake in Recreation, *Parks and Recreation,* vol. 10, no. 3, March 1975.
7 Hendrix, Jack H.: Recreation in the Tennessee Valley, *Parks and Recreation,* vol. 8, no. 4, April 1973.
8 LeMaster, Dennis C.: The BLM Organic Act, *Journal of Forestry,* vol. 75, no. 2, February 1977.
9 Murphy, Robert: "Wild Sanctuaries, Our National Wildlife Refuges—A Heritage Restored," Dutton, New York, 1968.
10 Outdoor Recreation Resources Review Commission: "Outdoor Recreation for America: A Report to the President and to the Congress by the ORRRC," U.S. Government Printing Office, Washington, 1962.
11 Tennessee Valley Authority: Personal communication, December 1976.
12 U.S. Congress: "Federal Land Policy and Management Act of 1976," (P.L. 94-579), U.S. Government Printing Office, Washington, 1976.
13 U.S. Department of the Interior, Bureau of Land Management: Red Rock Canyon Recreation Lands, *Our Public Lands,* vol. 18, no 1, Winter 1968.
14 U.S. Department of the Interior, Bureau of Land Management: "Summary of BLM's Outdoor Recreation Programs" (Statement by George L. Turcott, Associate Director, Bureau of Land Management, before Subcommittee on Parks and Recreation, Committee on Internal and Insular Affairs, U.S. Senate), Washington, Feb. 5, 1975.
15 U.S. Department of the Interior, Bureau of Land Management: "Bureau of Land Management Recreation Policy" (Instruction memorandum No. 75-543; updated statement of existing recreation policies contained in BLM Manual and in Title 43, Part 6000 of Code of Federal Regulations), Washington, Nov. 7, 1975.

16 U.S. Department of the Interior, Bureau of Land Management: "Public Land Statistics, 1975," U.S. Government Printing Office, Washington, 1976.

17 U.S. Department of the Interior, Bureau of Reclamation: "Federal Reclamation Projects: Water and Land Resource Accomplishments, 1975," Washington, 1976.

18 U.S. Department of the Interior, Bureau of Reclamation: Personal communication, January 1977.

19 U.S. Department of the Interior, Fish and Wildlife Service: Personal communication, November 1976.

Chapter 11

State
and Local
Agencies

Recreational areas administered by various state and local agencies provide recreational opportunities of great importance and considerable diversity. Because state lands are generally larger and have a more truly natural character, they are particularly important to wildland recreation.

FUNCTIONS AND TYPES OF STATE RECREATIONAL LANDS

State recreational lands serve a purpose midway between the generally more remote federal lands and the readily accessible areas administered by municipal, county, and regional or district park agencies, supplementing and accentuating public outdoor recreational opportunities to varying degrees in different sections of the country. They are most important in the more populous states, particularly those with rather small proportions of federal land. In the East, where they are especially vital, they serve as major outdoor recreational outlets.

Large numbers of people find many federal recreational areas too distant for regular or convenient use. On the other hand, in the more readily accessible municipal, county or regional areas, limited size, greater physical development, larger crowds, and the largely modified conditions usually typical of them militate against outdoor interests and activities which require more expansive and less artificial terrain. To a large degree, state recreational lands bridge this gap. They provide reasonably accessible outlets for those who wish a more natural setting than is customarily available in local areas but, for various reasons, do not desire or are not demanding of unmodified, primitive surroundings, or for those who cannot afford the time and expense of a journey to more remote federal lands.

Among state recreational lands are state parks, forests, fish and wildlife areas, historic and cultural sites, areas along roads and highways or related to reservoirs and other public works developments, and miscellaneous natural resource lands. Some of these areas were established and are managed primarily for recreation; on others recreation is coordinated with their primary function.[1] Best known and most heavily used of state recreational areas are those administered by state park agencies; they are given special emphasis later in this chapter.

Geographic location within a state or region is an important consideration in the establishment of state recreational lands, for availability to large numbers of people is one reason for their existence. Many such areas provide for high-density use; in others, absolute maintenance of undistrubed natural conditions is not a primary consideration; and some are sufficiently large and of such character that localized development for large crowds can be undertaken without materially damaging their attractiveness.

Acquisition of State Recreational Lands

Until passage of the Land and Water Conservation Fund Act state acquisition of adequate acreage of land for outdoor recreational purposes was often difficult. There are two reasons for this. First, except for Texas, the states had no public domain lands from which to form areas comparable to the parks, forests, and wildlife refuges established by the federal government.[2] Second, private acquisition of extensive areas of land throughout much of the nation had taken place long before the need for state recreational areas became acute. The nature of development and rising costs

---

[1] Management policy of state forests is generally similar, on a state level, to that of national forests. In some states, particularly in the Great Lakes region and New York, recreation is a primary use of state forest land. Management of state fish and wildlife areas (including refuges, sanctuaries, public hunting areas, fish hatcheries) is not unlike that of areas administered by the U.S. Fish and Wildlife Service.

[2] The residue of original public domain lands is the property of the federal government, subject to sale or other transfer under federal laws; most national parks and national forests were established from the public domain either by congressional action or by Presidential proclamation. Unoccupied and unappropriated lands within the present boundary of Texas, following its annexation, remained as public lands of that state instead of becoming part of the public domain [13].

often made it impossible to reestablish certain areas of prime recreational value under public ownership.

Early state recreational areas, particularly state parks, were acquired largely by the following methods:

1 *By gift from private citizens.* Gifts varied from small contributions of money from numerous individuals, accumulated for the purchases of specific areas, to extensive acreage given by one person.

2 *Transfer of federal lands to state ownership [10].* Outstanding examples of such transfers include the Yosemite Grant, entrusted to the state of California by the federal government in 1864, and Mackinac Island, acquired by the state of Michigan from the federal government in 1885. Originally such transfers had to be accomplished by specific congressional action, but in 1927 Congress passed the Recreational Act,[3] eliminating that necessity in connection with such transfers. Later, additional laws passed by Congress relative to the disposal of surplus federal lands provided further assistance in the development of state recreational systems.

3 *Exchange of school lands [10,11].* Sections 16 and 36 of each township were originally given by the federal government to all but the original thirteen states, as well as the states created from them, and Texas, for support of schools. Many of these school sections were scattered throughout the western national forests. To promote efficient administration of the national forests, Congress authorized the Forest Service to negotiate with the states for the exchange of school sections within national forest boundaries for a consolidated, equivalent national forest area within the same state. Some exchanges of this nature were prompted by the recreational values of lands derived from the Forest Service. Custer State Park in South Dakota was formed largely in this manner [10].

4 *Purchase, through funds derived in a variety of ways.* In some states land for state parks and related recreational areas has been purchased from a percentage of fish and game receipts reserved for that purpose,[4] as provided by the Federal Aid in Wildlife Restoration Act, 1937 (P.L. 415, 75th Cong., 1st Sess.) and the Federal Aid in Fisheries Restoration Act, 1950 (P.L. 681, 81st Cong., 2nd Sess.) Recreational lands have been purchased also from funds derived from tax levy, or by authority of legislative action and appropriation.[5]

Increasingly, bond issues have provided funds for purchase of state recreation lands.[6] This procedure was first justified on the basis of the rela-

[3] The Recreational Act permitted a discount by the Bureau of Land Management of up to 70 percent for land only; timber involved had to be acquired at full value. This act also permitted a 50 percent discount for land and timber by the General Services Administration.
[4] An important source of funds in Missouri, Nebraska, and Kansas [10].
[5] A number of state parks in Iowa, Massachusetts, and Washington owe their origin to funds provided by special legislative appropriation [10].
[6] The states of New York, Illinois, New Hampshire, Rhode Island, and California were pioneers in financing purchase of land for state recreational areas [11].

tion of outdoor recreation to public health and welfare, but in later years the general public showed an increasing willingness to invest in outdoor recreation by such means. Today many states have either bond financing or the authority to issue bonds to finance outdoor recreation programs [8]. However, some states (e.g., Indiana) do not view this method of fund raising for recreational purposes with favor.[7]

5   *Land and Water Conservation Fund.* Since 1965 the Land and Water Conservation Fund Act, as amended, has provided a most important source of funds for acquisition of recreational lands, as well as for development of recreational facilities and services, not only for the states but also for their various political subdivisions [16,17]. The nature and administration of the Land and Water Conservation Fund is outlined in Chapter 7.

Comprehensive State Recreational Land Data

Authoritative long-term data on state recreational lands (number of areas, aggregate acreage, public use, personnel, funds, costs, revenues) are important in assessing recreational values of different types of such areas, in evaluating trends in public recreational demand and use, and in comparing these values and trends to those of recreational lands administered by other public and private agencies. Such data has been collected specifically for state parks since 1941 (Table 11-1). Similar data for all types of state recreational lands has been developed as a result of surveys conducted by the Bureau of Outdoor Recreation,[8] following establishment of that agency in 1962.

The Bureau of Outdoor Recreation Survey[8] for 1962 [14] indicated that over 200 agencies were involved in management of state lands for various forms of recreation; such fragmented responsibility implies the difficulties encountered in collection of such comprehensive data. The 1962 survey also noted that there were about 30,000 state recreational areas of various types, ranging from small highway waysides to larger state parks and the, generally, more extensive wildlife and forest lands, with an aggregate area of nearly 50,000,000 acres (20,250,000 hectares). Public recreational use of all these lands in 1962 was estimated to exceed 400 million visits, about 90 percent representing day-use, and with state parks accounting for about 70 percent of that total. Also in 1962, nearly 30,000 employees were directly concerned in some way with recreation on all types of state land, about 60 percent being employed year-round; in addition, more than 10,000 employees were concerned with recreation on a part-time basis. Total expenditures in 1962, including operation and maintenance (salaries and wages; supplies and

[7] However, the Indiana Division of State Parks will assume responsibility for management of lands purchased by individual counties, through county bond issues, for state park purposes.

[8] As noted in Chapter 7, the Bureau of Outdoor Recreation was reconstructed in 1978 as the Heritage Conservation and Recreation Service.

equipment) and capital outlays (land acquisition and development) totalled $225,000,000.

Data for 1972 [15] indicated that the states managed almost 42,000,000 acres (17,010,000 hectares) of recreational land of various types. Public use data are not noted in the report but a rough estimate of about 700 million visits to all state recreational lands can be made by a comparison with the number of state park visits at about the same time.[9] The number of employees also continued at a high level in 1972, with year-round personnel being slightly in the majority.[10] Most significantly, there was a considerable increase in state expenditures for recreation between 1962 and 1972. Total expenditures in 1972 were nearly $614,000,000, almost three times greater than total expenditures a decade earlier. In large measure, this increase in total expenditures reflects the impact of the Land and Water Conservation Fund. Further, between 1960 and 1970, states passed bond issues for outdoor recreational land and facility development totalling nearly 2.8 billion dollars.

STATE PARK SYSTEMS

Except for municipal areas, state parks have a longer history than any other category of recreational lands, dating from the establishment of the Yosemite Grant in 1864 (Chapter 3). However, state parks did not begin to assume the position of importance they occupy today until public interest in outdoor recreation and protection of environmental interests developed sufficient social and political force to prompt widespread establishment of such areas.

Today every one of the fifty states has a state park system. These areas are managed for the protection, preservation and public enjoyment of the scenic, geological, biological, historic and prehistoric, and recreational resources characteristic of the various states. Though they vary widely in type and size, they may be logically grouped into three categories.

1 *Utilitarian areas* (mostly classes I, high-density, and II, general, though other classes may be included). Developed primarily to foster physically active recreation (swimming, boating, picnicking, camping, winter sports, and related activities); generally without significant natural, historic or prehistoric interests. Many state parks are in this category.

2 *Significant areas* (mostly classes III, natural environment; IV, outstanding natural areas; V, primitive; and VI, historic and cultural sites). Contain unique or important geological, biological, archeological, or histor-

---

[9] Assuming that state park visits continued as 70 percent of the total number of visits to all state recreational areas, as noted in 1962, 70 percent of 700 million is approximately the number of state park visits in 1972 (Table 11-1).

[10] Relationship of year-round and seasonal employees varies with agency; for instance, the majority of state park employees are seasonal (Table 11-1).

Table 11-1 : Comparative Summary of State Park Statistics

	1941(a)	1950	1955	1960	1970	1975
Areas: number	1,335	1,725	2,034	2,664	3,425	3,804
acres (1,000)	4,260	4,657	5,086	5,602	8,555	9,838
hectares (1,000)	1,725	1,886	2,060	2,269	3,464	3,984
Attendance: total (1,000)	97,489	114,291	183,188(b)	259,001	482,536	565,715(c)
day (1,000)	94,571	108,212	169,212	169,123	431,964	465,302
overnight (1,000)	2,918	6,079	11,057(b)	20,569(b)	50,572	51,488
cabins, hotels (1,000)	(d)	1,223	1,576	1,697	2,920	3,107
organization camps (1,000)	(d)	1,480	1,697	2,235	1,910	5,731
tent, trailer camps (1,000)	(d)	3,377	7,650	16,217	45,742	40,436
Personnel: total	5,486	10,626	13,637	17,537	34,334	44,929
seasonal	2,856	6,435	7,980	10,125	21,021	26,845
year-round	2,630	4,191	5,657	7,412	13,313	18,083
professional	(d)	401	373	731	3,391	6,186(e)
Expenditures: total ($1,000)	10,022(c)	36,399(b)	55,093(b)	87,373	385,752(b)	648,905(c)
salaries, wages ($1,000)	4,186	13,622	22,673	37,137	121,546	218,101
supplies, equipment ($1,000)	2,756	7,738	11,351	19,132	65,280	98,993
lands ($1,000)	1,560	2,651	5,523	12,077	71,685	150,076
improvements ($1,000)	1,449	12,364	15,293	19,026	125,794	167,395
grants to other agencies ($1,000)	–	–	–	–	16,155	55,459
other ($1,000)	–	–	–	–	8,749	6,925

Funds available for expenditure:						
total ($1,000)	10,477	52,283	69,075	131,419	619,194	1,467,313
appropriations ($1,000)	7,093	28,421	43,382	69,294	259,835	483,100
bond issues ($1,000)	–	–	–	–	–	540,318
L&W Conservation Fund ($1,000)	–	–	–	–	–	76,668
other ($1,000)	3,384	28,862	25,693	61,794	359,259	267,227
Operations revenue ($1,000)	3,072	6,646	13,817	22,641	70,956	115,406
Land acquisition: total (acres)	(d)	62,042	70,148	68,326	1,100,148	402,600
(hectares)	(d)	25,127	28,410	21,672	445,560	163,053

(a) Includes many state forests, wildlife refuges, waysides, and related areas not administered by state park agencies, that have not been included in subsequent tabulations.

(b) Includes data from which detailed breakdown is not available.

(c) Total does not equal sum of component parts; some agencies reported no breakdown of total.

(d) Data unavailable.

(e) Includes year-round (4,755) and seasonal (1,431); does not include about 800 consultants and consulting firms.

Sources: "State Park Statistics, 1956–1961," National Park Service, Division of Resources Planning, Washington, 1957–1961; "Statistical Abstracts of the United States, 1976," Bureau of the Census, Washington, 1976; "Parks and Recreation, August 1971," National Recreation and Parks Association, Arlington, Va.; and "State Park Statistics, 1975," National Recreation and Parks Association, National Society for Park Resources, Arlington, Va., 1977 (NRPA data copyrighted).

ical features typical of a particular state. Such state parks are designed to foster public understanding of the primary interests of such areas; physical facilities are usually held to a minimum. State parks such as Ginkgo Petrified Forest (Washington), Spring Mill (Indiana), and Valley Forge (Pennsylvania) fall in this category.

3 *Scenic or dual-purpose areas* (mostly class II, general, though other classes may be included). Owing to their larger size, these often combine the qualities of the two former types. Generally they offer opportunity for various outdoor recreational activities (hiking, camping, horseback riding, swimming, boating, and related activities) in a scenically attractive and usually natural setting. Necessary physical facilities are developed with regard to preservation of scenic beauty and natural environmental interests. Such state parks as Moran (Washington), Fall Creek Falls (Tennessee), Mattheisson (Illinois), Turkey Run (Indiana), Bear Mountain (New York), and Custer (South Dakota) are in this category.

Administration of State Parks

State park systems generally operate within bounds of well-defined policies which, although they vary in detail owing to differences in local conditions, are somewhat similar to the policy of the National Park Service, though on a state rather than national level [11]. Various state park policy statements indicate:

1 A definite recognition of the value of preserving areas containing typical state scenery

2 A definite recognition of the value of preserving significant historical, geological, or biological interests characteristic of the state

3 That development of state parks should be carried out under a carefully considered plan, and that their public use should be governed by regulations which will ensure perpetuation of the values which make them interesting

4 That, consistent with the preservation of inherent interests, development of state parks should be guided by the policy that, if such development is not compatible with public use of certain state parks, other areas adapted to such needs should be provided

5 That a definite minimum size limit exists for state parks having interesting or unique scenic values

6 That, wherever possible, accessibility to centers of population should be given adequate consideration in selection of various types of state park lands, particularly those designed for high-density use

7 That, while the greater effort will be made for citizens of a particular state, the interests of out-of-state visitors should not be neglected

Over the years state park organizations have assumed positions of importance equal to other state agencies in state government. Inadequacies of state park organizations which often typified early years of their existence, if, indeed, such organizations existed at all, have been largely remedied.

Most state park organizations now operate upon a higher professional level of efficiency. There are, of course, exceptions.

However, responsibility for state park administration is variously assigned in different states [5,11,14]. Local needs, together with historical and political considerations have largely determined the relation of state park organizations to other agencies of state government. Although there are differences in specific details, in most states, state parks are administered by one of two or more separate divisions within a major department concerned with management of several other natural resources (forests, fish and wildlife, land, waters).[11] Such organization reflects the close affinity between outdoor recreation and other land values. The importance of recreation to economics is inferred from the close relation that exists in some states between state park departments and state agencies concerned with economic development or tourism.[12] In Oregon inclusion of the Division of State Parks in the Highway Department is considered conducive of efficient and economical maintenance of state park areas by existing highway department personnel skilled in and equipped for such activity. A variation of this plan exists in Rhode Island where the Division of Parks and Recreation is under the Department of Public Works. State parks in a number of states are administered by an autonomous department independent of other state agencies.[13]

It should be noted, however, that park agencies operated as adjunct divisions of larger nonrelated agencies often suffer loss of identity and subordination of goals to the overpowering drive of the major department. For example, park lands administered by highway organizations are likely to be good sources of inexpensive rights-of-way for new road construction.

In some states certain specific state parks, or areas closely related to them, are separately administered by recognized historical, scientific, or educational bodies, or by special commissions established particularly for such purposes[14] As a result, administration of state park areas in some states is entrusted to more than one agency.

[11] E.g., Alabama, Alaska, California, Colorado, Connecticut, Hawaii, Illinois, Indiana, Iowa, Kansas, Maryland, Massachusetts, Michigan, Minnesota, Montana, Nebraska, Nevada, New Jersey, New York, North Carolina, Ohio, Pennsylvania, South Dakota, Tennessee, Texas, Utah, Vermont, Virginia, West Virginia, and Wisconsin.

[12] E.g., Arkansas, New Hampshire, Oklahoma, and South Carolina.

[13] E.g., Arizona, Delaware, Florida, Georgia, Idaho, Kentucky, Louisiana, Maine, Mississippi, Missouri, New Mexico, North Dakota, Washington, and Wyoming.

[14] Examples include the State Historical Society of Colorado, Franklin D. Roosevelt Warm Springs Memorial Commission in Georgia, Kansas State Historical Society, Baxter State Park Authority in Maine, two specific reservation commissions in Massachusetts, the Mackinac Island State Park Commission in Michigan, Minnesota Historical Society, Palisades Interstate Park Commission in New Jersey, East Hudson Parkway Authority in New York, Division of Historical Sites of the North Carolina Department of Archives and History, State Historical Society of North Dakota, Ohio Historical Society, Will Rogers Memorial Commission in Oklahoma, two independent commissions in Pennsylvania, and the Wisconsin State Historical Society.

State Park Statistics

Earliest reliable data concerning state parks is available for 1941. Trends in state park administration and public use since that time (Table 11-1) indicate the importance of state parks in outdoor recreation and the increasingly vital role such areas are destined to play in the future. Further, in the absence of equally reliable long-term data on other types of state lands used for public recreation, state park statistics serve as a barometer of public interest in the recreational values of other state lands. Striking changes in all aspects of state park development took place between 1960 and 1970; these changes can largely be attributed to the effect of the Land and Water Conservation Fund Act (see Chapters 5 and 7).

A summary of statistical data in Table 11-1 reveals the following:

Areas and Acreage. In 1975 the number of state parks was nearly three times that of 1941, having increased from 1,335 to 3,804. During the same period the aggregate area of state parks more than doubled—from 4,260,000 acres (1,725,000 hectares) to 9,838,000 acres (3,984,000 hectares).

Public Use. Attendance in 1975 (565,715,000 visits) was nearly six times that in 1941 (97,489,000 visits).

Although state park attendance has always consisted primarily of day visits, the percentage of day visits declined from 97 percent of total attendance in 1941 to 82 percent in 1975. Campers have always accounted for the majority of overnight visits and there has been a notable increase in the percentage of total overnight use by campers over the years—from nearly 55 percent in 1950 to about 92 percent in 1975. This highlights the growing problem of accomodating the increasing number of campers in many state parks designed for overnight use.

Personnel   Rapid increase in the number and aggregate area of state parks, and general expansion of their public use, is reflected in increased personnel. State parks had more than eight times as many employees in 1975 than in 1941. Since the busiest period in most state parks is during the summer months, seasonal employees have always outnumbered those employed throughout the year. However, while the number of seasonal employees has greatly increased, their number in relation to total staff has increased only about 10 percent—from a little over 50 percent in 1941 to slightly less than 60 percent in 1975.

Statistical data on personnel tell only part of the story. Opportunities for meaningful careers with state park agencies, once dubious by comparison with better established federal and municipal organizations, have greatly improved. Conditions typical of early years which were largely responsible for low salaries, job insecurity, and lack of public and official recognition of personnel initiative, have been altered. Complex social, economic, and biological problems have developed as a result of expanding use of state parks; solution of these problems has demanded continually higher standards of performance in planning, development, protection, and improvement of public understanding and responsibility in the care of these areas. These demands have placed a premium on professional competence in a variety of fields relating to state park management. As a result, the number of both seasonal and year-round employees with varied types of professional expertise in recreational land management has steadily increased. State park employees trained in some professional capacity (engineers, architects, landscape architects, foresters, park planners, naturalists, historians, interpreters, recreation leaders) were more than fifteen times greater in 1975 than in 1950.

Costs and Revenues Sizeable increases in costs and revenues since 1941 are reflections of public interest in expanding recreational opportunities in state park systems, including acceptance of accompanying higher costs.

Total state park expenditures in 1975 were nearly sixty five times greater than in 1941. When specific details are related to total expenditures it will be noted that relative expenditures for employee salaries dropped from 41 percent in 1941 to about 33 percent in 1975. There was also a corresponding drop in the relative amount spent on supplies and equipment between 1941 and 1975. However, expenditures for land increased from 15 percent in 1941 to about 23 percent in 1975, and expenditures for improvements to state parks increased from 14 percent in 1941 to over 26 percent in 1975.

The total amount of funds available for expenditure was nearly 140 times greater in 1975 than in 1941. The breakdown of these figures reveals that financial support of state parks from legislative appropriations dropped from 67 percent in 1941 to nearly 33 percent in 1975, but that support from other sources (including bond issues and L&WC Funds) increased from 32 percent in 1941 to over 67 percent in 1975. These changes, in part, reflect the effect of financial support provided by the federal government through provisions of the Land and Water Conservation Fund Act of 1965.

It is also significant that revenues from operations[15] in 1941 were about 30 percent of total expenditures, while in 1975 they were but 7 percent of the total.

There has been a striking rise in the cost per state park visit since 1941, due largely to inflationary trends relfected in increases in operational and

---

[15] Operational revenue includes returns from concessions, entrance and parking fees and related charges. Revenue is also derived in certain instances from such sources as special leases (air beacons, radio and television towers erected on state park lands) and sale of special products (sand, gravel, coal, salvage timber).

capital expenditures. Net *total cost* per visit was about twelve times greater in 1975 than in 1941, rising from 7 to 90 cents.[16] However, net *operational cost* per visit has not climbed as rapidly; it was about nine times greater in 1975 than in 1941, rising from approximately 4 to 35 cents per visit.[17]

Land Acquisition The aggregate area of state park lands more than doubled between 1941 and 1975. In large part, this increase reflects the effect of land acquisition resulting from assistance provided by the Land and Water Conservation Fund since 1965.

RECREATIONAL LANDS OF LOCAL GOVERNMENT AGENCIES

Cities and towns, counties, and district, regional, or metropolitan park authorities administer various types of recreational areas that are vital to outdoor recreation.[18] They are readily available for use for short periods of time—a few hours, a week end—which can readily be coordinated with job and other responsibilities by individuals, families, and special groups. The opportunities they provide range from sports to nature study and cultural interests. They are especially adapted to simple forms of outdoor recreation within the interests and capabilities of people of both sexes, all ages, varying family obligations, and different social, cultural, and economic background. To many people who lack time, money, and experience necessary for recreational use of more distant wild lands, they offer the major—often the only—contact with the outdoors. In certain instances, enjoyment of these areas develops interests that may eventually lead to recreation on wild lands. The need for conservation of gasoline, as well as the increasing cost of motor fuel, also emphasizes the value of recreational areas near where most people live and work.

[16] Total operational (salaries and wages plus supplies and equipment) and capital (lands and improvements) expenditures less total revenue from operations, prorated among total visits.

[17] Total operational expenditures (salaries and wages plus supplies and equipment) less total revenue from operations, prorated among total visits.

[18] Municipal parks are usually socio-activity–oriented, artifically developed, high-density recreational lands; they have a different management philosophy from that of most wild land recreational areas. However, many county, district, regional, or metropolitan park systems, established in the rural countryside near large cities, include areas of extensive size typified by largely natural conditions. Their management emphasizes the protection and preservation of natural features, thus enhancing recreational opportunities for both city and rural residents. For example, the Hennepin County Park Reserve District, near Minneapolis-St. Paul, Minnesota, embraces about 19,000 acres (7,700 hectares) of land, including several major areas ranging in size from 1,000 to 5,000 acres (405 to 2,025 hectares).

In addition, certain public recreation activities are permitted on municipal power reservoirs, city forests, and, in some cases, municipal watersheds. Areas controlled by private philanthropic organizations may also be available for public recreation.

Primarily because of the foregoing factors, expansion of localized recreational acreage is recognized as one of the more critical of today's outdoor recreational needs. Studies by the Bureau of Outdoor Recreation (reconstituted as The Heritage Conservation and Recreation Service in 1978) have been addressed to this problem. Moreover, several National Recreation Areas administered by the National Park Service have been established near a number of large cities by means of funds provided by the federal government [4,17,18].

Recreational areas within and near large population centers also aid in preservation of wild land interests. They not only serve as recreational outlets for vast numbers of people but, in providing for many interests and activities inappropriate on more truly wild or natural areas, they reduce public pressure for ill-advised developments on wild lands. This is particularly important where administrative policy emphasizes preservation of unique values, as in national parks. Thus, recreational workers who deal primarily with wild lands should understand the important role of recreational areas of various local agencies—and vice versa. Neither group stands alone. Though operating on somewhat different administrative philosophies, recreation workers on wild land and those on more highly developed areas administered by local agencies should strive for proper coordination of effort which yields many reciprocal benefits.

In the broad view, small neighborhood parks with minimum facilities for simple activities are as important as more extensive, more famous, and more distant recreational lands. Properly coordinated, each type of recreational area serves particular outdoor recreational functions. Each supplies particular needs for different people at different times, supplementing, accentuating, and protecting the basic values of other areas. By planning for adequate distribution of different types of recreational areas best able to accomodate different recreational interests and activities the maximum number of people can be served at minimum cost and with minimum damage to environmental values. Also, problems related to conflicts of recreational interests of different groups will be minimized.

Local Recreational Area Statistics

Completely reliable statistics on areas administered by local park and recreation agencies are unavailable. Collection of such information is a difficult matter. The agencies concerned are too numerous, too widely dispersed, and too varied in size; also, they usually lack time to collect, organize and report such data. Further, charges are not applied to most recreational uses of such lands so automatic accounting of visitor patronage is minimized.

However, as noted in Chapter 3, the number of municipalities having public parks accelerated rapidly during the early part of the century; this

trend has continued. Recent years have also witnessed a change in administrative emphasis, from largely passive to a more logical combination of
passive and vigorous activities.

Though incomplete, earliest reliable data on city and county parks
were collected in 1925-1926 [20]. At that time the aggregate area of such
parks in the United States was noted as about 316,000 acres (128,000 hectares); by 1970 the aggregate area had increased almost five-fold [12]. The
number of city and county parks, first noted for 1950 as slightly more than
17,000, had exceeded 31,000 by 1970 [12]. In 1972 nearly 11 million acres
(4,455,000 hectares) of land were being administered by various local agencies for recreation [15].

Some idea of the magnitude of public use of city and county parks can
be deduced from an estimate made in 1938 which indicated that total patronage exceeded 600 million visits annually [20]. More recent data [12]
indicated that for twenty six of the more popular facilities best adapted to
taking attendance[19] the number of users in 1955 totaled nearly 300 million;
by 1960 use of the same type of facilities had increased to 415 million.

Increases in the total number of city and county park employees over
the years has been accompanied by increases in both full-time and part-
time professional personnel.[20] Total professional personnel increased from
slightly more than 24,000 in 1940 to nearly 90,000 by 1970; during the same
period the number of professionals employed full-time increased from
about 3,500 to over 17,000 [12].

Operational and capital costs of city and courty parks has also mounted [12]. Expenditures for operation increased from nearly $26,000,000 in
1940 to over $600,000,000 by 1965. During the same period capital expendi-
tures rose from $5,000,000 to over $290,000,000. Public appropriations, derived primarily from local property taxes, continue to be the major source
of funds for support of parks administered by local government agencies
but because of the increasing importance of such areas local revenue
sources have been augmented by various types of state and federal grants,
including those from the Land and Water Conservation Fund [4]. Also
significant is the fact that $450,000,000 was obtained from bond issues
between 1965 and 1972 for support of local recreational programs.

Finally, recent years have witnessed an increasing amount of attention
on the part of localized park agencies in development of recreational opportunities for special groups (handicapped, low-income individuals, senior cit-

---

[19] Included athletic fields, stadiums, and related facilities, beaches and pools, picnic
areas, campgrounds, winter sports areas, boating facilities, arboretums, nature trails, zoos,
museums, and outdoor theaters.

[20] Includes engineers, architects, landscape architects, park planners, naturalists, historians, interpreters, recreation leaders, security personnel.

izens), as well as an extension of cooperation between park and school authorities. In the latter instance, school facilities are utilized for public recreation at times when they are not required in educational programs [4].

SUMMARY

State recreational lands fall midway between the readily accessible and generally more highly developed municipal parks and federal areas which usually are undeveloped, as well as almost inaccessible for many people. There are many types of state recreational lands, including: state parks, forests, wildlife areas, historic and cultural sites, areas bordering highways and those around public works developments, and miscellaneous natural resource lands. Some have been established primarily for recreational use; in others recreational uses are coordinated with their primary purposes.

In the past, acquisition of land for state recreation areas was often difficult but in recent years citizens of many states have become more willing to finance purchase of land for recreation through bond issues. Grants from the Land and Water Conservation Fund and related sources have also favored such purchases. In 1972 the states managed nearly 42,000,000 acres (17,010,000 hectares) of recreational land, the estimated number of visits was about 700 million, and total expenditure for recreation, including land acquisition, was nearly $614,000,000.

State parks are the best known and most heavily used of state recreational lands. Though state park organization policy is similar to that of the National Park Service, there are many variations ranging from highly organized programs, as in California, to custodial holding operations. Statistical data on state parks have been collected since 1941. These data indicate a constant increase in the number and aggregate area of state parks, amount of public use, number of employees and cost of operation. In 1975 there were about 3,800 state parks with an aggregate area of nearly 10 million acres (4,050,000 hectares); their combined annual public use was over 565 million visits.

One of today's critical needs is increased recreational lands administered by municipal, county, and regional or district park authorities. Such lands, located near where most people live and work, are readily available for short periods of time and provide recreational outlets for people who are unable to travel great distances to many of our wildland recreational areas. They also provide for many types of recreational interests and activities which may be inappropriate on recreational lands where preservation of natural conditions is a primary concern.

For various reasons, completely reliable statistics on recreational areas administered by local agencies are lacking. However, estimates indicate that public recreational use of such lands exceeds that of all state and federal areas combined.

SELECTED REFERENCES

1 Buechner, Robert D.: State Park Systems, *Parks and Recreation,* vol. 11, no. 7, July 1976.

2 Carstensen, Vernon (ed.): "The Public Lands: Studies in the History of the Public Domain," University of Wisconsin Press, Madison, 1963.

3 Clawson, Marion: "Man and Land in the United States," University of Nebraska Press, Lincoln, 1964.

4 Lancaster, Roger A.: Municipal Services, *Parks and Recreation,* vol. 11, no. 7, July 1976.

5 National Conference on State Parks, National Recreation and Park Association: "1967 State Park Statistics," Washington, June 1968.

6 National Recreation Association: "Recreation and Park Yearbook, Mid-Century Edition: A Review of Local and County Recreation and Park Developments, 1900–1950," New York, 1951.

7 National Recreation Association: "1956 Recreation and Park Yearbook: A Nationwide Inventory of Public Recreation and Park Services of Local, County, State and Federal Agencies for the Year Ending December 31, 1960," New York, 1961.

8 National Recreation and Park Association: "Recreation and Park Yearbook, 1966," Washington, 1967.

9 National Recreation and Park Association, National Society of Park Resources: "State Park Statistics, 1975," Arlington, Va. 1977.

10 Nelson, Beatrice: "State Recreation," National Conference on State Parks, Washington, 1928.

11 Tilden, Freeman: "The State Parks: Their Meaning in American Life," Knopf, New York, 1962.

12 U.S. Department of Commerce, Bureau of the Census: "Statistical Abstracts of the United States, 1976," U.S. Government Printing Office, Washington, 1976.

13 U.S. Department of the Interior, Bureau of Land Management: "Landmarks in Public Land Management," U.S. Government Printing Office, Washington, 1963.

14 U.S. Department of the Interior, Bureau of Outdoor Recreation, Department of Research and Education: "State Outdoor Recreation Statistics, 1962," U.S. Government Printing Office, Washington, 1963.

15 U.S. Department of the Interior, Bureau of Outdoor Recreation: "Outdoor Recreation: A Legacy for America" U.S. Government Printing Office, Washington, 1973.

16 U.S. Department of the Interior, Bureau of Outdoor Recreation: "Administrative and Legislative Directives of the Bureau of Outdoor Recreation," U.S. Government Printing Office, Washington, January 1975.

17 U.S. Department of the Interior, Bureau of Outdoor Recreation: "The Bureau of Outdoor Recreation: Focal Point for Outdoor America," U.S. Government Printing Office, Washington, 1975.

18 U.S. Department of the Interior, Bureau of Outdoor Recreation: *Outdoor Recreation Action, Fall 1976,* U.S. Government Printing Office, Washington, 1976.

19 U.S. Department of the Interior, National Park Service: "State Park Statistics, 1956–1961," Washington, June, 1957–1962.

20 U.S. Department of Labor, Bureau of Labor Statistics: "Park and Recreation Areas in the United States," U.S. Government Printing Office, Washington, 1928.

Recreation on Private Lands

Though public lands serve as the major base for outdoor recreation, they cannot continually accommodate all rapidly growing recreational demands. For many reasons, private lands will play an increasingly vital role in outdoor recreation.

IMPORTANCE OF PRIVATE LANDS FOR RECREATION

Approximately 60 percent of our land is privately owned [6]. Large portions of private land are more readily accessible from population centers than much of our public land and, thus, are available to large numbers of people. Estimates indicate that at least 50 percent of recreational opportunity is directly attributable to the private sector [16].

Recreational use of private land is highly diversified. It embraces a wide variety of activities, facilities, and types of land. Included are areas important for hunting and fishing, privately operated campgrounds and trailer parks, organization camps, privately owned summer or winter homes, and highly developed commercial resorts with related enterprises providing relevant needs of patrons. Also involved are privately owned agricultural and industrial forest lands, including dude ranches and vacation farms and tree-farm parks. Lands owned or otherwise controlled by scientific, educational, philanthropic, and outdoor-oriented or conservation-oriented organizations are also important, as are quasi-public lands such as those of Indian reservations and The Nature Conservancy.

In many cases recreational use of private lands offers opportunity for profit, as well as other benefits, to landowners. Many privately owned recreational enterprises are full-time undertakings; others operate part-time or seasonally. Some exist wholly on private land; others depend largely upon interests of nearby recreation areas on public lands, or are developed on public land by agreement with public land management agencies.

A number of government agencies[1] and various private organizations provide assistance in developing the recreational potential of private land and in the solution of many problems related to such developments [9,10, 13-20].

RELATIONSHIP OF PRIVATE AND PUBLIC LANDS FOR RECREATION

Many recreational areas on public land are overcrowded and overused. Overcrowding causes problems of public health and safety, vandalism, antisocial behavior, and conflicts of interest between different groups of recreationists. Overcrowding also promotes public pressure for development of facilities and activities which may not be appropriate to certain types of recreational areas on public lands. In particular, fragile values in areas of unique quality are endangered by overcrowding and development of inappropriate facilities and activities. Recreational use of private lands aids in relieving such situations.

A wide variety of outdoor recreational needs can be satisfied on private lands, some of which are better adapted to certain outdoor recreational uses than public lands. Private lands, particularly those where natural conditions have already been modified or where maintenance of natural conditions is not a major concern, are often the most logical sites for the more elaborate facilities (hotels and motels, trailer parks, sophisticated campgrounds). Thus, disturbance of high-quality recreational values of nearby

---

[1] Federal agencies include the Heritage Conservation and Recreation Service (see Chapter 7), the National Park Service and Fish and Wildlife Service of the Department of the Interior; Forest Service of the Department of Agriculture; the Economic Development Administration of the Department of Commerce; and the Small Business Administration. The Food and Agriculture Act of 1962 (P.L. 87-703), as amended, provides for the cooperation of the Department of Agriculture, through the Rural Areas Development Program, in developing the recreational potential of agricultural lands. Principal agencies so involved include the Soil Conservation Service, Agricultural Stabilization and Conservation Service, and Farmers Home Administration.

public lands may be minimized. In addition, the cost of these more elaborate facilities and services is borne by patrons through charges for their use, benefiting the local economy and freeing public funds for achievement of management objectives relevant to protection of high-quality recreational values for long-term public use and enjoyment.

FACTORS INFLUENCING RECREATIONAL USE OF PRIVATE LANDS

Important factors which influence use of private lands for outdoor recreation include:

1 The desire of landowners to earn a profit, either from some form of exclusive recreational operation (resorts) or from a part-time adjunct of some major land management program (fees for varied outdoor recreational privileges on farms, ranches, industrial forests)

2 Provision of facilities, services, and recreational opportunities adapted to needs of special groups (hunting, outdoor, or boating clubs; fraternal, church, union, or youth organizations; employees of large industrial enterprises)

3 Philanthropic programs of protection, management, and use which, although in the public interest, typify various types of land not administered by public agencies (privately organized scientific, educational, and conservation organizations)

4 Provision of public recreational facilities and services for public relations purposes, or the improvement of the "image," of an industry (industrial forest lands and tree-farm parks)

PRIVATELY OWNED COMMERCIAL RESORTS

Commercial resorts on private land are the oldest and most familiar type of outdoor recreational operations (p.38). They range from simple developments, sometimes but a few acres with a campground, to elaborate, extensive areas with varied types of overnight accommodations, related food services, entertainment, and subsidiary recreational facilities. Most commercial operations are conducted by individuals or families, though the more extensive are generally controlled by companies or corporations. They exist in all sections of the country but are most common in regions where climate is favorable for a maximum period of productive, long-term operation. Practically all offer a variety of scenic or related interests (mountains, deserts, ocean or lake shores, regions of prime hunting, fishing, water-related activities, or winter sports), and many are near well-known public recreational areas, such as national and state parks and forests. Most private enterprises of this sort rarely own, or lease, more than the minimum area necessary for housing and related physical facilities for their patrons. Certain recreational facilities may be provided (swimming pools, tennis courts, golf courses), but principal attractions and the site of most recreational activities of visitors are nearby peripheral lands which, in most cases, are publicly owned.

Many recreational facilities and services on public land are provided by private individuals or firms operating as concessionaires through contractual agreements with land managing agencies [16]. In some cases total investment of facilities is assumed by private parties; in others facilities are constructed by government for lease to private operators.

Private investment and management eliminates the need for public financing. Since government agencies are not geared for such activities many facilities and services desired by the public can be more easily provided and conducted with greater efficiency by private operators, with a percentage of the profits reverting to the public agency. However, difficulties may arise if differences in objectives develop between the concessionaire and the agency, the seasonal nature of certain recreation businesses reduces profits or results in financial troubles, or annoyances result from necessary agency supervision to ensure acceptable standards of service. In addition, since concessionaires do not hold title to the land, they may have difficulty in obtaining loans for their operation and they may also be affected by changes in public policies.

OUTDOOR RECREATION ON AGRICULTURAL LAND

Private agricultural land is of increasing importance for outdoor recreation. Attractive, well-managed farmland offers opportunity for many types of recreational interests and activities which, if properly developed and operated, can provide an important source of supplementary farm income through charges made for fishing and hunting, in season, as well as picnicking, camping, swimming and boating, and holidays at vacation farms and dude ranches.

Good agricultural practices are productive of conditions conducive to adequate numbers of fish and game species. Many farms are adjacent to public lakes or rivers, or have fishing streams running through them. In others, ponds and artificial lakes, developed primarily for other purposes, are stocked and managed by the landowners for fishing. To prevent overcrowding, public patronage of such privately stocked ponds, as well as privately controlled fishing spots on public waters, can be regulated by charging a fee, which many fishing enthusiasts are willing to pay. Agricultural land also provides habitat for many kinds of birds and mammals, particularly waterfowl and upland game birds. Although game species are public property, landowners have the right to control access to their property; thus, payment of fees to owners is for the privilege of access to and use of the area for hunting rather than for any game which may be secured.

Even if the landowners do not elect to make charges for hunting or fishing privileges on their land, control of such activities serves to reduce damage to private property.

The extent of such activities,[2] as well as the nature of landowner charges and restrictions, depends upon hunting and fishing pressure and consequent demand for privileges, as well as the nature and abundance of fish and game species. Most agricultural landowners, aware of the potential of supplementary income, work closely with state game departments for the improvement of local game populations by following prescribed agricultural practices, habitat improvement, and propagation of game species. Groups of properties are often managed cooperatively. In some cases lodging, meals, equipment, supplies, and services are provided.

Farm interests and activities themselves have assumed recreational significance, largely as a result of urbanization of our population and lack of knowledge of how our food is produced. This has resulted in a growing number of vacation farms and dude ranches catering to paying city guests. Their operations may be strictly commercial, with guests merely as observers, or the guests may assume varying degrees of responsibility in actual farm or ranch tasks. The dude ranch concept has the longer history, since it is related to the romanticism of the "Old West," which began to decline about the turn of the century. Thus, it is more firmly established and better defined than that of vacation farms, and supports several associations which have been in existence for many years.

Retention of rural open space as greenbelts within and adjacent to rapidly expanding urban centers is important in regional planning. The beauty of a well-managed rural countryside is an important aspect of our environment, and it is basic to enjoyment of the outdoors.

Difficulties

Development of recreational opportunities on privately owned agricultural land is a venture that should not be approached carelessly. Like any business enterprise it requires special abilities, interests, and aptitudes, and it demands attention to detail. Also, in granting permission to use the land, with or without payment of a fee, the owner assumes certain definite responsibilities. To most agricultural landowners these present numerous, unfamiliar, and often vexing problems.

An element of any recreational enterprise on private agricultural land is the owner's interest in the general public along with a tolerance of urban people's unfamiliarity with the rural environment, which may require patience and diplomacy. There are also many problems relative to adequate

---

[2] Approximately one million farms with a total of about 400 million acres (162 million hectares) of land are open to those who wish to hunt or fish [14].

financing, planning and development, maintenance of health and safety standards, legal matters, liability, and varied requirements of the general operation of the recreation business. In addition, the possibility of vandalism and carelessness, as well as behavior problems, common on any area catering to strangers, cannot be disregarded. Awareness of likely problems, provision for their solution, and advance planning of all aspects of the operation are the best guarantees for success.

PUBLIC RECREATIONAL USE OF PRIVATE FOREST LAND

As noted in Chapter 4, public demand has prompted extended recreational use of privately owned, industrial forest lands. Several surveys conducted by the American Forest Institute[3] indicate the increasingly important recreational role of these lands [1-4,15].

The 1968 survey, latest and most complete compiled, covered nearly 66 million acres (26,730,000 hectares) representing over 88 percent of forest industry lands in the United States owned or otherwise controlled by 234 companies. It provides an idea of what the forest industry is doing for outdoor recreation.

Lands of more than 95 percent of these companies are open to the public for various forms of recreation. In addition to such traditional activities as hunting, fishing, and related informal uses for which few facilities are required, provisions are also made for such activities as hiking, picnicking, camping, boating, swimming, winter sports, and the use of various kinds of specialized recreation vehicles. Specific recreational sites have been established which, in addition to basic facilities, include tent and trailer campsites, outdoor kitchens, and covered shelters. In some instances boat ramps, nature trails, ski lifts, ice skating rinks, swimming facilities with floats and bath houses with showers, and children's playground equipment are also included. There is even a beagle dog training ground.

Industrial forestry concerns have also established 122 tree-farm parks with a visitor-day capacity of nearly 14,000; 175 campgrounds with a visitor-day capacity of over 7,000; and 191 picnic areas with a visitor-day capacity of nearly 8,000. Over 86,000 miles (138.460 kilometers) of company roads and 14,000 miles (22.540 kilometers) of hiking trails are also available. Nearly 27 percent of the companies published descriptive literature and maps to aid in recreational use of their lands. A few companies employ recreational planners for development of long-range recreational programs coordinated with commercial utilization of timber. A larger number employ wildlife managers. The total expenditure for recreation is estimated to exceed 7 million dollars annually.

[3] Known prior to 1968 as American Forest Products Industries.

In most cases, recreational privileges and facilities on industrial forest lands are provided free, primarily as a public relations gesture. However, ever-present and growing vandalism (in 1968 estimated to cost over $400,000 annually), rising costs (including taxes and cost of more sophisticated facilities expected by recreationists), increasing recreation use, and increasing landowner responsibilities with respect to that use, have caused owners to seek better control of public recreation on their lands.

Some companies require permits, at no charge, for recreational use of their lands; other charge nominal fees for such use. There is also an increasing trend toward leasing land for recreation. The total number of recreational leases in 1968 (exclusive of hunting and fishing) exceeded 1,300 and involved nearly 20,000 acres (8,100 hectares). The total number of permanent campsite leases in 1968 was 27,590 and involved an area of over 33,000 acres (13,365 hectares). Campgrounds and picnic areas built by companies are often leased to state and quasi-public organizations for operation; such leases increased from 582 in 1960 to 714 in 1968.

Because of difficulties in compiling public use data, the 1968 survey did not note the extent of total public recreational use of industrial forest lands. However, earlier estimates indicated an increase in total number of recreation visits from 1.5 million in 1956 to over 6 million in 1960. This upward trend in public recreational use of privately owned industrial forest land will undoubtedly continue, providing that recreationists cooperate by exercising good manners in such use as a gesture of appreciation of such privileges.

LANDS OWNED OR CONTROLLED BY SPECIAL GROUPS

Various private organizations own or otherwise control considerable land for the use of their members. Included are outdoor and mountaineering clubs (Sierra Club, Appalachian Mountain Club); fraternal and union organizations; churches and religious denominations; groups catering to youth (Boy Scouts, Girl Scouts, Campfire Girls, 4-H) or elderly people; privately sponsored social service bodies (Salvation Army); private game, hunting, fishing, yacht or boat, and ski clubs; and various scientific, educational, and conservation associations (Audubon Society). Some large industrial concerns also sponsor diversified recreational programs for their employees, some of which involve areas of wild land.

Quasi-public Lands

Some privately owned areas are operated for public benefit and various types of recreational interest and use. Among noted examples of such areas are Mount Vernon, George Washington's home near Washington, D.C., owned and operated by the Mount Vernon Ladies Association, and the colonial city of Williamsburg, Virginia, restored by funds provided by John

D. Rockefeller, Jr. (p. 64). Areas more relevant to the scope of this book, however, are the wild quasi-public lands that include Indian reservations as well as reserves owned or otherwise controlled by The Nature Conservancy.

Indian Reservations [10,12,13]   Indian lands, totaling about 51 million acres (20,655,000 hectares), are those granted to various Indian tribes by treaty with the United States Government. They are essentially private lands, administered by tribal councils with technical assistance provided by the Bureau of Indian Affairs of the U.S. Department of the Interior, for the benefit of Indian residents. All recreational activities on Indian lands, including hunting and fishing, are dependent upon permission of the Indians. These lands, especially large reservations, have a wide variety of outdoor recreational interests. Many reservations are highly scenic and contain significant geological, biological, or archeological and historical interests. In addition, traditional activities of the Indians themselves are highly appealing. Though Indians have been reluctant to share recreational potentials of their reservations with non-Indians, obvious economic advantages derived from such activities have prompted a more liberal point of view on the part of some tribes in recent years.

There are a number of noteworthy examples. Public hunting and fishing are permitted on the Fort Apache Reservation in Arizona, but conditional on the purchase of a reservation as well as a state license. Recreational facilities (motels, boat rentals, gas stations, guide services, campgrounds) have been developed at Lake Hawley and Tonto Lake. A large part of the highly scenic Monument Valley on the Utah-Arizona border has been designated a tribal park by the Navajo tribe; the Navajos have designated also a number of other tribal parks and have established a Navajo Park Commission, which has plans for the improvement of public recreational facilities on their large reservation. Recreation facilities are operated also on the Warm Springs Reservation in central Oregon, the Pyramid Lake Indian Reservation in Nevada, the Colorado River Reservation north of Blythe, California, and the Cherokee Indian Reservation adjacent to Great Smoky Mountains National Park.

The Bureau of Indian Affairs encourages such interests on the part of various tribes, and a revolving fund provided by congressional appropriation (P.L. 87-250) and (P.L. 93-262) assists in financing such operations, which are economically beneficial to various tribes, provide opportunity for employment and individual enterprise of local residents, and aid in improved relations between Indians and non-Indians. Though the recreational potential of Indian reservations is as yet not fully understood or utilized, it offers great opportunities for the future if properly handled.

The Nature Conservancy [5]   The objective of The Nature Conservancy[4] is to identify, acquire, and protect outstanding natural areas and the diversity of life they support. It also provides expert advice to governmental bodies regarding the protection of natural areas, assists in providing protection to significant natural areas on an international level, and engages in educational programs to broaden public recognition of the importance of land preservation. In many cases, the Conservancy assists other conservation agencies (federal, state, and private) in acquiring and preserving natural areas.

Since establishment of its first preserve in 1954, The Nature Conservancy has been instrumental in completing over 1,700 projects in the United States, Canada, the Caribbean, and Latin America, and has preserved over 1 million acres (405,000 hectares) of land. These preserves and sanctuaries range in size from a few acres to several thousands of acres and are representative of every type of biological environment (forests, prairies, wetlands, mountains, inlands, and similar lands).

The Nature Conservancy retains ownership of a majority of the areas acquired. Management of these preserves is usually the responsibility of interested volunteers frequently associated with educational or or scientific institutions or, in certain cases, by paid personnel. A number of areas, however, have been acquired and transferred to existing public land-managing agencies or private conservation, scientific, or educational organizations for administration and protection. In most cases such transfers are subject to certain restrictions relative to public use and protected by a "reverter clause" in the transfer agreement.

Areas acquired by The Nature Conservancy, including those transferred to other organizations or agencies, are maintained so that the natural character of the land endures. Nondestructive uses (nature photography, hiking, canoeing, nature study) may be permitted. Scientific research and outdoor education are nearly always encouraged, subject to certain controls. Habitat manipulation is practiced only where necessary to protect and maintain threatened and endangered animal or plant species. However, construction of artificial features (roads, dams, buildings) is not permitted.

IMPACT OF PUBLIC RECREATIONAL USE OF PRIVATE LAND

Accurate data on the total impact of public recreational use of private lands

[4] A national, nonprofit, publically supported, nongovernmental, scientific and educational organization incorporated under laws of the District of Columbia in 1951. Headquarters are in Arlington, Virginia; there are also 4 regional offices, 7 field offices, and over 30 chapters located throughout the United States. It is exempt from taxation under Section 501 (c) (3) of the Internal Revenue Code. Contributions to The Conservancy are tax deductible up to the maximum limitations allowed by law. Financial support is derived from membership dues, general contributions, grants from foundations, recovery of expenses, and gifts from individuals and corporations. Lands are acquired by gift or purchase. Gifts may be by deed or legacy; purchases are made using several basic revolving funds established to further current and long-range objectives of the Conservancy.

is difficult to determine. It is too highly diversified in type and objective, too widely scattered geographically, and many operators of recreational enterprises do not regard information about their business as public property. No central body exists for collection and correlation of information which might be regarded as a complete overview of the importance of public recreation on private lands. Various associations that have been formed relate to recreational operations of similar character; they exist largely for exchange of ideas and solution of common problems and surveys that have been made are limited in application. However, from these limited sources it is obvious that the aggregate land area involved, the number of individual recreational enterprises that exist, and the extent of public recreational patronage of recreational opportunities on private land is considerable.

Most authoritative over-all estimates of the impact of public recreational use of private lands have been made by the Bureau of Outdoor Recreation [16].[5] In 1965, exclusive of commercial recreational facilities and services relating to amusement and spectator sports activities, there were over one million privately operated recreational enterprises[6] involving the use of over 470 million acres (191 million hectares) of land[7] which attracted about one and one-half billion visits annually.[8]

The foregoing data indicate that provision of recreational opportunities by the private sector involves a greater area of land, more people, and a wider variety of organizations and interests than recreation on public land. In many ways it relates to recreation on wild lands and, while complete and accurate data are not available, investments in privately owned recreational operations together with expenditures by their patrons are an important factor in the economic stability of many towns, cities, and regions of the country. In itself, the amount of travel advertising and literature available indicates the importance of the recreation "industry," not only in the United States but in many countries of the world.

SUMMARY

Public lands are the major base for outdoor recreation on wild lands. However, private lands, which amount to about 60 percent of the area of the United States, are becoming increasingly important. About 50 percent of recreational opportunity is attributed to the private sector.

[5] As noted in Chap. 7, the Bureau of Outdoor Recreation was reconstructed in 1978 as the Heritage Conservation and Recreation Service.

[6] Profit-oriented, 39,000; full-time operations, 37,000 and part-time, 2,000; nonprofit operations, 1,039,000.

[7] Profit-oriented, 5 million acres (2,025,000 hectares); full-time operations, 4 million acres (1,620,000 hectares) and part-time, 1 million acres (405,000 hectares); nonprofit operations, 467 million acres (189,135,000 hectares).

[8] Profit-oriented, 750,000,000; full-time operations, 600,000,000 and part-time, 150,000,000; nonprofit operations, 800,000,000.

Many private lands are better adapted to certain aspects of outdoor recreation than public lands; in particular, they are often the most logical sites for the more elaborate facilities and services desired by many people. Coordination of recreational uses of private and public land aids in reducing overcrowded conditions typical of many outdoor recreational areas, thus fostering the preservation of fragile, high-quality values which are primary recreational attractions of certain public recreational lands. Coordination of such uses also provides for a diversity of recreational opportunities for more people, minimizes duplication of recreational functions, and reduces overall costs.

Increasing use of privately owned land for recreation is prompted by a desire for profit, to provide for the interests of particular groups or organizations, for fulfillment of philanthropic interests in environmental protection and use, and for improving the image of an industry. Many types of commercial resorts serve as the backbone of the tourist industry, which is of great economic importance to many communities and regions. Agricultural and ranch lands are characterized by expanding recreational use involving payment of charges for a wide variety of activities, ranging from hunting and fishing privileges to guest accommodations. Youth groups, outdoor clubs, church and fraternal organizations, and related bodies own or lease various kinds of recreational land for the benefit of their membership and friends. Scientific, educational, and professional societies often acquire lands for public benefit for philanthropic reasons. Certain quasi-public agencies, such as Indian reservations and lands owned or controlled by The Nature Conservancy are also important. Industrial forest lands, long used by the general public for dispersed recreational activities, such as hunting, are being made increasingly available for camping, picnicking, and other types of more general recreational uses, largely as a public relations gesture.

The diversity of private involvements in outdoor recreation makes it difficult to assess their overall impact. However, studies of that nature, though limited in application, indicate that opportunity for recreation on private land involves a larger aggregate area, more individual enterprises, and use by a greater number of people than that on public land.

SELECTED REFERENCES

1 American Forest Products Industries: "Recreation on Forest Industry Lands in the United States," Washington, 1957 (mimeographed).
2 American Forest Products Industries: "Forest Industry Recreation Survey," Washington, 1958 (mimeographed).
3 American Forest Products Industries: "Recreation on Forest Industry Lands: Results of a Survey by AFPI, 1960," Washington, 1960.
4 American Forest Institute: "Public Outdoor Recreation: Results of a Survey by

American Forest Institute, 1968," Washington, 1968.

5   Nature Conservancy: "The Nature Conservancy—Annual Report, 1975," Arlington, Va. 1975.

6   Outdoor Recreation Resources Review Commission: "Outdoor Recreation for America: A Report to the President and to the Congress by the ORRRC," U.S. Government Printing Office, Washington, 1962.

7   Reinhardt, James A.: Private Resources for Public Recreation, *Parks and Recreation,* vol. 11, no. 4, April 1976.

8   U.S. Department of Agriculture, Forest Service: "Forest Recreation for Profit" (Agriculture Information Bulletin No. 226), U.S. Government Printing Office, Washington, 1962.

9   U.S. Department of Agriculture: "Rural Recreation: A New Family Farm Business," U.S. Government Printing Office, Washington, 1963.

10   U.S. Department of Agriculture: "Recreation Enterprises Can Boost Farm and Ranch Income," U.S. Government Printing Office, Washington, 1966.

11   U.S. Department of the Interior, Bureau of Indian Affairs: Personal communication, Dec. 29, 1976.

12   U.S. Department of the Interior: "The Race for Inner Space," U.S. Government Printing Office, Washington, 1964.

13   U.S. Department of the Interior, Bureau of Outdoor Recreation: "Federal Assistance in Outdoor Recreation," U.S. Government Printing Office, Washington, 1970.

14   U.S. Department of the Interior, Bureau of Outdoor Recreation: "Developing America's Outdoor Recreation Opportunities: Campgrounds," U.S. Government Printing Office, Washington, 1972.

15   U.S. Department of the Interior, Bureau of Outdoor Recreation: "Sources of Assistance in Developing Boating Facilities," U.S. Government Printing Office, Washington, 1972.

16   U.S. Department of the Interior, Bureau of Outdoor Recreation: "Outdoor Recreation: A Legacy for America," U.S. Government Printing Office, Washington, 1973.

17   U.S. Department of the Interior, Bureau of Outdoor Recreation: *Outdoor Recreation Action, Spring 1975,* U.S. Government Printing Office, Washington, 1975.

18   U.S. Department of the Interior, Bureau of Outdoor Recreation: "The Bureau of Outdoor Recreation: Focal Point for Outdoor America," U.S. Government Printing Office, Washington, 1975.

19   U.S. Department of the Interior, Bureau of Outdoor Recreation: "Private Assistance in Outdoor Recreation," U.S. Government Printing Office, Washington, 1975.

20   U.S. Department of the Interior, Bureau of Outdoor Recreation: "Liability and Insurance Protection for Private Recreation Enterprises," U.S. Government Printing Office, Washington, 1975.

Development of state park systems was prompted largely by public demand for more diversified and accessible outdoor recreational opportunities; old covered bridge, Turkey Run State Park, Indiana. *(Ken Williams, courtesy of Indiana Department of Natural Resources.)*

Section Five

Economics

Allocation of Recreational Land and Activities[1]

To many who are interested in outdoor recreation the subject of economics is distasteful. To perform an economic analysis of outdoor recreation is even worse. Economists are preoccupied with prices, profits, markets, supply, and demand. The outdoor recreation enthusiast is likely to be inspired by natural beauty, and the peace and serenity to be found far-removed from commercial activity. Bridging the communications gap between these two worlds is a difficult task. Some of the most knowledgeable noneconomists, who are responsible for the outdoor environment and its recreational use, have difficulty understanding the contribution economists might make in analyzing their problems.

Contrary to this impression, economists have much to offer in deciding how to obtain maximum net benefits from land and other resources allocated to outdoor recreation. If their talents are to be utilized efficiently, however, a meaningful dialogue must be established. The purpose of this chapter is to discuss recreation as an economic problem; to provide a *basic introduction* to the role of economics in the recreational management of wild lands. This involves discussion of what an economic problem is, insti-

[1] Prepared by Barney Dowdle, Professor of Forest Resources and Adjunct Professor of Economics, University of Washington.

tutional frameworks within which economic choices are made, and some of the consequences of making economic choices.

WHY ECONOMICS?

The emergence of outdoor recreation as an economic problem is a rather recent occurrence. Most of the literature on the economics of outdoor recreation has been published within the past twenty years. Other disciplines have also allocated increasing time and effort to outdoor recreation as public demands for outdoor recreation have increased. Reasons for growing interest in outdoor recreation are well understood, but worth emphasizing. In the past we had fewer people than today, less leisure time, and less income to spend on outdoor recreational activities. Translated into economic terms, this meant there was less demand for outdoor recreational facitilites and services. Lower demand on the relatively fixed supply of resources considered suitable for providing recreational services meant fewer problems in deciding how resources would be used. If there is no demand, there is no economic problem. Placed in an economic context, outdoor recreation is not a problem for which we will find a solution in the usual sense of the term. The economic problem will intensify as population grows, and as our income and leisure time increase.

The fundamental cause of the outdoor recreation problem is scarcity. In other words, nature has not provided us with sufficient resources to provide all the recreational activities we would like. When the recreational desires of all the people are summed, they far exceed the capacity of available resources. Additionally, many recreational activities are incompatible with each other; e.g., water-skiing and swimming. Some recreational areas are incompatible with nonrecreational activities; e.g., wilderness and logging. The nature of the dilemma is often publicized as a "crisis," and the search for "solutions" is correspondingly frenzied. Not uncommonly, greed and selfishness are cited as contributory causes, and the proposed solution is to overcome these somewhat undesirable human traits.

To be sure, if we could overcome the pursuit of self-interests, perhaps the problem in outdoor recreation might be resolved. One should note, however, a "cure" of this kind might be worse than the disease. Self-interest motivates people to produce many of the items we consume daily, such as food, clothing, books. These items are usually taken for granted. Much of the prosperity of our nation depends upon the acquisitive efforts of its citizens. If we overcame self-interest, what would be the motivating force to our prosperity?

The pursuit of self-interest, and the often mistaken belief that it is glorified by economists, appears to be a divisive issue in the dialogue between economists and specialists from other disciplines interested in outdoor recreation. This is unfortunate. Economists may be preoccupied with the market economy, an institutional framework within which people pursue self-interest and serve society in the process. On the other hand, they do recognize that other institutional arrangements are necessary for some kinds of economic problems. Some of these problems are in the realm of outdoor recreation.

The task of economics in outdoor recreation is to determine the optimal set of institutions for producing optimally various recreational facilities and activities. If the activities people desire are not being provided in appropriate quantities, or places, perhaps our institutions need changing. There is nothing sacred about an institutional arrangement that serves no useful social function. Economists are interested in the costs and benefits of making institutional changes. They are also aware that institutional changes may create problems that noneconomists are unlikely to anticipate.

The economic approach is different from disciplines which often attribute bad outcomes to human misbehavior and suggest that solutions lie in educating people to behave in a more socially responsible manner. The economist generally accepts human nature as a constraint and attempts to design an institutional framework, a penalty and reward system, which results in individual behavior contributing to social welfare.

INSTITUTIONAL FRAMEWORKS FOR MAKING ECONOMIC CHOICES

The basic economic problem which necessitates choice, as noted above, is scarcity. Resources which can be used to produce goods and services are limited in supply; our desires are insatiable. Even in the most affluent societies there is little evidence to suggest that an individual's appetite diminishes as more is obtained. Quite the contrary appears to be true, in spite of numerous philosophical and religious questions continually being raised about the propriety of such behavior. If we always want more, we are always living in a state of scarcity. We do not have enough to fulfill our desires.

The implication of scarcity is that we must make choices regarding the use of our limited resources. A corollary to this situation is that we must make sacrifices. Many outdoor recreational activities are dependent upon the use of rather large amounts of land. Hunting, camping, and wilderness hiking are good examples. If land is used only for these activities, it cannot be available for homesites, highways, or many agricultural uses. How should society use land that is suitable for both purposes? If desires change, what kinds of arrangements should be made to facilitate changing land from one use to another? One of the more important problems in outdoor recreation results from the fact that society is not a homogeneous mass of people all of whom have similar desires. Some like highly accessible, commercially developed facilities. Others prefer that areas remain inaccessible and that development be kept to a minimum. Whose preferences will prevail? Who will get the benefits? Who will pay the cost? The latter two questions are especially important to economists because of their interest in whether or not the same people who benefit also pay. If not, socially undesirable inequities may be perpetrated.

An obvious outcome of having to answer the questions posed is competition. We have limited resources which have alternative uses; hence we must compete with each other for the alternative—or alternatives—best suited to our personal interests, however selfish or altruistic they may be. The competitive process, it should be emphasized, results in both winners and losers. Society has evolved a number of institutional frameworks within which this competition can take place.

MARKET

In Western societies most choices regarding the use of scarce resources are made within the framework of a market economy. A market economy, alternatively called a capitalistic, or free enterprise, economy, has a number of characteristics which are essential to its operation. Among the most important, from the standpoint of understanding the economics of outdoor recreation, are private property and freedom of choice on the part of both consumers and producers.

None of the characteristics listed is absolute. Private property rights are subject to numerous restrictions including easements, the power of the state to condemn private property for alternative uses, and zoning regulations. Creation of public parks from private property is an example relevant to outdoor recreation. Freedom of choice is limited by legal restrictions on certain kinds of consumption, although restrictions vary widely by area and the extent to which laws are enforced. Examples include gambling and the use of alcoholic beverages. For the most part, however, individuals are endowed with the right to use their income as they please. They can purchase goods offered on the market, divide income between savings and consumption, and incur debt.

Regulations on production include the type of technology that may be used, pollution-control measures, workers' benefits, and the location of plant and facilities. The use of regulations to facilitate the production of environmental amenities is especially relevant to forest land management. Within the limits of various kinds of regulations and restrictions, production is directed by management, which is free to acquire resources by purchase, rental, or hire. They are also free to organize these resources to produce what they desire. They may also choose to produce nothing. Permitting land to lie fallow is an example. Producers may sell their output when and where the objectives of the firm are best served.

Numerous products and services, either directly or indirectly associated with outdoor recreational activities, are produced and organized within the framework of a market economy. Equipment for hunting, fishing, skiing, and camping is produced almost exclusively within the private sector of the economy. Most tourist facilities and overnight accommodations are privately owned and operated. Market-produced recreational activities extend into the area of hunting and fishing rights.

In economic theory the objective of decision makers in a market economy is to maximize their welfare—to pursue their self-interests. By doing so they promote the public interest. A producer is assumed to maximize expected net returns from buying and hiring resources, and producing and selling output. Consumers are assumed to maximize satisfaction received from spending their income and allocating their time between work and leisure. How well they achieve these objectives is determined by the rules of the game.

The ability of decision makers in a market economy to perform correctly and efficiently is the basis of the penalty and reward system. Profits are especially important in production for judging the soundness of decisions regarding investment, innovation, and the efficiency of management of an enterprise. Poor performance on the part of producers means losses. Low profits, or losses, are the punishment for inefficiency. They are assumed eventually to drive inefficient producers out of business.

The rules of the private market are not absolute, and economists have spent considerable time and effort evaluating exceptions, flaws, and qualifications. It is well known, for example, that many companies are not single-purpose profit maximizers. Other objectives commonly pursued include long-run security, welfare of employees, and service to the community. Many companies in the forest products industry, which have large land holdings useful for recreational activities, are under public pressure to open their lands for recreational use. Many have responded and are permitting use of their lands without user fees. It would be difficult to explain these actions in terms of profit maximization. Perhaps a desire to contribute to community welfare has some bearing on this demonstration of corporate responsibility.

The elimination of inefficiencies which result from poor performance in a market economy may be delayed for numerous reasons. Nevertheless, the rules discussed above generally predominate, and exceptions are limited where competition exists. Competition forces producers to seek improvements, to introduce innovations, to experiment, and to take risks. Producers who neglect the pursuit of profits in a competitive situation are eliminated. Their performance is constantly being tested, and failure to pass the test cannot be continued long. If competition does not exist, producers may enjoy security and relax in their task to produce goods which satisfy human desires.

PLANNING

The importance of state planning as an alternative to the market for making decisions regarding the use of scarce resources is especially significant in outdoor recreation because of federal ownership of large amounts of public land. Approximately 24 percent of the land area of the continental United States is in some form of federal ownership. Most federal ownership is in the Western United States; 56 percent of the Mountain states and about 46 percent of the Pacific Coast states. Within this area federal ownership ranges from a low of 36 percent in Washington to a high of 84 percent in Nevada.

Federal ownership in the Eastern United States is very small. In the New England states federal ownership ranges from a low of 1.2 percent in Connecticut to a high of about 4.4 percent in New Hampshire. Most of the states on the Atlantic Coast have very little federal ownership.

The significance of federal ownership for outdoor recreation should be obvious. Many public lands are used primarily for recreational purposes. These include national parks and related areas of the National Park System, wildlife refuges, wilderness areas, and numerous areas of the national forests. If lands are publicly owned, decisions regarding their use are made within the framework of the policital arena and the planning processes. Central planning is highly important in the Western United States because of the heavy concentration of public lands in the West. In the Eastern states, on the other hand, where most of the land is privately owned, outdoor recreational activities will be largely produced and organized within the framework of a market economy.

In contrast to the market economy, where producers serve the public interest by pursuing their own self-interest, the objective of public officials (planners) is to serve the public interest directly. Much of the ideological dispute over the merits of the two systems is over this difference. People who believe in public ownership and planning commonly fail to appreciate that the pursuit of self-interest, as measured by profits, may be a useful means of serving the public interest. Unfortunately, if the debate is conducted at this level, the most likely result is. to raise blood pressures.

Public officials often disagree on the best way to promote the "public interest." Indeed, ambiguities and controversy in the literature of public administration provide ample evidence of how elusive the concept of public interest is. Some suggest the public interest is no more than the sum of private interests. Others regard it as something that transcends the desires of the community. Much of the recent work in political science on the question of the public interest has been directed towards refuting certain notions of a "public interest," and emphasizing that public decisions essentially involve who is going to gain and who is going to lose.

In spite of the difficulties indicated, the planning process, however organized, can be assumed to serve at least some members of the general public. In the United States most planning is done within the executive and legislative branches of government and various administrative agencies. The Department of the Interior, the Department of Agriculture, and numerous other federal and state agencies play a major role in making decisions in the field of outdoor recreation. Viewed as a producer of goods and services, they interpret consumer demands, both present and future, and prepare budgets which provide the resources for meeting these demands. Alternatively, decisions regarding what to produce can originate within the executive or legislative branch of government.

In the market, purchasing power and dollar expenditures dictate what is produced; but in the political and administrative processes, votes and political power largely dictate the kinds of decisions that will be made. As noted earlier, the planning process is like the market in the sense that it serves as an arena within which competition takes place over the use of scarce resources. Public involvement programs are increasingly being adopted by public agencies to promote competition of this kind. Not all members of society have similar desires; hence they would have scarce resources used to produce different goods and services. The production of one good may preclude producing another. People with similar desires form groups or lobbies to bring maximum pressure to bear on the political decision-making process in order to serve the interests of their groups. The extent of these pressures and their degree of sophistication is obviously dependent upon the amount of benefit involved and the resources of the pressure group. Not all groups in society have power proportional to their numbers. Herein lie some of the inequities of the planning process.

The role of lobbyists in the field of outdoor recreation has grown more or less proportionately with outdoor recreation activities. In the past, for example, administrators of public lands faced little opposition in making decisions which today would have them embroiled in controversy. Land was relatively less scarce, because demands were lower or nonexistent; therefore, decisions were relatively less important. Given the fixed supply of land and the expected rise in the demand for outdoor recreation activities, controversies over land use can be expected to increase. Unfortunately, increased controversy is likely to consist of more sophisticated hypocrisy and inconsistency in argument. Policies will increasingly be advocated, ostensibly to serve the public interest, which will serve primarily to benefit special-interest groups.

PUBLIC AND PRIVATE GOODS AND SERVICES

Whether to use the market or the planning process for making resources allocation decisions is fundamentally related to whether or not goods and services are "public" or "private." The distinction is not related to the producer; rather it is characteristic of the good itself. In general, public goods will not be produced efficiently within the framework of a market economy.

The market involves exchange. For example, a person exchanges a day's work for a day's pay; one exchanges $10 for a fishing rod. In order for this exchange to be satisfactory to both sides, the benefits and the costs must be restricted to the two parties involved. In economics, this is known as the exclusion principle. The exclusion principle is the basis of private property rights, the right to control a good in one's interest, and the right to enjoy it while in one's possession.

If the costs and benefits involved in exchange are not restricted to the two parties involved, the market exchange system begins to break down. At the extreme, where people can benefit from production without having to pay, we have what economists have labeled public goods. Economists have long been aware of the difficulties of getting public goods produced in a market economy. Adam Smith devoted considerable attention to these problems in his "Wealth of Nations," a classic treatise in economics published in 1776.

Commonly cited examples of public goods are law and order, national defense, flood control, and environmental amenities. Examples with some relevance to outdoor recreation include fire, insect, and disease prevention activities, and landscaping. An individual could benefit from all these activities without paying anything for their production.

Private industry is the source of numerous goods and services to which the exclusion principle does not apply. In Table 13-1 examples of public and private goods, whether produced by public or by private industry, are listed.

It should be emphasized that the listings in Table 13-1 are primarily illustrative. Some of the public goods listed are restricted to a particular region. Residents of New England benefit very little from flood-control projects in the Columbia River basin. TV signals can be transmitted through a cable, in which case they are private goods. The person who does not pay does not receive the signal.

Landscape beauty is directly related to outdoor recreation. The general public is not excluded from enjoying landscaping produced by, say, a home owner or a timberland owner. The private owner bears the cost of producing the beauty, and the general public can enjoy it as they drive by. If one has a neighbor who keeps a beautiful yard and home, quite possibly this will result in an increase in the price of adjacent property. The reverse would be true if one had a neighbor who neglected the property and it became unsightly.

Table 13-1 Producers of public and private goods

Producer	Type of goods or service	
	Private use	Public use
Private industry	Skis, fishing rods, camping equipment	Radio and television signals and landscape beauty
Public industry	Timber, electricity, irrigation water	National defense, law and order, flood control, etc.

Private goods produced by public agencies include timber used in the forest products industry and electricity. Both represent products the consumer will not receive if the consumer does not pay the price. The price paid is on a per unit use basis. The more one uses, the more one pays.

There are numerous reasons for public involvement in the production of private goods. Government ownership and management of timberlands has its roots in land disposal policies of the past and historical attitudes regarding conservation of natural resources. Public power is quite different. As previously noted, flood control is a public good. If a dam is constructed to produce flood-control benefits, it may as well be used to produce power too; it may also provide for varied outdoor recreational benefits. The additional cost of equipment to generate electricity or to provide for outdoor recreation is relatively small. Indeed, resources are not likely to be used efficiently if electricity and recreational benefits are not produced.

Much of the controversy over public versus private power has to do with the way the costs of the dam are allocated between flood control and power production. Proponents of private power are inclined to allocate much of the cost of constructing the dam to electricity. Proponents of public power are inclined to allocate the cost of constructing the dam to flood-control benefits. The decision on how to allocate these joint production costs is somewhat arbitrary; hence, it is difficult to make a definitive statement about whether public power or private power is the more economical.

The categories listed in Table 13–1 do not include a number of goods and services which have both public and private good characteristics. Examples more commonly cited include educational and health benefits.

An educated, healthy individual is an asset to society, and so the argument is made that society should bear part of the cost. Similarly, outdoor recreational facilities contribute to emotional stability by providing a place to release the frustrations of urban living; therefore, they should be provided by the society. It is difficult, of course, to evaluate statements of these kinds empirically, or to reach agreement on the ethical issue of how far society should go in providing these services. Most people might agree on the desirability of parks and playgrounds in urban areas; there would be much less agreement on the appropriate size to make a wilderness area.

CHANGING ROLE OF GOVERNMENT IN OUTDOOR RECREATION

We have sketched an outline in which the market and the political processes are alternative systems for making decisions in the use of scarce resources. Additionally, we have indicated the market will not function efficiently in the production of certain kinds of goods and services. Even the most staunch supporter of a laissez faire economy will assign certain activities to government.

The role of government in outdoor recreation is becoming increasingly important for two reasons. Consumers are demanding relatively more goods that are of a public-good nature. Pressures for more parks and a cleaner environment are good examples. Secondly, public ownership of large acreages of land places public agencies in the position of having to arbitrate increasingly controversial conflicts in land use. The latter may or may not be related to the public versus private goods issue.

Whatever the reason, public agencies do require more resources to carry out their functions. This raises the question of government finance. Should government activities be financed by charging users where feasible, or should they be financed through government powers of taxation?

The distinction between these two means of providing benefits is much more subtle than might appear. Consider the issue of landscaping logging operations on public forest lands. Landscape beauty, as noted earlier, is a public good in the sense that once it is produced, viewers do not have to pay to view it. Not all people will be viewers, however, and some of the non-viewers will be consumers of wood products. Decisions to landscape may, therefore, result in a redistribution of income from the latter group to the former. Is this equitable or in the public interest? Numerous "answers" that sound authoritative are given to questions of these kinds. None can be objective. If direct taxation is used, policy makers must face the issue of whether to tax users or people who have the ability to bear heavier tax burdens.

An additional consideration facing policy makers is whether or not government entry, or expansion of activities, in the field of outdoor recreation will adversely affect private efforts in these areas. Public campgrounds are clearly substitutes for private campgrounds. If public facilities are available at zero, or a low price, this may preclude private investments in these activities. In short, government activities can lead to a demand for still more government activities.

PRICING DECISIONS

In the private sector of the economy prices serve the dual role of allocating scarce resources, or output, among competing users, and generating the revenues necessary to continue or expand production. Profits and losses are different, and a private producer without some form of subsidy who fails to cover production costs from sales revenues is not likely to continue in business.

In the public sector this is not the case. Many public agencies, such as the National Park Service and the U.S. Forest Service, have no responsibility to show a profit from their activities. If revenues collected from users of the goods and services these agencies provide fail to cover operating costs, deficits are covered by tax revenues. As long as taxpayers are willing to bear the burdens of these deficits, economic survival is not an issue. Moreover, willingness on the part of taxpayers to cover these deficits in the past appears to have established precedents against pricing certain kinds of output. Recreational use of public lands is one of the best examples. Another reason for not pricing recreational activities on public lands is the difficulty of controlling access. In many cases, the cost of administering a pricing system would exceed revenues collected.

In addition to generating revenues to offset production costs, prices serve the important function of rationing use. As demands for outdoor recreational activities have increased, the problem of rationing, or restricting, the use of recreational facilities has become increasingly troublesome. How does one control the crowds? Past precedents of not pricing now plague public administrators who must meet ever-increasing demands with limited recreational facilities. If supplies cannot be expanded, as is the case of unique natural resources, demands must be controlled. Recreational facilities do have capacity limits, even though they may not be very rigid. If charging the public is not politically feasible, congestion, queuing, and deterioration of facilities generally result. Some of our national parks are currently suffering these problems. Without adequate means of controlling scarce space—the amount of space that can be used without damaging the unique features of the area—people may damage the very features parks were established to preserve.

Unless funds are available to expand the capacity of recreational facilities, public administrators are hung on the horns of a dilemma. Charging, or raising prices, to control intensity of use is hardly popular with the using public. Users are also likely to be dissatisfied with congestion, waiting, and deterioration in the quality of facilities. The plea for more funds to solve this recreational "crisis" is hardly surprising. It is a predictable reaction of one who does not like to make painful decisions. Moreover, it will have the full support of users who stand to benefit from an expansion of output of services they prefer. The benefits are even greater if the cost of expanded output is borne primarily by others.

If scarce resources are to be used to produce goods and services which will maximize long-run social welfare, there is a major difficulty in the above approach. One of the virtues of the price system is that it generates information regarding consumer preferences. Even though this information may be imperfect, it does provide reasonably good guidelines. If consumers are willing to pay twice as much for one good as another, there is a reasonably good presumption they get twice as much satisfaction from it. Expenditures for altruistic reasons would be included in these calculations.

If the price system is not used to generate information regarding relative consumer demands, information with which to plan production decisions must be obtained in some other way. Methods of collecting information for use in making public decisions range from congressional and public agency hearings to consumer surveys. The growth of sociological and statistical research in the field of outdoor recreation is a manifestation of the need for information to determine what people want in the way of recreational services. In the private sector price offerings serve this function. A major objective of marketing research is to determine the consumer's willingness to pay. If consumers do not have to pay, their desires are very likely to exceed the productive possibilities of limited resources. To the extent that this is true, survey information will be inadequate to make the kinds of choices among competing resources that are necessary to achieve maximum social welfare. Perhaps more important, there is no assurance that public officials will use all the information given to them. History provides ample evidence of public decisions made on the basis of faulty information and disregard of accurate information.

A technique commonly used by public agencies to evaluate benefits for which prices are not available is benefit-cost analysis. Many public investment funds are allocated on the basis of analyses of these kinds. Increasing use of benefit-cost analysis as a guide for making public investment decisions has resulted in considerable effort being devoted to the development of techniques for estimating the "value" of various kinds of benefits. What is the value of the beauty provided by, say, a timbered hillside if the alternative is to look at a logged area? What is the value of fly-fishing in a stream if the alternative is to construct a dam and flood the area? Numerous questions of these kinds continually arise in the field of outdoor recreation, particularly in making decisions regarding competing land uses.

Economic analysis can provide insights into these problems; it does not provide answers. Value is a measure of satisfaction and will vary among individuals according to their preferences. Even though two individuals may pay the same price for an item, they may value it quite differently. Cost is a measure of the sacrifice made if one alternative is selected rather than another.

Placing a monetary valuation on nonpriced recreational benefits is necessarily arbitrary and puts a rather severe strain on the objectivity of those who make these estimates, as well as those who use them. The major contribution of analyses of nonmarket costs and benefits is that they provide guidance in making decisions by identifying the relevant factors which should be considered. A dollar measure of the quality of human life, and the benefits people enjoy, may be imaginary. Nevertheless, it can be a useful first approximation for making difficult choices, where sacrifices (costs) must be made if one alternative is chosen rather than another. Some guidelines are necessary unless the choices are to be made on the basis of political expediency, personal whim, or perhaps even random selection.

The economist's preoccupation with prices in making decisions of these kinds arises because of two fundamental economic considerations: (1) all costs should be counted, whether they are easily countable or not, and (2) all benefits should be evaluated, however difficult this may be. The crude yardstick used for this purpose is merely scaled in monetary units. It is to be expected that different estimates would be obtained by different people. As long as the relevant cost and benefit variables are considered in the analysis, different numerical estimates may be useful in reaching compromise agreements.

SUMMARY

The demand for outdoor recreational facilities in the United States, as well as most other countries of the world, will continue to increase as incomes rise and people exchange additional income for more leisure time. Resources suitable for supplying recreational demands are both publicly and privately owned. The institutional frameworks for making public and private decisions are quite different with respect to immediate objectives and the means of achieving objectives. Private enterprise must pursue profits for reasons of survival. Theoretically, the public interest is served in the process. Governmental ownership and control of the means of production is presumably to serve the public interest directly.

If society's demand for public goods increases, which is apparent in increased public concern over the quality of the environment, the role of government is likely to expand. The kinds of public policies and programs adopted will have significant effects on the efficient utilization of both public and private resources. Where public ownership of land is relatively negligible, as in the eastern United States, private enterprise can be expected to respond to certain kinds of increased recreational demands, specifically, those for which prices can be charged and the costs of production recovered. Other kinds may have to be provided by government purchase of land, or restrictions being placed on the management of private lands. Which approach is used will be largely dependent upon whether goods are public or private, that is, whether or not the exclusion principle applies and the extent to which the general public will accept encroachments on private property rights.

Where large amounts of land are in public ownership, such as the western United States, the impact of public actions on private efforts in providing outdoor recreational activities will be considerably different from that in the eastern United States. Many public activities will involve the production of recreational services for which the exclusion principle would apply; campgrounds are an example. In other words, private producers would be expected to respond and provide facilities. Prices would be charged, and revenues collected would be expected to cover cost of production. If public agencies supply services of these kinds without charge, and costs are covered through tax revenues, private incentive to provide facilities could be adversely affected. Consumers can hardly be expected to patronize private facilities, where they must pay a fee, if zero, or lower-fee, publicly operated substitutes are available. Adverse effects of this kind could distort resource use by placing a heavier burden on public lands than would be necessary.

A further problem in public management is the possible adverse redistributive effects that may occur largely as a result of the effects of political pressure groups who are able to obtain a disproportionate share of public benefits. This problem is particularly difficult to resolve because administrators must weigh conflicting values. Given the impossibility of doing this objectively, there is a tendency to bow to political pressures. It is not obvious that decisions made in this manner are always consistent with maximum social welfare.

The contribution of economics to outdoor recreation is primarily to provide insights and to raise relevant questions. Even though answers may not be immediately forthcoming, economic analysis can lead to greater efficiency and equity in allocation of resources to outdoor recreation.

SELECTED REFERENCES

1 Ackerman, Bruce A., et al.: "The Uncertain Search for Environmental Quality," The Free Press, New York, 1974.
2 Alchian, Armen A., and William R. Allen: "Exchange and Production: Theory In Use," Wadsworth, Belmont, Calif., 1964.
3 Baxter, William F.: "People or Penguins: The Case for Optional Pollution Control," Columbia University Press, New York, 1974.
4 Clawson, Marion, and Jack L. Knetsch: "Economics of Outdoor Recreation," Johns Hopkins University Press, Baltimore, 1966.
5 Kohler, Heinz: "Welfare and Planning: An Analysis of Capitalism versus Socialism," Wiley, New York, 1966.
6 Krutilla, John, and Anthony Fisher: "The Economics of Natural Environments: Studies in the Valuation of Commodity and Amenity Resources," Johns Hopkins University Press, Baltimore, 1975.
7 Musgrave, Richard A.: "The Theory of Public Finance," McGraw-Hill, New York, 1959.
8 Rourke, Francis E.: "Bureaucracy, Politics and Public Policy," Little, Brown, Boston, 1969.
9 Shonfield, Andrew: "Modern Capitalism: The Changing Balance of Public and Private Power," Oxford, New York, 1968.
10 Sirkin, Gerald: "The Visible Hand: The Fundamentals of Economic Planning," McGraw-Hill, New York, 1968.
11 U.S. Congress: "The Analysis and Evaluation of Public Expenditures: The PPB System," compendium of papers submitted to the subcommittee on economy in government, Joint Econ. Comm., U.S. Cong., vol XVII, 1969.

Suitably designed roads and other physical facilities, by aiding visitors in proper use of many wild-land recreational areas, are a means to an end rather than an end in themselves. Blue Ridge Parkway, Virginia and North Carolina. *(National Park Service.)*

Section Six

Providing Recreational Opportunities

Recreational
Land-Use Planning

Since outdoor recreation involves many diverse pursuits and activities, no one area can provide opportunities for all types. Many outdoor recreational activities are incompatible, and some can be engaged in only in areas with suitable terrain or at certain seasons of the year. Thus, different kinds of areas for different basic recreational purposes are desirable; their number, distribution, character, and size in various sections of the country depend upon public demand and the availability of suitable land.

Recreation represents but one aspect of land use [4,7,32]. Modern technological society requires consideration of other needs as well. Industry must have a continuing source of raw materials (timber, minerals, hydroelectric power). Production of food for expanding populations depends upon adequate agricultural and range land. Expanding metropolitan areas require space for homes, businesses, and a multiplicity of supporting services and utilities. On lands where such needs are dominant, outdoor recreation may be minimized, developed on an urban pattern, or, in some cases, even eliminated from consideration. Conversely, on some kinds of wild lands outdoor recreational benefits are dominant; under such conditions commercial use of natural resources, however well-managed, should be materially reduced or even totally excluded. Between these two extremes are lands with resources of such character that, by proper planning and subsequent careful development considering the nature of the environment, both recreational and nonrecreational needs can be served with minimum impact. Also, conflicts among recreation uses may present use and management problems.

BASIC ELEMENTS OF RECREATIONAL LAND-USE PLANNING

For our purposes, planning concerns advanced preparation of policies, procedures, or designs to achieve desired goals and objectives. With recreation lands this varies from comprehensive planning relating land uses and developments to public needs over a large region, such as a state or county, down to the design or arrangement of specific facilities on a particular piece of land or site.

The *plan* may be a publication of policies, programs, and priorities, such as a state comprehensive outdoor recreation plan (SCORP). It may also be a specific design and drawings for development of a tract of land— a site plan. Also the *plan* may be a combination of the above, as a park feasibility study or master plan.

Planning is a continuing process dealing with present conditions in terms of projected future needs, allowing for flexibility and revision with the evolution of new socioeconomic concerns and technological change [13]. There is also a control implication in planning as directions and procedures are formalized, restricting use of some areas (e.g., class V—primitive or wilderness lands) and concentrating activities in others (e.g., class I— high-density recreation areas). Thus recreation planning ideally should involve latest knowledge, all concerned parties—public administrators, owners, plannees (visitors, local residents, interest groups, resource users), as well as others affected by the plan. Planning will be effective to the extent that it is comprehensive and coordinates all concerned groups and affected resources. This includes adequate public involvement and review procedures. It is limited by those aspects excluded, or overlooked, and may impose undue control on omitted plannees.

Basic land planning coordinates various uses of land, on either the same or separate areas. Proper coordination among agencies and landowners with concern for the plannee maximizes the net benefit to society on a sustained basis. This basic principle applies when recreation is the primary concern of land planning, when lands have both multipurpose recreational and nonrecreational values, or when they have other primary functions which exclude recreation.

LEVELS OF PLANNING

Individual recreational areas, whether small urban neighborhood playgrounds or extensive, remote wilderness areas, are not completely independent entities. Each type of area has singular importance, featuring some particular recreational opportunity important to large segments of the population. Though ideal situations are not common, planning seeks to provide varied types of recreational areas, suitably developed; adequate in number, size and distribution; and appropriate to the need so that they will supplement one another in kind and quality of recreational opportunities. Coordinated planning offers maximum variety for the largest number of people, at minimum cost, and with maximum consideration for environmental maintenance. The reader should also be aware of the levels of planning, starting with national and state comprehensive plans and going to area and site plans [5], including:

1 Broadscale comprehensive planning on a national, regional, state or local level
2 Specific planning of individual areas, parks or forests
3 Planning for specific individual sites within areas (e.g., campgrounds and picnic areas), often involving small tracts of land

COMPREHENSIVE PLANNING

Although comprehensive recreational land planning on a local level typified a number of more heavily populated sections of the country at an early date, it was not until after publication of the Outdoor Recreation Resources Review Commission report in 1962 that planning on a broader scale was undertaken. Development of a national recreational plan was delegated to the Bureau of Outdoor Recreation. Since 1978, when the Bureau of Outdoor Recreation was reconstructed as the Heritage Conservation and Recreation Service, the HCRS has been responsible for development of the national recreational plan. Parallel programs were developed by various states as a prerequisite for securing financial assistance from the Land and Water Conservation Fund for acquisition of necessary lands and for development of suitable recreational programs. County and municipal needs as presented by various appropriate local agencies were incorporated in various state plans. It is the intention of these operations to coordinate typical recreational opportunities, and to provide for such modifications as future conditions and demands may require.

The Heritage Conservation and Recreation Service coordinates planning with states and also local governments through administration of the Land and Water Conservation Fund. Thus recreation planning at state and local levels is, in part, directed by the national government [31].

Both public and private lands are considered in comprehensive planning conducted on a national, regional, state, or localized basis. Comprehensive planning can promote cooperation between public and private agencies relative to coordinated recreational use of various types of land, together with development of legislation and administrative decisions with respect to such coordinated use. Though we are far from Utopia with relation to adequate coordination in recreational use of public and private lands, a framework for such coordination is slowly developing. The steps in comprehensive recreation planning are (1) to identify recreational resources, both public and private, (2) to relate these resources to determined public need for outdoor recreation, and (3) to develop a program of action relative to the funding and fulfillment of outdoor recreational opportunities which will most equitably satisfy necessary requirements.

At the federal level the foregoing steps have been followed to produce a national outdoor recreation plan [30,31]. Moving to the states, the process becomes more complex. A diagram of the state comprehensive planning process based on the procedure followed in Minnesota [20] is shown in Table 14-1.

In Minnesota, the Governor is the designated authority concerned with Land and Water Conservation (LAWCON) funds. He has designated the Commissioner of Natural Resources as the state liaison officer. The Natural Resources planning staff prepares the plan with the aid of advisory committees, the Heritage Conservation and Recreation Service and other federal agencies, and state, regional, and local government representatives. Although each state has its own relationship between the Governor and the planning staff, other states generally follow the planning process described here.

Public input in the planning process is sought through meetings, discussions, and formal hearings at various points in the planning process. Goals, objectives and operational standards are determined early in the process. These guide the inventory and facility need procedures.

An inventory of existing recreational lands and facilities, including potential lands, provides a basis of comparison for facility needs. With the use of statewide surveys, an indication is obtained of past recreation participation and potential future needs.

The reader will perhaps question the use of past participation, as well as preferences for future recreational activity, as a basis for projecting needs. There are limitations due to changes in family and personal life styles, taste changes, and also technological advances. Given these limitations, participation is presently used in absence of better operationalized methods.

Deficiencies in needed recreation facilities and lands are determined by comparing facility needs with the supply of available recreational land

Table 14-1   State Comprehensive Outdoor Recreation Planning Process—
adopted from Minnesota State Comprehensive Outdoor Recreation Plan
(SCORP), 1974 (20).

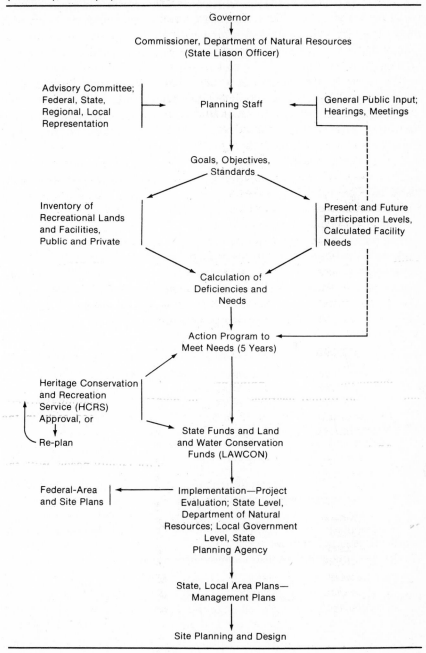

and facilities. For example, needed additional hiking trails are projected from past use by population changes to the present and future and then compared to existing trails by geographic or political unit.

A five-year action program with investment priorities is prepared, giving needs by region and county against which the state or local government units can program area plans to bring needs and supply into harmony. The plan is subject to review and approval by the State Legislature, and the Heritage Conservation and Recreation Service as well as the public.

State funds and federal Land and Water Conservation Fund monies are made available to state and local government units in the implementation phase. Such funding is in accordance with HCRS-state rules and criteria usually including a project area plan. The Department of Natural Resources in Minnesota administers the state agency needs, while the State Planning Agency works with the regional and local government units.

In theory, there is coordination with the federal agencies on their area plans and developments. However, they are somewhat removed from the SCORP funding process and may proceed independently [20].

Once the plan is completed, reviewed and accepted, the planners prepare to review the plan for the next five-year period. It is a continuing cycle. By law, to receive LAWCON assistance, a statewide comprehensive plan must be developed [31]. Also, for this plan, matching planning grants may be made from LAWCON funds, and HCRS provides technical assistance.

AREA RECREATION MANAGEMENT PLANS FOR SPECIFIC LANDS

Several important factors should be considered before area and later site planning is pursued. These factors and constraints include:

1 The nature of the basic recreational characteristics of areas in question; that is, both the physical characteristics of such lands and the recreational purposes which these areas are to serve
2 Public recreational interests and trends
3 Population patterns as related to wildland recreational use
4 Means of access
5 Socioeconomic factors affecting recreational use and demand
6 Variations in land-use patterns other than recreational
7 Modifications in the nature and ideology of political institutions
8 Degree of cooperation of public and private landowners and between planner and plannee
9 Budgetary limitations of the planning process

Careful consideration of the foregoing factors aids in relating the most suitable recreational uses to different types of land. Acceptable size and degree of development can be defined, ranging from small, readily accessible, highly developed areas for large numbers of people to remote areas of wild land typified by extensive size, lack of physical development, and freedom from modern distractions.

Incompatibility of recreational interests and activities adapted to varied multipurpose management with nonrecreational uses can be identified, and the activity assigned to appropriate multipurpose lands. The influence of activities distracting to recreational uses on nearby lands can be eliminated or modified by establishment of restrictive buffer zones, or related techniques. Thus, a variety of recreational resources will be perpetuated, in both quality and quantity for the benefit of future generations, and consistent with economic objectives.

Nature of Basic Recreational Characteristics

Basic recreational characteristics of wild land serve as principal attractions for varied recreational interests and activities. These are: (1) the physical character of the land including climate, topography, soils, and water resources; and (2) inherent recreational land values, such as significant geological, biological, archeological, or historical interests, scenic quality, natural or primitive conditions with varying degrees of solitude and the necessity for self-sufficiency, and conversely, various factors which lend themselves to mass recreational use. These characteristics vary widely with different lands in various sections of the country. They react differently to the impact of different types and intensity of recreational use. They are variously adapted to multipurpose management in conjunction with nonrecreational uses. They are also affected differently by activities carried out on adjacent lands.

The physical character of land affects both the type and the quality of recreational service which can be rendered best by different areas. Climate, as a major factor in the distribution of plant and animal life, strongly affects the characteristics of various recreational areas. Climate also affects the cultural patterns of people; consequently, ethnological and archeological interests vary widely in different sections of the country.

Topography is related to scenic interests, the nature of recreational activities and development, and the degree of hazard involved in recreational use. Mountain climbing, riding, skiing and related winter sports, boating and other water-oriented activities are dependent upon the character of the terrain. Topography is also important in determining the location of roads, trails, campgrounds, hotels, and similar developments. Topographical characteristics are also responsible for numerous public dangers which must be recognized, understood, and guarded against.

Various kinds of soils react differently to varying degrees and intensity of use. Water resources are also important. The presence of lakes, streams, expanses of salt water, or interesting waterfalls, can be responsible for both the interests and the hazards of recreational areas. Further, water resources are a determining factor in the nature of specific developments; campgrounds, hotels, sanitary facilities, and similar needs are dependent upon an adequate water supply.

The inherent recreational values typical of different types of wild land must also be carefully considered in recreational land planning. As noted in a few following examples, these primary values largely determine the character and intensity of public use. Some areas can accommodate large numbers of people without serious, irreparable loss of recreational interests. Their basic attractions may be more durable, may respond more readily to suitable maintenance and repair, or may simply not embody the irreplaceable unique qualities that demand restricted use and development. High-density areas are generally so characterized. On other types of recreational lands varying degrees of restriction in development and use may apply; their more delicately balanced qualities are more easily damaged by highly concentrated public use and accompanying physical development. On such lands the nature of permissible modifications and intensity of use varies from moderate to nil. In addition, some areas are typified by recreational values which can be more readily coordinated with nonrecreational uses (timber harvest, development of multipurpose reservoirs). Other areas managed primarily for recreation are often characterized by severe restrictions as to numbers of users and nature of physical development. In particular, areas typified by unique, irreplaceable geological, biological, archeological, or historical interests, as well as wilderness values, fall in the latter category. Therefore, it is imperative that recreational land planners correctly evaluate the primary recreational values of different types of land and understand the complex ecological relationships and related conditions which are basic to maintenance and perpetuation of inherent recreational benefits.

Where recreational benefits are dependent upon the maintenance of natural conditions, planners of recreational areas must give particular attention to ecological relations, weighing the values to be maintained against possible public hazards. For instance, extensive snag removal in a forest eliminates the nesting sites of many birds; indiscriminate clearing of brush and debris from the forest floor destroys elements of food, cover, and other conditions necessary to the survival of certain animals; the flooding of lands, and conversely, the draining of swamps or bogs, damage conditions upon which other plants and animals are dependent.

Public Recreational Interests and Trends
Winter sports, particularly skiing and snowmobiling, have extended the use of many established wild-land recreational areas and have prompted development of others specifically for such activities. Expanding public interest

in winter sports has induced a number of perplexing problems, such as visitor safety and the propriety of permanent winter sports developments in significant areas like national parks.

There has also been a rapid growth in water-related recreational interests, including those of wild rivers. Increasing popularity of boating, water skiing, and skin and scuba diving has created the need for marinas, boat-launching ramps and related developments, as well as more rigorous application of water safety rules and regulations. In addition to more extensive use of natural coastal and inland waters for such activities, many reservoirs, developed primarily for other public benefits, are widely used for water-related recreation. Further, a number of recreational areas have been established primarily because of their underwater interests; some of these feature underwater nature trails.

Changes in recreational interests and activities are closely related to improvements in means of travel, modernization of recreational equipment, and changes in types of recreational accommodations. These influence, along with cultural and human need changes, the nature and degree of recreational use of wild lands.

Areas formerly difficult to reach are now more readily accessible by four-wheel drive vehicles, trail bikes, and snowmobiles. Resultant problems are minimized by zoning of appropriate areas for the use of such vehicles. Better highways and automobiles, as well as faster and more versatile aircraft, have made formerly distant areas more accessbile to visitor use. The greater mobility of recreationists has resulted in less need for permanent summer-home sites on public land and for a greater variety and number of overnight accommodations for transients. For instance, compact motels and hotels have largely replaced the monstrous structures typical of many recreational areas several generations ago. In addition, with improved technology, camping has increased in popularity, resulting in expansion in the number of campgrounds. Even backpacking into remote areas is rendered less difficult by lightweight equipment and palatable dehydrated foods. Such changes have created problems as well as benefits, particularly with respect to changing character of campgrounds.

Increased use of trailers affects campground design and use. Modern campers insist on certain campground refinements which may be beyond budgetary limits of public agencies, or may result in such highly concentrated sophisticated use that natural conditions and related basic interests of an area are destroyed. Planning can minimize such difficulties by correlating type of campground with type of camping experience, and encourage greater participation by private industry in the provision of the more sophisicated camping facilities.

Over the years the term "last frontier" has been applied to progressively more remote wild lands. Deterioration of many such areas, including those remotely located, has resulted from improperly planned coordination of use and environment. Should current planning repeat such errors or fail to anticipate the constant changes in recreational needs and trends, future generations can expect continued depreciation of both the diversity and the quality of wild-land recreational experience.

Population as Related to Recreational Use of Wild Lands

The population pattern of various regions (density, dispersal, increase or decrease) affects all aspects of land use, including that for wild-land recreation. The greater the number of potential users of recreational lands, the greater the need for recreational areas of adequate size, proper distribution, and suitable diversity of interests; and the greater the difficulty of perpetuating relevant recreation quality. In particular, problems of congestion and overuse are intensified.

Each region has singular land-use problems that must be solved upon their own merits if all vital public needs, social as well as economic, are to be most advantageously served. Sections of the country with a highly concentrated population, as in parts of the Eastern United States, have particularly difficult land-use problems. Where population is rapidly expanding, different but equally difficult problems develop. Many Western areas exhibit evidences of "growing pains." Their complicated and controversial land-use problems can be reduced only by timely consideration of, and planning for, all varied public needs, recreational and otherwise, in proper relation to one another.

Severe fluctuations in the use of some recreational areas, particularly sudden weekend expansion of visitor population, subside as quickly as they start, which can be very troublesome. All types of recreational lands accessible to large centers of population are characterized by this kind of use pattern. Prohibitive costs make it unsound and uneconomic to gear the operation of such areas to their maximum patronage. As a result, they are plagued by overtaxed facilities and inadequate personnel during peak periods and by incomplete utilization at other times. Moreover, the physical character of most areas places definite limits on the extent and kind of physical development.

Many recreational interests and activities are compatible with commercial utilization of wild-land resources. In such instances, multiple-purpose use is not only feasible but desirable. Recreational use may be so great, however, that its benefits preclude, or at least severely limit, any other use. Additionally, recreational interests and activities themselves are not always compatible. Large concentrations of people and certain types of equipment (firearms, motorized trail bikes, snowmobiles) are not compatible with recreational use demanding privacy or solitude. Planning minimizes such conflicts by confining noncompatible interests and activities to different areas.

Large concentrations of people invariably cause deterioration of outdoor recreational areas. Besides increasing the likelihood of vandalism, the mere presence of large crowds has a wearing effect upon recreational lands and upon recreationists. Hazard from fire is increased; shrubs and vegetation may be literally tramped out. Certain soil types require definite limitations on the degree and type of public use [27].

Means of Access

The public use of different types of recreational lands both affects and is affected by the nature of related transportation facilities, both without and within such areas. In some cases established or impending future transportation patterns predispose certain areas to specific kinds of recreational uses. For instance, existing or definitely planned roads or customary mechanized equipment (aircraft, trail bikes, snowmobiles) may predispose an area to certain uses; or if several areas are being considered for winter sports development, lower operational costs of a location adjacent to a highway regularly maintained for winter travel may outweigh certain minor deficiencies in terrain.

The nature of transportation facilities also affects the character and the degree of patronage typical of different recreational lands. Where visitors come from, their background, economic status and interests, the distance they travel, the length of their stay, and the type of accommodations and services required are all related to the type of available transportation.

Increasing use of four-wheel drive vehicles, trail bikes, and snowmobiles, as well as light aircraft for reaching remote places, poses serious recreational land-management problems. Many recreational land planners contend that, under certain circumstances, roads are more damaging to scenic beauty and environmental interests, as well as more costly, than the various types of cableways, funiculars, or lifts that are common in mountainous areas in Europe.

**Socioeconomic Factors Affecting
Recreational Use and Demand**

Population patterns relating to age, sex, marital status, educational background, and economic status are important determining factors in the demand for and use of wild-land recreational areas. Differences in maturity and physical and emotional characteristics associated with various age groups promote different recreational interests. Recreational objectives and requirements of families differ from those of unattached individuals. There are differences in financial restrictions, and family recreation is often oriented toward the needs and interests of children.

Variations in Land-Use Patterns Other Than Recreation

Wild lands increasingly have been invaded by expanding industrial and urban developments and their various supporting services and facilities. In the future fewer areas of land will have to supply increasing amounts of food as well as necessary raw materials for industry (timber, minerals) if high material living standards are to be maintained.

The Outdoor Recreation Resources Review Commission reported that inadequate variety and distribution of recreational opportunities were due, not to lack of land area, but rather to lack of adequate planning for proper use of available land. There is a growing realization that we can and must adapt our activities to our environment, rather than subjugating our environment to our activities [11,15,23]. The latter policy, acceptable in pioneer times, when land and its varied resources were seemingly unlimited, is now recognized as both economically and socially shortsighted. In this connection we can learn from European concepts of land planning and natural-resource utilization.[1] There, where necessary intensive uses are properly related to environmental characteristics, many amenities as well as productivity and relatively high living standards have been maintained. Conversely, where past land use has ignored environmental limitations, both social and economic values and, consequently, general living standards have suffered. The latter situation applies in parts of Europe, as well as Asia and Africa, on the perimeter of the Mediterranean.

Changes in Nature and Ideology of Political Institutions

A variety of legislation, ranging from establishment of various types of parks and reserves to restrictive controls relative to water and air pollution, has brought about radical changes in policies of land use and natural-resource management since pioneer times. Old agencies have been reorganized or reoriented, new agencies have been formed, and deeply rooted institutional and personal concepts have been considerably modified. Many of these alterations reflect changing public attitudes toward the importance of recreational use of spare time and the maintenance of environmental quality.

Legislators and other public officials are understandably sensitive to the changing attitudes of their constituents [9,26]. Through the democratic process, resultant legislation bearing on such subjects reflects increasing

---

[1] The following is a policy statement of the State Forestry Administration, Bavaria, Germany, in 1914:

Considering landscape appearance and the educational role of the forest, it is desirable, at least in the vicinity of larger cities and favored travel points, to abstain from creating large, aesthetically offensive clear-cuts, and from producing only artificial forests of too-uniform appearance; moreover it is desirable to guide economic management so as to conform to the appearance and essence of an area, sustaining its appeal, and maintaining or, if necessary, recreating the character of the natural forest scene, with its varied plant community. [W. Mantel (ed.), "Wald und Forstwirtschaft in Bayern," p. 12, BLV Verlagsgesellschaft, München, 1963.]

public concern for the interests of the many as opposed to individual privilege (e.g., Wilderness Act of 1964).

Since land planning acitivites must be conducted within the framework of enabling legislation, the intent and purpose of relevant legislation, particularly its ambiguities and limitations, must be thoroughly understood. The underlying causes, as well as the history of events that brought such legislation into being, must also be recognized.

Cooperation of Public Agencies, Private Landowners and Plannees

Recreational planning at all levels generally involves a variety of lands controlled by different public agencies (federal, state, municipal) and private owners with varying primary management objectives. These objectives largely determine what the nature and degree of public recreational uses will be and how they may be coordinated to provide for a wide variety of interests and activities, thus favoring economy of operation as well as perpetuation of recreational values of different areas.

Planners usually have advisory rather than administrative functions in developing ideas and proposed courses of action. As planners develop ideas, it is important, where possible, to involve the recipients of the planning (plannees). Though the process is complicated by increased variety of opinions and interests, plans have a better chance of being accepted if plannees help in their creation.

Budgetary Limitations

If inadequate, available funds, whether derived from public or private sources, place obvious limitations on recreational land-planning activities.

It is important to recognize that financial aid from the Land and Water Conservation Fund, as well as many similar sources, is not the sole support of recreational developments. Such a fund, supplied on a matching basis, in effect serves as a catalyst in developing local concern and responsibility in the assumption of the planning task.

PREPARATION OF AREA PLANS

The planning of a particular designated park is one approach to area planning. Others concern larger and varied use areas, as in a national forest, where lands of several public agencies and owners may overlap. After area planning comes planning and design of definite sites such as campgrounds and picnic areas. Each site will reflect its relation to other sites in the overall "master" [2] or area plan.

Individual areas and projects are evaluated for selection based on such considerations as: unusual resource characteristics and opportunities, near-

---

[2] Individual park plans have been called master plans in the past. However, because of the connotation of finality with the term "master plan," it has been largely replaced by "area" or "management" plan.

ness to population, departmental responsibility, and political acceptance [10].

Detailed plans for specific recreational areas (national, state, or local parks; reclamation developments; seashores; wildlife refuges) are developed within a more generalized format. These include narrative and graphic materials. They define the function and purpose of individual areas, relate them to current and anticipated recreational needs of the region as defined in comprehensive plans discussed previously. Necessary facilities and services are indicated. Legislation and Executive orders generally establish policy and serve as the framework of these plans, especially in the case of public land. In some instances, particularly private lands, management policies are based upon institutional or personal objectives.

In effect, the area plan is a guide in dealing with the specific details of management. It prescribes the kinds of recreational activities that are compatible with the area's primary purpose. It outlines procedures for use and protection of recreational values (plant and animal life, scenic and environmental interest and beauty, archeological and historical features). It establishes standards for the degree and character of necessary physical development and public service (access, accommodation, health and safety, interpretation). It defines recreational objectives of each area in relation to other lands considered in the overall recreational program for the region, ensuring maximum economy of operation by elimination of expensive duplication of facilities and services through coordination of effort, wherever practical. And, while allowing for possible future changes as a result of unforeseen developments or public demands, the area plan provides for continuation of a well-balanced program and the preservation of intrinsic recreational values.

Preparation of the area plan should be preceded by examination of public recreational needs of the region and the general relationship of the proposed recreational area to them. These data should be available from state or local comprehensive plans, previously discussed.

First steps in the area plan include: (1) determination of proper size and boundaries of the proposed area, (2) predevelopment inventory, including recreation uses, (3) acquisition or other ways of controlling necessary land by means suited to anticipated recreational use (transfer of jurisdiction, purchase, lease, easement), and (4) cost data. It is recognized that these steps may not always follow in this order. Area plans may be developed before land is acquired, to explain feasibility to legislators or present ideas to plannees.

The predevelopment inventory should include a narrative report with maps of water areas, soil evaluation, vegetation, and topography as needed. It should note the character of various features of recreational interest (plant and animal life, geological importance, topography, scenic quality, archaeological and historical values, climate, soil conditions, adaptability to water-oriented or winter-oriented activities and physically active sports). The predevelopment inventory also should include the relation of the proposed recreational area to others of similar or different types and sizes in the region, so that proper coordination of recreational opportunities can be developed consistent with public demand. Data on location and accessibility of the area in relation to population provide a basis for estimating probable degree and character of use. Preliminary land designation using basic recreational land classes noted in Table 7-1 (p. 126) helps to indicate the interrelation of uses and activities. Definition of land ownership is also essential; this is directly related to costs and acquisition of necessary acreage suited to the anticipated program of development and use. In the case of areas on which certain modifications to enhance recreational use is permissible, the adaptability of the areas to planned modifications should be noted.

A statement on lands to be acquired, their costs, and conditions of purchase should be presented along with an estimate of costs of development and maintenance relative to probable recreational use.

In final form the area plan may be presented as a single complete unit, or as several separate but coordinated parts. Regardless of the final format, it includes a variety of necessary maps, charts, diagrams, and drawings developed in varying detail, augmented by explanatory text and complete specifications.

The complexity of the area plan depends on the size and type of area involved. Small areas, especially those related to a single type of activity (swimming, physically active sports), can usually be planned as single units. Larger, more complex areas involving numerous types of recreational interests, activities, and facilities (national parks, national recreation areas) must necessarily be broken down into coordinated units in order to include required detail.

The complete recreational management plan for a national park includes:

1 *An investigative or administrative statement.* This statement, one of the more important parts of the plan, sets forth all necessary facts supporting the functions of the proposed area. It includes and may expand the predevelopment inventory developed through in-depth studies of basic features of recreational interest, relation to other recreational areas in the region, location and accessibility of the area in relation to population and travel facilities, land ownership, adaptability of modification, and costs of development and maintenance. It also relates probable use to sources of attendance, differences in character of probable users, probable future trends in recreational interests and activities, and possible land-use problems. Location, and space requirements of planned facilities (roads, trails, accommodations) are noted, together with special considerations relevant to planned physical development (soil stability, water supply, waste and sewage disposal, public utilities) and control of visitor use and activities (visitor circulation within the area, enforcement of rules, regulations, and laws).

   2 *Maps of varied types relevant to the investigative statement.* These include (1) regional outline maps illustrating relation of various recreational areas in the region, population concentrations, and major transportation facilities (roads, airports, docks, and similar pertinent data); (2) topographic or aerial map of the area showing proposed boundaries and relief, location of streams, lakes, and similar details important in use, development, and protection of the area; (3) plat map indicating landownership together with dates of transfer, purchase, or other modifications in land control (easements, etc.); (4) soil and vegetation maps; (5) topographic maps of planned development, including roads, trails, centers of public concentration, administrative facilities, public utilities, and facilities for protection.

   Except for regional outline maps, it is advisable that these be prepared on the same scale for easy correlation. A good plan is to use the topographic map as a base and to prepare the others on plastic overlays. For large areas, general maps are supplemented by more detailed maps, on a larger scale, of principal sections of the area which involve most if not all of the foregoing considerations.

   Another type of area planning is that required for National Forests under the provisions of the Resources Planning Act of 1974 [28]. The act requires the U.S. Forest Service to develop an assessment of the forest and rangeland renewable resources under its administration and a 40-year program of managing them. For this there is a three-step hierarchy of plans:

   1 Area guide plans establishing goals and policy for National Forests in a given area
   2 Forest plans for each National Forest, providing forest policies with goals and targets for units
   3 Unit plans for portions of National Forests, and giving guidance to land managers

   At the National Forest level the planning process involves several steps which would include goals and targets for recreation. First, issues and assumptions are identified. Next, data on land use, needs and budgets are collected and analyzed. Alternatives for future land management are developed, and presented for public review.

   The review may include mailing out data on proposed alternatives, public information meetings or other means of obtaining input from citizens. The public input is used to revise and select the management alternative to be the basis of the forest plan. A final forest plan is prepared after further public review. In the forest plan the recreation component emphasizes dispersed recreation away from roads. Designated wilderness generally will be covered by a specific unit plan for the specific area. For example, a specific unit plan was drafted for the Boundary Waters Canoe Area of Minnesota. After public involvement, review, and the environmental impact statement process, it was completed in 1974, conforming also to the National Environmental Policy Act.

SITE PLANS FOR SPECIFIC LOCATIONS AND FUNCTIONS

Within a designated park or forest area there are locations for specific functions such as: campgrounds, picnic areas, lakeside recreation (e.g., swimming, boating, fishing) sites, ski areas, and special use sites (e.g., hotel, summer residences, youth camps, visitor and concession centers). All these sites must be carefully designated to fit the central area plan theme.

It is important to consider the reason for developments, including the effects of and on site factors such as soil, temperature, water, topography. Site developments are for human use, in which costs, function and beauty are key factors. The planner should be able to integrate improvements with the overall characteristic of the site [25]. In the words of the late planner-landscape architect O. B. Howell, speaking of outdoor recreation planning, ". . . for every site there is an ideal use, and for every use there is an ideal site."

The site planning process starts with selection and an assessment of suitability. This may include sketches and rough measurements of possible facility locations. The next step includes field topographic mapping of the site area. The design of structures including working drawings comes next and should include a cost estimate plus a description of the planned facility. The paper plan should then be checked with ground locations in the field to test practicality [17].

The plan is next ready for presentation and review by the client or higher agency administration. If it is approved, adjustments may again be necessary before it can be executed as an action plan.

SUMMARY

Wild lands in great variety are required for various types of recreational interests and activities, as well as for nonrecreational uses. Not all such uses are compatible with one another, or with particular types of land. Planning seeks to correlate various uses on the same or separate units of both public and private lands to which they are best adapted in order to maximize net benefit to society on a sustained basis.

Land planning for recreation and other public needs is a complex operation; it is not a one-person project and planners are only advisers. It involves expertise in a wide variety of fields including basic scientific knowledge of areas considered; socioeconomic factors related to the nature, degree, and variations of public use; legal and political considerations concerning land ownership patterns and philosophy of use; and budgetary limitations of the planning process.

In addition to determination of supply of lands and opportunities and data on current and proposed visitations, it is helpful to make economic analyses of proposed recreation alternatives and their impact on other resource uses. As planning develops, involvement of planners and broad groups of concerned people, though complicated, is a positive step toward plan acceptance and implementation. Broad comprehensive planning on a national, regional, state, or local level generates data for more detailed planning of individual areas, including that for specific sites within particular areas. Development of plans for each individual area serves as a basic guide in management, aimed at perpetuation of recreational and other values, and proper coordination with the purposes of other lands serving different needs.

The area plan may be developed as a single unit or, for larger, more complex areas, as several coordinated parts. Its development is preceded by an examination of broad recreational and other needs in the vicinity, a complete inventory of recreational values of the area, and determination of boundaries and adequate means of control of lands within boundaries. In final form the plan includes all relevant information concerning the function, nature, and degree of use of the area, including maps, charts, statistical data, detailed specifications of necessary physical developments, budgetary outlines, and supporting explanatory text. Within each park and area are specific sites to be designed and planned following landscape principles.

The planning process has been explained here in a series of steps. They are not always followed in the order as outlined. Planning means restricting some uses and allowing others. To the extent that all concerned (planners and plannees) are involved in the process, planning should result in optimum land use and perhaps maintenance of environmental integrity. However, some past planning has resulted in damage to people and environments. Good planning provides for flexibility with recurring evaluation and change. Management stems from and is related to planning.

SELECTED REFERENCES

1 Alden, Howard R., and Ralph S. Sampson: "So You're Planning an Outdoor Recreation Business," University of Idaho, College of Agriculture, Idaho Agricultural Extension Service Bulletin No. 493, Moscow, Idaho, February 1968.
2 Burch, William R., Jr.: Wilderness—the Life Cycle and Forest Recreation Choice, *Journal of Forestry,* vol. 69, no. 9, September 1966.

3 Burch, William R., Jr., and W. D. Wenger, Jr.,: "The Social Characteristics of Participants in Three Styles of Family Camping," U.S. Forest Service, Pacific Northwest Forest and Range Experiment Station, Research Paper PNW–48, Portland, 1967.

4 Coffman, John D.: How Much and What Kind of Forest Land Should Be Devoted Exclusively to Recreation and Aesthetics? *Journal of Forestry,* vol. 35, no. 2, February 1937.

5 Doell, Charles E., and Louis F. Twardzik: "Elements of Park and Recreation Administration," 3rd ed., Burgess, Minneapolis, 1973.

6 Driver, B. L. (ed.): "Elements of Outdoor Recreation Planning," University of Michigan Press, Ann Arbor, 1974.

7 Frank, Bernard: When Can Forest Recreation Be Considered as Exclusive or Dominant? *Journal of Forestry,* vol. 50, no. 4, April 1952.

8 Gilligan, James P.: The Contradiction of Wilderness Preservation in a Democracy, *Proceedings of the Society of American Foresters Annual Meeting,* Milwaukee, October 24–27, 1954, Washington, 1955.

9 Green, Arnold: "Recreation, Leisure, and Politics," McGraw-Hill, New York, 1964.

10 Gregerson, H. M.: "Criteria for Evaluation of Recreation Projects in Outdoor Recreation," Advances in Application of Economics, USDA, Forest Service, General Technical Report No. 2, March 1977.

11 Harris, F. B.: The Sancity of Open Spaces, *Living Wilderness,* vol. 22, no. 60, Spring 1957.

12 Hart, William J.: "A Systems Approach to Park Planning," IUCN, Morges, Switzerland, 1966.

13 Hawkes, A. L.: Coastal Wetlands—Problems and Opportunities, *Thirty-first North American Wildlife and Natural Resources Conference,* Pittsburg, 1966.

14 Hendee, John C., Wm. R. Catton, Jr., L. D. Marlow, and C. Frank Brockman: "Wilderness Users in the Pacific Northwest—Their Characteristics, Values, and Management Preferences," U.S. Forest Service, Pacific Northwest Forest and Range Experiment Station, Research Paper PNW–48, Portland, 1967.

15 Jackson, Henry M.: An Appeal for a Law of Environmental Rights, *Seattle Times,* May 25, 1969.

16 James, George A.: "Recreation Use Estimation of Forest Service Lands in the United States," U.S. Forest Service, Southeast Forest Experiment Station, Research Note SE–79, Ashville, 1967.

17 Jubenville, Alan: "Outdoor Recreation Planning," Saunders, Philadelphia, 1976.

18 Leopold, Aldo: Wilderness Values, *1941 Yearbook, Park and Recreation Progress,* U.S. National Park Service, Washington 1941.

19 Marshall, Robert: The Problem of Wilderness, *Scientific Monthly,* vol. 30, no. 2, Febtuary 1930.

20 Minnesota Department of Natural Resources: "Minnesota State Comprehensive Outdoor Recreational Plan, 1974," St. Paul, 1974.

21 Murie, Olas J.: Wild Country as a National Asset, *Living Wilderness,* vol. 18, no 45, Summer 1953.

22 Outdoor Recreation Resources Review Commission: "Outdoor Recreation for America: A Report to the President and to the Congress by the ORRRC," U.S.

Government Printing Office, Washington, 1962.

23 President's Council on Recreation and Natural Beauty: "From Sea to Shining Sea," U.S. Government Printing Office, Washington, 1968.

24 Recreation Advisory Council: "A National Program of Roads and Parkways," RAC Circular No. 4, U.S. Government Printing Office, Washington, 1964.

25 Rutledge, A. J.: "Anatomy of a Park," McGraw-Hill, New York, 1971.

26 Smith, F. E.: "Politics and Conservation," Pantheon, New York, 1966.

27 Stevens, M. E.: Soil Surveys as Applied to Recreation Site Planning, *Journal of Forestry,* vol. 64, no. 5, May 1966.

28 U.S. Department of Agriculture, Forest Service: "A Summary of a Renewable Resource Program," Washington, 1976.

29 U.S. Department of the Interior, Bureau of Outdoor Recreation: "Recreation Land Price Escalation," U.S. Government Printing Office, Washington, 1967.

30 U.S. Department of the Interior, Bureau of Outdoor Recreation: "Outdoor Recreation: A Legacy for America," U.S. Government Printing Office, Washington, 1973.

31 U.S. Department of the Interior, Bureau of Outdoor Recreation: "The Bureau of Outdoor Recreation, Focal Point for Outdoor America," U.S. Government Printing Office, Washington, 1975.

32 Wagar, J.V.K.: Some Major Principles of Recreational Land Use Planning, *Journal of Forestry,* vol. 49, no. 6, June 1951.

33 Zahnizer, Howard: The Need for Wilderness Areas, *Living Wilderness,* vol. 21, no. 59, Winter–Spring 1956–57.

Chapter 15

Recreational Land-Use Management

There is often much confusion as to the meaning of the words "management" and "administration." Management is frequently thought of as the carrying out of specific projects or functions in accordance with a definite plan or objective. Administration, on the other hand, concerns the organization of management tasks, together with supervision, direction, and control of personnel in management jobs. Thus management and administration overlap. For purposes of this book the term management will be used to include both basic administrative and managerial activities. Detailed tasks related to the operation of wild-land recreational areas, also part of management [19], are outlined separately in Chapter 16.

PRIMARY RECREATIONAL LAND MANAGEMENT OBJECTIVES

The primary objectives of the management of lands for recreation are the provision of optimum variety of rewarding recreational opportunities for the greatest number of people at the lowest possible cost and, at the same time, the perpetuation of recreational land values for the future. This last principle is particularly important with respect to wild lands.

However, the manager must be more specific in setting objectives concerning both the land and water resource and the visitor's experience. How much resource impact will be acceptable before controls are implemented? What are the effects of complete protection? What is to be accomplished by certain types of development? What is the visitor seeking from the experience? What services and facilities can be provided within existing laws and available funds and personnel? The effective manager will develop objectives related to these and other questions and direct programs toward meeting appropriate ends [22]. Recreation land-use planning, discussed in Chapter 14, is basic to the management process. Supplementary to this are the application of a variety of management "tools" and techniques, ranging from zoning and related controls to research.

At this point the reader is referred to the organizational framework of this book in the preface. We are now discussing management with an overlap to development as part of the larger management job. Differences in management approaches by various agencies and landowners, according to recreation land classes or zones, are inferred in Table 15–1 for recreation

Table 15-1　Framework for Recreation Management

Management responsibility	Recreational land classes (zoning)[a]	Owner-agency categories	Recreational uses	Management tools[a] and techniques
Local agencies: municipal, county, district, regional	I. High-density recreation areas			
State agencies: park, forest, fish and game, related departments	II. General outdoor recreation areas			
Federal agencies:	III. Natural environment areas			(Zoning) motor, canoe routes,
Federal agencies: National Park Service;	IV. Unique natural areas	Overlap to Classes III, IV, VI	Hiking, canoeing, camping,	(Development) trail construction and maintenance.
Forest Service	V. Primitive areas	Wilderness[b]	nature study, winter use,	(Environmental manipulation) fire management.
Fish and Wildlife Service; Bureau of Land Management; Water-based agencies	VI. Historic and cultural sites		fishing, hunting	(Rules, regulations) visitor contact, patrols, permits, enforcement. (Facilities) campsite location and maintenance.
Private: Company, individual, group				(Research) visitor-use studies.

Possible public involvement over land classification, uses, and management techniques.

[a] Tools of recreation management are indicated by parentheses.
[b] As specifically designated under the Wilderness Act of 1964, or subject to its provisions.

management. Examples can be given for each class and management responsibility combination. The specific example noted here concerns Class V, primitive areas, under Forest Service management. Even under the primitive area classification there are limitations in management techniques. For instance, areas classified as wilderness under the Wilderness Act of 1964 usually would have more restrictions on management than forest areas not so classified. In addition, techniques and uses will vary with agency and owner policies; e.g., Forest Service rules generally would allow hunting in wilderness whereas National Park Service rules would not.

The remaining columns in Table 15–1 show land categories (wilderness areas with overlaps), recreational uses, and management tools and techniques. In each case these are related to Forest Service Class V lands.

User and conservation groups may exert pressure regarding points of classification and the allocations for various types of recreational uses, as well as for certain management techniques. Also, the agency may seek public involvement about these points. This example is therefore a static one of a dynamic situation. At any stage conflict may develop within management circles, between user and management, and between users and potential users that would alter management proposals. Through such conflict the original area purposes, or objectives, may be threatened or changed.

"TOOLS" OF RECREATION MANAGEMENT

Various methods or "tools" for controlling the nature and degree of recreational use, as well as activities of users, are necessary to the perpetuation of recreational values of different types of lands. These tools include:

1 Zoning and related controls of land uses and user groups
2 Facility development—type, location, and design
3 Environmental manipulation and landscape management
4 Rules and regulations
5 Public relations and public involvement
6 Interpretation
7 Maintenance of area and facilities
8 Research

Zoning and Related Controls of Land Uses and User Groups

The recreational land classification initially suggested by the Outdoor Recreation Resources Review Commission can be usefully applied to designate and directly control land uses. Zoning of specific recreational areas, especially large ones, for particular types of outdoor concerns and activities, is an accepted management technique. Proper dispersal of compatible uses on different types of recreational land is important for protecting recreational values and enhancing visitor satisfaction. At the same time, use of

Class V (primitive area) designation, for example, is limited to resource uses. This class defines standards of access and management techniques.

Relationship to Environment and Recreation Uses Varied environmental characteristics of an area (soils, plant and animal life, natural scenic beauty, unique features) are affected in different ways by ecological laws and other natural changes. Different parts of recreational areas have varying degrees of durability against the impact of different uses. Further, recreational activities themselves have varying degrees of compatibility. Examples of groups of users with conflicting recreational objectives and needs are campers and picnickers; campers with different types of camping equipment (e.g., tents versus trailers); skiers of varying degrees of proficiency; water skiers and fishing enthusiasts; canoeists and motor boaters; hunters and those who simply observe wildlife; and hikers, horseback riders, and users of motorized trail equipment. Zoning, if accomplished with due consideration of all factors involved, separates incompatible uses in space and enhances the enjoyment and safe use of wild-land recreational areas [49].

Other Relevant Means of Zoning and Control Some other important means of controlling the use of recreation lands and user groups include boundary definition; consolidation of management objectives through ownership, easements, leases, or land exchange; and fees or rationing of patronage [2,7,32,34]. Public agency practices in land zoning and control can also establish the pattern for uses of private lands for recreation [34].

Clearly defined boundaries are vital; where possible, these should follow recognizeable topographical features (ridge crests, streams). In addition, all lands within boundaries should be subject to unified control and comparable management policies; otherwise, troublesome complications are inevitable. Though outright ownership is most desirable this may not always be possible; high costs and various other factors may prohibit purchase of necessary areas. Problems of ownership have been solved through negotiation of easements, leases, exchange of lands of equal value, and, in some cases, purchase with privilege of continued occupancy for given time periods.

Fees charged for use of recreational areas and facilities have served as a means of controlling use. However, their primary function is to provide a portion of financial support for recreation. On that basis they can be justified, even on public lands supported by taxes collected from the population at large. Since tax revenue pays only a portion of the cost of recreational management it is logical that those who actually utilize specific recreational areas and their facilities should assume a larger share of the cost by paying additional charges.

In many states a daily entrance fee is charged at parks and related recreation areas, or a visitor may purchase an annual permit for entry to all areas. A seasonal permit (Golden Eagle or Golden Age Passport) is also obtainable for entry to national parks and certain other federal recreational areas. A daily charge may also be made for use of camping facilities within many types of recreational areas which partially covers operation and maintenance costs to the agency. Through reservation systems [26], such as those used in several states (e.g., California), it is possible to reserve camp-sites in advance.

Rationing of campsites, when conducted on a "first come, first served" basis, is a less discriminating means of use control. The number of days of consecutive occupancy may be strictly limited, or the number of clearly defined, individually developed sites may be restricted to the assumed carrying capacity of the environment.

Another form of control is the restriction of private automobile traffic in highly congested recreation areas. Admittedly, this may be irksome but it is part of the price that must be paid if the superior qualities characteristic of many recreation areas are to be preserved for use and enjoyment of future generations. For example, in Yosemite National Park, California, a portion of Yosemite Valley once open to unrestricted use of private vehicles has been closed. Now access to the restricted area is accomplished by walking, by bicycle, or by use of regularly scheduled public buses which stop at major points within the restricted zone. As a result, the roads in that area are free of traffic, there is less noise, and the physical environment appears less impacted. Unrestricted access by private cars throughout Yosemite Valley has been reduced to protect the natural setting for which the park was established. In this case Yosemite Valley, a truly unique natural area (Class IV), was developed over the last century with roads, hotels, stores, and related facilities to a point where resultant high-density uses (Class I) overlapped the protected natural area. Restriction of roads was difficult to accomplish once use patterns were established. Variations of the Yosemite plan are also used in a number of other national parks.

In general, restrictions in degree of use may be accomplished by limiting facilities and services to those most appropriate to the basic purpose of an area and the character of its environment. Extraneous developments are omitted, or they may be provided by operations of the private sector located outside of, but reasonably accessible to, designated public recreational areas.

Wilderness Management Wilderness areas (Class V, as designated under the Wilderness Act) are examples of major recreational area zoning. Their uses relate to recreation under natural conditions, requiring self-sufficiency where development is virtually absent and conditions for solitude prevail. As Hendee, Stankey, and Lucas [15] so well state, management is necessary to maintain the wilderness resource. Such management is guided by basic principles, including the production of human benefits without degrading the resource. Wilderness-dependent activities are favored and regulation should be minimal to meet management plan objectives. Managers should limit possibilities of conflict between various types of wilderness uses (e.g., horse parties and hikers in congested locations).

With few exceptions (e.g., emergencies; established uses previous to designation as wilderness), the use of mechanized vehicles is prohibited. Though policy varies with agency, facilities are minimal and consistent with the protection of wilderness resources; they are not provided primarily for the comfort or convenience of users. In addition, through various forms of permit systems, management is also concerned with control, distribution, and regulation of visitors who are attracted to wilderness areas in ever-increasing numbers [14,15,24,25,26,27,28,37,38].

For such lands there are problems as to the amount of maintenance and structures needed for trail and campsite upkeep, visitor contact and regulation, fire control, area administration, and research. At the same time increasing wilderness use has prompted philosophical questions about the limitations in wilderness participation by some groups and the degree of visitor control.

Management of the Boundary Waters Canoe Area (BWCA) in Minnesota, administered by the Forest Service as part of the Superior National Forest, is outlined here as an example of problems in controlling and regulating wilderness use. Featuring over 1000 lakes, the BWCA is the largest wilderness in the Eastern United States (1,030,000 acreas; 417,150 hectares) designated under the Wilderness Act. Access to the area, which has 2000 designated campsites, is through 70 points of entry. Motorized vehicles (except motor boats in specifically designated sections) and roads are prohibited; most visitors travel by canoe. There are also limitations on the type of material that can be carried; no disposable cans or bottles are allowed. Also, since 1966, the Forest Service has required visitors to obtain permits [14,16] for travel or wilderness campfires in many parts of this area.

Despite such restrictions the BWCA has very heavy use (164,628 persons in 1976), primarily by canoeists. This use has been rising at an annual rate of 8.6 percent with similar increases in visitor congestion and resource damage [16]. The situation in the BWCA is further complicated by the aforementioned inclusion of motor boat- and canoe-only zones, as well as the designation of a portion (about 400,000 acres; 162,000 hectares) as a controversial portal zone in which commercial timber harvest has been allowed.

To protect the wilderness qualities of the BWCA and improve visitor experience quality within a set capacity, the Forest Service initiated a visitor distribution system in 1976, setting up entry point quotas and requiring visitors to obtain permits for each trip. Entry point limits were derived from computer simulation models of travel. However, visitors do not have to indicate their route stops.

This program, although perhaps causing some people to go elsewhere because of restrictions on entry, has had the effect of diverting users from some crowded routes to less-used areas. It is an attempt to balance natural area protection and wilderness experience with increasing popularity of wilderness travel.

Though not all national forest wilderness areas are subject to entry permits, there are restrictions on wilderness (backcountry) entry in many national parks. For example, permits are required for overnight hiking in Yosemite and Yellowstone National Parks. In Glacier National Park, Montana, wilderness visitors must obtain permits and designate their proposed routes of travel, with campsite locations. Only designated campsites may be used. The proposed itinerary is checked against current campsite occupancy and other restrictions for the desired locations. If there are sites available the itinerary is approved. If not, visitors must make alternate plans for open sites or forego their trip. Permits are returned to a ranger station at the end of the trip. Thus, the trip is controlled to protect the park and visitors usually contact other travelers at their campsite locations.

Semiwilderness Experience Opportunities   To maintain diversity of opportunity for many types of recreation, Class III (natural environment) lands, usually less restrictive in forms of access and development than Class V lands, provide for recreation uses between wilderness and the more highly developed Class I and II areas. On Class III lands visitors may pursue natural setting activities, though there may be other uses like timber harvest or grazing and perhaps more people, often obtaining many of the qualities of a wilderness experience such as solitude, naturalness, and challenge [28]. The range of wild-land recreation uses pursued on wilderness and the less restricted Class III lands fits the dispersed recreation policy emphasized by the Forest Service.

Facility Development—Type, Location, and Design

The nature and degree of physical development of an area are strong indications of the basic recreational purpose recognized by its management. Psychologically, the type, design, and location of facilities reflect interests and values of an area favored by management; these, in turn, develop public attitude toward an area and influence the character and degree of use. Such use may or may not be in accord with environment and related values. The development of several national parks has reflected inconsistency in preservation and use. The Yosemite National Park example given previously is a case in point. Thus, it is important that basic values of an area, whether they involve wilderness or other unique qualities or features suited to varying degrees of development, be properly related to primary values and environmental conditions. If they are, management difficulties resulting from inappropriate public use can often be minimized. It may be, as suggested in the discussion of bureau evolution in Chapter 5, that, over time, bureau leaders have changed management emphasis toward new goals. Thus, naturalistic preservation goals embraced by founding director Stephen T. Mather for national parks, though still stated in publications, in fact may be followed only to a limited degree in response to pressures for extensive development.

Further, where environmental conditions typical of different parts of a recreational area are suited to different types and intensity of use, the distribution of development serves to channel various uses into the most appropriate portions of the area. More vulnerable environments receive maximum protection through proper dispersal of impact of use. Development thus becomes an important means of visitor regulation and control.

Development need not be destructive to wild lands. If properly related to the basic purpose of an area and the nature of environment, development may favor perpetuation of an area's features with minimum restriction on public use. In addition to confining impact of use to limited sections of an area, development may also control patterns of visitor movement. For instance, in high-use areas, properly located hard-surface trails protect adjacent, attractive wild-flower meadows; visitors in "city" footgear find it unnecessary to wander indiscriminately, thus they avoid mud, water, excessive dust, and related unpleasant conditions. Similarly pleasure driving in scenic areas is favored by properly located one-way roads free from the danger and distraction of oncoming vehicles.

Necessary Facilities and Services   Many facilities and services are necessary to the development and proper public use of different types of recreational lands. Included are roads and trails, signs, campgrounds and picnic areas, commercial overnight accommodations and related requirements, organized camps, provision for such activities as water and winter sports, and varied structures required for administration, interpretation, and maintenance. These facilities and services are variously integrated through planning, along with such basic needs as water supply, sanitary facilities, sewage and waste disposal, and enforcement of laws and rules and regulations; such essentials are particularly relevant to the protection of public health, safety, and property. Salient points relative to the provision of such facilities and services, more closely related to more detailed operation of recreational areas, are outlined in Chapter 16.

Environmental Manipulation
Because of the nature and rapidly expanding use of wild lands for recreation, some sort of environmental management is generally necessary. Envi-

ronmental manipulation serves purposes of preservation of area attractions and values, and of public health and safety. It includes:

1   Hazard removal or salvage logging, particularly in campgrounds and picnic areas, along roads and trails, and similar areas of public concentration

2   Landscape management to maintain visual quality, including "vista cutting" along roads and trails in heavily forested areas to open up views or to improve scenic quality of strategic locations

3   Judicious plantings to ensure or to develop privacy

4   Supplementary watering, fertilizing, and related cultural treatments to maintain or to enhance vigor and character of vegetation

5   Maintaining animal populations in balance with environment, or stabilization of ecological succession at a particular stage

6   Varied practices in control of fire, if result of natural causes, and of destructive insects and fungi

Environmental manipulation varies with agency or owner policy and also with recreation land classes. More intensive efforts would be applied in Classes I and II, areas where higher-density recreation development and activities are most typical. In these classes vegetation plantings and cultural practices would be followed to maintain and enhance interests of recreation sites [23,31,47]. In Class III (natural environment) emphasis would be on natural conditions, but various forms of forest harvest might be practiced on areas adjoining specifically-designated recreation sites on national or state forest lands. In some park areas hazardous [30], dead, and down trees would be salvaged on Class III lands, as well as on Classes I and II. Vista cutting might also be more generally practiced in these areas.

Due in part to growing public pressure for change of forest cutting practices, and also to public agency and professional forestry awareness of the desirability of landscape management to maintain visual qualities of the forest, landscape architects working with the Forest Service have developed concepts and procedures for national forest landscape management. The basic concepts concern maintaining the natural characteristics of specific landscapes, maintaining visual variety rather than monotony, and designing deviations such as timber cutting to achieve acceptable variety—including vista cutting [33,42].

Landscape management is being effectively applied on national forests in the Pacific Northwest, particularly on Class II lands with highly variable topography. Road, pipeline, trail and building location, and power line siting are also of concern in landscape management, in addition to recreational facility development.

On Class IV (unique natural area), Class V (primitive area) and Class VI (historic and cultural sites), natural conditions would be altered as little as possible. This might mean not disturbing blow-down, diseased, insect-killed, or fire-killed forests, as they occur from natural causes rather than from artificially induced forces. In the case of highly valued species of both sacred park and commercial value (e.g., California redwoods; New Zealand kauri forests) downed trees may be of as much interest for preservation as standing trees. Such practices, of course, present problems. It is often difficult to tell what is the result of natural causes or where such conditions were due to human-related activities or carelessness.

As a result of research on the role of fire in natural ecosystems, the attitude on "natural" fire (e.g., lightning-caused) in areas managed for maintenance of intrinsic natural conditions has changed. There is evidence that where national parks and wildernesses are protected from all fires, potentially more hazardous fire conditions may develop than if periodic, natural fires had occurred. This is the case in some groves of *Sequoia gigantea* in Sequoia-Kings Canyon National Park, California [18]. Similarly, damage by indigenous insects and pathogens (disease) is being more carefully evaluated.

Recreation research has also resulted in development of ameliorative practices which are followed in restoring wilderness campsites and other abused locations after vegetation and soil loss due to heavy visitor impact [12,20,22,24,31,38,45-47].

The procedures in hazard removal, salvage operations, landscape management, and vista cutting are all important to adequate maintenance of the natural environment and public safety. When cutting and removal are to be done by private contractors, material to be removed must be carefully measured, marked, and evaluated. Area boundaries should be carefully defined, as should access routes, loading zones, or temporary roads. Special operating conditions should be carefully enumerated in a legal contract to include limitations on loading equipment, size of tractors, preparation of site, weather limitations, cleanup, and planting. Performance bonding of operators is recommended as is very careful supervision of all operations from beginning to end.

Because this process is very demanding, some managers prefer to use special contractors with whom sales can be negotiated or to do the work with their own personnel. Maintenance of the quality of the forest or wildland environment should be the main consideration rather than the monetary return from the sale of forest products. The application of the above procedures has been successfully used in the Pacific Northwest.

Rules and Regulations

Definite guidelines of use, among the first tools of recreational land management, are important to area administration. Regulatory restrictions, some of which may be irksome, will be increasingly necessary as greater numbers of people engage in outdoor recreation. Greater emphasis is placed upon a positive approach, the objective being to encourage public cooperation in the proper use of an area through greater understanding and appreciation of the values involved, and the development of individual responsibility in their perpetuation for the future. The effectiveness of rules and regulations is enhanced by use of other relevant methods such as interpretive programs, which guide user interest and activities into channels appropriate to specific recreational areas, or even parts of a particular area.

Deliberate vandalism is attributed to only a small percentage of users. In large measure, improper or destructive actions result from unfamiliarity with requirements in the use of an area and the lack of understanding of the ultimate effects of improper behavior on the environment and other people.

However, the phenomenal expansion in the use of recreational areas has, unfortunately, been accompanied by a rise in various acts of antisocial behavior [4,6,17]. Such acts range from nuisances to serious crimes. Rules and regulations should define the legitimate uses of an area and clearly indicate varied restrictions of such uses. Those guilty of infractions must be dealt with promptly and firmly, but fairly, in such manner as defined by law.

Of even greater importance is a well-organized interpretive program which, besides developing greater enjoyment of an area, also fosters public understanding of different hazards and how to recognize, anticipate, and cope with them. Interpretive programs explain the vagaries of nature, identify poisonous plants, and give information on patterns of animal behavior dangerous to humans. Coupled with public relations and general public education programs, they bridge the gap in understanding between visitor and manager. They should also impart to the visitor a feeling of self-responsibility as a citizen and owner of public recreation lands. Hopefully, the manager will also learn from the visitor-resource user as a part of these educational efforts.

Public Relations and Involvement

The importance of proper, well-coordinated management policies that are understood and supported by the general public is apparent in the increasing need for all products and services of wild lands. Problems induced by the rapid growth in recreational use of land, including protection of environmental features and beauty are particularly troublesome. As a result, attention has been focused upon all available types of land suited to varied, rapidly expanding, and increasingly diverse recreational activities.

Various types of both private and public lands are involved. Many conflicts of interest have developed among vociferous and politically effective groups who champion numerous land-use philosophies. Many techniques of natural-resource extraction and use, acceptable when land was plentiful and use competition less severe, have become outmoded and require reevaluation and improvement.

The number of agencies concerned with recreation has greatly increased. Their responsibilities to recreation are not always completely clear; personnel trained for development of other objectives are often puzzled by unfamiliar requirements of recreational management. In some cases the language of legislative acts establishing and defining the purposes of certain areas is outmoded. Titles applied to some areas may be somewhat ambiguous; "wilderness area," "recreation area," and "wildlife refuge" are definitive, but the term "park" is subject to various interpretations, especially when applied to areas of unique quality (national parks). Both biological and economic principles upon which different types of land uses are based are often misunderstood by the general public. Many recreational activities, in addition to being incompatible with some other forms of land use, are incompatible with one another. Properly organized programs of public information contribute to and assist in the solution of such land management problems [11]. All forms of communications media are utilized in developing suitable understanding of varied land uses.

On new planning and management proposals for recreation areas, public input is solicited. For federal lands this is required by the National Environmental Policy Act of 1969. It is important to give the public a real role in planning and management so that they can contribute ideas and understand the reasons for agency policies. Merely counting votes for or against programs may be self-defeating [9]. The objective of public information efforts is to enlarge public interest in logical land-management policies so that development and use of various recreational and other values of wild land may be properly related to one another and to the environment. However, they are effective only if based upon factual information presented in a manner both interesting and understandable to the layperson, and if supported by appropriate management practices in the field.

Interpretation

Interpretative activities (visitor centers or museums, nature trails, guided field trips, campfire programs, publications) were initiated primarily to enhance public enjoyment of outdoor recreation through appreciation of the areas involved. It was soon apparent, however, that such activities were of equal importance in directing recreational land use into proper channels and in developing public responsibility in environmental protection. In brief, public interest in perpetuation of recreational values is increased by understanding and appreciation of the interests involved [35,39].

Specifically, if the archeological importance of a remarkable cliff dwelling is understood and its value to society is recognized, one's approach to it, both physically and psychologically, will be more in keeping with the dignity which should characterize such treasures, and wear and damage will be minimized. Similarly, flora, fauna, and ecological interests will be less subject to modification by selfish removal of plants, disturbance of animals, or thoughtless meandering from developed trails. Moreover, the danger of fire or acts of vandalism which ravage the beauty of unique forests will be materially reduced. Even features of geological excellence, generally more resistant to damage, will be more likely to escape defacement if their significance is recognized. At some national parks, entering visitors are encouraged to stop first at the main visitor center to see a movie of the park featuring its varied attractions, the best means of reaching and observing them, and the purposes of the park's management. This introduction meets the three basic objectives of interpretation—improvement of visitor understanding of the area, accomplishing management goals, and promoting the agency and its programs [35].

Interpretation as a management tool is not limited to areas of highly unique quality, such as national parks, where early developments took place. Today interpretation is an accepted technique on many other types of recreational lands, including national forests, state parks and forests, county and municipal parks, and even some recreational areas on privately owned, commercial forest land. The most highly developed interpretive programs generally occur on Class I, II, IV, and VI lands; occasionally, very simple interpretive aids are provided on Class III and V lands.

Interpretation is a specialized aspect of recreational land management. Principles concerning the organization of interpretive services and development of relevant facilities, most closely related to the operation of recreational areas, are outlined in Chapter 16.

Organized Maintenance of Area and Facilities

As with facility development and interpretation, the numerous details related to maintenance of recreational areas and their facilities are more closely related to operational aspects of management. However, in large measure the manner in which a recreational area is maintained determines public reaction in its use. A neat, orderly appearance—evidence of good housekeeping—is an indication of agency sincerity in area protection and relates positively to development of personal visitor responsibility in the care and perpetuation of recreational values, and vice versa. Thus, good maintenance is an important management tool. Its varied details are suggested in Chapter 16.

Research

Research is an important tool in the solution of wild-land recreational problems and the improvement of wild-land recreational services [5,43,44]. In recent years recreational research has expanded in many directions, covering numerous relevant topics. Most have implications for policy or direct application to an area, but some are basic studies to test theories.

General Research Topics Studies of human relationships relate to public attitudes and perceptions in the use of various types of recreational lands; visitor behavior, with emphasis on vandalism and antisocial activities; visitor motivation, preferences and use-patterns; and public reaction to restrictions in recreational uses and land allocation proposals. Investigations of the physical resources involve existing ecosystems; plant succession; the impact of existing and proposed developments on soils and plant and animal associations; the effects of public concentrations on wildlife and vice versa; the effects of fire on environment; and archeological and historical studies.

Research emphasis concerning management techniques relates to studies of human carrying capacity of recreational lands and waters, including wilderness and wild rivers; measurement of control of visitor numbers and degree of use of specific sites; cultural activities in maintenance and rehabilitation of heavily used locations; and public response to interpretive efforts. Studies of structural design and effectiveness of various materials under different conditions favor economy, practicability, and esthetics in development of physical facilities.

Economic implications are revealed through investigations of the relationship between operational costs and returns from existing or contemplated charges for various services; and the impact of recreational expenditures on the stability of communities near recreational areas.

In particular, recreational innovations are being closely scrutinized, including the increasing use and impact of snowmobiles and various types of off-road recreational vehicles [3]. Further, the computer is being put to ever-increasing research use to simulate recreationist behavior and analyze use.

Research and Management Personnel Research and management are distinct activities which appeal to people of quite different interests and qualifications. Except in certain instances, research is not the province of management personnel [11]. It is generally conducted by individuals who are especially motivated, trained, and qualified for such duties. The multitude of details dealt with by management personnel leaves them little time for significant participation in research tasks.

Recreation researchers may be permanently or seasonally employed, as in the case at Forest Service Experiment Stations.[1] They may also be engaged on a cooperative or consulting basis through universities or similar institutions. Many disciplines are involved, including sociology, geography,

---

[1] The Forest Service has an experiment station in each of its regions (see Figure 9–1). Units attached to several of these experiment stations concentrate on specific aspects of wildland recreation research (e.g., recreational demand, benefits, depreciative behavior, planning and management techniques, dispersed use, wilderness and wild rivers), coordinating these in-depth programs to provide data to aid in solution of a wide range of problems.

forestry, biology, ecology, economics, engineering, architecture and landscape architecture, business, and recreation.

However, management personnel have an important relationship to research activity. They are close to practical "grass roots" problems and are in a position to aid in establishing direction and emphasis to research efforts. They are also in a singular position to implement the results of research findings. The validity of their opinions, based on experience, can sometimes be substantiated and strengthened by research results; or research may expose important factors which bear upon the solution of problems which might have been overlooked, ignored, or misinterpreted. In particular, it is important that management personnel, policy makers, administrators, interpreters, and extension specialists be capable of evaluating research results and subsequently applying them in the field. In certain cases suitably qualified management personnel may contribute to research programs, particularly when they involve periodic detailed field checking over an extended span of time.

Coordination between research and management personnel is implied in recommendations of the Advisory Board on Wildlife Management (Leopold Committee) for the National Park Service, where the objective is the maintenance or restoration of original biotic communities. In its report to the Secretary of the Interior [21] it suggested the following procedure:

> The first step in park management is historical research, to ascertain as accurately as possible what plants and animals and biotic associations existed originally in each locality. Much of this has been done already.
>
> A second step should be ecological research on plant-animal relationships leading to formulation of a management hypothesis.
>
> Next should come small scale experimentation to test the hypothesis in practice. Experimental plots can be situated out of sight of roads and visitor centers.
>
> Lastly, application of tested management methods can be undertaken on critical areas.
>
> By this process of study and pretesting, mistakes can be minimized. Likewise, public groups vitally interested in park management can be shown the results of research and testing before general application, thereby eliminating possible misunderstanding and friction.

Since 1965 the National Park Service has been working on implementation of the recommendations of the Leopold Report, with varied studies within the national parks. These have been done under direct agency contract, by universities, scientific organizations, and qualified individuals.

SUMMARY

The objectives of administration and management of recreational lands are to provide opportunities for an optimum number of people at the lowest cost and, to provide for, the perpetuation of varied recreational features and values. Control and manipulation of both the environment and its users are involved. Management tasks are difficult, often frustrating, and even disagreeable. Their successful accomplishment is favored when the best uses of various recreational lands are clearly defined, with both lands and uses properly correlated in a management plan. The management approaches will vary with land class and the policy objectives of the agencies or owner controlling the land.

A number of tools are useful in varied administrative and management tasks. These include zoning and related controls of land and activities, development, environmental manipulation and landscape management, rules and regulations, public relations and involvement, interpretation, maintenance, and research. Such activities minimize the impact of use upon environment by channeling various pursuits onto lands best able to accommodate them. When public understanding is improved through education and interpretation, visitors may assume better responsibility for the care of recreational lands. Also perhaps managers may learn from visitors in a two-way education process.

We have used the medium of the basic recreation land classes as originally proposed by the Outdoor Recreation Resources Review Commission to explain some of the differences in agency-owner management policies and use of tools of management. It is, of course, but one approach. However, if it serves to show the reader some of the modern management process and to raise questions, its use is justified.

SELECTED REFERENCES

1 Alfano, Sam S., and Arthur W. Magill: "Vandalism in Outdoor Recreation," U.S. Forest Service, Pacific Southwest Forest and Range Experiment Station, General Technical Report, PSW–17, Berkeley, 1976.
2 Argow, Keith A., and John Fedkiw: Recreation User Fee Income—How Far Does It Go toward Meeting Costs? *Journal of Forestry,* vol. 61, no. 10, October 1963.
2a Brockman, C. Frank: Park Naturalists and the Evolution of National Park Service Interpretation through World War II, *Journal of Forest History,* vol. 22, no. 1, January 1978.
3 Bury, R. L., R. C. Wendling, and S. F. McCool: "Off-road Recreation Vehicles—A Research Summary, 1965–1975," Texas A&M University, College Station, Texas, 1976.
4 Campbell, Fred L., John C. Hendee, and Roger Clark: Law and Order in Public Parks, *Parks and Recreation,* vol. 3, no. 12, December 1968.
5 Clawson, Marion, and Jack L. Knetsch: Recreation Research: Some Basic Analytical Concepts and Suggestions, *Proceedings of the National Conference on Outdoor Recreation Research,* Ann Arbor, Mich., 1963.

6 Davis, C.: Legal Problems and Liability in Outdoor Recreation, *Park Maintenance,* vol. 19, no. 12, December 1966.

7 Doell, Charles E., and Louis F. Twardzik: "Elements of Park and Recreation Administration," 3rd ed., Burgess, Minneapolis, 1973.

8 Douglas, Robert W.: "Forest Recreation," 2nd ed., Pergamon, New York, 1975.

9 Fairfax, Sally K.: Public Involvement in the Forest Service, *Journal of Forestry,* vol. 73, no. 10, October 1975.

10 Frissell, S. S., and Donald E. Duncan: Campsite Preference and Deterioration in the Quetico-Superior Canoe Country, *Journal of Forestry,* vol. 63, no. 4, April 1965.

11 Gilbert, Douglas L.: "Public Relations in Natural Resource Management," Burgess, Minneapolis, 1964.

12 Heinselman, M. L.: Vegetation Management in Wilderness Areas and Primitive Parks, *Journal of Forestry,* vol. 63, no. 6, June 1965.

13 Hendee, John C., William R. Catton, Jr., Larry D. Marlow, and C. Frank Brockman: "Wilderness Users in the Pacific Northwest—Their Characteristics, Values, and Management Preferences," U.S. Forest Service, Pacific Northwest Forest and Range Experiment Station, Research Paper PNW-61, Portland, 1968.

14 Hendee, John C., and Robert C. Lucas: Mandatory Wilderness Permits—A Necessary Management Tool, *Journal of Forestry,* vol. 71, no. 4, April 1973.

15 Hendee, John C., George Stankey, and Robert C. Lucas: "Wilderness Management," U.S. Government Printing Office, Washington, 1978.

16 Hulbert, James H., and Joseph F. Higgins: BWCA Visitor Distribution System, *Journal of Forestry,* vol. 75, no. 6, June 1977.

17 Hunkins, R. B.: Criminal Jurisdiction in the National Parks, *Land and Water Review,* vol. 2, no. 1, January 1967.

18 Kilgore, Bruce M.: Restoring Fire in The Sequoias, *National Parks and Conservation,* vol. 44, October 1970.

19 Koontz, Harold (ed.): "Toward a Unified Theory of Management," McGraw-Hill, New York, 1964.

20 LaPage, Wilbur F.: "Some Observations on Campground Trampling and Ground Cover Response," U.S. Forest Service, Northeast Forest Experiment Station, Research Paper NE-68, Upper Darby, Pa., 1967.

21 Leopold, A. Starker, et al.: "Wildlife Management in the National Parks," Report to the Secretary of the Interior, March 1963.

22 Lime, David W.: Principles of Recreational Carrying Capacity, *Proceedings, Southern States Recreation Research Application Workshop,* Ashville, N.C., Sept. 15–18, 1975.

23 Litton, R. B., and Robert M. Twiss: The Forest Landscape—Some Elements of Visual Analysis, *Proceedings, Society of American Foresters Annual Meeting,* Seattle, Washington, Sept. 12–15, 1968, Washington, 1967.

24 Lucas, Robert C.: User Concepts of Wilderness and Their Implication for Resource Management, *Western Resource Papers, 1964,* New Horizons for Resources Research: Issues and Methodology, University of Colorado Press, Boulder, Colo., 1964.

25 Lucas Robert C.: Wilderness—A Management Framework, *Journal of Soil and Water Conservation,* vol. 28, no. 4, July–August 1973.

26 Magill, Arthur W.: "Campsite Reservation Systems, The Camper's Viewpoint," U.S. Forest Service, Pacific Southwest Forest and Range Experiment Station, Research Paper PSW–121, Berkeley, 1976.

27 Merriam, L. C., Jr., et al.: "Newly Developed Campsites in the Boundary Waters Canoe Area—A Study of Five Years Use," University of Minnesota, Agric. Exper. Sta. Bulletin 511, St. Paul, 1973.

28 Merriam, L. C., Jr., and T. B. Knopp: Meeting the Wilderness Needs of the Many, *Western Wildlands,* vol. 3, no. 1, Spring 1976.

29 Mills, A. S., L. C. Merriam, Jr., and C. E. Ramsey: "Public Opinion and Park Development," University of Minnesota, Agric. Exper. Sta. Bulletin 510, St. Paul, 1973.

30 Paine, L. A.: "Accidents Caused by Hazardous Trees in California Recreation Sites," U.S. Forest Service, Pacific Southwest Forest and Range Experiment Station, Research Note PSW–133, Berkeley, 1966.

31 Ripley, Thomas M.: Rehabilitation of Forest Recreation Sites, *Proceedings, Society of American Foresters Annual Meeting,* Detroit, Oct. 24–28, 1966, Washington.

32 Rubini, F. F.: Revenue Facilities and Services by Lease, *Parks and Recreation,* vol. 2, no. 1, January 1967, and vol. 2, no. 3, March 1967.

33 Rutherford, Wm., Jr., and Elwood L. Shafer, Jr.: Selected Cuts Increased Natural Beauty of Two Adirondack Forest Stands, *Journal of Forestry,* vol. 67, no. 6, June 1968.

34 Schuster, E. G., H. H. Webster, and R. D. Ulrich: "Land-Use Controls for Outdoor Recreation Areas," Agric. and Home Econ. Experiment Station, Special Report No. 78, Iowa State University, 1976.

34a Schoenfeld, Clarence A. and John C. Hendee: "Wildlife Management In Wilderness," Boxwood Press, Pacific Grove, Calif., 1978.

35 Sharpe, Grant W. (ed.) "Interpreting the Environment," Wiley, New York, 1976.

36 Society of American Foresters: Wilderness Policy (The Coming of a New Deal—Senator Frank Church; Wilderness Allocation: Directions for the New Administration—M. Rupert Cutler; and A Colloquy Between Congressman Weaver and Assistant Secretary Cutler), *Journal of Forestry,* vol. 75, no. 7, July 1977.

37 Stankey, Geo. H., Robert C. Lucas, and David M. Lime: Crowding in Parks and Wilderness, *Design and Environment,* Fall 1976.

38 Sumner, Lowell: Regulation of High Country Pack Stock Use, *Proceedings, Region IV Park Naturalist's Conference,* Yosemite National Park, April 14–18, 1948, National Park Service, 1948 (mimeo.).

39 Tilden, Freeman: "Interpreting Our Heritage," University of North Carolina Press, Chapel Hill, N.C., 1967.

40 U.S. Department of Agriculture, Forest Service, California Region: "Collecting User Fees on National Forest Recreation Sites," San Francisco, 1963.

41 U.S. Department of Agriculture, Forest Service: "A Summary of the Renewa-

ble Resource Assessment and a Recommended Renewable Resource Program," Washington, 1976.

42 U.S. Department of Agriculture, Forest Service: "National Forest Landscape Management," vols. 1 and 2, Agriculture Handbooks 434, 462, and 483, U.S. Government Printing Office, Washington, 1973, 1974, and 1977.

43 U.S. Department of Agriculture, Forest Service: *Proceedings of the Southern States Recreation Research Applications Workshop,* Ashville, N.C., Sept. 15–18, 1975, General Technical Report SE–9, Ashville, June 1976.

44 U.S. Department of the Interior, National Park Service: Research in the Parks, *Transactions of the National Park Centennial Symposium,* Dec. 28–29, 1971, Washington, 1976.

45 Wagar, J. Alan: "The Carrying Capacity of Wildlands for Recreation," Forest Service Monograph No. 7, Society of American Foresters, Washington, 1964.

46 Wagar, J. Alan: How To Predict Which Vegetated Areas Will Stand Up Best Under "Active" Recreation, *American Recreation Jounral,* vol. 1, no. 7, July 1967.

47 Wagar, J. Alan: Cultural Treatment of Vegetation and Recreation Sites, *Proceedings, Society of American Foresters Annual Meeting,* Detroit, Oct. 24–28, 1965, Washington, 1967.

48 Wagar, J. V. K.: Services and Facilities for Forest Recreation, *Journal of Forestry,* vol. 44, no. 11, November 1946.

49 Whyte, William H.: "The Last Landscape," Doubleday, New York, 1968.

Recreational
Land-Use Operation

Since recreational land management is concerned with people, as users, and the environment, as well as with basic tools of management, the successful accomplishment of a manager's tasks can be exasperating as well as rewarding. Patience, diplomacy, resourcefulness, and initiative, along with varied technical skills, are required. Management of environment per se presents many difficult problems, but likely reactions to certain stimuli can often be determined by experience or research. Public reactions are not so predictable. Understanding what prompts human actions and reactions under certain circumstances in outdoor recreation is very difficult and requires particularly dedicated, open-minded and trained personnel.

In addition to perpetuation of basic recreational needs and environmental quality by proper planning and basic management, as discussed in Chapters 14 and 15, there is the highly important job of operation of recreational areas. This involves a variety of tasks related to:

1 Protection of health, safety, and property of both visitors and employees
2 Development of facilities
3 Maintenance details—facilities and areas
4 Budget preparation and proper handling of funds

5   Organization of interpretive programs
6   Relationship between management and operators of commercial services
7   Personnel requirements and training

PROTECTION OF VISITOR HEALTH, SAFETY, AND PROPERTY

Whenever recreational lands are provided for public use, the administering agency has an obligation to guard patrons, as well as employees and their families, from conditions which may adversely affect their physical well-being or endanger their property. There are a number of basic reasons for taking such precautions on wild-land recreational areas.

Because of increasing urbanization, wild land is an unfamiliar environment for many people; too often its hazards are unrecognized or improperly understood. Also, recreational attractions of the outdoors often develop localized overcrowding, which promotes a variety of conditions disadvantageous to public health; crowded conditions and resultant disruption of normal living patterns increases the possibility of contamination of food and water and the spread of contagious diseases. Further, the informality typical of a recreational outing often causes visitors to become lax in the protection of personal belongings; the outdoors seems to foster a feeling of trust which, unfortunately, is not always justified. Thievery and other crimes are matters of growing concern, particularly in areas used by large crowds [2,5].

In many recreational areas normal traffic dangers are complicated by rough mountainous terrain with steep, narrow, winding roads. In addition, a variety of attractions generally compete for the attention of the driver. Attractive scenic vistas, wild animals, colorful wild flowers, or interesting geological formations along the way militate against traffic safety.

The behavior of hikers also poses a variety of problems. For instance, rapid descent of a steep trail may make footing unsure and speed unsafe. Short-cutting switchbacks in an unfamiliar area may lead hikers into dangerous situations. Special precautions are also required when trails are used by foot or mounted travelers or by mechanized trail bike riders. The character of the surface over which hikers travel, such as snow, glacial ice, bogs, or rocky footing on steep, mountainous terrain, often necessitates special precautions.

The peculiarities of climate, such as fog, high winds, lightning, or extremes of temperature, can be dangerous if not properly understood. The unsuspected or changeable power of stream or ocean currents and the hidden dangers of unfamiliar waters are ever-present threats in some areas.

The presence of poisonous plants and dangerous animals involves potential danger. Obviously dangerous animals (grizzly bear, poisonous reptiles) are only part of the problem. There is danger also in overfamiliarity with less aggressive native animals that have lost their fear of people (American black bear). Such animals are not tame; their response to unexpected movement or misunderstood actions can often result in severe injury to the uninformed person. Under conditions of complete protection, many wild animals lose their fear of human beings, yet react instinctively when startled, frightened, or bewildered. Under such circumstances even ordinarily inoffensive animals can inflict injury.

Basic Precautions

The nature and degree of various hazards to public health and safety, and to property, vary with specific types of wild-land recreational areas; each type has particular problems which must be understood and solved by management. While it is impossible to detail necessary safeguards for all possible situations in this general text, some basic precautions can be noted. These include:

1 Competent personnel experienced in, and responsible for, various specialized duties
2 Organization and training of personnel to meet emergencies wherever and whenever they occur
3 Safe design and construction of facilities and efficient organization of services, together with regular inspection of both facilities and services
4 Development of an adequate program of general information and interpretation to enhance public understanding of the particular recreational function of an area and the nature of potential hazards in the wild-land environment
5 Fair, unbiased enforcement of adequate rules and regulations

The existence of a competent staff is taken for granted. Most employees of wild-land recreational areas either have regular duties which relate in some way to protection of public health, safety, and property, or may be called upon to assist in various ways in emergency situations. Of particular importance are employees whose regular duties involve enforcement of laws and related rules and regulations, or the construction, operation, maintenance, and inspection of facilities and services most likely to be involved in hazards to public health and safety. Certain areas (mountainous terrain, deserts, potentially dangerous waters) require employees capable of assuming leadership in various kinds of rescue operations and first-aid treatment. Other types of wild lands have other potential dangers. For instance, if rock and earth slides, avalanches, falling trees, tidal rips, and similar dangers are potential hazards in locations generally frequented by the public, employees should be skilled in recognizing likely signs of them.

However, despite the effectiveness of precautionary measures, emergency situations invariably arise. Emergency organization of staff, supported by regular training under simulated emergency conditions, and development of preplanned emergency procedures promote quick and effective action when real emergencies occur. Organization and training should involve all personnel. Tasks relevant to different emergency situations and suited to individual competence should be assigned to various individuals on several levels—first call, follow-up, support, and standby.

Safely constructed facilities and efficiently operated services have minimal hazard to public health and safety. Road and trail construction should conform to acceptable engineering standards. Signs must be properly located and clearly legible; in particular, directional signs contribute to safe use of roads and trails. Water supply, sanitary facilities and sewage disposal, and methods of refuse and garbage disposal for all parks and recreation area units should conform to public health standards [17,19,25]. The same criteria should apply to public food services, which should be inspected regularly by qualified personnel to ensure continuation of acceptable standards.

Cooperation of visitors in guarding against hazards is also necessary. Since recreational areas are established for public benefit and enjoyment, those who use them must recognize that this privilege entails definite personal responsibility. For example, before starting on an extended back-country hike it is wise to register and post an anticipated itinerary, and to check out upon return. Such precautions should be automatic on wild-land recreational areas where hikers are required to obtain permits for wilderness trail and fire use.

Visitors should also be informed of the particular function of the area in question, of the kinds of recreational opportunities which it is intended to provide, and how these differ from opportunities available on other types of recreational lands. Efforts toward such public understanding should be reinforced by adequate, sensible rules and regulations which protect both area and visitor. Enforcement is the responsibility of management personnel equipped and trained for the task. Infraction of laws which involve more serious situations than those covered by rules and regulations are handled by duly constituted officers (federal, state, county). How the authority is shared by the local recreational staff and "outside" law enforcement officers varies with the situation. Some situations are complicated and characterized by overlapping authority.

The trend toward unacceptable behavior and more serious crimes in recreational areas [2,3,5] has prompted more effective law enforcement methods, including addition of police to recreational management personnel. Also, regular and seasonal personnel in park and recreation areas receive training in effective law enforcement. In addition to traffic enforcement, including safe approach to violators, and instruction on reporting incidents, this may include background on types of violations, arrests, collection of evidence, and investigation [24].

DEVELOPMENT OF FACILITIES

Some basic considerations concerning development of principal facilities of recreational areas follow. These are intended merely as guides; limited space prohibits presentation of details.

Roads and Trails   Roads and trails in recreational areas are a means to an end, rather than an end in themselves. Their primary function is to facilitate proper mobility, circulation, and distribution of visitors, and to bring visitors in contact with representative attractions. Although these roads and trails should conform to sound engineering principles, they should be so located, designed, and constructed as to avoid extensive modification of scenic beauty or damage to natural features of interest. The same principle applies to trail development.

Extensive cuts and fills should be avoided if possible, especially if they result in scars visible from a distance. If scars are unavoidable, they should be rehabilitated by suitable plantings of native trees and shrubs. The road surface, bridges and culverts, walls, and similar features should blend with natural surroundings.

Roads, and to a lesser degree, trails, are no longer considered the sole means of visitor access to points of interest within recreational areas. Highway construction and maintenance are costly. Available roads invariably attract crowds which often seriously damage or modify the environment [18]. Crowded conditions typical of many recreational areas have prompted studies of other means of access. Overhead lifts and tramways have received consideration, and in portions of some areas of high quality visitors now travel by public vehicle rather than in private cars.

Signs   Public use of recreational areas necessitates a variety of signs. These serve to direct public movements, designate features and facilities, identify hazards, caution against improper actions or activities, define rules, and regulations, or point out particular attractions.

In large measure signs indicate the motif of recreational areas. Proper placement, scale, design, materials, and nature and clarity of text are important features of their serviceability; decisions on these factors come from careful consideration of the purpose to be served. Protection from vandalism should also receive careful consideration. The location of signs should be related to the average sight distance for various rates of travel, varying from a few feet for stationary viewing or for foot or horse travel to approximately 300 feet for fast motor traffic on main highways. Scale, design, and materials used should be in accord with the character of the region, cost of maintenance, and cost of occasional replacement. Wherever possible text should be positive; emphasis should be placed upon desirable actions rather than prohibitions. Long lines and all-capital letters should be avoided. The size of letters and the nature and extent of the text depend on the purpose. A few words in large, readily visible letters serve directional or cautionary needs; regulatory or informational signs require more extensive text. In any event, brevity, consistent with clarity and completeness, is paramount. Unnecessarily wordy signs are ineffective.

Campgrounds and Picnic Areas The location and development of campgrounds should conform to their primary purpose [4,8,9,13,14,26]. Their clientele may be motorists, horseback riders, canoeists, or hikers. A variety of types of campgrounds provide for differing visitor needs. The traveler stopping for one night has different needs from the long-term camper. Simple campgrounds would be found on Class III lands, with primitive camps on Class V, and the majority of developed campgrounds on Class I and II lands. However, it is also possible to have a range of campground types from primitive to developed within a single recreation area. Recent studies indicate the desirability to visitors of such a range, which can also reduce total development costs [14].

Some campgrounds serve as centers of operation from which attractions of a given region may be conveniently explored within a specified time. Others serve to accommodate overflow crowds during peak-use periods or to satisfy transient visitors enroute to more distant objectives. The demand for special modern facilities such as showers, laundries, stores, and related features has encouraged the development of large private campgrounds (e.g., KOA Campgrounds) located outside or adjacent to public parks and forests. Some new public parks rely on the private sector to provide these more sophisticated services. Facilities in the public area are then limited to simple or primitive camps costing less public money to develop and maintain.

Campgrounds serve to control and guide public use of the outdoors, thus aiding overall preservation of the attractiveness of recreational lands without too great a limitation of visitor use and enjoyment. Limiting camping to specific, well-defined sections within an area, however, often results in large concentrations of people in a relatively small space. Unless campgrounds are properly planned, designed, constructed with adequate spacing, such concentrations will bring about serious modification of campground features [8,12,13].

Destruction of vegetation is one of the first indications of campground overuse. In extreme cases herbaceous plants, even shrubs and small trees may be literally tramped out. In campgrounds designed and developed for large numbers of people, portions of the more heavily used camp spaces may be paved with some appropriate hard-surface material. Though this introduces an element of artificiality into the camping experience, it has the advantage of preventing adjacent environmental damage.

Proper selection of an area for a campground depends upon a number of important factors. These include the features of the area, its topography, nature and proximity of water supply, the type of soil and vegetation, climate, accessibility, expected degree of public use and its seasonal or periodic variations, the requirements of users (including the kinds of vehicles or mode of transportation), and the proximity of the campground to public needs (food and automotive supplies) and points of interest.

The attractions of a campground (vegetation and forest cover, nearby lakes and streams and other topographic features, scenic beauty or outlook, animal life) may be hazardous as well as charming. Consideration must be given to fire hazard, public health and safety, possible depredations of certain animals (American black bear), and, in some cases, the existence of poisonous plants or reptiles. Although level terrain simplifies campground layout and facilitates greater economy of space, a reasonable degree of irregularity in topography often lends itself to development of a plan which provides maximum individual privacy. The nature and proximity of water supply are important to economy of operation and to public health. The reaction of soils and types of vegetation to different degrees of use must be understood, for they react variously to similar conditions; further, some types of vegetation can be more easily replaced than others, if excessive use of an area necessitates rehabilitation. Climatic conditions (including elevation, temperature, prevailing winds, rainfall, and snow quantity) and accessibility to centers of population bear strongly upon the degree and fluctuation of campground use. Such factors are important in determining the location, size, and arrangement of camping facilities.

The mode of transportation generally used by campers must also be considered. For instance, use by trailers requires certain modifications in campground design. Increased use of pickup trucks with campers and growing demand for utility connections (water, power) further complicate the problems of campground planning. Campgrounds in remote areas for those traveling on foot or horseback or by canoe must obviously be laid out differently from those adjacent to primary highways. Individual campsites with pit toilets have been developed in some heavily used wilderness backcountry areas (e.g., Boundary Waters Canoe Area, Glacier National Park) to concentrate use in designated areas and avoid individual party site development.

An adequate site plan is basic to proper development of campgrounds, particularly those of large size. This is necessary because roads, campsites, and related developments must be tailored to the terrain and associated characteristics. One effective form of layout embraces a system of one-way roads which should be 10 feet wide with an additional 3-foot width to accommodate bordering gutters. The resultant traffic pattern eliminates congestion and minimizes the damage to vegetation and trees that is almost inevitable in a two-way system. Short individual parking spurs branching from the primary campground road give access to single campsites which, in addition to a parking spur for the car, provide a fixed tent site, table, and outdoor fireplace; approximately 750 square feet of space is required. Trailer camp units occupy about 1,200 square feet of space, though newer trailer types need less. Campgrounds combining trailer and tent sites in various arrangements are now in general use. Maximum efficiency of such individual campsites is accomplished by definitely locating units in proper relation to each other, to existing vegetation, and to prevailing winds. Spacing between individual campsites will be dependent upon topography, vegetation, and the degree and character of expected use. Maximum privacy may be provided by placing each unit behind screens of vegetation. Each camp unit should be within 200 to 250 feet of safe drinking water, and no more than 300 to 400 feet from sanitary facilities.

Protection of trees and other vegetation from damage through undesirable movement of automobiles can be effected by the erection of solid log or rock barriers at critical locations bordering roads and parking spurs. Trees and shrubs which unnecessarily interfere with proper visitor movement in campgrounds should be removed; otherwise the damage which will inevitably occur to such vegetation will set a pattern for more extensive, undesirable modification of the area [13].

Where space is not a major problem, large campground developments preferably can be planned in distinct but harmonious sections that are separated by suitable buffer zones. This permits ready increase or decrease of available camp space according to fluctuations of seasonal travel. Also, under some conditions use of entire sections may be rotated annually in order to minimize the likelihood of damage by distributing public pressures over a wider camping area.

Special Requirements of Picnickers   Since those who utilize the outdoors for picnicking are more transient than campers and have different objectives, it is advisable to provide separate areas whenever possible. This not only avoids temporary, periodic overcrowding of campgrounds, with resultant ills, but also eliminates possible friction between campers and picnickers.

In many cases, because of the larger number of picnickers, natural conditions are more likely to be sacrificed in planning adequate picnic areas than in developing campgrounds. Further, design and arrangement of picnic areas are different from those of campgrounds. The one-way road pattern still applies, and for the same reasons, but group rather than individual parking facilities are the rule. These should be located within easy walking distance of permanent tables, outdoor fireplaces, water, and sanitary facilities. The size of parking areas required for a number of cars is computed on the basis of 300 square feet per car; this allows a 10- by 20-foot space for static parking plus the necessary room for backing and turning. Individual picnic spaces, suitable for small groups not exceeding eight individuals and including a table, camp stove, and trash can, require an area of 225 square feet [8].

Utility, economy of construction and maintenance, and a design which is in harmony with the region are guiding principles in the construction of tables, camp stoves, and other necessary items in campgrounds and picnic areas [8].

Picnic or camp tables made of sawed or native wood products, different forms of masonry or metal, or various combinations of these are suitable to many types of terrain and conditions of use. Wooden facilities should be adequately protected from the weather by proper preservatives. Where weather conditions make seasonal storage necessary, tables should be constructed so that they can be handled by two persons so that they can be dismantled and reassembled readily.

Camp stoves must be economical to construct and maintain and must be planned for ease and economy of operation. As in the case of tables, the type and design of camp stoves are largely a matter of local determination and should be based upon the nature and degree of their use, as well as the character of the region. Increasing use of gasoline stoves by campers does not necessarily eliminate the need for camp fireplaces. Not all people have gasoline equipment, and a fire is often a necessity as well as a pleasure in outdoor living. The same principle does not always apply to picnic areas, especially those of excessive use, where camp stoves are often replaced by community kitchens with wood stoves or metered gas ranges.

Pure water supplies, proper refuse disposal, and adequate sanitary facilities are vital to campgrounds and picnic areas [7,17,25]. An uncontaminated water source must be maintained by proper development and regular inspection, and the design of taps and drinking fountains should conform to modern sanitary requirements. The nature and degree of development depends upon local conditions. An estimate of water requirements per person per day for picnickers is 3.1 gallons; for campers, 5.5 gallons; for occupants of cabins, 18.4 gallons; and for those in organized camps, 15 gallons.

Adequate refuse and garbage disposal requires a sufficient number of properly placed containers, the development of public responsibility in the proper use of such facilities, and a system of frequent, regular servicing.

Sanitary facilities, whether they are of a modern flush type or not, should conform to regulatory laws governing such features. They should be adequately lighted, properly ventilated, and designed for easy regular cleaning and maintenance. Where there is danger of freezing in winter, adequate provision must be made for complete draining of all pipes and related equipment, unless there is sufficient use to justify heating of the buildings. The exterior of sanitary buildings should be in harmony with the surroundings.

Facilities Necessary to Operators of Commercial Services on Public Lands.

Among the more difficult problems of recreational land management are those concerned with the location and design of buildings required by concessionaires. These apply to extensive developments (hotels, lodges, cabins, and associated facilities for overnight use) or minor needs (food stores, photo and souvenir shops, and refreshment stands). Harmonious relations between administrators and concessionaires enhance the quality of public service. To remain financially solvent, concessionaires must attract sufficient patronage. It is to their advantage to seek and obtain locations for their enterprises which are alongside visitor traffic or which command strategic viewpoints, and to conduct their operations in buildings which readily proclaim the nature of their specific service.

Although varied types of commercial services and facilities are necessary on many recreational areas, the best long-term interest of both the public and the concessionaire will be served if commercial activities do not usurp the primary values of such lands. While the financial solvency of those who provide necessary commercial services must be considered by the administration, concessionaires must also recognize that the existence of their enterprises depends upon the maintenance of the attractions of an area. To this end administrators of recreational lands should:

1 Permit establishment of only those commercial facilities that are in keeping with the character of a given area, and only if they are definitely necessary to its proper public use. For instance, overnight accommodations should not be provided if they merely offer a convenient stopping point in an extended itinerary, or if adequate services of this kind are available nearby.

2 Give proper consideration to all factors concerned in preparation of an operating contract. If a given commercial development is acceptable on an area, the administration and the operator should understand their particular responsibilities clearly.

3 If possible, locate, design, and construct necessary commercial facilities for lease to suitable operators. By assuming responsibility for capital investment and holding title to buildings, the administration can better control the location and design of commercial buildings, as well as the character and propriety of the operation which they are designed to serve.

4 If possible, it is usually best for the protection of public natural areas and parks to have hotels and related buildings in peripheral zones away from major features, or outside park boundaries.

Hotels and other commercial structures in recreational areas should be planned so as not to detract from natural features; their design should reflect the character of the region. Native materials are usually preferred, but their use must be carefully gauged for economy of construction, since much handwork entails higher costs than commercial materials. This factor is important, since commercial buildings must pay their way; their cost is reflected in charges for the public services which they provide. Proper design and skillful use of less expensive materials can often produce attractive results, since cost may rule against more expensive native materials.

Organized Camps Camps designed for organized groups have an important place in outdoor recreation. Sponsored by a wide variety of organizations (churches, lodges, schools, youth groups, clubs, and even towns and cities), they serve diverse purposes, catering to specific age groups, boys or girls, families, the infirm, or the underprivileged.

The nature and the extent of facilities, as well as the camp layout, should be in accord with the purpose to be served. For instance, the facilities and layout of family camps differ from those of youth groups. Further, many camps must necessarily be used consecutively by several organizations; in such cases it is necessary that they be designed to satisfy diverse needs.

Proper layout of an organized camp is important for efficiency of operation, maximum enjoyment of the recreational interests of an area, and proper care of the health and physical well-being of its patrons. Regimented arrangement of barracklike structures, promoting close confinement of many individuals on a small area, is impractical and undesirable; instead, large camp populations are broken up into small groups having similar interests or abilities. This is accomplished best by an arrangement consisting of a central headquarters in which all campers have a common interest and supplemented by a number of separate but closely coordinated sleeping units. Occupants of different sleeping units engage in activities as specific groups, frequently joining in overall camp programs.

The camp headquarters include the main lodge (including dining hall, kitchen and related facilities, camp store, office, and the like), the service road, visitor parking area, and the central washhouse and laundry. In large camps a separate administration building may be needed. The lodge kitchen should be so related to the service road that refuse and bulky supplies may be handled conveniently, unobtrusively, and with dispatch. Parking space for visitors should be so located that a pleasing approach to the camp is provided. Two or more units of sleeping accommodations, each with necessary sanitary facilities and with responsible supervision and leadership, augment camp headquarters; small specific units of from four to eight tents or cabins, each housing four individuals, are recommended as a means of reducing behavior problems, especially in youth camps. Each of these group facilities should be located so as to provide satisfactory privacy and yet be convenient to the central lodge and features of special interest. Finally, the infirmary should be suitably isolated from the main body of the camp.

The development and operation of camps for organized groups should give careful consideration to the following:

1 *Adequate, experienced leadership and supervision.* Qualified leadership should be provided for the development of all values typical of the region wherein the camp is located, including various forms of physical activity (swimming, boating, hiking, riding) and cultural interests (nature study, handicrafts, dramatics). Poor, unqualified, or inadequate administrative supervisory personnel greatly reduce the value of individual camping experience.

2 *Character of buildings.* Building design should be attractive and insofar as possible, should reflect the spirit of the region. Permanent structures should be designed for economy of operation and ease of maintenance.

3 *Fire hazard.* Electrical wiring, flues, and other details of building construction should conform to accepted safety regulations.

4 *Health and safety.* Clean, healthful surroundings, personal cleanliness, good food, and proper supervision of activities are basic to the health and safety of any group. Experienced first aid and medical attention, if not provided in camp, must be readily available.

Facilities for Swimming and Boating

An understanding of the hazards involved, proper supervision, and provision of adequate equipment for public health and safety are necessary wherever swimming, boating, and related water sports are made available on public lands. Where possible, swimming should be separated from water skiing, boating, and other water-competitive uses.

Bathhouses must be designed in accordance with proper sanitary practice and for numerous public needs. Adequate shower, sanitary, and staff facilities are also necessary for swimming areas.

Docks, for use by either swimmers or boaters, should be constructed of proper materials, treated with suitable preservatives to prolong life. Fluctuating water levels, ice, marine animals, and many other factors which affect the serviceability of docks should be taken into account. Boat-launching facilities should include adequate turning space for car trailers used in transporting boats to the launching site. Usually, launching facilities for motor boats should be separated from those used by canoes and related smaller craft to avoid congestion.

Since canoes and racing shells must be removed from the water when not in use, suitable storage racks are necessary. Transportation of this equipment, to and from the water, whether for current use or for seasonal storage, is made easier by large overhead or barn-type boathouse doors.

Winter Sports Facilities Downhill skiing dominates the winter sports picture, but cross-country skiing, snowmobiling, skating, tobogganing, sledding, sleighing, and ski jumping are also important. These uses are somewhat competitive and usually require their own special areas. Besides, many people simply enjoy the beauty of the winter landscape or watching various activities. Children especially like to play in the snow, often with various types of informal sliding equipment.

The basic requirements of a ski area are proper terrain, snow conditions, and climate. Snow must be of dependable depth and quality. In order to reduce accidents, topography should allow development of different sections for beginner, intermediate, and expert skiers; the ratio of steep to gentle slopes depends upon the number and proficiency of users. Specific zones, defined by topographical boundaries or patches of trees, separate groups of skiers of varying ability, snowmobile routes, and cross-country trails. Patch cutting on heavily timbered terrain sometimes provides a suitable substitute for natural ski slopes, if logging debris is removed.

Climate, in addition to affecting visitor enjoyment of winter sports areas, is responsible for numerous hazards. Storms and heavy fog create considerable danger. Extremes of temperature or prolonged periods of high wind often develop a dangerous surface crust on snow slopes. Wide variations in altitude have equally diverse snow conditions owing to differences in temperature and wind velocity at varying levels. The probability of avalanches or slides is increased by certain combinations of climate, snow condition, and topography [22].

Careful evaluation of proposed areas should be made by experienced participants before development is undertaken. Further, before a final decision is reached, areas under consideration should be examined carefully during the summer as well as during winter. Separated trails for use of snowmobiles and cross-country skiing should be carefully planned and laid out to avoid unnecessary hazards, wild-life habitat, and impact on vegetation. As solitude is often a major attraction of cross-country skiing, it is well to avoid overlaps between this use and snowmobiling.

Accessibility of ski areas and types of transportation used in reaching them will largely determine the character and degree of their development. Access roads should be located and constructed so as to minimize the difficulty, hazard, and expense of snow removal. Cost of road maintenance due to winter sports developments may be materially reduced by locating ski areas along or near highways which are regularly maintained for general winter travel. Where ski areas are adjacent to busy main highways, access to parking areas and related facilities should be provided by spur roads.

Necessary buildings, although located conveniently to the ski area, should be sufficiently removed from ski runs to avoid any danger of collision between skiers and buildings or between skiers and groups of spectators. Overnight accommodations are necessary only if ski areas are located at a considerable distance from centers of population and if such facilities are not already available nearby.

Some form of uphill transportation, varying from a simple rope tow to several types of chairlifts, is necessary on modern downhill ski areas. Rope tows may be suitable on areas where there is not enough patronage to justify more extensive development or where it is necessary to preserve significant or scenic values in summer, as in national parks. Such less elaborate developments can be installed each fall and removed at the end of the winter season.

Personnel concerned with the public use of winter sports areas should be experienced and with a thorough, first-hand knowledge of the area and its hazards; they should also be able to perform first aid and rescue work.

Off-Road Recreation Vehicles   In recent years off-road recreation vehicles (ORVs) of many designs have become popular for wild land use. Along with motorcyles, these vehicles are used on various types of rural public lands, particularly in the West. The ORV is of major concern in management of rural lands for recreation [1].

Careful planning for and management of the use of ORVs is needed to avoid damage to delicate ecosystems. It is not adequate to allow uncontrolled use of ORVs on what some people might consider unused land. Control is necessary, or ORV users can be hazardous to each other as well as to the environment. In addition to difficulties with behavior of some ORV users, management is further complicated by differences in attitudes toward such equipment between users and nonusers and between ORV manufacturers and environmentally oriented organizations.

ROUTINE MAINTENANCE OF FACILITIES AND AREAS

Of prime importance in the management and operation of all types of recreation areas on wild land is proper maintenance of such areas once they have been established, as well as maintenance of their facilities once they have been developed. While this seems obvious, it is surprising how many recreational areas were established in the past, and how many facilities were developed, without adequate planning or budgeting for maintenance. Careful planning can make the maintenance task simpler; for example, where roads or trails are constructed on stable soil, and where screening vegetation is left between campsites, excessive erosion and extreme trampling and soil compaction is reduced.

Further, the removal of carelessly discarded litter is an expensive and time-consuming task. Campground and picnic tables must be stained or painted and repaired. Latrines must be cleaned; where such facilities are of modern type, fixtures must be protected from freezing in winter. Trail hazards must be removed and eroded spots filled and properly drained. In our example of a national forest wilderness, the Boundary Waters Canoe Area, maintenance may include trail or portage repair and construction, campsite restoration and littler removal, fireplace and tent area restoration, latrine replacement; in addition, water sources may be checked for purity and water quality of lakes tested, particularly near campsite landings.

In wilderness areas where outfitter horse camps are allowed under special-use permit, compliance with rules on proper protection of the site, removal of equipment and corrals, and general area cleanup are checked by agency personnel. These and many other details are part of the overall maintenance activity.

BUDGETS

Estimates of receipts and expenditures for operations during a given period of time are as important to recreational management and operation of land as to any enterprise. They provide for efficient utilization of funds provided by taxes, bond issues, grants, bequests, and similar sources, or available through other means such as profit from operations, rents or leases, and sale of miscellaneous products. They are also required for periodic presentation and justification of programs for official approval by legislative bodies or corporate boards. In addition, by means of carefully stated operational procedures they become a financial plan for the expenditure of funds for approved programs.

Budgets vary in type and complexity [6], depending upon their purpose and the specific information desired by management. They may be related to items in an accounting system (personnel, supplies and materials, travel), to functions of an operation (maintenance, improvements, facilities and services), or, if more than one area is involved, to specific recreational land units. In many cases they may incorporate all three of the foregoing aspects, properly detailed and cross-referenced, to satisfy varied requirements and to enable management to visualize the relation of expenditures of the different segments of operational procedures to the progress of intended plans. Today many private and government organizations use program budgeting. In this form the budgets are designed to cover readily identified work units [11]. Budgets should provide fiscal responsibility in park and recreation operations.

ORGANIZATION OF INTERPRETIVE PROGRAMS [20]

Interpretive programs are a major feature of many wild land recreational areas. Such programs involve a variety of services and facilities designed to enhance visitor enjoyment, appreciation, and understanding of such lands. The techniques include both attended and unattended services, many with the latest audiovisual devices. They also contribute to development of visitor responsibility in the protection of recreational values for the future. However, the primary ingredients of a good interpretive program are the interpreters themselves. The successful interpreter, in addition to having a sound knowledge of an area, likes people, is concerned with their interests, and can project ideas to them.

Visitor Centers or Museums[1]

These facilities are generally the focal point of the interpretive program. They are to a recreational area what a table of contents is to a book or a display window is to a department store; they inform and stimulate interests in an area. Well-planned exhibits in a strategically located and attractively designed building present, outline, and briefly explain the area's significant points, thus encouraging people to go afield and observe such interests at first hand. Exhibits should not be so complete that the visitors become jaded or feel no need to explore further on their own [27]. The features of an area are primary; visitor centers or museums encourage responsible public use and enjoyment of recreational areas through understanding. Consequently, the scope of the exhibit "story" should not go beyond the immediate area involved except where necessary for perspective. Extraneous material should not be included. For instance, regardless of the interest or value under other conditions, a display of weapons of modern warfare would be inappropriate in an area of unique biological significance.

A successful visitor center or museum project in a recreational area is dependent upon the following:

1 The quality of the scientific foundation of the project or the character of the research program which develops such a foundation.
2 An understanding of public psychology by those who plan and prepare the exhibits. Since the displays will be available to people of all ages, interests, and backgrounds, their effectiveness will depend greatly on how scientific fact is simplified and dramatized. Modern museum displays borrow considerably from good advertising technique, for their objectives are similar in spite of radically different "products." The objective of advertising displays is to "sell" some type of commercial product; that of museum displays is to arouse interest in and understanding of the significance of scenery and related attractions. Eye-catching arrangements and judicious use of color have great value.

[1] The term "visitor center" is more widely used in recreational areas than "museum," mainly because the general public often associates the latter term with old-fashioned and often unattractive displays of poorly arranged subjects. However, modern museums utilize advanced techniques in arrangement, color, and materials which dramatize factual data and excite public curiosity.

3 The location of the building. Since visitor centers or museums are designed to foster public understanding of an area, they must be strategically located in relation to public activity. However, they should not become a major feature in themselves.

4 The design and plan of the building. In addition to an attractive appearance, a visitor center or museum should have public display rooms arranged to foster proper visitor circulation. Adequate space for necessary staff activities must also be provided. It is extremely important that the design and plan of the building be adapted to the exhibit plan.

Roadside and Trailside Exhibits

These are actually small-scale museums or visitor centers related to specific rather than generalized features. They vary from simple, attractive, informative signs to more elaborate semi-enclosed structures; the latter contain exhibit cases with interpretive displays which explain nearby localized interests (fossil remains, a biological association of particular note, or a geological feature).

Self-guiding Trails

Facilities of this type feature on-the-spot contact between visitors and more detailed attractions of an area. They usually involve little cost and effort and are so adaptable that they should be included in recreational areas wherever possible. A short trail that is readily accessible to centers of public concentration, which offers typical views of the area, and which provides opportunity to observe nearby features of interest usually serves this purpose. Two systems of development prevail. In one system individual features along the way (trees, wildflowers, geological or historical objects) are marked by small signs attached to movable stakes. In the other, a small, attractive leaflet describes specific interests at points along the trail, marked by permanent, numbered posts. The descriptive leaflets are made available in a container located at the beginning of the trail; these may be purchased on the honor system (box for coin deposit is attached to the container) and retained by visitors or returned to the container after they have served their purpose.

The latter system has many advantages. A minimum of maintenance is required. The leaflets are appropriate souvenirs. Such trails are always available during daylight, at the convenience of the visitor; thus, the number of people served is often greater than on officially conducted walks and field trips. In addition, visitors have greater privacy than is possible in large crowds usually typical of conducted walks. They can also proceed at their own pace, and if leaflets are carefully prepared, answers to questions may be obtained more readily than in the confusion normally typical of large groups.

Interpretive Talks

Informal talks or campfire programs on an area's attractions are often important features of interpretive programs. Such activities generally require campfire circles or outdoor amphitheaters of different type and design. These should be readily accessible but in a setting which will inspire the visitor and arouse interest in the topics discussed. Surroundings should be typical of the area and emphasize its principal interests. The site should be as free as possible from distractions which will destroy the mood of the program; forests, topographical features, water surfaces, and other characteristics of a natural setting have varied acoustical properties which must be taken into account. Since it is desirable to illustrate such programs, proper visibility to the audience is essential and provision must be made for convenient use and safe storage of projection equipment. If large crowds are the rule, an amplifying system may be necessary.

In certain instances programs may have to be given indoors. In such cases community buildings and related suitable structures, or even hotel lobbies, may be utilized.

Guided Field Trips

Led by an interpreter, these may involve a short walk of an hour to a hike of several days, or a trip by bus, boat or horseback. The success of such ventures is largely dependent upon the qualifications and experience of the leader; a sound scientific background relevant to features along the way, an understanding of people, and an interesting technique of explaining various subjects to one's group are vitally important. Each type of trip involves specific problems. The leader should confine explanations to specific points, properly spaced along the way in accordance with the capabilities of the group or the location of special attractions. While the main purpose of such trips is interpretation, it is also necessary that the group be impressed with the importance of good outdoor manners. The leader should also understand the hazards of the route to be taken, see that members of the party show proper respect for safety precautions, and in the event of accidents, know how to cope with emergencies.

Libraries

In addition to its importance as a research tool for interpretation, the library of a recreational area is also of use to the general administrative staff; size and content vary with the nature of the area. It is also a source of information to special visitors.

While most people who use and enjoy wild-land recreational areas have merely a casual interest in various detailed features, some have a much deeper perception. For these people, as well as for the administrative and interpretive staff, a well-chosen collection of books about the region is of great value.

Interpretive Literature

Distribution, publication, and sale of literature and related material dealing with an area may also be desirable, particularly where recreational lands are characterized by diverse and dramatic qualities. In addition to serving as acceptable souvenirs, such publications promote a broader under-standing of a region and contribute to the visitor's continual pleasure after returning home. In addition to leaflets and brochures containing general background information, rules and regulations, and maps, such literature may also include booklets and more elaborate books on specific subjects (wild flowers, animal life, geology, history, wilderness). They may be han-dled directly by the administrative agency or sold through private channels or, in some cases, by approved subsidiary organizations established for such purpose.

Various natural history and museum associations which operate in many national parks and monuments are examples of such subsidiary orga-nizations. They are organized so that accumulated small profits derived from their operation accrue to the benefit of the local interpretive program.

RELATION BETWEEN ADMINISTRATION AND COMMERCIAL OPERATORS

A variety of specific commerical facilities and services is necessary to full enjoyment of many outdoor recreational areas. Hotel accommodations, meals, equipment and supplies, public transportation, and other necessities must be provided. Many recreational lands are administered by various public agencies prohibited from providing commercial services. Thus they must be provided by concessionaires who usually operate under a franchise or permit granted by the administrative agency.

It is important that the nature of these services be in accord with the purpose of the area, that necessary commercial structures be designed and located to harmonize with the environment, and that the public be given maximum value at reasonable cost. It is also necessary to ensure the opera-tor opportunity for fair profit.

A written agreement or contract between the administration and the operator should define the nature of the service, the quality and standard desired, costs to the public, and similar considerations. In many instances the administrative agency shares in revenues above a determined figure which, although rarely applied directly to the operating costs of the area, nevertheless aid indirectly in its support. By this means, as well as by regu-lar inspection of facilities and financial records, the administration controls the activities of the operators and ensures proper performance of their du-ties. Inadequate or inappropriate concessionaire facilities and services re-flect discredit upon the entire management of a recreational area.

Formerly, in agreements of this kind the operator was required to fi-nance and construct necessary buildings. Later, some administrative agen-cies built and retained title to necessary commercial structures, which were leased to suitable bidders who provided required services. Since the administrative agency assumes responsibility for major capital investment, this system facilitates greater control over commercial activity.

PERSONNEL REQUIREMENTS AND TRAINING

Proper management of wild lands for recreation requires employees possessed of a wide variety of interests and abilities. Ideally the personnel of specific organizations are suited to the recreational values in areas under their jurisdiction and, as determined by the management plan, the manner in which these values are offered to the public. Recreational management of wild lands involves a great deal of hard, sometimes disagreeable, work. Most duties are deeply concerned with people as well as with the environment.

The basic qualities desired of a staff member of a wild-land recreation area are:

1 An interest in and an understanding of people. Employees must recognize and understand the reasons for varied public recreational demands, have patience and insight into the vagaries of human nature, and be able to guide the public diplomatically in the proper area use.

2 An awareness of environmental interrelations responsible for varied recreational attractions, and recognition of the fact that perpetuation of such attractions is related to understanding environmental effects of use and development.

3 An interest in, appreciation for, and understanding of, the area in which one works. The feeling of an employee for an area will be reflected in the person's attitude toward the work, no matter how menial the task.

4 Ability to recognize the relation of one's particular responsibilities to the broader recreational objectives pertinent to the area involved, its relation to other recreational lands in the region, and the importance of both recreational and other land uses.

5 Capability in specific assigned tasks, ranging from maintenance to policy-making responsibilities.

The individual in charge of a recreational area has a major responsibility to get maximum performance from the staff and also to keep happy working conditions. The primary administrative officer must be wise and exemplary; must know when to be firm and when to be sympathetic. Frequent staff meetings to maintain personnel communication, rotation of duties, and fair distribution of responsibilities are steps to maintain harmony [20]. A sense of humor and an awareness of trivia can be major leadership assets.

Several park and recreation management agencies provide special training programs to improve personnel performance, increase job awareness, and orient new employees. Such approaches may be the organization's attempt to compensate for bigness and to increase communication and cooperation among all levels of employees. The National Park Service has two training centers which provide orientation training, management, and professional development courses for employees, and some special courses for nonemployees [23].

SUMMARY

The operation of recreational areas involves numerous tasks involving various aspects of protection, development, and maintenance; responsible handling of funds; interpretation; supervision of concessionaires; maintenance details, and formation and training of staff. Though highly technical skills and hard work are required of various employees, technical perfection and application to the duties at hand are not the only criteria for success. Since their activities deal in large measure with people, patience, and diplomacy—often under trying circumstances—as well as initiative and resourcefulness are demanded. Workers at all levels of a recreational staff should recognize and be interested in their responsibilities to visitors, be aware of and understand the effects of public use on the recreational value of the area in which they are employed. They should also understand the relation of their particular area and the specific recreational opportunities it offers to other recreational lands. Finally, recreational staff should be willing to learn from their association with their visitor clientele.

SELECTED REFERENCES

1 Bury, R. L., R. C. Wendling, and S. F. McCool: "Off-Road Recreation Vehicles—A Research Summary, 1965–1975," Texas A&M University, College Station, Texas, 1976.
2 Campbell, Fred L., John C. Hendee, and Roger Clark: Law and Order in Public Parks, *Parks and Recreation,* vol. 3, no. 12, December 1968.
3 Clark, Roger N., John C. Hendee, and Fred L. Campbell: "Depreciative Behavior in Forest Campgrounds," U.S. Forest Service, Pacific Northwest Forest and Range Experiment Station, Research Note PNW–161, Portland, Ore., 1971.
4 Dailey, Tom and Dave Redman: "Guidelines for Roadless Area Campsite Spacing to Minimize Impact of Human-related Noises," U.S. Forest Service, Pacific Northwest Forest and Range Experiment Station, Technical Report PNW–35, 1975.
5 David, C.: Legal Problems and Liability in Outdoor Recreation, *Park Maintenance,* vol. 19, no. 12, December 1966.
6 Doell, Charles E., and Louis F. Twardzik: "Elements of Park and Recreation Administration," 3rd ed., Burgess, Minneapolis, 1973.
7 Douglas, Robert W.: "Forest Recreation," 2nd ed., Pergamon, New York, 1975.

8   Frissell, S. S., and Donald P. Duncan: Campsite Preference and Deterioration in the Quetico-Superior Canoe Country, *Journal of Forestry,* vol. 63, no. 4, April 1965.

9   Hendee, John C., Mack L. Hogans, and Russell W. Koch: "Dispersed Recreation on Three Forest Road Systems in Washington and Oregon," U.S. Forest Service, Pacific Northwest Forest and Range Experiment Station, Research Note, PNW–280, Portland, Ore., 1976.

10 Hendee, John C., et al.: "Code-A-Site—A System for Inventory of Dispersed Recreation Sites in Roaded Areas, Back Country, and Wilderness," U.S. Forest Service, Pacific Northwest Forest and Range Experiment Station, Research Paper, PNW–209, Portland, Ore., 1976.

11 Kraus, Richard C., and J. E. Curtis: "Creative Administration in Recreation and Parks," Mosby, St. Louis, 1973.

12 LaPage, Wilbur F.: "Some Observations on Campground Trampling and Ground Cover Response," U.S. Forest Service, Northeast Forest Experiment Station, Research Paper NE–68, Upper Darby, Pa., 1967.

13 Meinecke, E. P.: "A Campground Policy," U.S. Forest Service, Intermountain Region, Ogden, Utah, 1932.

14 Merriam, L. C., Jr., et al.: "The Camper in Minnesota State Parks and Forests," University of Minnesota, Agricultural Experiment Station Bulletin 516, St. Paul, 1976.

15 National Recreation and Park Association: "Outdoor Recreation Space Standards," New York, 1966.

16 National Recreation and Park Association and National Park Service: "Trends," Park Practice Program, National Society for Park Resources, Arlington, Va., var. dates.

17 Ort, Don E.: Recommended Campground Sanitation Requirements, *Guidelines for Developing Land for Outdoor Recreation Use,* Cooperative Extension Service, Purdue University, West Lafayette, Ind., 1963.

18 Potter, Dale R., and Alan J. Wagar: "Techniques for Inventorying Manmade Impacts in Roadway Environments," U.S. Forest Service, Pacific Northwest Forest and Range Experiment Station, Research Paper, PNW–121, Portland, Ore., 1971.

19 Recreation Advisory Council: "Policy Governing the Water Pollution and Public Health Aspects of Outdoor Recreation," RAC Circular No. 3, U.S. Government Printing Office, Washington, 1964.

20 Sharpe, Grant W. (ed.): "Interpreting the Environment," Wiley, New York, 1976.

21 Sternloff, Robert E. and Roger Warren: "Park and Recreation Maintenance Management," Holbrook Press, Boston, 1977.

22 U.S. Department of Agriculture, Forest Service: "Avalanche Handbook," A.H. 489, U.S. Government Printing Office, Washington, 1976.

23 U.S. Department of the Interior, National Park Service: "Training Opportunities," Washington, 1969.

24 U.S. Department of the Interior, National Park Service: "Seasonal Law Enforcement Training Material," Washington, 1973.

25 U.S. Public Health Service: "Environmental Health Practice in Recreation Areas," PHS Publication 1195, National Technical Information Service, Washington, 1966.

26 Wagar, J. Alan: "Campgrounds for Many Tastes," U.S. Forest Service, Intermountain Forest and Range Experiment Station, Research Paper INT–6, Ogden, Utah, 1963.

27 Washburne, Randal F., and J. Alan Wagar: Evaluating Visitor Response to Exhibit Content, *Curator,* vol. 13, no. 3, 1972.

National Parks and related reserves on other continents have distinctive recreational interests; African areas are outstanding for their abundant fauna, as noted in this assemblage about a waterhole. *(South African National Parks Board.)*

International Relationships

Foreign National Parks
and Related Areas

The subject of national parks and related areas throughout the world is a large one. The necessarily brief treatment in this chapter only alludes to its more fascinating aspects. For instance, the many features of national parks and related reserves in faraway places are only suggested, and multiple administrative and management concepts are only briefly outlined. However, all workers in wild-land recreation should be aware of activities of their counterparts in other countries. Thus, an attempt has been made to provide the reader with the fundamentals and scope of foreign national parks and related reserves so that they may be compared with similar areas in the United States. While our country has an enviable record in wild land recreation and environmental conservation we do not have all the answers. We can learn from others as others can learn from us. Details of foreign national parks and reserves may be obtained in a number of excellent publications, some of which are included in the chapter references.[1]

NATURE OF BENEFITS [1,10,11,13,14,30]

Values inherent in the features of natural environment, as well as in varied objects of antiquity, have international importance. Public responsibility in

[1] Most complete references to national parks and equivalent reserves throughout the world have been issued by the International Union for the Conservation of Nature and Natural Resources [11,14]. There is also a good, popular two-volume handbook on this subject [5].

their protection and preservation transcends national boundaries and political ideologies. Today, over 100 nations on all continents have established national parks, floral and faunal sanctuaries or reserves, recreational forests, and similar areas, or have placed sites of archeological and historical importance under the protection of public agencies. Though methods of accomplishing such purposes vary, their generally similar objectives emphasize maintenance of environmental interests for varying benefits important to future as well as present generations.

International interest in the establishment of national parks and related reserves is motivated by (1) concern for the preservation of significant world interests, (2) enhancement of educational and cultural values, (3) improvement of scientific knowledge, (4) development of coordinated land-management programs, (5) stimulation of economic benefits through tourism, and (6) identification with a viewpoint of political maturity.

Preservation of Significant Interests

The natural concern of most people with their surroundings, and their curiosity regarding things about them, are fundamental to the reserve concept and to environmental protection. There is an inherent interest in the preservation of plant and animal species and significant ecological associations; of dramatic segments of terrain, scenic or not, which reflect the nature of past geological changes; and of archeological remains or historic sites indicative of the nature, accomplishments, and trials and tribulations of our predecessors. Modern society has recognized the importance of guarding such areas against unnecessary encroachment. As heirlooms of our heritage they are worth their cost.

Enhancement of Educational and Cultural Values

Representative bits of natural and significant environment, lands on which various activities are conducted in harmony with scenic or environmental interests, and evidence of our early forbears have recognized educational and cultural value. Similarly, archeological and historical sites enable us to identify closely with significant events of the past.

High-quality reserves, representative of interests typical of various countries, are also a source of national pride. They also promote understanding of cultural differences between the world's peoples.

Improvement of Scientific Knowledge

Knowledge of nature's methods, as expressed in the characteristics of varied natural environmental associations, aid us in living in harmony with our surroundings. In particular, large natural areas are important as "bench marks," or "control plots," for necessary research on the varied effects of environmental manipulation resulting from different methods in the management and use of both renewable and nonrenewable resources.

Development of Coordinated Land-Management Programs

As units of properly planned land-use programs, various types of reserves, with their cultural, educational, inspirational, scientific, and related values, provide necessary balance between our varied needs. Though a major share of the Earth's land and water area must necessarily serve utilitarian requirements, natural areas, as well as areas of carefully controlled use, are also important to our existence. Systematized allocation of land on the basis of primary benefits offers the most suitable substitute to unnecessary sacrifice of important esthetic values.

Stimulation of Economic Benefits thorugh Tourism

Varied interests typical of different areas of the world are magnets for increasing global travel favored by all forms of modern transportation facilities, particularly fast, dependable, relatively inexpensive jet aircraft. Maintenance and development of the important economic returns from tourism, as well as competition for such benefits, are largely dependent upon perpetuation of the varied basic attractions. Not the least of these attractions are the significant geological, biological, archeological, and historical features contained in various types of reserves, and the scenic qualities of an attractive landscape. A number of countries have developed these concepts to a high level. In particular, a number of more recently independent nations have given high priority to considerations of this nature, largely because of economic returns resulting from foreign travel.

Identification with a Viewpoint of Political Maturity

Various types of reserves throughout the world, including most national parks and related areas in former colonies of European nations, were largely instituted by older, established countries. When these former colonies achieved independence, it was generally assumed that their reserves might be abolished for, though vital to farsighted conservation programs, they were entwined with colonial policies not always in public favor with indigenous inhabitants. However, officials of many of the new governments, often with the assistance of dedicated former conservation officials, recognized the very practical aspects of maintaining the integrity of their national parks and related reserves. Money brought in by tourists was, and is, an important to our existence. Systematized allocation of land on the basis of primary benefits offers the most suitable substitute to unnecessary sacrifice of important esthetic values.
[9].

HISTORY OF INTERNATIONAL INTEREST IN PARKS AND RESERVES

The concept of governmental responsibility to environmental protection has been characterized by slow but accelerating growth over many years.

Although natural conditions throughout much of Europe have been greatly modified by centuries of use, concern for the preservation of the environment and conservation of natural resources has long been associated with the culture of many European peoples. Conservation laws, designed primarily to prevent the extinction of certain species of fauna and flora, were adopted in various parts of Europe at an early date.

This concern for conservation accompanied the expansion of European culture to far-flung corners of the globe, particularly in North America, Africa, and parts of southeast Asia.

Modern Reserve Concept

Tangible action in establishing specific reserves was first manifested in different parts of the world during the nineteenth and early years of the twentieth century. Its growth has not been uniform. Greater progress has been made in some regions than others; in fact, unenlightened practices in the use of natural resources are still typical in many parts of the world.

Early reserves of the world varied in type and size, and had equally varying objectives. Although the establishment of Yellowstone National Park in 1872 is generally credited with being the first indication of this movement, it was not the first of the world's wild-land reserves. Yellowstone National Park was antedated by the establishment of several other reserves, including the Hot Springs Reserve in 1832; Fountainebleau, near Paris, France, in 1853 [10]; and the Yosemite Grant in 1864. Nevertheless, the significance of the establishment of the Yellowstone area was that this action was responsible for the introduction of the national park concept, which crystallized interest in the establishment of similar areas in other countries. It also gave added emphasis to conservation in general.

However, according to Ann and Myron Sutton [27], Yellowstone was not established as a national park; initial legislation in 1872 merely stated that this area was "set aside as a public park." Still, even though the specific nomenclature "national park" was lacking in the initial legislation, Yellowstone represents the first land set aside for purposes of a national park. In the Yellowstone (1872) and Mackinac Island (1874) legislation Congress had not refined the term "national park" sufficiently to include it in the body of those acts. A Parliamentary document of New South Wales, Australia, establishing "The National Park," now Royal National Park, near Sydney, was the world's first legislative document to make specific reference to this term. United States legislation did not refer to "Yellowstone National Park" until 1883.

Another early example of the expansion of the national park concept occurred in Canada in 1885. In that year an area of 10 square miles surrounding the hot springs at Banff, in the Province of Alberta, was designated as a health resort; two years later this area was enlarged to 250 square miles and christened Rocky Mountains, later Banff, National Park. This area was the nucleus of the extensive present-day Canadian National Park System. [1,11,14,30].

National parks were nonexistent in Europe until 1909, when the first one was established in Sweden [11,14,30]. However, as early as 1880 a Finnish scientist proposed that certain areas in Europe be reserved in their natural state for posterity [17], and in 1884 James Bryce, member of the British House of Commons, introduced the Access to the Mountains Bill which sought to preserve public rights of access to certain types of "open country" which has been seriously curtailed. Bryce's bill, which applied only to Scotland, did not pass, but it was a harbinger of developments in Britain in later years [7].

In Africa initial efforts to prohibit the ruthless slaughter of wildlife were made in 1846 in Transvaal, now a part of the Republic of South Africa. The earliest area set aside specifically for the protection of native African fauna and flora was a small reserve established in 1889 by King Leopold of Belgium in what was then the Belgian Congo, primarily for the protection of elephants. Soon thereafter, in 1897, the Hluhluwe, Umfolozi, and Saint Lucia reserves were established in Natal, Republic of South Africa, and in 1898 the Sabie Game Reserve in Transvaal, forerunner of South Africa's famous Kruger National Park, was established [11,26,30,31].

Creation of various types of reserves in several Australian states dates from establishment of Royal National Park by New South Wales in 1879 and other land laws of the 1880s. A few areas came into being before 1900, but most Australian national parks and reserves are more recent [1,11,14,21,22,30]. In New Zealand some reserves were established under authority of the Land Act of 1892; and in 1894 Tongariro National Park became the basis of New Zealand's Park System [11,14,23,30].

Though reservation of wild lands in Asia has little consistency, parts of that continent have a long history of nature conservation. It was initiated in Indonesia during the Dutch colonial period. In 1889, a section of the primeval jungle forest on the slopes of Mount Tjibodas, on the island of Java, was placed under the protection of the Botanical Institute of Buitenzorg, primarily to serve as a natural science research laboratory [3]. In 1912, the Society for Nature Protection aided the colonial government in the establishment of the first of over 100 nature reserves. Since independence such areas have been administered by the government of the Republic of Indonesia [11]. It is also significant that establishment of national parks in Asia was first suggested in Japan toward the end of the last century by Nagaroni Okabe,[2] member of the House of Peers, who had developed

---

[2] Early interest in establishment of national parks in Japan is also credited to efforts of Edwin von Baeltz, about 1911 [1].

interest in Yellowstone National Park during a period of study in the United States [15]. However, there were no national parks in Asia until 1934, when the first eight areas of the Japanese National Park System were established. This action followed adoption of Japan's initial National Park Law by both houses of the Japanese Diet; this law became effective in 1934 (revised 1950) through Imperial Edict. Adoption of the National Park Law resulted largely from public interest developed by the Japanese National Park Association, formed in 1927 [1,11,15,16].

Establishment of Yellowstone National Park also prompted the initial suggestion of similar reserves in South America. This idea was voiced in Brazil in 1876 by Andre Rebouces, an engineer [1], but it did not bear fruit—and then not in Brazil—until much later. The first South American national park was established by Argentina.[3]

Organization of the IUCN

Interest in the preservation of significant wild-land values on an international level began to develop early in the present century. Such interest, resulting largely from recognition of the basic similarity of conservation problems, was reflected in cooperative efforts by localized groups of nations in various parts of the world. In time, such efforts were approached on a continental and, eventually, on a worldwide basis.

Among the more noteworthy of early international conferences on natural resource conservation were the International Conference for the Protection of Fauna and Flora of Africa, held in London in 1933 [6], and the Pan American Convention on Nature Protection and Wildlife Preservation in the Western Hemisphere, held in Washington, D.C. in 1942 [24].

The desirability of an international approach to nature conservation was first suggested by Paul Sarasin, Swiss naturalist, who proposed the establishment of an international advisory committee before World War I. This movement, interrupted by World War I, was reactivated following the end of hostilities by P. G. Tienhoven of the Netherlands. Largely through his efforts the International Office for the Protection of Nature was founded in Brussels in 1928. This organization was active until 1940. After World War II a Provisional International Union for the Protection of Nature was organized by the Swiss League for the Protection of Nature. The Swiss League, working closely with the French Government and UNESCO, organized a conference held at Fountainebleau in 1948, at which the International Union for the Protection of Nature was officially established. Later,

---

[3] National parks in Argentina are established under authority of the National Park Law of 1934 (with later modifications). However, Argentina's National Park System is considered to have originated in 1903, when Dr. Francisco P. Moreno donated approximately 15,000 acres (6,075 hectares) of land for a national park. This area comprises part of Nahuel Huapi National Park [11].

the name of this organization was changed to the International Union for the Conservation of Nature and Natural Resources; it is generally referred to as the IUCN [4,30].

FACTORS OF IMPORTANCE IN ESTABLISHMENT OF PARKS AND RESERVES

National parks and equivalent reserves throughout the world, as well as systems of such areas, vary widely in type, size, conservation objectives, and philosophy of administration and management. Even their nomenclature lacks a standardization which adequately portrays the purpose of specific types of areas and their relationship to one another. The terms used often imply a similarity which does not actually exist. Conversely, the character of identical types may be hidden by dissimilar terminology. For instance, "national park" is a generic term which is interpreted differently in the light of local conditions and needs.

The need for some sort of standardized nomenclature was recognized at both the International Conference for the Protection of Fauna and Flora of Africa and the Pan American Convention on Nature Protection and Wildlife Preservation in the Western Hemisphere [6,24]. In both cases definitions applicable to various types of reserves were adopted.[4] However, these definitions were related primarily to conditions typical of continents under discussion; they were not designed to be uniformly applicable to reserves throughout the world. Futher, the term national park was the only one defined at both these international meetings. Though essentially similar, neither of these definitions of a national park is relevant to some areas known as national parks in densely populated countries where local conditions require controlled utilization of natural resources of such areas, and consequent departure from principles of strict preservation.

At the First World Conference on National Parks, held in Seattle, Washington, in 1962,[5] it was noted that various types of reserves throughout the world were designated in about two dozen different ways [30]. Later, the IUCN developed standards for national parks and related reserves having natural interests [11], but areas with significant archeological or historical values worthy of national park status were not included. More definitely, on December 1, 1969, the Tenth General Assembly of the IUCN, meeting in New Delhi, India, adopted a resolution defining the term na-

[4] The International Conference for the Protection of Fauna and Flora of Africa defined the terms national park, strict natural reserve, fauna and flora reserve, and reserve with prohibition of hunting and collecting. Reserve definitions adopted by the Pan American Convention on Nature Protection and Wildlife Preservation in the Western Hemisphere were those for national park, national reserve, strict wilderness reserve, and nature monument.

[5] Second World Conference on National Parks, held in Yellowstone National Park, September 1972, commemorated the 100th anniversary of the "national park idea" [13].

tional park which emphasized the necessity for (1) an essentially natural environment; (2) control by some national authority; and (3) specialized—inspirational, educational, cultural, recreational—public use. This resolution recommended that all governments adhere to IUCN standards in designating national parks, and requested that the term not be applied to areas lacking expressed essential characteristics [12].

It is important that factors underlying variations in type, size, objective, administrative philosophy, and nomenclature be understood and carefully considered when discussing and comparing reserves in different parts of the world. Among the most vital of these factors are (1) the primary interests of the areas concerned, (2) regional population density, (3) economic level of countries involved, (4) nature and stability of the political system of various governments, and (5) the history and cultural background of the people [1,10,11,13,14,30].

Primary Interests

These vary with such basic characteristics of various continents as topography, flora and fauna, and archeology and history. These basic characteristics are related to global geographic positions of different continents; their climate, geology, nature of development, history; and the cultural and ethnic background of their people. Thus, understanding of the world's varied reserves is predicated upon a knowledge of the many interrelating factors responsible for their principal interests, the perpetuation of which responds to different management programs as well as to varying types and degrees of use.

Population Density

Very large reserves are feasible only in regions where economic pressure for land, by reason of low population density or resource demand, is not acute. For instance, in contrast with sparsely populated, less developed nations, most European countries and Japan have relatively little land that is not required for production of utilitarian needs. In Europe and Japan a modified form of national parks and related reserves has evolved. Establishment of large, unmodified, wholly government-owned areas is impossible; Europeans and the Japanese have sought to reconcile modern individuals and nature to joint occupation of their reserves. Land-ownership patterns are not disturbed; private as well as public land is generally included; and private industry is not completely curtailed. The objective of such policy is to safeguard areas of exceptional interest, scenic beauty, and similar values against damage or destruction.

Economic Level

The establishment and maintenance of reserves, whatever their nature, are largely dependent upon the economic level of the nations involved. The probability of their establishment is in direct ratio to per capita income. A country must not only be able to afford designation of land for such use; it must also be able to meet the cost of adequate protection, administration, and management. Primarily for this reason national parks and related reserves are more numerous, larger, and generally better planned, protected, and administered, as well as better known, in countries typified by a more affluent society.

Nature and Stability of Government

Since establishment of reserves and related maintenance of environmental interest and beauty must be based upon long-term objectives, it follows that desired results cannot be achieved without governmental stability. Countries recognized as world leaders in this aspect of conservation are all characterized by stable governmental structure.

The nature of the political system under which a government operates is also important. In nature conservation, effects of varying political systems may be reflected in either a positive or negative manner. Certain totalitarian countries have adequate, often extensive, reserves of various types. These, largely reflections of the political objectives of governmental hierarchy, can be expected to be maintained so long as current policies are continued. Countries which operate on a system reflecting greater freedom of individual expression would seem to offer maximum opportunity for progress in nature conservation. However, under such a system, the attainment of a desired result is dependent upon a responsible citizenry, properly informed on the requirements and values of such objectives, and the nature and effects of alternate choices.

History

The extent and nature of various types of reserves throughout the world are often connected to the history of the countries involved. Since some European areas originated as private estates of the nobility, they were withdrawn from public use and maintained in an essentially natural condition. Later, when converted to public status, they remained largely unaltered. Similarly, reserves established as parts of colonial empires are maintained by recently independent governments, largely for economic and political reasons.

Further, wherever government has encouraged individual initiative in land and resource acquisition, this has materially affected the location and distribution as well as the size and character of reserves.

Cultural Background

Public attitudes toward the natural scene, and toward past heritage, play a role in the establishment of reserves; cultural importance and value must warrant their formation. It was not an accident that the national park idea originated in the United States, and that this concept of land use was quickly adapted by other countries with a similar heritage. The emotional appeal of this idea is so strong that even in Europe and Japan, where virgin lands are largely nonexistent, the most satisfactory substitutes have been devised. Awareness of cultural values of reserves by leaders of emerging nations encourages their fellow citizens to accede even though the aura of a colonial past is yet to be erased, and despite the fact that, historically, native fauna is viewed primarily as a source of food.

ADMINISTRATION AND MANAGEMENT OF FOREIGN PARKS AND RESERVES

In addition to differences in administrative philosophy and degree of protection in various types of reserves, the relationship between public and private responsibility in the discharge of such matters is dissimilar. Further, where such areas are entirely under some form of governmental authority, this responsibility is organized in several ways. The nature and degree of their public use also varies. Still, in spite of such basic differences, there is similarity in the problems encountered in different areas.

Concepts of Administrative Philosophy and Use

On some reserves, established primarily as field laboratories for natural resource research, recreation activity is limited and access is controlled. The general public is restricted to limited portions of the total area or to well-defined routes of travel, or the number of visitors is rigidly controlled— often through provision of only primitive facilities.

Other reserves are managed in an opposite manner, with emphasis placed upon public use and enjoyment. Though care is taken to see that the interest and beauty of the environment are not destroyed, nature is appropriately manipulated in a manner favorable to public use with minimum impact on environmental interests. In certain cases the truly natural character of the area may be completely modified, though it may still be attractive. Controlled resource use may be permitted and there is little, if any, interference with private land ownership. In such cases public access and use are provided for through agreement with private owners, though rights of private landowners are respected by designation of specific routes of public travel and concentration.

The great majority of reserves are administered on concepts somewhere between these two extremes. Standards and means of public access range widely. Accommodations of varying types and standards may be operated by the administrative agency or by concessionaires under contract, subject to agency control. In some cases overnight accommodations are outside reserve boundaries, though in close proximity, and completely under private management. Other facilities and services necessary to public use also differ greatly, and visitor activities and movement, including speed on roads and highways, are subject to varying controls, dependent upon the area's interests. The general objective in such cases is to permit maximum, appropriate public use consistent with the perpetuation of specific interests of the area.

Since it is impractical, if not impossible and uneconomic, to provide for all types of public interest and activity on any one type of reserve, competing interests and activities are often accommodated on several distinct areas. Though sometimes contiguous they are generally separate, with coordination of specific uses related on the basis of regional needs.

Administrative Relationships

Varying objectives of different types of reserves prompt diversity in administrative relations. Areas noted for their geological, biological, or scenic interests are usually controlled by some public agency (federal, state, provincial), generally a park, forest, fish and game, or land department. In some cases, however, administration is by a semipublic organization (boards, commissions, authorities) whose members are private citizens with interest in and knowledge of the problems involved, and who are appointed for varying terms by an officer of an appropriate government agency. In some cases administrative responsibility is entrusted to the professional staff of a recognized university, museum, or related educational or scientific institution. The degree of government control exercised over the activities of such semipublic bodies varies, but they generally operate with considerable autonomy, within specific limitations subject to only minimal official supervision.

Archeological and historical areas and sites are generally, but not always, administered by organizations similarly constituted. However, these areas and sites are distinct from those concerned with geological, biological, and related scenic interests.

Foreign Park and Reserve Examples

Examples from several foreign countries will serve to illustrate the nature of reserves and their problems.

Many African reserves [1,5,11,14,26,31,32] which feature natural or scenic interests are of extensive size. Some embrace areas larger than a number of American states. Though protection of their basic interests is generally of primary concern, administrative policies with respect to protection and visitor use are variable, being dependent upon the nature of attractions, the degree of land-use pressure in the region, and the importance of the reserve to the economics of the country. A few are restricted to scientific study,[6] while in others the general public is limited to small portions of the area.[7] However, in most reserves more liberal policies prevail, though per-

---

[6] Example: Monts Nimba Nature Reserve (81,250 acres; 36,906 hectares) on border between Ivory Coast and Guinea.

[7] Example: Virunga, formerly Albert, National Park (2,022,500 acres; 819,113 hectares), Zaire.

missible visitor activities are carefully controlled and regulated. This is particularly the case in wildlife areas which are often sensitive to disturbance or where the presence of certain animals embodies hazard to visitors. In some wildlife reserves roads and accommodations are primitive or nonexistent and visitors must accompany guided parties. A few are in close proximity to modern cities or are readily accessible by public transportation.[8] Many more remote areas have adequate facilities; however, overnight accommodations, including campgrounds, are available only at specific places which are often enclosed by a protective fence.[9] Visitors in such reserves are generally required to make advance reservations and remain within protected places during the night. Further, public travel is restricted to specific roads during daylight hours, speed limits are rigidly defined, only closed vehicles are permitted and, except for designated places, visitors are not permitted to leave their vehicle.

In certain regions policies of strict protection and controlled public use, including restricted hunting, are accommodated by coordination of several kinds of contiguous reserves which provide for various types and degrees of visitor use.[10] There are also a number of reserves and reserve complexes, composed of one or more types of protection, which straddle national boundaries.[11]

Many Asiatic countries have established national parks and related reserves [1,2,3,5,11,14,16], but, with the possible exception of Japan and the U.S.S.R., this concept of land use lacks adequate support. Because of economic, population, and political difficulties, in many countries in Asia, its reserves have problems related to personnel, boundary definition, and enforcement of protective measures. Asiatic reserves vary in size from a few acres to over 2,000 square miles.[12] The U.S.S.R., in Europe as well as in

[8] Examples: Nairobi National Park (28,160 acres: 11,405 hectares), Kenya; Victoria Falls National Park (132,250 acres; 53,561 hectares), Rhodesia.

[9] Examples: Tsavo National Park (5,141,760 acres; 2,086,414 hectares), Kenya; Gorongosa National Park (988,420 acres; 400,310 hectares), Mozambique; Wankie National Park (3,238,400 acres; 1,305,477 hectares) Rhodesia; Kruger National Park (4,697,600 acres; 1,902,528 hectares), Hluhluwe (57,000 acres; 23,085 hectares) and St. Lucia (91,000 acres; 36,855 hectares) Game Reserves, Republic of South Africa; Serengeti National Park (2,848,000 acres; 1,153,440 hectares), Tanzania; Murchinson Falls (962,500 acres; 389,814 hectares) and Queen Elizabeth (488,960 acres; 198,029 hectares) National Parks, Uganda; Kafue National Park (5,536,000 acres; 2,242,080 hectares), Zambia.

[10] Bamingui Bangoran National Park (2,500,000 acres; 1,021,500 hectares), Vassako-Bola Strict Nature Reserve (375,000 acres; 157,875 hectares), and three game reserves (agg. area 2,250,000 acres; 916,250 hectares), Central African Republic.

[11] National Park de "W" (825,000 acres; 334,125 hectares) in Niger is contiguous with Pendjari Strict Faunal Reserve (688,750 acres; 278,944 hectares) in Dahomey and Cortiagu Partial Faunal Reserve (127,500 acres; 51,638 hectares) in Upper Volta; Kalahari National Park (2,720,000 acres; 1,101,600 hectares) in the Republic of South Africa adjoins a game reserve of (2,400,000 acres; 972,000 hectares) in Botswana.

[12] Kranji Reserve (49 acres; 20 hectares), Singapore; Petchora-Ilych Nature Preserve (1,765,035 acres; 794,840 hectares) in Asiatic U.S.S.R.

Asia, has an extensive system of nature preserves *(zapovedniki)* [13] where management emphasizes protection for education and research; general public use is not a major consideration [2,11]. Conversely, the National Park System in Japan[14] gives major consideration to public use [11,16]. A wide variety of recreational activities are permitted and commercial use of natural resources is not completely eliminated; however, as in Europe, care is taken to maintain environmental interests insofar as possible.

Although Australia and New Zealand have a similar cultural and political heritage, we find added to the obvious dissimilarity in physical size, differences in the size and distribution of population, climate, topography, economics and industrial activity, governmental structure, and attitudes of the people. These differences affect the character and nature of administration of reserves.

The expanse of relatively undeveloped land and the comparatively small population would seem to simplify problems of nature conservation in Australia. However, the Australian environment is delicately balanced and vulnerable to disturbance. Intensive agriculture, industry, and urban development are concentrated in the relatively small, most habitable portion of the continent, so inevitably environmental modification is also concentrated. Even pastoral activity, typical of much of the "outback," has a severe impact on that arid, even more fragile region. In addition, Australia's political system is not conducive to centralized conservation efforts for the states have soverign powers over their own land, and flora and fauna. The Commonwealth government plays a minor role in conservation; its primary responsibility in this field relates to parks and reserves in the Northern and Capital Territories. There is no nationally uniform conservation policy or procedure. Control of various parks and reserves is vested in about 16 different organizations [20].

Australian parks and reserves have been established independently by all of the six states, as well as by several territories, often by a variety of administrative acts. Further, the degree of progress in such matters, as well as administrative philosophy, standards, protection, and nature of manage-

[13] No central administrative agency. Management is by various agencies of the Council of Ministers of the Union Republics, or the Academies of Science of either the U.S.S.R. or the Union Republics. A few nature preserves were established in the 1920s; most were set up at a later date. A national park, managed for more general public use, has been established in the Lake Baikal region.

[14] Includes over twenty areas (aggregate area about 4,500,000 acres; 1,822,500 hectares) administered by the National Park Division of the Ministry of Health and Welfare. These areas are supplemented by about twenty "quasi-national parks," areas of secondary scenic quality (aggregate area over 1,000,000 acres; 405,000 hectares) which absorb some of the tremenduous outdoor recreation pressure in Japan. Quasi-national parks are administered by local prefectures, in coordination with the Ministry of Health and Welfare and the National Parks Deliberative Council.

ment of such lands varies widely.[15] There are over 150 national parks (aggregate area between 6,000,000 and 7,000,000 acres; 2,430,000 and 2,835,000 hectares). There are also nearly 900 scenic, floral and faunal reserves, and sanctuaries (aggregate area about 14,000,000 acres; 5,670,000 hectares).[16] These areas vary widely in size, management and objective, location and degree of public use. Some have been established primarily for protection of particular features. Others are managed for general recreation; some of these, located near or within large urban centers, serve essentially as city parks. Many are remote, difficult of access, and largely wilderness. Visitor accommodations are provided in numerous areas. In certain cases management is carefully coordinated with such activities as grazing and certain industrial developments. For instance, Kosciusko National Park in New South Wales includes developments of the Snowy Mountain Hydro-electric Authority which predates the New South Wales National Parks and Wildlife Service Act of 1967. These deficiencies, however, are being modified by the growing influence of a number of conservation organizations such as the Australian Wildlife Protective Society, the Australian Academy of Science, the Australian Conservation Foundation, and National Park Associations in several states [11,20,21,22].

Despite its small size, New Zealand has greatly diverse features, ranging from volcanoes and hydrothermal areas to rugged, glacier-clad mountains and deeply incised coastal fiords. Forests and related vegetation are equally varied. The superb New Zealand National Park System includes ten areas[17] representative of the many scenic attractions of this island nation [11,14,23].

[15] National parks and reserves in Queensland are administered by the National Parks and Wildlife Service, formed 1975; in Victoria by the National Parks Authority, established 1957, while wildlife reserves and forest parks are administered, respectively, by the Fisheries and Wildlife Department and the Forestry Commission; in South Australia by the National Parks and Wildlife Service; in Western Australia by either the National Parks Board or the Wildlife Authority; in Tasmania by the National Parks and Conservation Board; and in the Northern Territory by the Northern Territory Reserve Board. The strongest centralized Australian park organization exists in New South Wales; it was established in 1967 and is patterned after the U.S. National Park Service.

[16] Noteworthy areas include Simpson Desert National Park (1,218,000 acres; 493,290 hectares) and many national parks in, or in the vicinity of, the Great Barrier Reef, Queensland. Kosciusko (1,322,000 acres; 535,400 hectares) and Blue Mountains (244,986 acres; 99,220 hectares) National Parks, New South Wales; Wilson's Promontory National Park (102,379 acres; 41,463 hectares) and Healsville Sanctuary (432 acres; 175 hectares), Victoria; Cradle Mountain-Lake St. Clair National Park (338,496 acres; 137,091 hectares), Tasmania; Ayres Rock-Mount Olga National Park (331,680 acres; 134,330 hectares), Northern Territory; Flinders Chase National Park (135,680 acres; 54,950 hectares), South Australia; Walpole-Nornalup National Park (32,229 acres; 13,053 hectares), Western Australia.

[17] Included are Tongariro (161,552 acres; 65,429 hectares) which, in addition to having an active volcano, is a winter sports center; Fiordland (2,422,883 acres; 981,180 hectares) containing spectacular scenic fiords and wilderness country; and Mount Cook (172,979 acres; 70,056 hectares) and Westland (210,000 acres; 85,050 hectares), characterized by spectacular mountains with extensive glacier systems. There are also reserves and sanctuaries administered by the Lands and Survey Department. In addition, Tronson Kauri Park (1,241 acres; 503 hectares) is jointly administered by the New Zealand Forest Service and National Parks Authority.

The nature of their development and public use resembles, in some respects, that of many national parks in the United States. The Tourist Hotel Corporation, a government agency, operates most of the park concessions. Of particular note is the fact that regulated hunting is allowed in New Zealand National Parks in order to reduce large populations of exotic animals destructive to native vegetation and habitat. Natural predators are largely nonexistent in New Zealand [20].

Initially, early national parks in New Zealand, which date from the late years of the nineteenth century, were administered by independent boards of trustees. In 1952 the New Zealand Parliament passed the National Park Act establishing the New Zealand National Parks Authority. The National Parks Authority consists of nine members representative of government and interested private organizations, together with individual park boards, to control and administer all national parks. Individual parks are placed under park-board control and administration. The Department of Lands and Survey acts as executive agency of the Authority and the park boards [11,14,20,23].

In Europe establishment of large reserves primarily for exclusive protection of their interests is impractical. Still most European countries have established national parks and reserves adapted to local conditions and needs.[18] As in Japan, use of natural resources is generally permitted, but care is taken to protect the environment. Administrative responsibility for European national parks and reserves is vested in a variety of public or quasi-public agencies.

Great Britain has a variety of protected areas having different functions. By authority of the National Parks and Access to the Countryside Act of 1949, ten national parks have been established in England and Wales; these, essentially "landscape control zones," have an aggregate area of over 3 million acres (1,200,000 hectares) [7]. They are augmented by twenty-one "Areas of Outstanding Scenic Beauty" (aggregate area about 2,500,000 acres; 1,012,500 hectares; first one designated 1956) and six "Long Distance Footpaths and Bridleways" (total of 1,273 miles; 2,048 kilometers; first one designated 1951). These areas are administered by local planning authorities, subject to supervision of the National Parks Commission, Ministry of Housing and Local Government. There are also

---

[18] France has a number of reserves of varying size; some, like Fontainebleau, date from early days. After passage of its National Park Act in 1960, France established Vanoise National Park (147,000 acres; 59,525 hectares) in the Alps; it adjoins Gran Paradiso National Park (140,000 acres; 56,700 hectares), one of the larger Italian National Parks [11,14]. Bialowiesa National Park (12,682 acres; 5,136 hectares), one of Poland's areas, is noteworthy as a habitat for the remaining European bison [8,11,14]. Sweden's National Park System [11,14,29] includes areas of diverse types; included are Dalby Soderskog (89 acres; 36 hectares), a typical early-day Swedish farm, and Sarek (470,490 acres; 190,548 hectares), the largest wild area in Europe. West Germany has numerous nature parks, e.g., Lüneberger Heide (49,420 acres; 20,015 hectares) and smaller nature reserves [11,14]. Natural resources are utilized, consistent with environmental protection; use of motorized vehicles is also greatly restricted.

ten National Forest Parks (aggregate area nearly 500,000 acres; 202,500 hectares) in England, Scotland, Wales, and North Ireland, administered by the Forestry Commission.

The New Forest, established in 1087 by William I (see page 32), is under the administration of Special Acts of Parliament. Timber production, protection of wildlife and commoners' animals, and safeguarding of public amenity and recreation are major management concerns. Its management illustrates the importance of tradition in Britain and in the continuity of ancient laws and rights as well as the resistance to change.

In addition, the National Trust owns areas of historic as well as of natural interest. Great Britain also has a system of about 100 National Nature Reserves (aggregate area about 400,000 acres; 161,875 hectares) where greater restriction is placed on general public use; these areas are administered by the Nature Conservancy, established in 1949.

In Switzerland multiple-use forest management is common in the alpine forest region, yet the Swiss also have restricted access areas in the Alps where vegetation is preserved for scienfitic investigation. The Swiss National Park [18] near Zernez, in the Engadine Alps, is such a preserve. Although administered by a federal commission and not the forestry agency, the park is almost one-third forested and has been subject to intensive ecological study by the Swiss Forest Research Institute. Created in 1914, the 41,670-acre (16,876 hectares) park provides complete protection for all plant and animal life; no timber or other resource production is allowed (although the area was logged and mined for iron ore in the Middle Ages). The only visitor developments are closely restricted trails and a few information signs, yet many walk the trails, respecting the scientific controls.

North America's national parks and reserves range from those in extensive systems in Canada and the United States to small areas in a number of Central American countries. Canada's National Park System[19] is augmented by provincial reserves [11], a situation similar to that existing between national and state parks in the United States. Mexico has about fifty national parks, ranging in area from less than 100 acres (40.5 hectares) to more than 600,000 acres (243,000 hectares), with an aggregate area of over 2,500,000 acres (1,012,500 hectares);[20] for various reasons they have been excluded from the IUCN list. They are not well known, even by many Mexicans, being overshadowed by interest in Mexico's fabulous archeological areas which are under separate administration. In Central America a

[19] Nineteen natural scenic parks (aggregate area nearly 18,000,000 acres; 7,290,000 hectares), a similar number of national historic parks (aggregate area 14,000 acres; 5,670 hectares), and several hundred historic sites. They are administered by the National and Historic Parks Branch of the Department of Indian Affairs and Northern Development [11,14].

[20] Administered by the Department of National Parks, Division of Forestry and Game, Office of the Secretary of Agriculture and Animal Husbandry. Better known areas include Iztaccihuatl-Popocatepetl (64,198 acres; 26,000 hectares) and Pico de Orizaba (49,375 acres; 19,997 hectares), national parks which include Mexico's most important mountains [11,14].

number of countries have national parks and reserves, but their establishment and management is complicated by economic and political conditions and indifferent public attitude. Costa Rica is one exception. Much progress in establishment and administration of national parks and related reserves has occurred there.

South America has great potential for significant national parks and reserves. However, in most countries on this continent this concept of land use is also of fairly recent origin but all countries there are taking a more active role in that matter. In the establishment and management of such areas efforts are made to adhere to policies adopted at the Pan American Convention on Nature Protection and Wildlife Preservation in the Western Hemisphere, but certain departures from these standards often typify actual practice. Establishment and adequate management is often complicated by difficulties of boundary determination, land-ownership patterns, lack of personnel, and public attitude toward the use of natural resources. Most South American literature has not emphasized preservation. Thus, a precedent has not been established relative to values of national parks and equivalent reserves.

Although national parks and reserves exist in Bolivia, Colombia, Chile, Ecuador, Guyana, and Peru, most noteworthy systems in South America [11,14] are found in Argentina,[21] Brazil,[22] and Venezuela.[23] Argentina's best known national parks are Nahuel Huapi (1,900,000 acres; 768,905 hectares) in the Lake District east of the Andes and Iguazú (139,000 acres; 56,251 hectares) on the Argentine-Brazilian border. The latter includes part of Iguazú Falls, one of the great cataracts of the world, as well as diverse flora and fauna. It adjoins Iguacú National Park (445,000 acres; 180,225 hectares) in Brazil, forming an international park about the great cataract. Venezuela's national park system includes Canaima National Park (nearly 2,500,000 acres; 1,012,500 hectares) in the remote Guiana Highlands; it embraces Angel Falls, 2,648 feet (807 meters) high, highest free-leaping waterfall in the world.

Similarity of Problems

Despite dissimilarity in area characteristics, and differences in the sociological, economic, and political factors responsible for their existence, the problems concerned with reserve management often are quite similar. Basically, these problems concern perpetuation of the resource or environ-

[21] Eleven national parks and one natural monument (aggregate area about 6,500,000 acres; 2,631,500 hectares). They are administered by the National Parks Administration, Ministry of Agriculture.

[22] About eleven national parks and two biological reserves (aggregate area over 5,000,000 acres; 2,025,000 hectares). Brazilian national parks and reserves are administered by the Division of Research and Nature Conservation, Forest Service, Ministry of Agriculture.

[23] Seven national parks and three natural monuments (aggregate area about 3,500,000 acres; 1,417,500 hectares). They are administered by the National Parks Section, Division of Renewable Resources, Ministry of Agriculture and Animal Husbandry.

ment, and the people who use these resources. These fundamental concerns apply whether an area is located in Africa or North America, whether it is maintained as a natural field laboratory with public access strictly limited or as a modified environment with controlled resource uses primarily for enjoyment of large numbers of people. Nevertheless, human presence in an area, however controlled or limited, has a degree of impact. Even without human intrusion geological and biological dynamics exert slow but inevitable change in the appearance and characteristics of an area. When viewed in long-term perspective, it is impossible to "freeze" any biological association at a given stage of time. Even the concept of the "everlasting hills" is a myth.

The examples presented here of parks and reserves in other countries illustrate the broad range of policies and variations in management in different parts of the world. None of the examples is exactly like the United States, but they serve to show the spectrum from older to newer societies. As population rises with respect to available land, restrictions on land use increase. To protect wildlife, vegetation, and natural features, public use is restricted. The need for well-defined policy and coordinated planning becomes evident.

Superintendents, naturalists, and rangers in American national parks and their contemporaries elsewhere in the world find great uniformity in mutual problems, though they may deal with different plant and animal species; varying intensities of public use; or dissimilar degrees of social, economic and political pressures. For this reason each profits from the experience of others, a factor largely responsible for the establishment of the IUCN.

SUMMARY

National parks and related reserves exist today in over 100 nations throughout the world. Various reasons have motivated international interest in the reservation of such lands, ranging from concern for the preservation of significant interests to stimulation of economy through tourism and the development of an adequate world image of political maturity. Workers in wild-land recreational areas throughout the world can profit from study and understanding of each others' problems and methods of their solution.

Although there were earlier reserves in various parts of the world, the establishment of Yellowstone National Park is generally credited as initiating the modern reserve concept. Yellowstone, the first national park in the world, prompted the establishment of similar reserves in other countries, beginning in the latter part of the nineteenth and early portion of the twentieth centuries. Such activity was favored by gradually expanding international interest which began to develop tangible form in the 1930s and culminated in 1948 with the organization of the International Union for the Conservation of Nature and Natural Resources (IUCN).

However, growth in this form of conservation has not been uniform; greater progress has been made in some countries than in others. Even the nomenclature of various types of areas lacks standardization which adequately portrays their character and their relationship with one another. Often terms used imply a similarity of purpose that does not actually exist; for instance, national park is a generic term interpreted differently by some countries in the light of local conditions. In addition, national parks and related reserves throughout the world vary widely in type, size, objective, and the philosophy of their administration and management. Such differences, in addition to variations in primary interests of various continents, are the result of variations in population density, economics, the nature and stability of government, and the history and cultural background of people.

Some reserves have been established primarily as a means of protecting rare or endangered interests, or as field laboratories for scientific research; these are not readily accessible to the general public, and activities which adversely affect basic values are not tolerated. In other reserves public use is emphasized, or their management is coordinated with other public needs; in some of these there is little interference with private land ownership, though resource use is carefully controlled. The great majority of reserves are administered on concepts between these two extremes, with a general objective of permitting maximum, appropriate public use consistent with perpetuation of primary interests. In addition, the nature of the administrative authority ranges from government agencies to semipublic bodies which operate with considerable autonomy.

However, despite differences in the world's national parks and related reserves there is considerable uniformity in the problems of recreational use of wild lands in the United States and in other countries. Careful planning and well-defined management policy become increasingly important as populations rise and area visitation increases.

SELECTED REFERENCES

1 American Committee for International Wildlife Protection: "National Parks— A World Need," Victor H. Cahalane, ed., Special Publication No. 14, New York, 1962.

2 Bannikov, A. G.: "Nature Reserves of the USSR" (Trans. from Russian by IPST Staff, D. Greenberg, ed.) Published for the U.S. Department of the Interior and National Science Foundation, Washington by the Israel Program for Scientific Translations, Jerusalem, 1969.

3 Buitenzorg Scientific Centre: "Buitenzorg Scientific Centre," Archipel Drukkerjii en 't Bockhuis, Buitenzorg, Java, 1948.

4 Coolidge, Harold J.: The Birth of a Union: Fountainebleau, October 1948, *National Parks Magazine,* vol. 23, no. 97, April–June 1949.

5 Curry-Lindahl, Kai, and Jean-Paul Harroy: "National Parks of the World," 2 vols., Golden Press, New York, 1972.

6 Great Britain, Parliament, House of Commons: "International Convention for the Protection of Fauna and Flora, with Protocol, Treaty Series No. 27, 1936, London, November 8, 1933," His Majesty's Stationery Office, London, 1936.

7 Great Britain, Ministry of Town and Country Planning and Central Office of Information: "National Parks and Access to the Countryside," His Majesty's Stationery Office, London, n.d.

8 Gut, Stephen: "National Parks in Poland," State Council for Conservation of Nature, Warsaw, 1960.

9 Hays, G. D.: How Independence Saved an African Reserve, *Oryx,* vol 8, no. 6, December 1966.

10 IUCN: "International Commission on National Parks," Washington, n.d.

11 IUCN, International Commission on National Parks: "United Nations List of National Parks and Equivalent Reserves," Hayez, Brussels (French ed.), 1967; (English ed.), 1971.

12 IUCN: Resolutions Adopted by the Tenth General Assembly of IUCN, *IUCN Bulletin,* vol. 2, no. 14, January–March 1970.

13 IUCN: "Second World Conference on National Parks," Arts Graphiques Heliographia SA, Lausanne, Switzerland, 1974.

14 IUCN: "World Directory of National Parks and Other Protected Areas," Morges, Switzerland, 1975.

15 Japan, National Parks Association: "Chronological History of the National Parks of Japan," Welfare Ministry, Tokyo, August 1952.

16 Japan, National Parks Association: "The National Parks Portfolio of Japan," Tokyo, 1954.

17 Kalliola, Reino: Protection of Nature, Soumi: A General Handbook on the Geography of Finland, *Fennia Series,* vol. 72, no. 17, pp. 274–284, Geographic Society of Finland, Helsinki, 1952.

18 Menzi, W., and D. Feuerstein: "Kleiner Fahrer durch den Schweizerichen Nationalparks," 2nd ed., Verehrverein fur Graubunden, Chur, Switzerland, 1948.

19 Merriam, L. C., Jr.: European Forest Recreation Policies and Possible United States Implications, *Journal of Forestry,* vol. 67, no. 12, December 1969.

20 Merriam, L. C., Jr.: "Notes on the National Parks of New Zealand and Australia," unpublished report to National Parks and Conservation Association, August 1974.

21 Morcombe, Michael: "Australia's National Parks," Landsdowne Press, Melbourne, 1969.

22 Mosley, J. G.: "National Parks and Equivalent Reserves in Australia: Guide to Legislation, Administration, and Areas," Australian Conservation Foundation Special Publication No. 2, Canberra, Australia, 1968.

23 New Zealand, National Parks Authority: "National Parks of New Zealand," Government Printer, Wellington, 1965.

24 Pan American Union: "Nature Protection and Wildlife Preservation in the

Western Hemisphere," Convention between the United States of America and Other American Republics, Washington, 1940, Treaty Series No. 981, U.S. Government Printing Office, Washington, 1943.

25 Pop, Emil, and N. Salageanu: "Nature Reserves in Romania," Meridiane Publishing House, Bucharest, 1965.

26 South Africa, National Parks Board of Trustees: "60 Years Kruger Park" (comp. by R. J. Labusschagne), Pretoria, 1958.

27 Sutton, Ann, and Myron Sutton: "Yellowstone: A Century of the Wilderness Idea," Macmillan, New York, 1972.

28 Sweden, Forest Service: "Swedish National Parks," National Board of Crown Forests and Lands, Stockholm, n.d.

29 Tindall, Barry S.: National Parks in the World Community, *Parks and Recreation,* vol. 8, no. 2, February 1973.

30 U.S. Department of the Interior, National Park Service: "First World Conference on National Parks, Seattle, Washington, June 30–July 7, 1962, Proceedings," Alexander B. Adams, ed., U.S. Government Printing Office, Washington, 1964.

31 Van Der Merwe, Nico J.: "The Position of Nature Conservation in South Africa," South African National Parks Board, Pretoria, 1962.

32 Williams, John G.: "National Parks of East Africa," Collins, London, 1967.

Index

Acadia National Park, Maine, 50
Access to the Mountains Bill, Great Britain, 309
Adirondack Forest Preserve, 61
Administration of recreational lands (*see* Management of recreational lands)
Advisory Board on Wildlife Management, 273
Africa:
  early wildlife conservation in, 308, 309
  International Conference for the Protection of Fauna and Flora of, 310, 311
  national parks and reserves in, examples of, 308, 309, 315–316
Age classes, effects of variation on recreation, 8, 105–106, 249
Agencies for recreational land management:
  city and county, 16, 35, 62–63, 124, 189, 200–203
  district and regional, 62, 63, 124, 189, 200
  federal: Corps of Engineers, 59, 61, 80, 185–186
    Tennessee Valley Authority, 59–60, 181–184
    U.S. Bureau of Indian Affairs, 79, 213
    U.S. Bureau of Land Management, 57–58, 177–181
    U.S. Bureau of Reclamation, 59, 60, 184–185
    U.S. Fish and Wildlife Service, 42, 58–59, 61, 170–176

Agencies for recreational land management:
  federal: U.S. Forest Service, 42, 47, 50–57, 74, 79, 82–84, 134*n.*, 146–169
    U.S. National Park Service, 42–50, 62, 74, 79, 82–84, 131–144
  interstate, 61
  private, 63–66, 206–215
  state, 16, 42, 61–62, 124, 189–200
  (*See also specific agencies*)
Agricultural lands, recreational use of, 13, 20, 65, 209–211
Agricultural Stabilization and Conservation Service, 207*n.*
Aircraft, effect on recreation, 10, 19, 249, 307
Aker, W. N., 48
Alaska Native Claims Settlement Act, 80, 132*n.*, 174, 178*n.*
Albright, Horace, 49
Allocation of recreational land and activities, economic (*see* Economics of outdoor recreation)
American Association for the Advancement of Science, 45*n.*, 51
American Colonial period, parks of, 35
American conservation movement (*see* Conservation movement)